Netflix, Dark Fantastic Genres and Intergenerational Viewing

Focusing on Netflix's child and family-orientated platform exclusive content, this book offers the first exploration of a controversial genre cycle of dark science fiction, horror, and fantasy television under Netflix's "Family Watch Together TV" tag.

Using a ground-breaking mix of methods including audience research, interface, and textual analysis, this book demonstrates how Netflix is producing dark family telefantasy content that is both reshaping child and family-friendly TV genres and challenging earlier broadcast TV models around child-appropriate family viewing. It illuminates how Netflix encourages family audiences to "watch together" through intergenerational dynamics that work on and offscreen. The chapters in this book explore how this "Netflixication" of family television developed across landmark examples including *Stranger Things*, *A Series of Unfortunate Events*, *The Dark Crystal: Age of Resistance*, and even *Squid Game*. This book outlines how Netflix is consolidating a new dark family terrain in the streaming sector, which is unsettling older concepts of family viewing, leading to considerable audience and critical confusion around target audiences and viewer expectations.

This book will be of particular interest to upper-level undergraduates, graduates, and scholars in the fields of television studies, screen genre studies, childhood studies, and cultural studies.

Djoymi Baker is a Lecturer in Cinema Studies at RMIT University, Australia. She has published work on children's television history, film and television genres, stardom, and intergenerational fandom. Djoymi is the author of *To Boldly Go: Marketing the Myth of Star Trek* (2018) and the co-author of *The Encyclopedia of Epic Films* (2014).

Jessica Balanzategui is a Senior Lecturer in Media at RMIT University, Australia, and was previously Deputy Director of the Centre for Transformative Media Technologies at Swinburne University of Technology. She has published widely on "problematic" children's screen genres in journals including *New Media Society* and *Convergence*, and is the author of *The Uncanny Child in Transnational Cinema* (Amsterdam UP, 2018).

Diana Sandars is an academic in the School of Culture and Communication at the University of Melbourne, Australia. She has published widely on the children of Australian and Hollywood screens. Diana is the author of *What a Feeling: The Hollywood Musical After MTV* (Intellect, forthcoming) and co-editor of *Gothic in the Oceanic South: Maritime, Marine and Aquatic Uncanny in Southern Waters* (Routledge, forthcoming).

Routledge Advances in Television Studies

14 Creating Reality in Factual Television
The Frankenbite and Other Fakes
Manfred W. Becker

15 A European Television Fiction Renaissance
Premium Production Models and Transnational Circulation
Edited by Luca Barra and Massimo Scaglioni

16 Difficult Women on Television Drama
The Gender Politics of Complex Women in Serial Narratives
Isabel C. Pinedo

17 Global Trafficking Networks on Film and Television
Hollywood's Cartel Wars
César Albarrán-Torres

18 Cognition, Emotion, and Aesthetics in Contemporary Serial Television
Edited by Ted Nannicelli and Héctor J. Pérez

19 Children, Youth, and International Television
Edited by Debbie Olson and Adrian Schober

20 Quality Telefantasy
How US Quality TV Brought Zombies, Dragons and Androids into the Mainstream
Andrew Lynch

21 Speculative Television and the Doing and Undoing of Religion
Gregory Erickson

22 Post-heritage Perspectives on British Period Drama Television
Will Stanford Abbiss

23 Netflix, Dark Fantastic Genres and Intergenerational Viewing: Family Watch Together TV
Djoymi Baker, Jessica Balanzategui and Diana Sandars

Netflix, Dark Fantastic Genres and Intergenerational Viewing

Family Watch Together TV

Djoymi Baker, Jessica Balanzategui, and Diana Sandars

Routledge
Taylor & Francis Group
LONDON AND NEW YORK

First published 2024
by Routledge
4 Park Square, Milton Park, Abingdon, Oxon OX14 4RN

and by Routledge
605 Third Avenue, New York, NY 10158

Routledge is an imprint of the Taylor & Francis Group, an informa business

British Library Cataloguing-in-Publication Data
A catalogue record for this book is available from the British Library

Library of Congress Cataloguing-in-Publication Data
Names: Baker, Djoymi, 1972- author. | Balanzategui, Jessica, author. | Sandars, Diana, author.
Title: Netflix, dark fantastic genres and intergenerational viewing : family watch together TV / Djoymi Baker, Jessica Balanzategui, Diana Sandars.
Description: New York : Routledge, 2023. | Series: Routledge advances in television studies | Includes bibliographical references and index. |
Identifiers: LCCN 2022061417 (print) | LCCN 2022061418 (ebook) | ISBN 9781032121895 (hardback) | ISBN 9781032121888 (paperback) | ISBN 9781003223498 (ebook)
Subjects: LCSH: Netflix (Firm) | Television and families. | Science fiction television programs. | Animated television programs. | Streaming technology (Telecommunications)
Classification: LCC HD9697.V544 N4823525 2023 (print) | LCC HD9697.V544 (ebook) | DDC 384.55/54--dc23/eng/2023-02-17
LC record available at https://lccn.loc.gov/2022061417
LC ebook record available at https://lccn.loc.gov/2022061418

ISBN: 978-1-032-12189-5 (hbk)
ISBN: 978-1-032-12188-8 (pbk)
ISBN: 978-1-003-22349-8 (ebk)

DOI: 10.4324/9781003223498

Typeset in Times New Roman
by MPS Limited, Dehradun

Contents

1 Family Viewing in the Age of Netflix

This book tells the story of how Netflix developed a cycle of dark family telefantasy programs in order to reposition the world's most popular subscription video on demand (SVOD) service as a go-to destination for family content. We argue that Netflix initiated new frontiers for "family television" as a genre, industry model, and cultural construct through its cycle of dark family telefantasies under its "Family Watch Together TV" catalogue label. In so doing, throughout this book, we illuminate how this move created a new model of family viewing tailored for the era of on-demand streaming.

When Netflix launched its first "Netflix Original" series, *House of Cards* (2013–2019),[1] the SVOD was strategically rebranded from simply being a streaming service reliant on pre-existing licensed content into a content creator (Burroughs 2019: 5; Lobato 2018: 244). From this juncture onwards, Netflix promised to be a superior alternative to broadcast and cable TV not just via its distinctive algorithmically driven approach to digital content distribution, but also by offering "prestige, plenitude, and participation to its subscribers, through a mix of technological and aesthetic appeals" (Tryon 2015). While the streaming service landscape has since become increasingly crowded and competitive, Netflix has so far remained the dominant and most culturally influential SVOD service.[2] Netflix's influence includes popularising the SVOD "binge-watch" (Jenner 2020), the prioritisation of "Original" and exclusive rather than licensed content (Burroughs 2019; Lobato 2018), and algorithmically "personalised" viewing recommendations (Van Esler 2020), all domains that have received careful scholarly attention. One key element of Netflix's strategy and influence that has not yet been adequately addressed, however, is its new approach to "family television". Netflix's identity has shifted significantly since it began as a DVD distribution service in 1997, with multiple key junctures of change including its pivot to video streaming from 2007 into the early 2010s, its heavy investment in exclusive "Originals" from 2013 onwards, and its efforts to operate as a "fully global television service" (Lobato 2019: 1) since 2016. We argue that from the mid-2010s to the early 2020s, the platform's "Family Watch Together TV" category represents another such transformational juncture, operating as a key site of cultural and industrial renegotiation in Netflix's

DOI: 10.4324/9781003223498-1

ongoing process of redefinition. Ramon Lobato details how, as a "disruptive media phenomena", Netflix has throughout its over 20-year history operated as a "boundary object that exists between, and inevitably problematises, the conceptual categories used to think about media" in ways that produce "definitional tension" even in Netflix's own marketing and strategic discursive positioning (2019: 20).

We contend that the company's strategy around "Family Watch Together TV" illuminates a major but to date underexplored transition in Netflix's identity at a point of maturity for both the company and the SVOD ecology more generally, which raises significant "definitional tension" around:

1 How Netflix is positioned in relation to legacies and futures of "TV" as a media form.
2 How "family television" operates as a longstanding but ambiguously defined genre that solicits and constructs a particular type of viewing.
3 How the "Family Watch Together TV" category and Netflix more broadly relate to not just the key legacy media formats of film and television but also adjacent entertainment media such as social media and video-sharing streaming platforms such as YouTube.

Both Catherine Johnson (2012) and Amanda Lotz (2017) influentially suggest that streaming video services like Netflix function as "portals", shifting the television viewing experience from choosing from a linear schedule to choosing "on-demand" from an extensive library menu. Despite enacting such fundamental changes to the way video content is distributed and accessed, Netflix and the SVOD ecology more broadly are typically positioned as Internet-enabled continuations of television as a media form, technology, and industry sector, and thus are examined within the disciplinary terrain of television studies. As Lotz articulates:

> the revolutionary impact of new media upon television has not been as a replacement medium, but as a new mechanism of distribution that allows evolution of legacy companies and the creation of a sector – maybe sectors – of Internet-distributed television. (2017: 1)

While the terminology Internet-distributed television has become commonplace to describe Netflix and other SVOD services, Lobato suggests we conceive of Netflix "as a hybrid TV-cinema-digital media distribution system with a unique set of experiential and aesthetic connections to older media" (2019: 44–45). Netflix is strategic in its use of such terms and aesthetic connections at different times and in different contexts. For example, in 2016, when Netflix's focus was on international expansion, Co-founder and Chief Executive Reed Hastings called Netflix "a new global Internet TV network" (Netflix 2016b), while in 2022 Netflix's "What Is Netflix" website defined it as "a subscription-based streaming service". Ultimately, as Derek

Johnson argues, "even as a new portal logic dominates the space of Internet-delivered television, its relationship to the television channel may not be one of opposition and obliteration so much as evolution and adaptation" (2018a: 9). From its interface tagging to its legacy media promotions, Netflix frequently (and even inconsistently) uses the rhetoric of different media forms. In this context of persistent "definitional tension", we analyse Netflix's "Family Watch Together TV" interface label and category as a deliberate and strategic evocation of television, family television, and family viewing, even as its delivery mode clearly reframes what these concepts might mean in the streaming era.

Attempting to expand its core territory, Netflix started to commission original family content in 2014 (Andreeva 2014). Building on its 2014 "Watch Together" family movie night campaign (Brouwer 2014), Netflix sought Original productions to pitch as "Family Watch Together TV" on the platform. Netflix was also seeking to counter public narratives that the streaming era had brought about a "Golden Age" of gritty adult content but a perceived decline of family television content and family communal viewing (Cobb 2015) – types of content and modes of viewing associated primarily with broadcast television and its linear, schedule-based mode of distribution. By 2016, Netflix's Chief Content Officer Ted Sarandos announced that the streaming service was committing to "doubling down on kids and families" through increased child and family-oriented Originals (quoted in Flint 2016; Littleton 2017).

The way Netflix addresses the family audience through content, distribution, and paratextual promotion is the site of a significant intervention in television studies. Throughout this book, we draw on screen genre and television studies frameworks including textual and paratextual analysis and audience research to elucidate how "Family Watch Together TV" repositions pre-existing approaches to family audiences and genres. Indeed, as Balanzategui (2020b) has argued, established screen genre and related audience studies frameworks have been underutilised in considerations of how children's genres operate and have been transformed in the streaming era. Yet, as Lobato cautions, specific interpretive frames such as television, Internet, or digital platform studies carry with them sets of assumptions and specific histories of technological development, necessitating critical reflection on how these frameworks "shape the kind of thinking we bring to the analysis" (2019: 21). In accordance with Lobato, Balanzategui advocates for the integration of genre studies frameworks with emergent analytical approaches to SVODs as digital platforms, such as interface and catalogue analysis (Balanzategui 2020b; Balanzategui and Lynch 2022). Taking up such an integrated approach that combines a tight historicised focus on Netflix's development as an SVOD platform 2016–2022 with how this development relates to the complex history of "family television", our research addresses the area of definitional and *transformational* tension represented by Netflix's "Family Watch Together TV" category. We demonstrate how this category's high-profile flagship content type, dark family telefantasy, is built around and motivates shifting notions of "family viewing" in the streaming era.

This book focuses on Netflix's Original dark family telefantasy as a genre cycle, with each chapter capturing how the cycle unfolded chronologically: *Stranger Things* (2016-), *A Series of Unfortunate Events* (2017–2019), *Lost in Space* (2018–2021), *Dark Crystal: Age of Resistance* (2019), and *Raising Dion* (2019–2022). We conclude with a chapter that revisits *Stranger Things*, focusing on Season 4 (2022), alongside *Squid Game* (2021-) to consider the cycle's new frontiers in 2021–2022. By telling the combined stories of Netflix's dark family telefantasy and "Family Watch Together TV", we outline how this genre cycle reconstructs family viewing for the on-demand, non-linear streaming era, in so doing troubling cultural expectations shaped in large part by broadcast television and film around child-appropriate "family" content. Yet simultaneously, this genre cycle harnesses personal and cultural nostalgia for these pre-streaming era content types and modes of viewing.

Genres, Alt-Genres, and Cycles in the Streaming Era

Netflix includes "Family Watch Together TV" as one of its "genres" on the interface, even though the term reads more like a recommendation around audience suitability and age – and a directive around *how* to watch this sort of content – rather than a *genre*. As Maire Messenger-Davies notes, while children's television tends to be deployed as a genre label, it is "an unusual genre in that its title is defined by the people who watch it, rather than by the characteristics of the text" (2001: 96). In turn, the intergenerational viewing experience associated with the *family* category assumes a different function from that of children's television as a "babysitter" (Beyens and Eggermont 2014) or "educator" (Bryant 2014: 50), instead inviting a shared spectatorship across different age groups (Brown 2013: 1; Cantor 1991). Derek Johnson refers to this communal construct of spectatorship that spans generations as "co-viewing", which operates "as a means of building bridges across age demographics to navigate the significant economic, technological, and social shifts facing television" (2019: 24). Netflix's "Family Watch Together TV" is built around the solicitation of an SVOD-specific type of co-viewing via a variety of genres, but is dominated by family sitcoms on the one hand, and its flagship cycle of dark family telefantasy shows on the other.

Netflix's family sitcoms, beginning with a sequel to the popular (if critically dismissed) family sitcom *Full House* (1987–1995), constituted the company's first attempt to "reinvent family-friendly viewing" in the streaming era (Loock 2018: 362). The family sitcom has historically been a key genre through which shared family viewing has been most obviously constructed as a cultural category. Furthermore, as Derek Johnson points out, "as media industries change, so too do ideas about the family" (2019: 27), and as such the legacies of both prior models of family viewing and of family reverberate in and are transformed by Netflix's "Family Watch Together TV" category. The family sitcom emerged in the 1950s, with programs such as *Father Knows Best* (1954–1960) and *Leave It to Beaver* (1957–1963) delivering stories revolving around all members of the onscreen family, designed to "appeal to the entire family" audience (Haralovich 1992: 114). Lynn Spigel suggests these "wholesome" onscreen families were a way of mitigating the concerns that television itself was disrupting the family home (1992: 142) – concerns that echo contemporary fears about how on-demand, platform-neutral SVOD viewing can fracture and atomise families within a single household, as children retreat to their bedrooms to stream (Ofcom 2019: 7). Just as in the 21st century, Netflix is reconstituting ideas about family viewing and togetherness via its "Family Watch Together TV" content, in the 1950s the family sitcom reflected and informed the dominant post-war nuclear family ideal in the 1950s (Cantor 1991; Kutulas 2005). By the mid-1960s, family sitcoms such as *The Patty Duke Show* (1963–1966) started to include stories revolving around an emerging generational gap (Kutulas 2005: 52–54). In the 1970s, *The Brady Bunch* (1969–1974) depicted a blended family just as no-fault divorce was starting to change the structure of many families in the US (Pugh 2018). Around this time, a wave of family sitcoms focused on Black families also emerged, including *Julia* (1969–1971), a sitcom about a widowed African-American nurse raising her six-year-old son on her own, *Good Times* (1974–1979), which follows the struggles of an African-American family living in a Chicago Housing projects, and *The Jeffersons* (1975–1985) a "fish out of water" comedy spin off from *All in the Family* (1971–1979). This trend continued into the 1980s with the hit shows *Diff'rent Strokes* (1978–1985) and *The Cosby Show* (1984–1992). As Muriel G. Cantor asserts, across the decades, the family (or "domestic") sitcoms "have both changed and stayed the same", in that despite changing families, the resolution of any conflict upholds the family as a desirable ideal (1991: 215).

In the streaming era, media commentator Kayla Cobb (2015) suggests that the dominance of "dark, gritty, and sexy programs" left little room for the family sitcom and other family programming, with streamers such as Netflix following the cable trend of preferring to offer distinct content for adults and children respectively (Johnson 2019: 30). Nonetheless, Derek Johnson charts how in the 2010s in particular, parental co-viewing was increasingly seen as creating an important secondary market for kids' shows on cable facilitated through nostalgic revivals, a trajectory also mirrored by streaming services (2019: 40). While Johnson focuses on the role of *children's* programs in this transition, it can also be seen in legacy *family* genres and programs. When Netflix announced its *Full House* revival, Cobb (2015) proclaimed: "Family TV is dying. Can Netflix's bet on 'Fuller House' save it?" *Fuller House* (2016–2020), like the original program, received consistently negative reviews yet initially attracted a strong audience, only to fall off after the first season (Clark 2019a). Its remaining fan base was sufficient to take the series to five seasons before it was cancelled. As Mareike Jenner notes, sitcoms like *Fuller House* marked Netflix's transition away from its initial focus on quality branding and towards its revival of popularist linear television genres (2018: 139). By tagging *Fuller House* as "Family Watch Together TV", Netflix was also overtly marking its shift from separate adult and children's content towards family content, but its reception was hardly helpful to Netflix's brand image. *Fuller House* was dismissed as "treacly garbage" (Tiffany 2017) that made reboot "a dirty word" (Mitchell 2022).

Family sitcoms function as a well-recognised family viewing staple nestled under the "Family Watch Together TV" tag on the interface, but we argue that it has been through its Original dark family telefantasy programming that the streaming service sought to articulate a narrative around a new form of family television touted as matching the quality of its adult content. This approach to family content is positioned as being aligned with Netflix's brand reputation for edgy content that, like its personalised algorithmic distribution model, supersedes broadcast TV. Prior to the foregrounding of its "Family Watch Together TV" category, Netflix was primarily distinguished from linear television via its "personalized delivery of content independent from a schedule" (Lotz 2017: 2), yet Netflix's dark family telefantasy content strategically repositions this feature as an agent not of atomisation and individualisation, but as a means of bringing families together to watch TV. Netflix's dark family telefantasy genre cycle thus aligns with Derek Johnson's contention that in the post-network climate of disruption, instability, and change, co-viewing has become a valuable means of transforming "engagement of consumers in the past and present into a platform for building future generations of viewers" (2019: 25). In tandem, he asserts, "the idea of *family* promises to reproduce continuity while adapting to change" (2019: 25), thus positioning the "family" audience as newly significant.

As we highlight throughout this book, "Family Watch Together TV" is a Netflixification of family viewing that can be considered a continuation of co-viewing – which became increasingly prominent in television industry discourse and strategies from 2005 onwards (Johnson 2019: 24, 29). However, this Netflixified model of family viewing is built around distinct and specific strategies that sought to reposition Netflix in both the market and cultural consciousness between 2016 and 2022. Notably, this repositioning occurred at a juncture during which Netflix was focused on solidifying its newly global presence, and at a time when its once novel mode of distribution had become increasingly mainstream as the SVOD ecology became more crowded. In this context, Netflix articulated its approach to *family* content along different lines than the transgenerational viewing around *children's* shows that Johnson (2019) canvasses. Brian Wright, VP of Family Content for Netflix, asserted that Netflix's goal was to make family content that was "just as good" as their high-profile adult Originals *House of Cards* and *Orange Is the New Black* (2013–2019) (quoted in Tiffany 2017). Netflix was thereby attempting to associate its family programming with the critical acclaim and cultural prestige more commonly associated with *adult*

Quality TV (Auster 2005: 226–227; Baker 2017: 43–44; Feuer 1984: 34, 56). Indeed, scholarship on Quality TV links the "quality" associated with this mode of television with distinctively "adult" themes, styles, and modes of address (Kelso 2008: 51; McCabe and Akass 2008: 88; Williamson 2008: 109). While Netflix's family sitcoms such as *Fuller House* lacked the cultural capital of Quality TV and received poor critical reception (Mitchell 2022; Tiffany 2017), Netflix found a successful family television strategy when it turned to telefantasy, a mix of science fiction, horror, and fantasy.

Telefantasy is a term that emerged in fan magazines in the 1980s, to acknowledge the often-blurred lines between science fiction, fantasy, and horror TV (Johnson 2015: 3, 56). While Steven Gil notes telefantasy's "problematic … broadness of scope" as a term for scholars (2012: 80), by contrast, Catherine Johnson argues telefantasy operates

> as a cultural category that emerges precisely as a broad catch-all designed to bring together a range of different programmes united by their representation of the otherworldly and unreal, on the one hand, and their tendency to defy easy generic classification, on the other. (2015: 57; 2005: 4)

More than a convenient umbrella term bringing together related genres of the "unreal" (Johnson 2015: 57–59), Johnson's conception of telefantasy as a "cultural category" speaks to the way television genres circulate and are constructed discursively (Altman 1999: 101; Mittell 2004: 11). Johnson notes telefantasy is subject to slippage between various elements of science fiction, fantasy, and horror and therefore lacks a clearly defined generic social contract (2005: 2), and that this ambiguous social contract is continually renegotiated.

In turn, Netflix's cycle of dark family telefantasy under the "Family Watch Together TV" label on its interface necessarily curtails the severe violence of these programs, yet nonetheless offers younger audiences what Karl Mannheim calls "fresh contact" (1997: 171) with dark and challenging genres such as horror and dark fantasy. Indeed, many of the programs in the cycle have been called the family-friendly (or *almost* family-friendly) answer to Quality Telefantasy programs such as *Game of Thrones* in the public press (Allen 2020; Robinson 2019), confronting contemporary cultural and regulatory expectations around appropriate family viewing. In the attempt to attract and maintain a wide cross-section of new subscribers, Netflix's dark family telefantasy reimagines the family audience as an edgier, more knowing, intergenerational audience than prior models of family viewing associated with television, cable, and film. Netflix has used its dark family telefantasy programs as its "tentpole" or "flagship" Original content (Baker 2017: 44; Klarer 2014: 204; San Filippo 2017: 79) to strategically promote its new family profile as a point of branding.

As Noel Brown notes, historically in film and television, "the so-called 'family audience' symbolised respectability, profitability and mass cultural acceptance" (Brown 2013: 1; Cantor 1991). By contrast, as we chart throughout this book, ambiguities around the age-appropriateness and classifications of Netflix's dark family telefantasy programs have fuelled controversy, questioning their suitability as "Family Watch Together TV". Mike Hastings, Director of Enhanced Content at Netflix, has attempted to play down such tensions and position them in relation to Netflix's celebrated personalisation and freedom of choice, stating: "We understand that every family is different and that parents have differing perspectives on what they feel is appropriate to watch at different ages" (quoted in Spangler 2018a). Hastings' comment invites a discursive approach to Netflix's cycle of telefantasy within "Family Watch Together TV", through a consideration of "the larger cultural operations" of genre at a given historical moment (Mittell 2004: 13).

While the family sitcom sitting under its "Family Watch Together TV" label attracted a dedicated niche audience but critical scorn, by contrast Netflix's cycle of dark family telefantasy attracted critical acclaim and awards, functioning as a successful branding strategy. Leger Grindon explains that the genre cycle is "a distinctive and more focused category" than "genre", as it denotes a series of works produced during "a limited period of time and linked by a dominant trend", often by a single studio (2012: 44). For example, Rick Altman notes that during the studio era of Hollywood, individual studios developed their own proprietary genre cycles as a form of company branding (1999: 120). Despite this overt production strategy, the studio itself might nonetheless demonstrate "scrupulous avoidance of generic terminology" in its promotions (Altman 1999: 120). As such, Steve Neale argues that genres are not simply a "groups of texts" that may share shifting conventions at a given time, but also "systems of expectation, categories and labels" (2000: 2; Altman 1999: 101; Naremore 1998; Wallin 2019: 3–4). Similarly, Jason Mittell suggests, "genres do run through texts, but also operate within the practices of critics, audience and industries" that together constitute an understanding of genre (2004: 12). Altman terms this "genrification", an ongoing process, in which genres function as "discursive claims made by real speakers for particular purposes in specific situations" (1999: 101).[3] Mittell builds on this work in his approach to television genres as "*discursive practices*" (2004: 11, emphasis in original). Netflix, for example, does not have a telefantasy category per se, yet acknowledges the shared genre terrain across these categories by combining "TV Sci-Fi & Horror" and "TV Sci-Fi & Fantasy", respectively.

Throughout this book, we explore the ways that Netflix has produced a cycle of dark family telefantasy programs that it presents under its "Family Watch Together TV" label on the interface, prioritising the solicitation of a specific viewing practice and audience over more traditional genre labels. Zoë Wallin argues, "cycles work alongside a discursive approach to genre" but can take into account texts "that fall outside of established generic categories" (2019: 4). She outlines how "cycles are not simply about increases in production of a particular type of film but are formed through the distribution and release of films in close proximity" (2019: 2). As such, a cycle reflects "production policies", but in addition the way texts are released and promoted reveals a cycle's different discursive functions (Wallin 2019: 2). Across each of the chapters, we explore the way that Netflix greenlit, promoted and released its cycle of dark family telefantasy, nestled under its preferred category of "Family Watch Together TV".

More broadly, the streaming era constitutes a significant shift in the discursive practices around genre. In line with its carefully cultivated identity around personalised content delivery, Netflix uses its data analysis to create "genres of programming tailored to particular audiences" (Barker and Wiatrowski 2017: 1). Netflix famously developed a range of constantly changing and "oddly specific" micro-genres or "alt-genres" in its catalogue, such as "Action & Adventure based on real life from the 1980s" (Madrigal 2014; Moore 2021; Smith-Rowsey 2016: 64; Van Esler 2020: 8). As Daniel Smith-Rowsey notes, Netflix's approach seems to run counter to established ideas about genre (2016: 67), particularly the notion articulated by Altman that "if it is not defined by the industry and recognized by the mass audience, then it cannot be a genre" (1999: 16). This distinctive approach to generic categorisation in turn shapes how Netflix foregrounds and "recommends" content to subscribers on the platform's home page. As Mattias Frey points out, on SVOD platforms like Netflix, "recommendation is integrated into the consumption interface" in what he describes as "the culmination of a consumerist fantasy: personalization" (2019: 165). Although prior viewing helps generate the recommendations, the genre connections between viewing and recommendations are not necessarily made visible or obvious in the alt-genre tags (Madrigal 2014). For example, *Raising Dion* (2019–2022), one of the case studies analysed in this book, turned up in a search for "TV Sci-Fi & Horror" at the time of writing. However, when clicking on the title and bringing up the program "tile" on the interface, these genres were not listed at all. Instead, under "genres" the program was called "Kids' TV Shows", "TV Shows Based on Comics", and "Family Watch Together TV". The overlapping genre tags used by Netflix indicate what Smith-Rowsey calls an "intentional instability" in how Netflix uses and constructs genre on the interface (2016: 67). As such we disagree with Mareike Jenner when she asserts that Netflix doesn't challenge "already existing consensus about genre" (2018: 132). The selection of programs that appear under a specific alt-genre tag is changeable over time and fluid. Not all programs tagged on thumbnails or tiles as "Family Watch Together TV" will necessarily always come up in a search for this category, depending on the subscriber's prior viewing history, what Netflix is overtly promoting at the time, and, as Lobato points out, which territory the subscriber resides in (2018: 245).

The discursive practices through which both family viewing and telefantasy are articulated in the current era are thereby informed by the slippery nature of streaming interfaces and digital ephemera more broadly (Johnson 2017: 123; 2019: 123; Kelly 2020; Van Esler 2020: 2–3). Derek Johnson notes that "while the transgenerational character of the media industries is not necessarily new … that potential takes on added significance amid digital transformations that demand negotiation of the borderlands between old and new" (2019: 5). We expand on this to highlight how the Netflix interface also functions as such a "borderland" which contributes to the negotiation of genre and its solicitation of intergenerational viewing. Netflix's cycle of dark family telefantasy overtly labelled as "Family Watch Together TV" is constructed not just via the content of the shows, but via the interface aesthetics, recommendation algorithms, and distinctive approaches to generic categorisation in the Netflix catalogue, all of which demonstrate how streaming services such as Netflix address their subscribers and frame their holdings (Johnson 2019: 110–113).

Family Television and Family Telefantasy

While Kathleen Loock (2018) suggests that Netflix turned to the family sitcom to reintroduce family viewing into the streaming era, its fashioning of dark family telefantasy under the "Family Watch Together TV" tag enters into a more contested history around suitable family viewing. In its early years, television was constructed as a family medium par excellence, even as it continued in a new guise much older debates around children's entertainment (Spigel 1992: 52). Organising television history according to categories associated with key timeframes is in some ways problematic in its neat compartmentalisation of complex and layered industrial and cultural changes. Nonetheless, the periods commonly known in television studies as TVI (mid-1950s to early 1980s) and TVII (mid to late 1980s to late 1990s) sedimented a construct of the "family" audience tied to broadcast distribution, a model that we argue Netflix is actively and self-reflexively deconstructing with its own Original dark family telefantasy content, while also (and seemingly paradoxically) trying to nostalgically *re*construct it. Roberta Pearson explains that the TVI period is the "era of channel scarcity, the mass audience, and three-network hegemony", while TVII represents a time of "channel/network expansion, quality television, and network branding strategies" (2011: 107). The subsequent TVIII period is "the era of proliferating digital distribution strategies" and increasing fragmentation of audiences and platforms (Pearson 2011: 107). Jenner (2016) presents the provocation that Netflix and other SVODs may be advancing this fragmentation further into the realm of "TVIV", which is characterised by "a move away from the television set", and its associated viewing practices and "social connotations" (Jenner 2016: 259). Netflix's "Family Watch Together TV" category by contrast serves to encourage a return to an older model of communal family viewing, yet also subversively disrupts this model through the dark family telefantasy cycle.

During the TVI period, when television was an expensive novelty, the local community would flock to the houses of neighbours and family members to gather around a TV set and watch together (Hartley and O'Regan 1992: 206; Spigel 2001: 45). Once set ownership became more common later in the TVI period, this social dimension shifted to the family within the home in an idealised cultural image of family togetherness (Hartley 1992: 112; Hartley and O'Regan 1992: 206). The cultural associations between family and television viewing were exemplified with the emergence of the post-war suburban "family room" in which the television would take the central position (Spigel 1992: 39). As Lynn Spigel notes, advertisements for television sets in the 1950s showed the family audience watching their new set together as the ideal imagined audience (Spigel 1992: 43). Although television would soon be implicated as one cause of juvenile delinquency in the 1950s, paradoxically it was also seen as a potential cure, in that it was thought to help keep children home with their families (Spigel 1992: 45, 50, 53–54). Alongside moves to control content, parents were urged to control the television set itself (Spigel 1992: 55). This public discourse established a perception of television as a (highly contested) family medium.

Further contributing to television's privileged but contested status as a family medium, the edges between children's, family, and adult television were blurred even early in the medium's history. However, broadcast distribution's attachment to timeslots that interact with the broadly defined lifestyle habits and routines of the mass audience worked to establish certain expectations and boundaries – albeit fluid and continually shifting – around each type of content. Paul Witty reports on a 1951 questionnaire in the US which found:

> Televiewing for children was heaviest during the dinner and after-dinner hours – from 6.30 to 8.30. Since this period is later than the time many children's programs are presented, it appears that adult programs form a large part of children's fare on TV. (1952: 253)

A similar tendency was found in the UK in the 1950s (Buckingham et al 1999; Davies 2001: 115). Conversely, as Spigel argues, "adults seem to have watched the shows supposedly aimed at children. Since children's shows were often scheduled during the late afternoon and early evening hours, adults would have ample occasion to view these programs" (2001: 200). In other words, there were crossovers in the audience in both directions. By the late 1950s, the US industry started to address this shared audience with "kidult" programming that appealed to both children and their parents (Woolery 1985: 396). Similarly, programs initially designed for adults shifted to overtly address their newfound family audience (Spigel 1992: 57). Shows aimed solely at children or adults persisted, but a new shared family television terrain was being established that operated across and between these two distinct demographics.

Efforts to control children's television in the 1950s were based on adult tastes, whereas surveys indicated children were drawn to genres that their parents frequently disapproved of – at least for children – among them science fiction and horror (Spigel 1992: 57). Early science fiction television in the US was aimed primarily at children, partly because science fiction cinema serials were popular with a young audience, and partly because limited television production budgets meant a distinctly lo-fi approach to the genre (Baker 2020: 112; Duchovnay 2008: 69–70; Sconce 2004: 2026–2027). The first US science fiction program, *Captain Video and His Video Rangers* (1949–1955), was continually decried by parents and commentators for its perceived violence, yet remained a favourite among children (Baker 2020). Psychiatrist Frederic Wertham, best known for his campaign against crime and horror comic books, also criticised *Captain Video*'s science fiction violence on TV (1954: 369), as did the 1954 Senate Subcommittee on juvenile delinquency (Baker 2020: 114). The Subcommittee was also concerned about children's exposure to horror on TV (Spigel 1992: 55). These concerns continued cultural debates that had circulated in earlier decades around film (discussed in Chapters 2 and 4), and were based at least in part on a "nostalgic adult fantasy" of "childhood innocence" that emerged in the 19th century and have informed attitudes to children's entertainment industries ever since (Cunningham 2020; Egan and Hawkes 2008: 637; Spigel 1992: 52).

During the 1950s in the US, parents protested when horror content was broadcast, while children protested when it was taken off air (Spigel 1992: 57). Although in this era science fiction TV was largely intended for children, while horror TV was intended for adults, these genres both became part of a shared and often fraught discourse around television genres and children. In the UK, by contrast, telefantasy was, in general, taken more seriously as a television genre from as early as the 1950s (Coleman 2009; 142, 145; Hills 2005: 117; Jancovich and Johnson 2009: 77; Peirse 2010; Wheatley 2012). However, telefantasy struggled for legitimacy on early US television (Jancovich and Johnson 2009: 75), despite the emergence of anthology science fiction programs for adults in the mid-1950s onwards such as *Science Fiction Theatre* (1955–1957) and *The Twilight Zone* (1959–1964).

Furthermore, while they are typically understood as adult shows, popular telefantasy anthology programs that leaned heavily into horror such as *The Twilight Zone* and *Alfred Hitchcock Presents* (1955–1965) often featured child characters and engaged prominently with childhood themes (Mogg 2018), and also attracted child audiences (Schober 2018: 44; Zicree 1982: 96). However, the dynamics of broadcast distribution meant that airing timeslots could be used as a regulatory device to limit children's engagement with these programs, and indeed *The Twilight Zone*, *Alfred Hitchcock Presents*, and *Night Gallery* (1970–1973) aired after the 9:00 pm watershed in supposedly "child-free" time slots. Nevertheless, the popularity of these shows – including the interest they sparked amongst children – laid the groundwork for later comedy-horror sitcoms of the TVI period such as *The Munsters*

(1964–1966) and *The Addams Family* (1964–1966), both of which "trafficked in audience familiarity with horror iconography while introducing even broader audiences to the genre in the guise of the family sitcom" (Balanzategui 2018a: 204). These two horror-comedy sitcoms aired pre-9:00 pm in family-friendly timeslots, reinforcing their suitability for a "family" audience consisting of both parents and children.

The subsequent transition into the TVII era in the late 1970s and 1980s was paralleled by a boom in family or children's horror films from the US (Antunes 2013; Balanzategui, 2018a; Lester 2016; 2021). TVII conditions were driven by the deregulation of cable networks and increasing fragmentation and competition between networks, which created a space for television shows for children that engaged with the horror genre more explicitly. Catherine Johnson points out that these industrial changes undermined "the networks' ability to attract large consensus audiences", so a strategy emerged of programming that targeted "differently defined (although not necessarily mutually 'exclusive') niche audiences" (2005: 98). The TVII period thus saw the emergence of US cable channels tailored for youth and child audiences, such as Nickelodeon, MTV, and YTV (the Canadian sister channel to Nickelodeon), and this transformation also "diminished the effectiveness of traditional regulatory devices driven by television scheduling, such as the 9:00pm watershed" (Balanzategui 2018a: 217) because they facilitated 24-hour children's and youth programming. Subsequently, during the 1990s, the internationally popular US-Canadian children's horror anthology shows *Goosebumps* (1995–1998) and *Are You Afraid of the Dark?* (1992–1996; 1999–2000) – both of which were the product of cable networks YTV/Fox Kids and YTV/Nickelodeon, respectively – contributed to the mainstreaming of horror programming for children. Notably, both of these shows were aimed squarely at *child* rather than *family* audiences. As Balanzategui articulates, they self-reflexively adjust the themes, structure, aesthetics, and affectual resonances of earlier adult-oriented telefantasy shows such as *The Twilight Zone* to render them "safe" for children (2018a: 208–218). Nevertheless, both shows were met with controversy and resistance (Balanzategui 2018a: 208, 212–213). They can therefore be seen as part of the ongoing trajectory in which dark telefantasy for child and family audiences mediates shifting ideas about television's relationships with children and their parents, and also influences changing understandings of "children", "parents", and "families" as cultural categories.

Although "dark" telefantasy programs in the TVI and into the early TVII era frequently attracted both young and adult viewers in the US and globally, the public discourse around the genre suggests it was seen as a challenge to the cultural notion of television as a family medium (Hills 2005: 118). For instance, Helen Wheatley notes that Gothic-inflected 70s and 80s British telefantasy shows had fantastic themes "both enthralling and terrifying" (2012: 385), while Alison Peirse points out that British program *Century Falls* (1993) pushed "the possible limits of horror in children's television" in ways that were quite controversial (2010: 119). Globally influential British telefantasy shows such as *Doctor Who* (1963–1989) also contributed to shifting ideas around the suitability of dark telefantasy content for children. As Lindsay Coleman notes, the initial run of *Doctor Who* "was viewed by children, but was not technically part of children's programming for the BBC. It was a series produced for the family, inclusive of parents and older siblings" (2009: 142, 145). As a science fiction show that frequently depicted violence and Gothic, horrific images, it came under frequent criticism by commentators such as Mary Whitehouse as being unsuitable for children (Coleman 2009: 142).

Thus, while "dark" telefantasy programming has attracted child and family viewers from the TVI period onwards, the discourse around it suggests a genre that needs to be carefully negotiated in a domestic medium. Comedic genre hybrids such as the aforementioned *The Addams Family* (1964–1966) and *The Munsters* (1964–1966) attempt to achieve this by acknowledging the popularity of horror for family audiences while safely containing it within the domestic sitcom (Hills 2005: 122). More broadly, the British television industry dealt with the problem by frequently moving away from using "horror" as a genre label in schedules and promotional materials in favour of the more literary and legitimate-sounding "Gothic TV" (Hills 2005: 119–120). Lorna Jowett and Stacey Abbott extend on this observation, noting that across television history, horror TV has often been hidden under other genre labels in paratextual materials, such as "police investigation series, hospital dramas, comedy and children's television" (2013: 17). In this way, industry discourse around genre labels appears to moderate and manage taste cultures around genre, in particular when it comes to darker telefantasy genres. Similarly, Jancovich and Johnson note that science fiction television has also been inconsistently labelled across its history, citing by way of example the fact that British program *The Quatermass Experiment* (1953) was initially billed as a "thriller" by the BBC (2009: 77), and was identified as horror by its producer Rudolph Cartier (Johnson 2005: 26), yet today is considered part of science fiction canon. The shifting labels assigned to science fiction and horror programs are examples of Altman's genrification (1999: 101) and Mittell's discursive practice (2004: 11), through which telefantasy has been both marketed and carefully managed in specific contexts.

In the streaming, or what Jenner (2016) polemically calls the "TVIV" era, on-demand, personalised access to a wide catalogue of content has come to supplant the linear distribution model, and as a result the long-contested terrain represented by "family" content and its audience is undergoing a renewed period of transformation. As we argue in this book, the cycle of dark family telefantasy Netflix Originals represent one of the most strategic sites of this transformational and definitional tension. Netflix features science fiction, horror, and fantasy heavily yet these programs are frequently "hidden" in plain sight under its "Family Watch Together TV" alt-genre tag on the interface. Emily Lawrence suggests Netflix's "non-canonical" alt-genres operate to manage and construct taste (2015: 358). As Lawrence points out, many of the terms used in Netflix alt-genres relate to adjectival "appeal elements" associated with the "feel" of a text that help to shape audience expectations (2015: 359–360), a labelling strategy that displaces focus on the generic identity of the content. In listing "Family Watch Together TV" as a genre, Netflix frequently obscures or sidelines the more traditional telefantasy labels of science fiction, horror, or fantasy, continuing a re-labelling practice seen since the 1960s, particularly prevalent in Britain (Hills 2005: 120). In the chapters that follow, we examine *why* Netflix is prioritising dark telefantasy and invested in circulating family discourse around this content in ways that revise dark telefantasy as a generic identity via marketing rhetoric, interface aesthetics, labelling, and catalogue organisation.

Dark Family Telefantasy and the Intergenerational Dynamic

Netflix's cycle of dark family telefantasy Original programs promoted under the "Family Watch Together TV" label employs a heightened intertextuality to solicit and appeal to younger audiences as well as adults – both with and without children. By paratextually framing these programs under the "Family Watch Together TV" tag, Netflix more specifically invites shared cultural transfer *between* family members, returning to a communal model of television viewing and, in so doing, to the cultural mythologies such viewing carries. As such, we argue that Netflix's dark family telefantasy is characterised by an *intergenerational dynamic* – a combination of paratextual framing and textual aesthetics, theme, and form – that invites dialogue and exchange between age-groups and generations, constructing a new type of family viewing for the SVOD era. Indeed, as we found in our audience research, detailed below and integrated throughout this book, ideas about "family viewing" remained attached to parents watching with kids – even though our methodology invited consideration of multiple different types of families not aligned with traditional ideas of the nuclear family. While we discovered that there are multiple motivations around committing to watch an entire program together as a family on Netflix, these reasons revolved around a desire to share content tastes, trends, genres, and nostalgia with the rest of the family. Netflix's strategy to cultivate an intergenerational dynamic *onscreen* and via paratexts invites intergenerational interactions and connections *offscreen*, which we found indeed connects with how families use Netflix to "watch together".

In theorising and centring the *intergenerational dynamic* constructed by Netflix's dark family telefantasy genre cycle, we expand in new directions Derek Johnson's work on the significance of co-viewing to what he describes as *transgenerational* media strategies. Johnson frames his analysis around the transgenerational because, he argues, "an approach imagined as cross-generational or intergenerational would lend itself to examining relations between discrete age cohorts", while the *trans-* prefix prevents such focus on "discrete, isolatable generations" in favour of "more complex processes in which the production and consumption of popular culture bends boundaries around adulthood and childhood" (2019: 4). While we concur with Johnson's point about the complexity of age-based boundary-crossing in contemporary media industries, when it comes to Netflix's dark family telefantasy cycle, we theorise throughout this book how these very "relations between discrete age cohorts" (Johnson 2019: 4) are cultivated in the paratextual framing, marketing, and composition of the texts that discursively construct this genre cycle. Netflix's dark family telefantasy genre cycle is thus notable for the way it balances the solicitation of specific modes of age-based, generational intimacy with the text with appeal across and *between* different generations and age groups. It is in this way that this genre cycle invites a mode of co-viewing tailored for the Netflix brand and SVOD era – "Family Watch Together TV".

While Netflix's much-hyped marketing rhetoric around on-demand and personalised content delivery is positioned as superseding the rigid infrastructure of linear television, at the same time – and seemingly conversely – the very idea of "Family Watch Together TV" nostalgically revives a broadcast TV era model of family viewing around a single TV set. As the following chapters demonstrate, the intergenerational dynamic in the dark family telefantasy genre cycle is built around familiarity and affective intimacy with a painstakingly reconstructed pop cultural past. It is a viewing experience premised on a nostalgic intertextually that invites parents and older viewers to share memories from their own youths with their children or younger family members, in so doing extending their nostalgic intimate connection with the text to their children. These are programs that can, of course, be watched by adults without the presence of children and vice versa. What interests us here is how the strategic use of the "Family Watch Together TV" label, in combination with the heightened intertextuality of the programs, together work to *solicit* intergenerational sharing and connection.

As such, within this intergenerational dynamic, Netflix is positioned as the gatekeeper charged with facilitating the generational transfer of not only personal memories but also, on a collective level, culture. In so doing, this type of content self-reflexively positions Netflix in line with television's status not just as a media form, but also as an "object, practice and cultural form" that has as a result long been "a deeply nostalgic technology" (Holdsworth 2011: 15). As we illuminate throughout this book, "Family Watch Together TV" programs invite the passing down of nostalgically beloved media, trends, and even mundane features of past ways of life – like drinking "Tab" out of red plastic cups – to younger members of the family. While Netflix's original content strategy is often underpinned by a commitment to nostalgically treasured pre-existing family products – such as television programs like *Lost in Space* (1965–1968), films like *The Dark Crystal* (Jim Henson and Frank Oz 1982), or the *Series of Unfortunate Events* books (1999–2006) – we argue its *intergenerational dynamic* is not merely based on adaptations, prequels, sequels, and reboots, but rather on a heightened intertextual system more broadly that invites affective intimacy between both the text and between family members. This provides the potential for comforting nostalgic familiarity or the excitement of Mannheim's "fresh contact" (1997: 171), depending on the age and generational identity of the audience member. Thus, the dark family telefantasy genre cycle foregrounds a viewing pleasure based on a knowing familiarity that sustains an interplay between nostalgic comfort and disruptive freshness, encouraging intergenerational sharing of memory and media experiences.

Do Families Watch Together?

The "age of choice" associated with the deregulated structure of programming within the SVOD ecology pervades content, run time, episode count within a season, and delivery. As a result, the relationships between family viewing structures and the content being consumed are undergoing rapid shifts. As we articulate in the chapters that follow, these changes are illuminated most clearly via a consideration of Netflix's dark telefantasy family content. Although broadcast TV offers ratings-controlled programming that ensures content delivered before 9 pm is of a family-friendly nature, and more predictable conventions around episode durations and quantity per season, streaming services offer a flexible and variegated approach to season structure that takes into account on-demand viewing and binge-watching practices. In this ecology, families ostensibly become the programmer of SVOD content, engaging in a diverse range of practices which incorporate these programs within their individual family's flow, rather than operating in accordance with a generalised understanding of "family" habits as part of an undifferentiated mass audience. This approach recalls Netflix's Mike Hastings' attempt to reassure subscribers that Netflix understands that every family is different, and that parents will accordingly have differing ideas about what is appropriate for their children (Spangler 2018a), a statement that subtly emphasises individual parental responsibility over regulatory mechanisms like ratings.

The "Family Watch Together TV" suite of Original titles at Netflix, and the dark family telefantasy genre cycle within this category, emerged over a period in which parental control over streaming on the platform had been undergoing revision in the face of consumer concern. As Jenner points out, the affordances of Netflix's personalised, non-linear delivery come with different sets of decision making on the part of viewers:

> Tasks previously performed by industry are now the viewer's responsibility, such as organising how much of a specific television text are shown each week, when they can see it, how long instalments should be, or in what order texts are placed in. (2018: 39)

These responsibilities are potentially more onerous for the parent who wants to actively control their children's streaming.

Parental oversight in this on-demand era interacts with issues of temporality (how much viewing is appropriate in one sitting, or over a week, and at what times of day), age suitability of the content, and access to devices. As outlined on "Habyts", a website which provides guidelines and resources for families around managing children's media use in the digital age, the 2019 Childwise Annual Report on children's use of media characterised 2017 as

> a turning point in kids' television viewing habits. That is, kids are now more likely to watch programmes and video on devices such as tablets and smartphones than on a TV … What this means is that watching television is no longer a family activity, it's a private one. (Habyts 2019)

The Childwise report suggests that control over family viewing is no longer primarily a matter of who holds the remote control (Jenner 2018: 60), or whether the V-chip has been programmed on the TV set (FCC 2019), but rather how devices and platforms are managed. The report is symptomatic of anxieties about the perceived shift in power balances associated with children's on-demand access to a vast library of streaming content across multiple devices and platforms, and suggests ways for parents to reclaim power in the streaming era. The Childwise report advises that adults should be responsible for streaming subscriptions and parental locking settings, which are new forms of adult gatekeeping that again place personal responsibility on individuals rather than aligning it with networks or broadcasters. Netflix's "Family Watch Together TV" tag on the interface similarly solicits the adults of the house to take charge of viewing arrangements, while repositioning the streaming service not as the *death* of family viewing, but rather a means of its *return*.

In this context in which different members of a family are able to stream content across different devices, potentially in separate rooms, Netflix's "Family Watch Together TV" alt-genre thereby represents a nostalgic appeal to come back to the television set once more as a family unit. Thus, while Jenner (2016) claims that the TVIV era is marked by a rejection of the cultural practices formerly associated with television as a medium, "Family Watch Together TV" represents Netflix's attempt to maintain some semblance of the communal viewing model and in so doing be repositioned as a cultural "glue" as the television medium once was (Holdsworth 2011). Beyond this appeal to nostalgia, though, "Family Watch Together TV" could mean something quite different in the streaming era, given content can easily be shared between different families, watched "together" but at different times of the day or week using separate devices in rooms or spaces other than the traditional loungeroom, or shared among family members dispersed across different geographic locations. Thus, Derek Johnson notes "co-viewing needs to happen simultaneously, but may speak to shared *engagement* with the same content across those different contexts" (2019: 24, emphasis added). The original 1950s image of family viewing "together" is thus both invoked and superseded. The "Family Watch Together TV" label is, therefore, a recommended mode of intergenerational viewing in which the "together" might be configured in different ways.

Indeed, given the Childwise findings, much attention has been on how parents can control children's viewing on Netflix when they are *not* in the room together. With a wide swathe of content in the catalogue, responsibility is placed on parents to activate the most appropriate parental locks for the family Netflix account if desired. Parents can set up restrictions in a child's profile and then let children choose what to watch, a practice found to be the case among 66% of parents in a 2020 US survey (Jacobson 2020). Although classification limits can be set for each child's profile, originally there was nothing to stop a child simply clicking on a parent or older sibling's profile to watch more adult content, a fact criticised in a 2017 report by The Parents Television Council (Henson 2017: 2). The report also cautioned,

> Netflix offers categories of content that viewers may find offensive, which often feature pornographic titles and cover art, and which often appear in close proximity to child-friendly categories – with no clear or obvious way of eliminating those categories from menu screens. (Henson 2017: 2)

An adult profile in Netflix might include not only thumbnail images implying sexual or violent content but also "auto-play trailers in the header" that may include adult content (Porter 2019). Netflix eventually responded with a new profile lock in 2020 that prevents children from accessing adult profiles entirely (Sattelberg 2020). Proposed legislation was drafted to "ban 'auto-play' sessions on websites and apps geared for children and young teens" (Derby 2020). More broadly, the legislation is intended to "require YouTube and Netflix to do more to protect children from viewing sex, violence, and drugs on their streaming services" (Abril 2019). Netflix's constantly evolving in-house measures to appease parents when families are *not* watching together has taken place in a shifting media regulatory landscape.

How Family Viewing Works on Netflix: Audience Research

Throughout this book, we draw on textual and paratextual analysis combined with social media and empirical audience research to highlight how Netflix's construction of family viewing both builds on and challenges previous television and film models. This multi-faceted analysis illuminates in new ways crucial key continuities and distinctions between these legacy media forms and SVOD platforms, while highlighting how shifting definitions of "family" content are pivotal to the cultural and industrial tensions underlying the rise of the SVOD sector.

Netflix is famously cagey about its viewing data.[4] In 2020, the streaming service began its "trending" list on the platform, but depending on what their algorithm decided about a customer's viewing habits, that list was not always easy to find on every profile. Netflix initially ranked its programs by a seemingly odd metric: whether viewers had watched the first two minutes of a program or film within the first 28 days of its release (Keck 2021). This means it counted a show as a success even if a viewer watched a few minutes and then decided not to keep watching. In September 2021, Netflix shifted to tracking the total number of viewing hours within the first 28 days of a title's release (Spangler 2021). In September 2021, Co-CEO Ted Sarandos announced, "We're trying to be more transparent with talent, with the market" (quoted in Spangler 2021), launching a dedicated "Top 10" website in November 2021 (Keck 2021). This was part of a promotional drive to lift subscriptions, which had gone up during the pandemic, but that dipped as restrictions lifted in many regions: indeed, Netflix lost subscribers in the US and Canada for the first time in mid-2021 (Faughnder 2021).

Even as Netflix releases more of its data to promote its top shows, ultimately their famous algorithm cannot tell them whether families actually watch their programs together (Baker et al 2020). In Australia where we reside, viewers reported more family co-viewing during the pandemic lockdowns of 2020 and 2021, both across households (Baker et al 2021), using extensions such as Netflix Party (Fogg 2020), and within households, drawing families back from their individual devices to the TV screen (Field 2021). As Derek Johnson notes, "streaming services such as Netflix construct discrete profiles and experiences for different family members" (2019: 23). Unless customers set up dedicated shared profiles for partners, or for the family, or the household as a whole, by default co-viewing occurs on one person's profile, messing up the algorithm for their "personal" tastes and leaving a big hole in Netflix's understanding of their audience.

Netflix cannot tell if people use each other's profiles and who else might be exposed to the content. As such, Netflix ultimately does not know whether families follow their recommendation to watch TV together. Further, as Sarah Arnold notes, the Netflix algorithm is a blunt instrument that "makes reductive claims about its users" (2016: 57). Lobato cautions that catalogue analysis alone can "help us understand patterns of distribution, not reception" (2018: 251). As Jason Mittell notes, critics and scholars of family and children's television need to "avoid simplistic arguments" and instead consider the ways real audiences watch TV (2015a: 113). Similarly, Jonathan Gray suggests "we know embarrassingly little about audiences" in the contemporary era (2017: 81). The most substantial studies of Netflix so far have not examined audiences (Barker and Wiatrowski 2017; Jenner 2018; Lobato 2018; McDonald and Smith-Rowsey 2016), with the exception of Mattias Frey, who notes in his extensive surveys and interviews in the US and the UK the importance that Netflix subscribers place on recommendations not from the platform but from family and friends (2021: 133, 170,

210, 213), and in one case, the reviews of other parents (2021: 176). He notes that Netflix operates within systems of "social exchange" whereby talking about programs and films constitutes another way "of watching, somehow, *together*" (2021: 172). Frey's research is a very welcome addition to the field, but for our purposes here, it is worth noting that his study does not otherwise delve into family and intergenerational viewing. More broadly, there has been a growth in surveys regarding binge-viewing in particular at the expense of other patterns of Netflix viewing (Fayelle et al 2020). Graeme Turner notes "a tendency towards the individualisation of consumption and the decline of the influence of the family upon the viewing habits of younger respondents" in Australia (Turner 2019: 224). However, Turner gives no additional information and does not delve further into the family dynamics of Netflix viewing.

Our audience research for the book was designed to understand how children and adults relate to Netflix's dark family telefantasy cycle, and consisted of a mixed method research design. This included a small-scale online survey from November 2021 to December 2021, as well as semi-structured interviews with six Netflix-subscribing families in June 2022, which included both parents and their children, ranging in ages from 5 to 15. We have combined both the qualitative and quantitative data in the surveys (Leavy 2017: 10), and qualitative data in the interviews, with textual and paratextual analysis throughout this book. The advantage of this combination is that it yields some indicative patterns, but also descriptive examples and expressive language in the interviews and open-ended questions (Leavy 2017: 19). As Greene notes, a mixed method approach "involves an openness to multiple ways … of making senses of the social world" (2007: xii). Snowball sampling (Leavy 2017: 80) was used by requesting people share the recruitment advertisement and survey details with people or communities who may be interested. While quantitative studies tend to favour larger sample sizes, by contrast qualitative studies tend to have smaller sample sizes. We are particularly interested in participants' qualitative reflections on the family viewing reported in the quantitative data captured from our survey.

Previous research with child audiences around horror film and television has yielded illuminating insights into what children make of genres adults deem inappropriate for them, and how they emotionally engage with such content (Buckingham 1996; Götz et al 2019), and in our semi-structured interviews we build on such work. We deployed a semi-structured interview methodology previously developed by Balanzategui (2020b; Balanzategui et al 2018). After obtaining signed approval from parents in line with the ethics approval process of our institutions, we spoke first to the child or children alone, then to their parent/s alone, and then to both the child/ren and parent/s together. This approach sought to capture the children's and parents' own versions of family viewing on Netflix and relationships with dark family telefantasy content, and finally to understand how both the parents and child/ren collectively understood their family viewing habits on Netflix.

We conducted these interviews via online meeting software so that families could remain in the comfortable environment of their home and thus respond more naturally, which was a particularly important methodological design for the child participants. Our findings from these semi-structured interviews are examined throughout the subsequent chapters, and are integrated with our textual and paratextual analysis.

Across both the survey and the interviews, we sought to investigate what people understand by the concept of family viewing in the contemporary era. We also asked how different families use the Netflix streaming service for viewing, whether separately or together. The survey included 11 multiple choice questions and 4 open-field questions taking less than 10 minutes to complete. All survey questionnaire respondents were anonymous through the online Qualtrics software. Our audience research approach intersects with reception studies, examining how groups and individuals make meaning from texts in different circumstances (Staiger 2005: 2; Willis 2017).

In the Australian context where we write, Netflix was the most watched streaming service in 2020, with over two thirds of Australians aged 14 or over watching the service in any given four-week period (Roy Morgan 2021). Despite a subsequent post-lockdown subscriber slump worldwide (Helmore 2022), in the Australian market Netflix actually grew, retaining their place as the largest streaming service with 28% of the market (Fang 2022). Eligible participants in the survey were English-speaking adults of 18+ years who have access to a Netflix streaming service account, while interviews included adults and children residing in the same household. Although some questions in the survey related to adult guardians with children under their care, we did not exclude families without children as we were interested in different types of families who use Netflix. The survey gathered 225 responses with a roughly equal mix of Australian and international participants. With approximately 222 million Netflix subscribers worldwide, this gives us a result generalisable to the general population with 90% confidence level and a ±6% margin of error. We can thus start to use these results as broadly indicative of trends within the Netflix customer base.

By clustering together programs under the "Family Watch Together TV" label, Netflix implicitly assumes and constructs this category of viewing and what constitutes a family. We asked respondents what Netflix's category of "Family Watch Together TV" means to them, with multiple possible answers and an open field option. Survey respondents were evenly split between those with children and those without. The vast majority of respondents with children were parents, with some grandparents, guardians, and one aunt. The questions we asked and our key findings from the surveys are tabled below. Respondents could select multiple options in some of the questions, which is indicated by those tables in which the percentages do not add up to 100%.

Netflix has a category called "Family Watch Together TV". What does this mean to me?

Programs designed for both adults and children to enjoy	59%
Watching TV with children	59%
Watching TV with several generations	29%
Watching TV with adult family members	15%
Watching TV with a partner	14%
Programs designed for young children	12%
Watching TV with companion animals	09%
Watching TV with close friends	05%
Other	03%

Our survey and interviews indicate that ideas about "family viewing" remain firmly attached to a cultural image of parents watching with children even as actual Netflix families vary. Indeed, respondents were evenly split between those with children under their care and those without. One respondent suggested they thought talking with adult family members about what they had been watching – rather than actually watching it together – should still be counted as part of a shared family TV experience, a finding that is supported by Frey's larger 2021 study.

On average, how often would your family watch a Netflix program together?

More than once a week	32%
Weekly	21%
Rarely	21%

If you watch a Netflix program together as a family, how do you most often watch it?

In the same room on the same device	84%
Across different households	6%
In the same household on different devices	4%

Do programs tagged as family content by Netflix (e.g. "Family Watch Together TV" motivate you to sit down and watch a whole Netflix program with your family?

	Never	*Sometimes*	*Often*
Parents	50%	39%	11%
Non-parents	85%	15%	0%

While 50% of parents sometimes or often paid attention to different "family" labels used on the Netflix interface, most other respondents were never motivated by those tags. This disparity suggests that the idea of family viewing, and in turn the "family" labels on the Netflix streaming interface, are strongly associated with parents and children, even among the many families where that model does not actually apply. Elsewhere in the survey, most respondents assumed references to family viewing meant any kind of family (including theirs), whereas a few indicated in their comments that they thought "family" excluded families without children. This is despite the fact that the survey explicitly asked respondents about different forms of family and family viewing, and overtly included families without children among the options.

What other factors motivate you to watch Netflix together as a family?

	Never	*Sometimes*	*Often*
It's your favourite genre	19%	52%	29%
You read a good review	9%	50%	41%
You want to introduce them to a program you like	9%	58%	32%
Nostalgia for a film or TV show you liked when you were younger	13%	59%	28%
You like the star of the show	20%	70%	10%
It has been recommended to you by Netflix in your profile	28%	65%	7%
It has diverse representation	21%	62%	17%

While respondents reported multiple motivations for gathering to watch an entire program together as a family "on-demand" via Netflix, our survey data reveal that watching Netflix together is tied to a critically praised show (the top choice when combining "sometimes" and "often"); the desire to share a favourite program with other family members; nostalgia; and genre preferences.

Conclusion

This book proceeds to tell the story of Netflix's cycle of dark family telefantasy in chronological order. We begin with the cycle's prototype and flagship show, *Stranger Things* (2016-), and then address the more explicitly child-oriented (but ambiguously child-appropriate) follow-up, *A Series of Unfortunate Events* (2017–2019). Our tale then turns to the slick but nostalgic sci-fi show *Lost in Space* (2018–2021), the puppet-animated prequel show *Dark Crystal: Age of Resistance* (2019), and the superhero spectacular *Raising Dion* (2019–2022). We finish the story by considering the evolution of this genre cycle from late 2021 onwards via key examples *Stranger Things 4* (2022) and *Squid Game* (2021). Both shows build on the success of the dark family telefantasy cycle to provoke new frontiers for "family viewing" in a new phase for the SVOD ecology, when Netflix is faced with increasing competition from the family-focused Disney+ in particular.

As we outline throughout the book, Netflix's dark family telefantasy cycle attempts to harness the recent popularity of adult Quality Telefantasy and in the process reconfigures the family audience for the on-demand streaming era. In this genre cycle, the labelling of the programs under the "Family Watch Together TV" interface tag, along with the content of the shows – their themes, forms, and aesthetics – solicit an *intergenerational dynamic*. Thus, as this book highlights, Netflix's dark family telefantasy does not necessarily target a specific *demographic* – an approach that was, pre-streaming, scaffolded by legacy media infrastructure such as ratings, scheduling, linear distribution, and mass viewing – but instead, in the absence of this infrastructure, invites a particular type of *viewing*. As Noel Brown (2012) argues, "we have entered a new era in 'family' entertainment, where it is increasingly difficult to gauge where the 'childish' elements end and the 'adult' aspects begin". He suggests that much of today's family content would once have been considered decidedly adult. Though Brown writes prior to the global mainstreaming of subscription video streaming services and discusses this trend in the case of feature films, his comments seem apt for Netflix's strategy around family content as well. While Netflix's family sitcoms lacked cultural prestige and were poorly received by critics (Dumaraog 2020; Tiffany 2017), by contrast Netflix was able to assert its identity as a prestige family service around its dark family telefantasy offerings. By showcasing creepy or violent science fiction and horror-inflected fantasy content under the "Family Watch Together TV" label, Netflix harnesses the appeal of Quality Telefantasy, drawing on the seriality and high production values associated with both Quality TV and Quality Telefantasy. Netflix thereby attempts to confer prestige upon family telefantasy programming for an intergenerational audience. As we explore in the next chapter, the success of *Stranger Things* formed a prototype for the dark family telefantasy genre cycle that would follow, even as it exposed tensions around its reimagining of a darker family viewing terrain.

Notes

1 *House of Cards* was both fully funded by Netflix and available only on Netflix, and explicitly branded as a Netflix exclusive via the "Netflix Original" title. As such it was the flagship program that announced Netflix's move into being a creator and distributor of exclusive content. Prior to this, Netflix experimented with content production, partly funding the Norwegian crime dramedy, *Lillyhammer* (2012–2014) which premiered on the TV network NRK1.

2 Although Disney+ is closing the gap, at the time of publication Netflix continues to be the dominant streaming service based on subscriptions and share of minutes spent watching streaming services. In the Third Quarter of 2022, Disney+ had 152.1 million subscribers. In comparison, in Q3 2022, Netflix had 223 million (Stoll 2022). Netflix was the preferred streaming service in the US in 2022 (Wise 2022) and it was also the leader in streaming minutes in 2022, achieving 22.4% of

the minutes audiences spent streaming, outpacing YouTube, Disney+, Hulu, and Prime (Iqbal 2022). The Walt Disney corporation is not to be confused with the individual subscription servers that it offers: Disney+, Hulu, and ESPN.

3 He notes by way of example how Universal Studios' 1930s horror films were re-branded for re-release in the 1950s as science fiction, by then the more popular genre (1999: 78–79).

4 In 2022, Netflix announced the introduction of an ad-supported tier in response to an unexpected drop in subscribers, which may necessitate a new strategy around data transparency to attract and sustain advertisers. While this change is outside the scope of the focus of this book, notably, at the time of writing, industry commentators remained uncertain about how much data would be made available to advertisers with the change in subscription structure (Shepherd 2022).

2 The Intergenerational Dynamic and "Family Watch Together TV" on Netflix

Stranger Things as Dark Family Telefantasy Prototype

Stranger Things (Duffer Brothers, 2016), one of Netflix's most successful and influential Original television programs, is the prototypical dark telefantasy "Family Watch Together TV" show, even though it pre-dated this label's operation as a prominent and consistent organisational category on the platform. *Stranger Things* occasionally appears in searches for "Family Watch Together TV", but more consistently in "Explore titles *related to*: Family Watch Together TV" (emphasis added). As this chapter details, *Stranger Things* was Netflix's first experiment with dark family-oriented television content that strategically targets children, tweens, teenagers, and adults in ways that directly address each age group, while also cultivating dialogue across age-based and generational lines. In addition, via a distinctive approach to nostalgia – across aesthetics, form, and theme – the show simultaneously addresses "niche", seemingly highly personalised tastes in alignment with these age groups, as well as a wide audience. This chapter outlines how the launch of *Stranger Things* navigated a tense moment of transformational transition: at this time, Netflix was still seen as a disruptive innovator – displacing modes of viewing, regulation, and distribution associated with broadcast and cable television – yet at the same time, via family content like *Stranger Things*, the SVOD was being repositioned in relation to collective, communal modes of viewing. This repositioning complicates previous emphases in Netflix's branding, paratextual promotion, and related journalistic and scholarly commentary on individualised algorithmic content delivery and personalisation. Reflecting this transformational tension, *Stranger Things* has attracted confusion on social media around its ambiguous positioning in relation to the age of its intended audience. There is a wealth of such online commentary in which netizens ask for advice as to whether children should watch the show, for example, "Is *Stranger Things* too scary for a preteen to watch" (Quora 2020), "Is stranger things, a kids show?" (u/shmashes 2020), "Age for Netflix's "*Stranger Things*"? (u/PinkMoonrise 2018). This Reddit post is characteristic of this commentary:

> So my 10-year-old son has been practically begging to watch this show and my husband and I have said no so far. His friends at school are

DOI: 10.4324/9781003223498-2

> watching it, *and* my husband and I watch it … I'm really confused with this one guys. (u/PinkMoonrise 2018)

Our audience research further illuminated this confusion laced with concern, underpinned by the situation outlined above by the Redditor in which adults initially watched the show without their children and were unsure if they should also allow their children to watch. For instance, Emma, the mother of 15-year-old Tamara, explained in a semi-structured interview how at the age of 12 or 13, her daughter was very eager to watch *Stranger Things* because she "had heard about and seen shorts for it". Her daughter explained that she had seen it "all over Google and TikTok". Having seen the show, Emma was concerned because she

> thought it might be a little bit scary for her … . And I said, I don't know if you want to watch it, it might be a bit too scary. And she held out for a little while. But she ended up just watching it herself anyway.

Similarly, another interview participant, 12-year-old Cole, explained that he campaigned to watch the show, yet his mother, Madeline, originally resisted, having watched the show by herself. Madeline explained that she told Cole she "wouldn't let him watch that on his own – you have to watch that one with us". Despite this initial negotiation between mother and son, they both thoroughly enjoyed watching *Stranger Things* together for the conversations it sparked between them – Madeline explained that she enjoyed it much more when they watched it as a family than when she watched alone – as we further detail later in this chapter.

This chapter illuminates how, despite the evident cultural confusion around *Stranger Thing*'s demographic positioning, there was no ambiguity around Netflix's *strategy* in producing a show that occupies such a cultural grey area. We argue that the global success of the first season of *Stranger Things* in July 2016 cohered Netflix's approach to the family audience, as the show became a flagship Original for the SVOD which influenced and reinforced a shift away from high profile (but poorly received) family sitcom revivals such as *Fuller House* (2016–2020), and towards high-budget, heavily promoted dark telefantasy productions, namely those analysed in this book. In line with Wallin's (2019) explication of a genre cycle cited in our first chapter, we map this genre cycle in Table 2.1 to make clear when each show was greenlit and announced, when it went into production, and the time of release. The table thus provides a snapshot of the discursive formation of this genre cycle between November 2014 and October 2019. As Wallin articulates, a genre cycle involves not just an increase in production of a particular type of content by a studio, but "the distribution and release of films [or in this case, TV series] in close proximity" (2019: 2).

Table 2.1 also displays the order in which we address each of these shows in the book to tell the story of how dark family telefantasy crystallised as a

Table 2.1 Dark Family Telefantasy's Formation as a Netflix Genre Cycle Ordered Chronologically by Production and Release

Series	*Greenlit/Officially Announced*	*Into Production*	*Released*
Stranger Things	April 2015 (then titled *Montauk*)	November 2015	15 July 2016 – worldwide; all episodes. Still in production as of 2022. Season 5 planned to be final season (no release date at time of writing).
A Series of Unfortunate Events	November 2014	May 2016	13 January 2017 – worldwide; all episodes. Third and final season released 1 January 2019.
Lost in Space	June 2016	February 2017	31 April 2018 – worldwide; all episodes (pilot screened 31 March 2018 at Awesome Con, Washington DC). Third and final season released 1 December 2021.
The Dark Crystal: Age of Resistance	May 2017	November 2017	30 August 2019 – worldwide; all episodes, one season.
Raising Dion	October 2017	July 2018	4 October 2019 – worldwide; all episodes. Second and final season released 1 February 2022.

flagship Netflix genre cycle under the "Family Watch Together TV" label. *Stranger Things* – the second show in the cycle to be announced but the first to go into production and be released – lay the foundations for the cycle's distinctive regenrification of the prior cycle of *adult*-oriented gritty, dark, and high-budget Quality Telefantasy shows on cable television, such as *Game of Thrones* (HBO, 2011–2019) and *The Walking Dead* (AMC, 2010–2022). As Andrew Lynch points out, Quality Telefantasy was throughout the 2010s a major cultural force and served to legitimate fantastical TV content for adults (2022: 3). With *Stranger Things*, Netflix reframes this cultural elevation of Quality Telefantasy by repositioning it for families: Head of Family Content Brian Wright credits the show with "validating [the] theory that family content can be great content" (quoted in Tiffany 2017). This chapter focuses in particular on the first two seasons of *Stranger Things* as foundational to Netflix's dark family telefantasy cycle, outlining how the show served to not just legitimate Quality Telefantasy for *families,* but also to legitimate Netflix's ability to deliver family content that solicits "togetherness" and connection through communal viewing within a single household. We will return to Season 4 in the final chapter of this book to consider *Stranger Things* in relation to the late phase of this genre cycle's development in 2021–2022.

This chapter illustrates how the first season of *Stranger Things* showcased Netflix's distinctive capabilities at a moment when the tense transition from linear television to on-demand, personalised streaming was still central to cultural discourse about the transformation of home entertainment. At this juncture, *Stranger Things* highlighted how, in comparison to such legacy televisual media, Netflix was able to tactically operate relatively independently from age-based, regional classification frameworks and their associated regulation and production practices. Indeed, the show's creators and showrunners, Matt and Ross Duffer, claimed in an interview with *Rolling Stone* (quoted in Grow 2016) that the show was initially rejected between 15 and 20 times by various television networks and producers because of its liminal position between adult and child viewerships. They state that the television networks deemed that this horror-thriller-sci-fi show would only be suitable for broadcast if the content and focus were made more suitable for children, or if it was repositioned as an explicitly adult-oriented show, displacing the focus on the child characters.

Rejecting this legacy television demand to fit within either child or adult-oriented genre paradigms, the Duffer brothers subsequently sold the concept to Netflix, where it would become one of the biggest success stories of the early SVOD "Originals" era (Miller 2016; Moore 2017). *Stranger Things*' success helped to establish how dark family telefantasy as a flagship content type for Netflix could subversively push at the boundaries of linear television's approach to young and family audiences in a way that supported the SVOD's branding. Matt Duffer expands in an interview with *Empire* that the show parallels the creation of the PG-13 rating in the US in the 1980s, because "Spielberg movies" were:

> pushing it so dark and he upset a lot of parents. I liked that, though. I think that's good and healthy and great and some of our favourite experiences growing up were having the shit scared out of us. As we get further into the show, especially when you get into the final episode, it ratchets up a notch. But by then you've already got the kids watching, so then we can scare the shit out of them. Then the parents can get mad. (Quoted in Thrower 2016)

The controversial creation of the PG-13 rating in the 1980s – a contentious process sparked by *Poltergeist* (Hooper, written and produced by Spielberg, 1982) and solidified by the release of *Indiana Jones and the Temple of Doom* (Spielberg, 1984) and *Gremlins* (Dante, executive produced by Spielberg, 1984) – was indeed a cultural flashpoint in relation to the distinctions between child/adult and "family" content. Filipa Antunes points out that while "entertainment for families and children had previously been associated with Walt Disney, Norman Rockwell, and Spielberg's *E.T.*", during the mid-1980s these models were replaced by more "unconventional reference points, such as violent adventure and horror" (2017: 39). Catherine Lester articulates in her own work on children's horror films how

> the meeting of 'horror' and 'children' is an inherent contradiction on account of the horror genre's stereotypical associations with violence, depravity and other 'adult' content being incompatible with the cultural construction of childhood in Western modernity. (2021: 2)

She thus describes the introduction of the PG-13 rating in the US as a watershed moment that provided a "home for borderline content that did not sit neatly within the 'child-friendly' G and PG ratings nor the 'adult' ratings of R and above" (2021: 15, 17). Antunes similarly argues that children's horror films provoked "a drastic ideological shift" in considerations of child-appropriateness and related ideas about childhood innocence, as the blooming of "horror-flavored PG and PG-13 films" in the 1980s marked a transition that can be understood as a "a major milestone, not just industrial but also social and cultural" (2017: 39).

This "major milestone" reverberates in Netflix's "Family Watch Together TV" content, and thus it is notable that *Stranger Things* – the protoype for the flagship dark family telefantasy genre cycle that would come to be associated with this tag – was explicitly designed to hark back to this period of ratings and cultural flux in the mid-1980s. Indeed, as has been well established (Hassler-Forest 2020; Lizardi 2017; Mollet and Scott 2021; Wetmore 2018), *Stranger Things*' narrative world does not just *gesture to* but is *built out of* intertextual references to popular culture from this period, especially Spielberg films, the work of Stephen King and film adaptations of King novels. The King adaptations *Firestarter* (Lester, 1984), *Stand by Me* (Reiner, 1986), and the television mini-series *It* (Wallace, 1990)[1] are particularly prominent and obvious intertexts. Notably, King's horror literature, like mid-80s children's horror films, challenged boundaries between child and adult demographics, being very (and notoriously) popular with children (Beckett 2009: 20). *Stranger Things* – the first season of which is set in 1983, the year between the release of *Poltergeist* and *Gremlins* – constructs a bricolage around such texts in ways that solicit immersion in this period of cultural transition. In so doing, this flagship dark family telefantasy show establishes a parallel between the rise of horror films and books popular with child and family audiences and Netflix's own horror-tinged family television. The show thus implicitly positions *television* as the site of flux and contestation in relation to family and child audiences in the 2010s. This is notable because, as Balanzategui has pointed out previously in her analysis of children's TV horror anthologies, "unlike cinema, television is a mode that enters the domestic space, and thus the fabric and rhythms of children's everyday lives" (2018a: 201).

Stranger Things' nostalgia-steeped intertextual references have been the dominant focus of the substantial and growing body of scholarship on the influential series, to the point that Matt Hills describes this focus as "a critical orthodoxy" (2021: 189) that resembles a "1980s 'Choose Your Own Adventure' novel, where readers can decide which critical pathway to take" (190). In this book, we develop our own theorisations of the poetics and cultural operations of nostalgia, integrating the insights drawn from our audience research with textual and industry analysis. Building on prior work of key cultural theorists of nostalgia including Fredric Jameson (1991; 1992; 2014) and Svetlana Boym (2001; 2018), we explore the intergenerational dynamic and haunted nostalgia of Netflix's dark family telefantasy cycle. The "critical orthodoxy" (Hills 2021: 189) of analysing *Stranger Things* through frameworks of nostalgia is characterised by tellingly dichotomous perspectives. On the one hand, the nostalgia in *Stranger Things* has been read as regressive (Mollet and Scott 2021; Siranni 2019), conservative and reactionary (Hassler-Forest 2020), as a commodification of the past (Mascio 2021) deployed to cast the widest possible audience net to maintain and attract subscribers (Lizardi 2017: 113), and as operating in service of an anti-communist ethos that positions capitalism as the "only viable system of economic and political organization" (Knewitz 2022: 80). Yet the show has conversely been understood as evoking nostalgia in cynical and critical ways (Wetmore 2018: 3), to question our contemporary era of digital connectivity (Dodd 2021) and caution against the Reaganite principles of the 1980s so younger audiences can avoid the traps of neoliberalism as they shape their own futures (Ní Fhlainn 2021), and as a tool of Anthropocene recognition and thus environmental critique (Relidzyňska 2021). Notably, when it comes to how the series depicts the family – its target audience, particularly precariously defined in this moment of transition to on-demand streaming – it has been positioned as a critical deconstruction of the nostalgic notion of the nuclear family (Butler 2021), and also as imagining the family and family home as sites of a nostalgic "lost mythic childhood, community and United States" (Barnwell 2021: 169), and offering a "rose-coloured rear view" of the past (Bartlett 2017).

These varying and dichotomous perspectives highlight how ambivalently constructed the nostalgia is in *Stranger Things*, and the lack of consensus among scholars points more broadly to the underrecognised complexity of nostalgia as a conceptual, aesthetic, and cultural force. As this chapter illuminates, in *Stranger Things* nostalgia is deployed to cultivate a specifically *inter*generational dynamic that offers not just secure and cosy (re)imaginings of the past, but motivates new ways of thinking about and new forms of attachment to the past via television, in the process fostering interaction across different age groups. Our audience research highlighted this specific mode of interaction: the above-quoted mother Madeline, for instance, explained that the conversations the show sparked between her and her 12-year-old son made her "feel very connected to [him]" as he "enjoyed hearing stories from my childhood", stories associated with memories sparked by the show. She highlighted the show as an example of how "we tend to chat about more when we're watching Netflix together", as opposed to when her family watched movies together. She notes while they watched *Stranger Things* they would be so enjoying those conversations "about my childhood and we might just miss a whole section of the actual show", an experience that stood out to both Madeline and her son Cole as rewarding because of the depth of the "conversation we're having about what we're actually watching".

Stranger Things offers immersion in nostalgia for the 1980s in ways that directly appeal to Gen X and older Millennial audiences, but also to younger audiences who never experienced the 1980s outside of popular media constructions from and about the decade. This approach accords with Derek Johnson's theorisation of the transgenerationality of contemporary media industries, which entails "a process of transformation across generational lines that invites professionals and consumers alike to move between age-defined arenas of cultural participation" (2019: 3). Building on Johnson's work along new axes which emphasises instead the strategic *intergenerational dynamic* of Netflix's "Family Watch Together TV", this chapter considers how nostalgia is deployed in *Stranger Things* to cultivate intergenerational connections between older and younger characters – and in parallel older and younger *audiences* – in ways that encourage a model of communal viewing tailored for the streaming era. This distinctive form of nostalgically constructed communal viewing combines Netflix's much-hyped and platform-centric personalised, individuated on-demand streaming with the very practice Netflix itself has superseded: gathering around a TV set to "watch together" at a set time. Thus, without the synchronised infrastructure of broadcast viewing which sets up family viewing as a household event, Netflix finds new ways to bring families together via *Stranger Things*' nostalgic mode of address, encouraging complex modes of engagement and exchange across and between generational lines. Nostalgia is deployed in a way that makes wide demographic appeal *feel* personalised and niche – and in tandem, *Stranger Things*' aesthetic, formal, and thematic strategies atomise different age groups into separate segments yet also forges connections between them.

Stranger Things as "Family Watch Together TV" Prototype

While *Stranger Things* pre-existed Netflix's "Family Watch Together TV" as a prominently accessible "micro-genre" category on the interface, its success during a period of experimentation for the SVOD ushered in a distinctive approach to the family audience and in so doing established a template for the subsequent cycle of dark telefantasy, family-oriented Original series that would come to dominate this category. Leger Grindon notes that a genre cycle tends to be "sparked by a benchmark hit, a prototype that is imitated, refined, or resisted by those that follow" (2012: 44). Richard Nowell calls this the "Trailblazer Hit", adding that it prompts a cycle in part because "content-wise [it] is seen to differ significantly from contemporaneous hits" (2011: 46). *Stranger Things* represents the "trailblazing" or "benchmark hit" that became a prototype for Netflix's dark family telefantasy genre cycle. The strategic crafting of intergenerational appeal via dark telefantasy is a key feature of all the other case studies we address in this cycle throughout this book. Thus, the analysis of *Stranger Things* in this chapter helps to identify how *intergenerationality* operates as an aesthetic and formal strategy that aligns with Netflix's corporate goals during the period of growth and expansion that followed the company's pivot to investment in exclusive Originals from 2011 onwards (Lobato 2018: 244). *Stranger Things* has been the most enduring, and arguably, the most culturally impactful, of this early experimentation with Original series, a point to which we will return in Chapter 7.[2]

In the mid-2010s as Netflix started to build an increasingly mainstream and extensive global presence, journalistic commentary expressed concerns that television's "traditional" socio-cultural function as a communal, family medium was being threatened by the SVOD's personalised, on-demand distribution model (Lawson 2013; O'Keefe 2016; Ruddick 2017). In this context, *Stranger Things* was positioned by Netflix as the first of a number of forthcoming Original TV series designed for families to watch together. This framing sought to reposition Netflix's on-demand model as one that did not just cater to niche personal tastes in a way that atomises audience groups into unique individuals, but also, and seemingly conversely, as a means of connecting family members across age groups via communal viewing.

In an article in *The New York Times* from February 2016 – five months prior to the release of the first season of *Stranger Things* – Ted Sarandos, Chief Content Officer, and Cindy Holland, Vice-President of Originals, explained that the company was pivoting to the family audience with the hope that, to quote the author John Koblin, "families will watch these offerings at home together, just like in the old days". Sarandos describes the company's aim to produce programming "exciting for younger adults and more than tolerable for adults", and Holland points to the popularity of family-friendly movies from the 1980s, suggesting that viewing trends on the platform indicate that "families are looking for things to watch together when they're home" (quoted in Koblin 2016). Re-narrativising the concerns of the period that Netflix was responsible for the decline of communal family television viewing, Holland contends that it was *not* the rise of SVOD but the proliferation of channels on cable television that led to specialisation so niche that each member of the household was being targeted individually. Sarandos affirms that in response to this development, Netflix's new slate of Original family programming sought to fill "a significant hole in the market" (quoted in Koblin 2016).

Notably then, Netflix's professed strategy and discourse around "Family Watch Together TV" at its inception operates in tension with the company's initial branding around disruptive innovation via an algorithmically driven business model built around niche and ultra-personalised consumer tastes (Frey 2019). Instead, Netflix's pivot to family TV is described nostalgically – as reviving a communal experience reminiscent of "the old days" of broadcast television prior to cable's strategies around market segmentation – and foregrounds mass appeal rather than Netflix's then much talked about "micro" or "alt-genres". Thus, "Family Watch Together TV" incites the type of tensions to which Derek Johnson refers in his contention that "in contemporary television economies that privilege on-demand experiences personalised across myriad digital devices and narrowcast services, the ongoing industrial significance of family relations offers a paradox" (2019: 23). Yet Johnson argues that in this context "long gone is the idealized electronic hearth in which television provided the centerpiece of a domestic tableau" as services like Netflix's "construct discrete profiles and experiences for different family members, extending decades of efforts by the cable industry to offer generationally exclusive programming experiences" (2019: 23). Similarly, Amanda Lotz articulates how in the post-network, multichannel television era "narrowcasting" – "targeting a niche segment of the overall audience" so that "smaller, specific audiences gain value" (2006: 26) – replaces broadcast audience strategies. Streaming services engage audiences with even "narrower" devices of algorithmic personalisation. However, "Family Watch Together TV" highlights Netflix's attempt to balance such personalised and "generationally exclusive programming experiences" with mythologies and viewing dynamics that reposition the SVOD as an electronic hearth – to the point that Netflix representatives like Holland and Sarandos even highlight how they are counteracting, rather than extending, cable's niche programming structure. In harking back in this way, Netflix seems to suggest that their model for "watching together" does not necessarily mean one built around the affordances of on-demand, platform-neutral streaming, in which family members may all watch the same show but on different devices, in different rooms, and at different times. Instead, the TV-centred "togetherness" described in the 2016 *New York Times* article introducing Netflix's family audience strategy nostalgically implies a synchronised, collective gathering around a single TV set. This version of "watching together" was consistent with our audience research survey results: for those respondents who did regularly watch Netflix as a family, 84% reported doing so at the same time, in the same room, on the same device.

Stranger Things is introduced in this 2016 article as one of the key forthcoming shows to launch the new family focus for the company, being described as like "the 1980s movie *Stand by Me* with an added supernatural element" starring Winona Ryder. Both the mention of Ryder and the association with this beloved 1980s Stephen King adaptation serve to introduce this show via a nostalgic lens in tandem with the broader nostalgic rhetoric around bringing back "the old days" of families watching TV together. As Holland explains, this emphasis on nostalgia is part of the company's strategy to attract the interests of parents, and there is also an intention to echo the themes of films and television shows from the 1980s, because "parents are searching for the evolution of that and the 2016 version of that kind of programming" (quoted in Koblin 2016). Like the Duffer brother's own comments around the introduction of the PG-13 rating, Holland's comments suggest that *Stranger Things* does not just offer a pastiche of 1980s popular culture, but instead offers a *new version* of that kind of content for a 2016 audience. The foregrounding of the casting of Winona Ryder – the now middle-aged but previously beloved teen star of edgy horror-comedy films of the late 1980s and early 1990s such as *Beetlejuice* (Burton 1988), *Heathers* (Lehmann, 1990), and *Edward Scissorhands* (Burton, 1990) – highlights this attempt to "update" older content. Ryder's character Joyce in the show is a characteristically quirky but isolated and beleaguered single mother, connecting with an adult audience through a nostalgically constructed "grown up" version of her idiosyncratic, often borderline anti-social teen characters. Netflix's early paratextual framing of *Stranger Things* thus implies parallels between the rise of controversial new forms of dark or horror-tinged family films in the mid-1980s and Netflix's own 21st-century family television.

Nostalgia here is tied with "innovation", not necessarily in relation to Netflix's trademark on-demand distribution model, but instead to suggest that Netflix's family offerings will rejuvenate for the streaming era the beloved *themes, aesthetics*, and *forms* of the category-defying family films of the mid-1980s. In another article from January 2017, when this new "family watch together" strategy was in full flight, Netflix's then VP of Family Content Brian Wright explained that the company sought to create family shows that are "just as good" as their high-profile adult Originals. *Stranger Things* is the example Wright points to as part of a growing slate of "young adult" content: it is here that Wright, as we highlighted earlier, celebrates *Stranger Things* for "validating [the] theory that family content can be great content" (quoted in Tiffany 2017).

Stranger Things was thus introduced to the world as a key part of Netflix's pivot to family television, being positioned as the pillar of this new strategy to produce content that appeals across age groups within a single household in a way that will revive synchronised communal viewing as a regular family "event". Notably, as Holland's comments make clear, Gen X parents nostalgic for the 1980s are a key target of this strategy. Thus, *Stranger Things* is an example of the phenomenon Ryan Lizardi has identified in which media companies tend to target Gen X and older Millennials in their economically motivated attempts to craft "transgenerational nostalgic appeal" (2017: 2), in so doing encouraging parents to impose their own nostalgic media attachments onto their own children. Derek Johnson similarly outlines the growing interest of the post-network television sector in "building transgenerational bonds between millennials and their children" by harnessing legacy texts from the 1980s and 1990s (2019: 36). Lizardi relates this "dual audience methodology" to Netflix and to *Stranger Things*, which he argues deploys nostalgia in strategic ways that create a "safety net of older nostalgic viewers" if the show fails to attract younger viewers, while vice versa, seeking to attract younger viewers in case the show is not successful with older audiences, with younger audiences appealed to via child and teen characters and a cliff-hanger-filled narrative structure designed to fit Netflix's binge watching model (2017: 113). However, we contend throughout this book that the intergenerational dynamic crafted by this show and others in the genre cycle is not as straightforward in its multi-generational "mass appeal" approach as Lizardi's description implies.

Journalistic commentary around the show when it was first launched emphasises its combination of nostalgic appeal and youth-oriented novelty. Mark Lawson (2016) in *The Guardian* writes of the show's combination of "a distribution model that represents the future of screen entertainment with content that harks back to its past". Notably, Lawson refers to the show as a "watercooler smash" in the article's title – a nostalgic reference to the shared cultural "watercooler" moments associated with scheduled linear television – and this is the very same Mark Lawson who only three years earlier published a previously cited article in the same publication concerned for the death of the "big TV get-together" in the age of on-demand streaming. Lucy Managan (2016) suggests that *Stranger Things*

> is fun for almost all the family, depending on your juvenile cohorts' response to occasional gory scenes. The pace is (just about) fast enough to keep younger viewers hooked, and anyone old enough to remember 1983 for real is in for a richly enjoyable retro-feast.

Similarly, D'Addario (2016) in *Time* argues that while other nostalgic films and TV shows of the time indicate cultural and audience fatigue with "yesterday's news", *Stranger Things* deploys a nostalgia that feels "warm and inclusive" in a way that is "welcoming you into a fan club". The story, he contends, is both derivative and "wildly original": the nostalgia works, he suggests, because the nostalgic tone "succeeds less from discrete moment to moment than as an overall ambience ... the show is committed to selling you a sort of story that doesn't exist in mainstream pop culture anymore". D'Addario concludes that although he is not the show's "perfect audience" given his lack of 1980s pop cultural knowledge resulted in an "entire layer of references" lost on him, "I'd go back there anytime". All of this commentary around the initial release of *Stranger Things* thus associates the show's appeal to both younger and older audiences as driven by a seemingly disjunctive combination of "freshness" or innovation and nostalgia.

Thus, as indicated in Netflix's own comments around their strategy and these early reviewer responses, nostalgia is deployed in *Stranger Things* in a way that seeks to "welcome" multiple generations, rather than interpellating a specific generational group, inviting younger audiences who did not live through the 1980s into this world in a way that solicits connections between younger and older audiences. Lizardi points to the problematic elements of such "hyper-nostalgic" strategies, in which the tastes and pasts of Generation X are "consistently validated and regurgitated" in a way that displaces unique mediated experiences for the current younger generation that speak directly to their own present, creating instead for them a "surrogate nostalgic identity" (2017: 1). Lizardi thus does not see this process as potentially productive, nor does he focus on the possible generative connections produced by such content, instead positioning this mediated cultural and household dynamic as one that reinforces a generational hierarchy that diminishes the agency and contemporary positionality of young people. Lizard's framing is refracted in the interchangeable use of the terms *trans-*, *cross-*, and *inter*generational throughout his book. Along related but different lines, as we highlighted in the first chapter, Derek Johnson deploys the *trans-* prefix in his illuminating study of children's entertainment in transgenerational media industries to emphasise the complexity of age-based boundary crossing and to concomitantly avoid foregrounding relations between specific generational or age-based categories (2019: 3).

By contrast, throughout this book, we address the specifically *inter*generational strategies of texts like *Stranger Things* to illuminate how they seek to capture not just "the widest possible demographic net" (Lizardi 2017: 113), but specifically a *family* audience existing within a single household, which, in the on-demand streaming era Netflix itself was largely responsible for ushering in, is not a straightforward or simple task. Thus, while Lizard's contention that *Stranger Things* targets a wide demographic as a risk mitigation strategy may be accurate, at the same time, the intertwined aesthetic, thematic, and formal mechanisms of the show communicate with and *between* the different age groups that constitute "family" audiences in ways that are more precise, complex, and interesting than this characterisation suggests.

This mode of viewing continues the "co-viewing" strategies Johnson illuminates in relation to children's media in his own work, but in ways that target families and are distinctively attuned to Netflix's brand identity and the affordances of the SVOD platform. This intergenerational dynamic privileges and foregrounds the separate and distinct age-based frames of reference of different viewers, while encouraging connection between them.

In his research using four different generational focus groups, Göran Bolin illuminates complex and poignant processes of "intergenerational transfer" (2016b: 259) of musical and pop cultural experiences and tastes. He notes the affectively powerful "double meaning" of such transfer, which marks the "loss of childhood" for older generations, but also "points to the successful sharing of generational experience" (259). Lizardi engages with Bolin's work to highlight his findings around the melancholy realisation among Bolin's participants that the transfer of certain intergenerational experiences was incomplete or impossible due to "changes in the ('objective') media landscape" – a process which produces "a mourning of the ability to pass on media practices and communication experiences to one's own children" (Bolin 2016b: 260). However, Bolin's research also points to the importance placed on intergenerational knowledge transfer and to its complex value. Indeed, even the mourning Bolin elucidates when the sharing of intergenerational experience is blocked highlights the personal and cultural significance of this process.

Furthermore, Lizardi presents the perspective that while intergenerational transfer based on parental nostalgia and media tastes may offer affective rewards and affirm the identity of the older generation, the younger generations with which these experiences and tastes are shared do not benefit from this process, which he argues risks producing "an unprecedented generational identity crisis because [younger generations are] being consistently encouraged to consume nostalgic cultural output from eras before they were born" (2017: 8). Yet as Merrill et al outline in their psychological research on narratives shared between parents and their children, intergenerationally shared narratives "help frame a sense of connection between parent and child that reinforces family identity and values across generations" (2018: 753). While these narratives may originally be "told by parents and received by children", the continual retelling and exchange over time empowers children to "dynamically participate in the conversations such that they may begin to have a sense of 'ownership' over the stories", creating a type of "vicarious memory" for the young person that facilitates intergenerational connections even if they did not experience the events firsthand (2018: 753). Ultimately, the authors conclude, this intergenerational process offers young people a link to the past that enables them to "learn about the self in familial and cultural context, which can shape ongoing understanding of their identity" (2018: 769).

The complex nostalgia in *Stranger Things* invites children and young people to share in a narrative world associated with their parents' or older relatives' youth in a way that invites the kinds of intergenerational sharing of stories revealed to be so important to family and self-identity formation in Merill et al's (2018) research. The previously cited comments from our audience research participants Madeline and her 12-year-old son Cole about how connected they felt when watching and discussing the show reinforce the value of this intergenerational sharing, and we will detail further audience responses along these lines later in this chapter. Thus, we deploy the term *inter*generational throughout this book to denote the processes of exchange, communication, collaboration, and interaction *between* generations and age groups cultivated by family watch together content like *Stranger Things*.

Throughout this chapter and the book as a whole, we canvas how this intergenerational dynamic cultivates different modes of affective intimacy with both the texts themselves and with different family members. It is for this reason that we focus on the intergenerational dynamic fostered by dark family telefantasy on Netflix, instead of referring to the transgenerational or, more generally, to broad "all-ages" appeal. Indeed, Netflix's language around *Stranger Things* prior to and around the time of its launch – language later echoed by reviewers of the show – emphasises not necessarily "broad" appeal, but more specifically the pleasures of sharing mediated experiences and memories between different age groups.

Intergenerationality in this context can be understood in relation to the term "intercultural", which is used across multiple disciplines but in global communication studies particularly precisely to denote cultural dynamics that differ from those described by related terms "multi-", "trans-", or "cross-" cultural. While these terms tend to be used in different ways with differing theoretical scaffolding across film, cultural, globalisation, and communication studies, Kecskes explains succinctly in his outlining of the difference between cross-cultural and intercultural pragmatics that while:

> cross-cultural pragmatics compares different cultures, based on the investigation of certain aspects of language use, such as speech acts, behaviour patterns, and language behaviour, intercultural pragmatics focuses on intercultural interactions and investigates the nature of the communicative process among people from different cultures, speaking different first languages. (2017: np)

Expanding such conceptual underpinnings of "inter-" in new contexts, intergenerationality is deployed in this book to articulate a similar process focused on interactions, dialogues, and dialectics *between* age groups and generations, even if these groups at times "speak" in different generational languages.

Ultimately, *Stranger Things* and the discourse that surrounded it when it launched illuminates how Netflix initiated new definitions of and expectations around "family" content for the streaming era. Yet this newness was underpinned by nostalgia for both broadcast TV models of communal viewing and also, more specifically, for the period of pop cultural transition represented by the rise of the PG-13-rated "family" film in the mid-1980s. Notably then, the rhetorical devices used to describe and culturally position *Stranger Things* are an example of Mittell's "discursive practices" key to the crystallisation of TV genres, in which TV genres are constructed according to multilayered "cultural operations" including the "terms and definitions" that "circulate around and through" them (2001: 8–9). These rhetorical devices influenced how dark family telefantasy emerged as a genre cycle under the "Family Watch Together TV" label, working in tandem with the semantics and syntactics of the content itself (Altman 1999) and the way it was paratextually framed and categorised on the Netflix platform. While she does not engage with Mittell's work, Lawrence (2015) highlights how this discursive process of cultural definition works in relation to Netflix's positioning and descriptions of its alt-genres – and "Family Watch Together TV" certainly is one of Netflix's most prominent "alt-genres". Lawrence describes how within the platform's catalogue organisation infrastructure, alt-genres "possess a special kind of rhetorical power, forming a critical persuasive component of the personalized collections that Netflix presents to users" (2015: 358). Focusing on the tags and titles of these alt-genres, she notes that they "function as arguments about and for particular taste preferences and aesthetic experiences" (358), in ways that "operationalize customized vocabularies of appeal" (359).

The case of Netflix's "Family Watch Together TV", and the place of *Stranger Things* in instigating this category, illuminates how these "customized vocabularies of appeal" operate via discursive and reciprocal processes *beyond* the platform as well as within it. As the commentary around *Stranger Things* from Netflix representatives and reviewers highlights, the show was being positioned as key to a new wave of nostalgia-driven darker family content before the inception of "Family Watch Together TV" as a well-recognised category, and specific language around "watching together" features in this discourse, predating but predicting the cycle's critically persuasive "alt-genre" label. Indeed, *Stranger Things* may be the prototype for dark family telefantasy and more broadly for "Family Watch Together TV", but, as we detailed at the beginning of this chapter, the show preexisted the sedimentation of this cycle into an official category on the platform, and even now is not often positioned within it. In this case then, this high profile, prototypical example which sparked a subsequent genre cycle is "bigger than" the category it initiated, but played a pivotal role in, to return to Lawrence's terms, operationalising "customised vocabularies of appeal" (Lawrence 2015; 359). The selection of options that display when one selects the "More Like This" recommendation associated with *Stranger Things* highlights how the show operates as an ur-text for the subversive liminality of "Family Watch Together TV", which draws together "family" and adult-oriented dark telefantasy genres. The "More Like This" options that displayed in March 2022 included other dark telefantasy family shows

Figure 2.1 Image of "More Like This" content recommendations on the Netflix interface in relation to *Stranger Things*. Screenshot by authors, 31 March 2022.

addressed throughout this book (Figure 2.1). These include *Lost in Space*, *The Dark Crystal* (highlighted as an 81% match) and *Locke and Key* (highlighted as an 88% match), but also definitively *adult* horror shows, including the graphic, erotic horror series *Brand New Cherry Flavor* (2021) and the prestige, supernatural religious horror-drama directed by Netflix's horror "auteur", Mike Flanagan, *Midnight Mass* (2021) – both of which are rated MA15+ in Australia, a rating that demarcates strong content legally restricted to those under 15. This liminal positioning on the platform is another important example of Mittell's "discursive processes" that shape genre and Lawrence's "arguments about and for particular taste preferences and aesthetic experiences" (358). In this case, the taste preferences and aesthetic experiences offered by the programs bundled together as "like" *Stranger Things* defy distinctions between child-appropriate and adult-oriented dark telefantasy content.

Thus, *Stranger Things* ignited a new genre cycle of Netflix Originals that repositioned the platform's content delivery model as not just "personalised" but offering opportunities to "watch together", yet did so in a way that challenged broadcast-era classification and demographic segmentation expectations to occupy a provocative grey area between "adult" and child/family-oriented content. Furthermore, the discursive, rhetorical, and paratextual strategies used to position *Stranger Things* generically emphasise its intergenerational appeal and the act of communal household viewing, extratextual positioning that intersects with the show's aesthetics, themes, and form, as the next section illuminates. The genre cycle initiated by *Stranger Things* is an intriguing continuation along new axes of the ambiguous but audience-centric cultural operations of children's TV as a genre, because this diverse "genre" is defined, as Messenger-Davies points out, "by the people who watch it" – children – rather than any shared semantic and syntactic conventions (2001: 96). Yet in the case of the "Family Watch Together TV" genre cycle, this audience-led definition process points more specifically to a particular *type* of viewing, rather than a particular or age-based *demographic.*

As the cycle's prototype, *Stranger Things* models the dark family telefantasy's cultivation of a specific mode of intergenerational viewing via a combination of the following:

1 The merging of nostalgia with fantastic wonder, in a way that draws on nostalgic aesthetics, themes, and/or references in the crafting of a rich fantasy world.
2 The regenrification of Quality Telefantasy to position it for family audiences: *Stranger Things* and the other dark family telefantasy shows that follow it maintain Quality Telefantasy's combination of fantasy genres with Quality TV's prestige elements (in the form of actors, directors, or other related stamps of authorial quality) and high-budget, slick aesthetics. Although Quality Telefantasy emphasises gritty cultural realism, particularly in the form of sex and violence (Lynch 2022: 54), by contrast, dark family telefantasy tempers such gritty realism in favour of *generic verisimilitude* – a diegetic construction of ontological rules grounded on genre-specific conventions and expectations (Neale 2000: 28). In this way, dark family telefantasy reverses Quality Telefantasy's privileging of cultural realism over generic verisimilitude (Lynch 2022: 38) by playing up genre-based fantasy elements in ways that tone down the "grittiness" of the subject matter.
3 The deployment of a *dark* telefantasy mode to engage children and younger audiences, but also to solicit adult viewers with or without children. The "darkness" of these shows' approach to fantasy genres is thus key to the genre cycle's combined appeals to Quality and maturity, but within the bounds of an approach privileging generic verisimilitude over cultural realism, as outlined above. This generic darkness and/or flirtation with horror thus operates as a "family-friendly" substitute for the gritty cultural realism Lynch positions as a legitimating device for

adult-oriented Quality Telefantasy, as it balances (often precariously) appeals to adult tastes with suitability for child audiences.

4 A narrative structure designed for Netflix's personalised and on-demand affordances and distribution model, but which is also laced with nostalgia. For instance, while episodes tend to end on cliff-hangers that encourage binge-watching, on a macro level, each season of *Stranger Things* is built around a three-act structure, like an extended movie or 1980s/1990s telemovie, as is reinforced by season titles that follow film sequel rather than television conventions (*Stranger Things*; *Stranger Things 2*; *Stranger Things 3*).

The reconfiguration of older content, particularly from the 1980s and 1990s, is a device common to this genre cycle, and can be understood as part of this nostalgia-driven approach. As Netflix's own comments around their strategy with *Stranger Things* suggest, the "Family Watch Together TV" cycle is underpinned by the company's assumption (supposedly drawn from viewer data) that content for younger audiences is more entertaining and compelling for adults if it harks back to key texts of their own youth.

Nostalgia as a "Family Watch Together" Strategy

Stranger Things weaves a fictional, fantasy world that operates like an "alternative" mid-1980s. Each season is set in a particular year (starting in 1983) and the aesthetics and diegesis are crafted out of the clothing, objects, interior design, technologies, and popular culture from the time. Aside from the varied assortment of 1980s media texts, artefacts, and technologies constantly in the orbit of the child lead characters – from walkmans to ham radios – key cinematic examples are explicitly referenced in ways that emphasise and map on to the chronology of each series, contributing to a sense that the passage of time is unfolding as it previously did in the "real" mid-1980s. In the opening to Season 2, for instance, the child characters dress up in homemade *Ghostbusters* (Reitman 1984) uniforms for Halloween, and early in Season 3, they are seen in a cinema watching *Day of the Dead* (Romero 1985), which came out the year this season is set. Thus, while there is no specific focus on actual socio-political historical events in the series, films and media references throughout the series operate as temporal co-ordinates, cultivating the impression that narrative events occur in parallel to real historical chronology.

Yet despite this attention to nostalgic aesthetic and intertextual detail, the show does not set out to craft a realist, authentic rendition of the historical past, but an overtly fantastical one. The show is set in the fictional US small town of Hawkins, Indiana, and focuses on the tensions between the town and the Hawkins National Laboratory. The Lab's sinister scientists are experimenting with telekinesis using a supernaturally-empowered child, "Test Subject" Eleven (Mille Bobby Brown), to make contact with the

"Upside Down": a dystopian alternate dimension populated by betentacled beasts, including the sinister "Mind Flayer", who can psychically control both the other beasts and humans. Using her telekinetic powers, Eleven inadvertently opens a gate between Hawkins and the Upside Down in the course of the Lab's experiments – and when she escapes the Lab, she finds and befriends the show's other four central child characters, Mike (Finn Wolfhard), Dustin (Gaten Matarazzo), Will (Noah Schnapp), and Lucas (Gaten McLaughlin), who rename her "Elle".

Thus, the show is not presented in a way that attempts to immerse viewers in a past that aligns with "real" history. As a result, the series sits somewhere between the two types of films Fredric Jameson so famously accuses of being "nostalgia films" – movies that are about the historical past and "specific generational moments of that past" (Jameson 2014: 546) yet that displace genuine attentiveness to history in favour of romanticised nostalgic pastiche. While on the one hand (and most influentially), Jameson references historically rooted films such as *American Graffiti* (Lucas 1973) and *Chinatown* (Polanski 1974), he also mentions *Star Wars* (Lucas 1977), which, he argues, "reinvents" the experience of the Saturday afternoon TV serial. He suggests that *Star Wars* is a

> complex object in which on some first level children and adolescents can take the adventures straight, while the adult public is able to gratify a deeper and more properly nostalgic desire to return to that older period and to live its strange old aesthetic artifacts through once again. (2014: 547)

Stranger Things' nostalgic register operates in the liminal space between these examples by foregrounding how the diegesis maps chronologically on to history and carefully capturing the mundane texture of everyday life and media – the "specific generational moments" – of this period, while simultaneously constructing a fantasy realm that exists in parallel with this "real" history.

In so doing, *Stranger Things*' nostalgic pastiche of pastness invites continual comparisons between the viewers' lived experiences and memories of the 1980s and the fantasy alternate past depicted in the show: much like the Upside Down, this is the past positioned as an *alternate dimension*. As our audience research illuminates, this approach to nostalgia invites self-reflexive consideration of how this alternate past both intersects with and differs from the adult viewers' own, rather than cultivating straightforward identification with or longing for this past. As Pickering and Keightley articulate in their analysis of the culturally and conceptually productive elements of nostalgia – which are often dismissed or downplayed in the substantial body of scholarship and critical theory on nostalgia:

> we need to recognize the various ways in which people are involved in putting the situated past into some form of narrative order for themselves, or in critically negotiating mediated representations of the past for their relations to collective identities and experiences. (2006: 925)

In *Stranger Things*, this process of critically negotiating and narratively (re) situating the mediated past also works for younger viewers who did not experience the 1980s first-hand, or who do not have memories of this period. Mascio's (2021) audience research with viewers aged 20–25 supports that this complex process of nostalgic attachment and reflection is sparked for audiences who weren't alive in the 1980s. 76% of the survey respondents in this age group experienced the show as a

> reconstruction of the past removed from one's own experiences, but linked to a much wider range of media texts … the show is considered 'close' to experiences of the present and therefore capable of generating the kind of nostalgia that Appadurai (1996) considers as detached from any specific past. (238)

This connection to the past was reflected in different ways in our own audience research via its cultivation of intergenerational family connections: for instance, the above-quoted 12-year-old Cole we interviewed explained that he enjoyed the 1980s setting even though it "was very different to the way things are now" because it facilitated his mother's memory sharing with him.

Thus, while Jameson's description of *Star Wars*' dual layers of pleasure resonates with *Stranger Things*' nostalgic aesthetic and formal devices, *Stranger Things*' complex deployment of nostalgia fosters a dialogue and dialectic between its multiple generational layers. Just as older viewers are invited to draw comparisons between their lived and historical pasts and the show's diegesis, younger viewers are encouraged to reflect on how the show's fantastical but attentive and detailed depiction of the past might relate to their *mediated* experiences of this period. Indeed, while younger viewers may not have lived through the 1980s, the seemingly "perpetual cultural relevance" (Lizardi 2017: 2) of this period in contemporary entertainment media positions the 1980s as a component of contemporary young people's media diets. Thus, depictions of the 1980s in media have the ability to manifest as what Alison Landsberg calls "prosthetic memories" (2004) – mediated memories of times or places beyond the scope of lived experience. In a slightly different process, this type of interaction with media from or influenced by the 1980s has the potential to create what Merrill et al term in their research on intergenerational story sharing "vicarious memory" (2018: 753): the recollections of children's parents and other older family members and friends, which become personal memories of a different order for the younger generation via intergenerational exchange. Our interview with Madeline and her 12-year-old son Cole was an example of this – in separate, individual interviews, when Madeline and her son talked about watching the show together, they shared their memory of talking about the plastic red soft-drink cups featured in the show. Madeline had told her son about how she also used to drink out of these cups as a child living in the US in the 1980s, and how they often contained, as in the show, the soft drink "Tab" which had what Cole described as a "toxic chemical" that caused cancer. Cole explained that he liked hearing stories like this from his mother about her childhood, and evidently this memory around the cups and the tasty but toxic soft drink had become, via the show, a memory of personal connection shared between mother and son – a source of affective intimacy or what Madeline described as "feeling connected".

Thus, while Lizardi writes critically of the "surrogate nostalgia" (2017: 1) imposed on children by texts like *Stranger Things*, in the case of this series, the nostalgia invites intergenerational memory sharing that has the potential to forge new connections between generations and family members. The comparative reflection that the show's nostalgia invites also facilitates intergenerational sharing of these different versions of, and access points to, "pastness". Indeed, Netflix Head of Experiences and Vice President Greg Lombardo points to the intended intergenerational dynamics of the show's nostalgia in an interview anticipating the launch of the fourth season:

> You've got the '80s, that nostalgia. I watch this with my 13-year-old son, and I'm able to regale him with stories of what it was like when I was a kid. He's intrigued by, 'What's a Walkman?' When he sees these things, it's a really great way to unlock that sense of family. (Quoted in Castillo 2022)

This type of experience was highlighted by Madeline and Cole around the red plastic cups and Tab soft drink, which was foreign to the child but familiar to the mother, sparking a discovery that initiated a new sense of understanding between them. Such an experience of intergenerational connection ignited by the nostalgic objects of the show is also regularly gestured to in social media commentary. See, for instance, the below reflections on the show from various Twitter users, all of which are in a similar vein to both Madeline and Cole's and Lombardo's own recounted experiences:

> @TortoiseNHound (2020) My child "asked me 'what's that thing on my Stranger Things' sweatshirt' (it's a cassette) and 'what's a Walkman'".
>
> @TexasAngry (2022) "My son just finished Stranger Things season 1 through 3 and is infatuated with the '80s. We ordered him a Walkman and I got out the old cassette tapes. TIME WARP!"
>
> @PavelBains (2021) "My kid: How can you ride a bike with no hands? Me: Well from the age of 6–14 my friends and I biked everywhere. My Kid: Like in Stranger Things? Me: Yeah. Just like that".
>
> @raisinguprebels (2021) "Thank you @Stranger_Things, my 7yo is obsessed with Motley Crue now. First my mom in the 80s and now my kid in 2021. Okay okay maybe I showed him some videos …".

The heightened nostalgia of *Stranger Things* invites such affective intergenerational connections because it *feels* niche and personally targeted. As these social media reflections and our audience research indicates, the show's attentive focus on the minute details of everyday life in the 1980s such as drinking soft drink out of a red plastic cup, riding bikes with no hands, and making recordings on cassette tapes has the capacity to spark highly specific, mundane (but nevertheless important) personal memories for viewers who lived during this period and enjoyed similar experiences. The very specificity and mundanity of these memories – their association with the long-forgotten but suddenly resurfaced textures, sounds, and tastes of past modes of everyday life – is what renders them affectively potent and thus personal. Thus, the cultural nostalgia that seems to underpin *Stranger Things*' broad appeal can also seem narrowly targeted – in line with Netflix's "personalised" content delivery branding – due to the way the show's narrative world evocatively resonates with such specific and personal memories, in so doing fostering affective intimacy via intergenerational connection.

There are many examples of this seemingly "narrowly" targeted cultural nostalgia throughout the series as a whole. Some commentators have taken to describing this strategy as "80s Easter eggs", a term that captures the narrow-broad interplay of this cultivation of affective intimacy via nostalgia (Gomez 2019; Prahl 2022; Supplisson 2022). These "Easter Eggs", such as references to Coca-Cola's infamous failed rebrand of Coke, "New Coke", in Season 3, and the use of popular songs such as Kate Bush's "Running Up That Hill" (1985) and Metallica's "Master of Puppets" (1986) in Season 4, have often been extended to strategic nostalgia-driven paratextual tie-ins and marketing campaigns. For instance, *Metal Hammer* magazine in 2022 featured a story about Season 4's popular new "metal-head" character, Eddie Munson (played by Joseph Quinn), meeting Metallica to play "Master of Puppets" together, a meeting the magazine describes as "the metal story of the year" (Aldersalde 2022). We return to this deployment of specific 1980s "Easter Eggs" as a key aesthetic device in Chapter 7.

In tandem with this strategic deployment of cultural nostalgia, the affective power of personal nostalgia is regularly emphasised aesthetically in the show. One particularly compelling instance of this occurs in the beginning of Season 2, when the four central boy characters, Mike, Dustin, Will, and Lucas, are reintroduced. The boys are dressed up as the four "Ghostbusters" from the hit 1984 film, and the speedy expositional narrative momentum pauses as each boy is captured in his family home as his mother accosts him for a photograph, a sequence which evokes a scene from another nostalgically beloved 1980s film, *E.T: The Extra-terrestrial* (Spielberg, 1982). Each of the four times this photograph is taken, a polaroid image of the boy abruptly overtakes the entire screen, lingering for an extended beat to enable protracted appreciation and contemplation. Notably, following this season, Polaroid announced a tie-in *Stranger Things* branded edition of their camera. The continued strategy of 1980s Easter Eggs leads to paratextual play via merchandise with this "alternate dimension" rendering of the past.

What is striking about this aesthetic device in this first episode of Season 2 is the sharp disjuncture between the crisp and vibrant digital images that constitute the show's general aesthetic, and the grainy, poorly lit, faded and washed-out appearance of these polaroid photos. As Dodd (2021) points out, despite nostalgic aesthetic features like the much-discussed grainy, Stephen King-esque opening titles, "what is frequently unappreciated and unrecognised is the technological foundation upon which this retrospection is built" (134). Dodd notes the digital effects used to craft the "analogue" look in the opening titles, and also points out that while the soundtrack is indebted to John Carpenter, it is "more in the vein of the Synthwave genre that rose in popularity from the late 2000s to mid-2010s" (2021: 134). The polaroid images of each boy in costume at the beginning of Season 2 create acute momentary awareness that the show's nostalgic vision is delivered to us via the digital production and distribution technologies of the 21st century, breaking the nostalgic "illusion" for a moment, even as nostalgia for the aesthetic textures of the period is underscored. The images foster nostalgia for the (adult) viewers' own childhood or youth polaroids – and, in line with the examples pointed to above, in so doing encourage older viewers to share their knowledge of and experiences with polaroids with uninitiated younger viewers. But beyond this, this moment reminds the viewer of the selective and fictionalised nature of this fantastical recreation of the 1980s: these polaroids feel like a brief flash of the "real" mediated 1980s – only accessible to us now via personal memories or mediated "prosthetic" memories (Landsberg 2004) that form via media images that are grainy and low-resolution when compared to the high-definition aesthetic regimes of our digital present. In this way, the aesthetic disjuncture of this moment is jarring as it briefly interrupts immersion in the series' pastiche-driven nostalgia.

This example from the opening of Season 2 is thus a complex construction of nostalgia: the sequence is playful and thus comfortingly nostalgic in its celebration of the boys' fannish love for 1980s movies, but it simultaneously provokes the pain of loss and an uncanny *dis*comfort associated with digital/analogue aesthetic disjuncture. This can be further articulated via Roland Barthes' influential conceptualisation of "punctum" in relation to photography. While Barthes' notes that generally one is drawn to or becomes interested in a photograph because of its subject matter – "the figures, the faces, the gestures, the settings, the actions" (1981: 25–26) – the "punctum" interrupts this straightforward appreciation with a sudden recognition of the photograph's uncanny, temporally dislocative power. This element can "break (or punctuate) the *studium*" – like a "sting, speck, cut, little hole" – becoming an "accident which pricks me (but also bruises me, is poignant to me)" (26–27). Barthes' theorisation of studium/punctum establishes a contrast to the moving images of film and television, which inject images of people, places, and events lost to time with an illusion of constant movement, life, and presence. The stillness of the photograph, by contrast, offers access to a level of detail only accessible with visually "frozen" time, which carries with it concomitant recognition of the inevitable death of the individuals captured (whether that be because they are literally no longer alive, or because the photographed version of them is now gone). As Eric Jenkins explains of Barthes' model,

> cinematic movement blocks access to both the *punctum* of detail and of death, and it interferes with the *punctum* of death by portraying the illusion of life. … Rather than the stillness and silence of the photograph … cinema seems bustling with living movements. (2013: 577)

The flashes of still polaroid photographs at the beginning of *Stranger Things 2* incite moments of "punctum" that momentarily halt the flow of the show's fast-paced narrative, which is particularly lively in this montage sequence re-introducing the four central boys. This encourages adult viewers to relate these images to their own personal memories in ways that simultaneously enforce closeness and distance between their memories and the world of the show. While evocatively nostalgic – thanks to both the boys' homemade *Ghostbusters* costumes and the grainy aesthetic of the polaroid – these images also provoke cognizance that the photos capture fleeting moments that can never be relived or revived. Indeed, within the diegesis, the boys are already out the door by the time these photos have come into focus. Both the irretrievability and "prosthetic" nature of this moment are emphasised for the viewer by the polaroids' clash with the slick, crisp digital aesthetic of the rest of the show. The sequence underscores how neither these polaroid photos nor the viewers' own past polaroids neatly "mesh" with *Stranger Things*' narrative world, and thus, by extension, there is also an uncanny closeness and distance between the "real" 1980s and the viewers' own personal past and memories. This distance and disjuncture can never fully be overcome by the affective potency of this moment of nostalgia, and of the show's overall nostalgia-soaked tone. This moment thus captures how affectively and aesthetically complex the show's nostalgia can be, as it invites awareness of nostalgia's uncanny potentials. As Balanzategui has previously articulated in her work on the "haunting" and uncanny qualities of nostalgia (2016; 2019; 2020a), while there is a "distinctive combination of familiar unfamiliarity embedded in uncanny dread" such a combination can also be found in "nostalgic longing", which has the capacity to involve, as in this moment in the opening of *Stranger Things 2*, a "confrontation with a past that is not quite as we remember it" capturing "the very essence of the uncanny" (2020a: np). Dylan Trigg teases out the unfamiliarity lurking in nostalgia's comforting familiarity, pointing out how "nostalgic memory is necessarily untimely and uncanny. Nostalgia corresponds with the past, but only insofar as it replicates the past and forgets it" (2006: 245).

That this moment is deployed to reintroduce the boys' characters in Season 2 reinforces the conflicted and haunting nature of this incarnation of nostalgia: the actors and characters have grown up and changed between the first and second seasons, already looking somewhat different to the cute young children beloved by so many viewers child and adult. Indeed, the growth of the child actors between each season has been a source of fascination in news and social media commentary at the launch of each season (Fashingbauer Cooper 2022; Smith 2022; Stopera 2022). Thus, even for younger viewers, these "polaroid moments" invite recognition and felt awareness of the passage of time, as well as nostalgia for these characters as they once were in Season 1. On multiple levels, then, nostalgia in *Stranger Things* is deployed as an aesthetic device that can incite intensely personal memories and complex affectual resonances – a connection to the text that "feels" niche despite the show's broad appeal – as well as memories that invite connection, reflection, and dialogue between viewers of different ages.

Nostalgic Narrative Devices

Reinforcing the affective value and power of nostalgia, memories and nostalgia are also crucial to the show's narrative, being conjured in climactic ways in service of the child characters' individual identity formation and development, and also as a key component in the forging and strengthening of relationships between generations and age groups. On a macro level, for much of Season 1, the three key narrative strands are organised around and enforce clear demarcations between:

1 The child characters, Mike, Dustin, Will, and Lucas, and their new supernatural friend, Eleven.
2 The teen characters Nancy (Natalia Dyer, Mike's older sister), Jonathan (Charlie Heaton, Will's older brother), and Steve (Joe Keery, Nancy's boyfriend).
3 The adults, particularly Joyce (Ryder), Will's mother, and Hopper (David Harbour), the town's Chief of Police.

The boys exist in a world permeated by the role-playing game Dungeons and Dragons – indeed Bastow (2021) astutely points out that the structure of the narrative around the boys' adventures emulates a Dungeons and Dragons campaign – as well as playful communication using ham radios and long unsupervised bike rides around town. When Joyce's son Will goes missing, the boys' narrative focuses on their quest to find their friend – independent of parental help and guidance – which leads them to encounter the escaped Eleven, who introduces them to the sinister world of the "Upside Down". This eventually leads them to Will, who has been trapped in the alternate dimension. Throughout much of Season 1, Mike hides Eleven from his parents in his basement bedroom, a metonym for the children's occupation and navigation of their own spaces and worlds throughout much of the first season, independent from parental oversight and control.

The teenagers' narrative by comparison focuses around the high school and the houses of friends unattended by parents (the site of parties and romantic trysts), while the adults, Joyce and Hopper, embark on their own quests to find Will via frantic investigations centred around the living room of Joyce's home and the police station. In this way, for much of the series the characters across the three narrative strands occupy spaces and worlds aligned with their age-based frames of experience, and via this structure the show seeks to appeal to these three distinct demographics in separate, atomised ways. However, in the climactic episodes, all three groups come together to find and rescue Will from the Upside Down, working collectively and drawing together their age-based knowledge regimes to locate Will. In the penultimate episode, for instance, all the lead characters gather around Joyce's living room table to devise a plan to save Will, realising that each group has fragments of information and complementary but distinct skills that could help recover him from the alternate dimension. The boys for instance build a home-made "sensory-deprivation" tank out of a kiddie pool, so that Eleven can telepathically connect with Will, using knowledge garnered from their passionate junior school science teacher. By contrast, Joyce is able to bolster the frightened and confused Eleven, who has struggled to establish safe and secure contact with Will in the Upside Down, by drawing on her experiences as a single mother to offer her reassurance and maternal support. Joyce tells Eleven that she is a "very brave girl. … I'm going to be there with you the whole time. And if it ever gets too scary for you in that place, you just let me know, ok?" Notably, in this moment of connection, Ryder's Joyce nostalgically recalls but resituates previous beloved quirky teen outsiders played by Ryder in the 1980s and 1990s. In a moment of nostalgia-inflected catharsis, Joyce, a middle-aged mother burdened and enriched by her experiences of a difficult life, comforts an unconventional tween girl who, like most of Ryder's iconic teen characters, has until this moment felt misunderstood and isolated by all the adults she has encountered.

Such cathartic moments of connection occur not just across intergenerational lines during the Season 1 climax, but between different age groups within the same generation. Capturing the moment of recognition that they have both been focusing on and agonising about the same issues but concealing their struggles from one another, during this same episode teenage Nancy and her young brother Mike have the following conversation:

Nancy: I knew you were acting weird, I just thought it was because of Will.
Mike: I knew you were acting weird too, I thought it was because of Steve.
Nancy: Hey. No more secrets. Okay? From now on we tell each other everything.

Mike: Ok – do you like Jonathan now?
Nancy: No. No it's not like that. Do you like Eleven?
Mike: What?! No! Ew! Gross!

While this conversation concludes by emphasising the two characters' distinct age-based differences – Mike is still too young to have mature conversations about romantic relationships – it reinforces that the siblings need to work together and communicate across the gulf created by these differences. In a construction of onscreen intergenerational connection that invites parallel connections among collectives of viewers offscreen, in these climactic episodes, the characters are finally seen interacting in the same spaces and working together, rather than being atomised within "adult", "teen", or "child" spaces like the police station or child's bedroom.

In the course of this communal process of compiling information and communication, the adults, teens, and children discover that Will is almost catatonic in the "Upside Down" version of the fort that he regularly plays in with his friends in his front yard. We learn that Will's connection to the "real" world amidst the horrors of the Upside Down has been sustained by his repeating of The Clash's 1981 song "Should I Stay or Should I Go" as though it were a mantra. This song represents a cherished memory in which Jonathan shared the song with Will: earlier in the season, the viewer is provided access to this memory via a flashback from Jonathan's perspective, when he hears the song on the radio while still haunted by the mystery of his younger brother's disappearance. In Jonathan's memory, the teenager and Will are sitting together in Jonathan's bedroom, and Jonathan is playing Will the song and telling him that discovering such music will "totally change your life". Yet towards the end of the scene, it becomes clear that Jonathan is also using the sound of the music to cover over a loud argument between their mother Joyce and her ex-partner (the boys' uncaring father). Despite the painful undercurrent of this memory, what Will clearly treasures in this scene is his teenage brother's "passing down" of his favourite music to him, in so doing teaching him how to love and appreciate the song, and this memory tethers him to his identity and reality while he remains trapped in the Upside Down. Memories of media exchange between distinct age groups within the family are thus positioned in the climax of Season 1 as crucial to the security of the child's identity, and to his very connection to the world. The "nicheness" of nostalgia for media – its alignment with deeply personal, identity-forming memories – is thus positioned also as a source of deep connection between children and their older siblings. That this moment is first introduced as Jonathan's treasured memory of his lost brother and later revealed to also be precious (and literally "lifesaving") for Will in the climactic episodes positions this realisation as a key thematic thrust of the whole first season. In this way, the show validates the kind of interactions highlighted above in which older family members share their media tastes, memories, and passions with younger family members, a dynamic within the text that legitimates and encourages intergenerational communication and sharing among audience members.

Season 2 follows a similar structure, having three distinctive narrative strands that come together in the climactic episodes, as the child, teen, and adult characters must defeat the monsters that have escaped the Upside Down. In this season, the climax reinforces the value of memory and nostalgia to identity and intergenerational connection even more explicitly. In this season, while Will has been rescued from the Upside Down, he finds himself unable to withstand the power of the Mind Flayer, the powerful psychic monster that controls the other creatures of the alternative dimension. The Mind Flayer possesses Will, and Will struggles to free his mind and body from the powerful being. Will himself thus becomes a danger to Hawkins, his family, and friends, as the monster is able to use what Will calls his "Now Memories" to spy on the town's activities. Telling his mother and Detective Hopper about these memories, Will describes in hushed and fearful tones how these "now" memories are "happening all at once", "growing and spreading". He later tells his friend Mike: "At first, I just felt it in the back of my head. I didn't even really know it was there. Like when you have a dream and you can't remember it unless you think really hard. It's like that. But now I remember. I remember all the time". The implication is that these "Now Memories" threaten Will's own sense of a secure identity grounded in reality by pulling his psyche into the "Upside Down", as well as threatening the entire town of Hawkins: the "Now Memories" are starting to overtake the personal memories that connect Will to his sense of self, his friends and his family. These important memories are being replaced with Will's traumatic and depersonalising memories of being trapped in the Upside Down, and with the monster's own powerful and strategic perception of Hawkins in the present as the beast attempts to infiltrate the town.

These "Now Memories" are evocatively aesthetically rendered at the beginning of the first episode of Season 2. Will has just finished one of his favourite activities: playing the videogame Dig Dug at the arcade with his friends (an activity likely to raise potent nostalgia for adult viewers who also enjoyed Dig Dug). When Will steps outside of the arcade, the "Now Memories" overcome him and he looks up to suddenly see the world via the lens of the Upside Down – the arcade seems to be uninhabited, abandoned and rotting, and the spinning arcade sign, which was moments before pictured as a beacon for childhood fun, play and cherished memory formation, is suddenly strangled by vines, cloaked in an insidious grey hue and surrounded by black clouds and unnatural red flashing lightning. Throughout Season 2, the "Now Memories" are depicted as a horrifying threat to Will's developing subjectivity, as is neatly evoked by his changing drawings (one of his key passions). Previously, these colourful crayon drawings offered insight into Will's childish creativity and imagination, but overtaken by "Now Memories", they become oppressive dark grey spirals (which are revealed to have tactical use, because they expose how the Mind Flayer plans to access Hawkins – via a tunnel beneath the town).

To combat these "Now Memories", at the climax when the child, teen, and adult characters come together in Joyce's house as in Season 1 (this time in the shed), they inundate Will and his tormentor, the Mind Flayer, with their own favourite memories of personal connection with Will. Counteracting the creepy "Now Memory" drawings Will has produced in collaboration with the Mind Flayer, Joyce reminds her son when she gave him a huge box of crayons for his 8th birthday, and all he wanted to do was "draw with all your new colours. And you drew this big spaceship. But it wasn't from a movie, it was YOUR spaceship". Jonathan reminds Will of the day their father left, after which they stayed up all night building the fort, "Castle Byers" (the same fort Will retreated to when trapped in the Upside Down in Season 1). Jonathan lovingly recalls how it started pouring with rain, but the boys stayed out to finish the fort anyway. Will's childhood friend Mike reminds him of how they first met in kindergarten, when they both felt "so alone", and Mike approached Will while he was playing on the swings and asked him to be friends – which he describes as the "best thing I've ever done".

Memories shared communally between family and friends are thus positioned again as crucial links that ground Will in the world of Hawkins rather than the dystopian horrors of the Upside Down, providing a secure attachment to his own identity in a way that re-establishes links with the different members of the family unit as well as with his friends. This memory sharing exercise calms Will enough to start using his fingers to share "morse code" with his family, helping them to figure out how to expel the beast from his body (making him as hot as possible, given the Mind Flayer's inability to withstand heat). Again, while the show presents the independence and agency of the three key age groups featured as admirable and productive for much of the season – in ways that speak specifically with different demographics in the intended intergenerational audience – the climax also models the value of the intergenerational sharing of memories to sustain vital connections between these generational and age-based groups. Across the series, nostalgic memory is certainly not always "rose-tinted" – the memories Mike and Jonathan share to save Will are laced with trauma – but they are consistently depicted as being central to both individual and collective senses of identity.

Significantly, while nostalgia is typically positioned as the domain of adults – as it is in much of the writing on *Stranger Things* (Hassler-Forest 2020; Lizardi 2017) – the show highlights how children, too, engage with and even thrive on nostalgia, both their own and that of older friends, siblings, and parents, to narrativise and ground their sense of self. Furthermore, the nostalgia in *Stranger Things* is not only or simply comforting and conservative, but is often uncanny or intertwined with traumatic memory, in ways that the show and its characters often lean into or accept. In these ways, *Stranger Things* aesthetically, formally, and thematically models a specific mode of intergenerational interaction and viewing driven in complex ways by nostalgia. In these ways, the show lays the foundation for Netflix's dark family telefantasy cycle, offering a dark mode of telefantasy that appeals to adults and children, but beyond and more specifically than this, that celebrates and cultivates a complex *intergenerational dynamic* between viewers in different age groups.

Conclusion

Ultimately, the nostalgia in *Stranger Things* operates like a prism that engages viewers across different age groups in specific but complementary ways. The nostalgia thus underpins the show's aesthetic and thematic affective resonances in ways that make this prototypical dark family telefantasy Netflix Original *feel* niche and personally targeted despite its broad appeal. Such an approach would go on to become key to the flagship and most high profile content under the "Family Watch Together TV" tag. To return to the research of Merrill et al (2018) on the value of intergenerational narrative sharing, across its form, theme, and aesthetics the show cultivates a nostalgia that celebrates "the transmission of oral history" between age groups and generations within a family unit, a process important not just to adults but to young children for the way it enables "developing individuals [to] learn personal and cultural narratives" (2018: 753). *Stranger Things* offers complex nostalgic "access points" to an alternate 1980s, encouraging dialogue between different age groups offscreen in ways that emulate the conversations and interactions that occur between characters in the climax of each season. Thus, in establishing a template for Netflix's dark telefantasy "Family Watch Together TV" cycle, *Stranger Things* models a particular *mode of intergenerational viewing* – a mode that seeks to simultaneously uphold but modify the on-demand, personalised distribution model so central to Netflix's brand and algorithmic digital infrastructure. *Stranger Things*' celebration of memory sharing across age groups also invites celebration of the act of bringing different members of the family together around the television set, just as the characters come together around Joyce's living room table to save Will at the end of Season 1, in spite of their distinct and diverse age-based knowledges, attitudes, and habits.

By combining dark telefantasy content more commonly associated with an older demographic with younger onscreen characters, *Stranger Things* caused confusion around the intended audience (Grow 2016; Milbrand 2017; Renau 2018), yet its intergenerational dynamics on and off the screen were key to its success. Despite its US rating of TV-14, child-oriented *Stranger Things* merchandise, such as child-sized T-shirts, indicated its "broader reach" (Baker et al 2020). *Stranger Things* became the "benchmark hit" (Grindon 2012: 44) that formed the prototype for Netflix's dark telefantasy "Family Watch Together" genre cycle of exclusive "Originals" discussed in the remaining chapters, a prototype strategically developed around a rich and multilayered intergenerational dynamic.

Notes

1 We will return to the significance of *It* to Season 4 of *Stranger Things* in this book's final chapter.

2 "Family Watch Together TV" cohered as a label and category on the interface after the release of the first season of *Stranger Things*, although it may have been used to tag content on the "back-end" prior to this. Indeed, there are distinctions between how Netflix's "front-end" micro-genre categories are organised to overtly shape the catalogue in ways that enable users to find and select content, and how content is tagged on the "back-end" (Madrigal 2014). "Family Watch Together TV" is not included in pre-*Stranger Things* attempts to catalogue Netflix's extensive micro-genres (such as journalist Alexis Madrigal's extensive list of 76,897 genre tags in 2014). These attempts include an array of alternative idiosyncratic, strangely specific family-related tags (Ogre's Crypt 2016). Nor does "Family Watch Together TV" appear in Madrigal's 2014 user-generated spreadsheet of Netflix micro-genres. By contrast, after *Stranger Things,* "Family Watch Together TV" becomes a "front-end" genre label overtly displayed on the interface and as a tag displayed on individual program tiles.

3 The New "Family Watch Together TV"

A Series of Unfortunate Events

Released approximately six months after *Stranger Things*, *A Series of Unfortunate Events* (*ASoUE*) (2017–2019) was the first of the dark family telefantasy genre cycle shows to be consistently anchored to the "Family Watch Together TV" tag. While *Stranger Things* was a prototype and transitional text for Netflix's new suite of family content, *ASoUE* sedimented the key features of Netflix's dark family telefantasy cycle outlined in Chapter 2: the merging of multilayered nostalgia with fantastic wonder; a complex appeal to "Quality" via an excessively and performatively *dark* telefantasy mode (wherein the dark edge seeks to entertain adults but the fantastiscal mode tempers this darkness to maintain suitability for children); and a narrative structure designed for Netflix's personalised and on-demand affordances, but which also nostalgically looks back to prior media histories. *ASoUE* thus continues the discourses of category crisis in relation to family, children's, and adult content ignited by *Stranger Things*. Notably, while *Stranger Things* is a pastiche of US screen and popular culture from the 1980s, *ASoUE*'s engagement with nostalgia and construction of an intergenerational dynamic is buttressed by its status as a direct adaptation of a series of novels.

ASoUE is an adaptation of Daniel Handler's notoriously darkly satirical children's Gothic fairy tale series of the same name (1999–2006), written under the pen name "Lemony Snicket", with Snicket operating also as a character in the books via his role as narrator. As Cindy Holland, VP Original Content at Netflix, explained, "on the search for fantastic material that appeals to both parents and kids" they chose Snicket's books precisely because they are "darkly funny" and already had "generations of readers" who would be interested in the show (quoted in Andreeva 2014). Like *Stranger Things*, the show thus appeals to multiple niche audiences in a way that extends to broad demographic reach: the show targets millennial fans of the 13-novel series and its offshoot works; a child or tween audience new to the series; adults who recognise its broader network of nostalgic media references; and a family or intergenerational audience that combines these niche markets. Designed for the US TV-PG rating that explicitly targets families and children, *ASoUE* nonetheless displays an ambivalence to this

DOI: 10.4324/9781003223498-3

positioning in a similar manner to the US TV-14 rated *Stranger Things*, negotiating the dark Gothic terrain of the novels in ways that challenge family viewing. Continuing our consideration of the dark family telefantasy genre cycle's challenge to accepted understandings and assumptions around family television and viewing, this chapter examines how *ASoUE* deploys a strategy of playful adaptation to subversively destabilise discourses around family viewing and intergenerational relationships, childhood and child-appropriate content, and nostalgia in ways that resonate with *Stranger Things*.

ASoUE is set in an eclectic Gothic, anachronistic steampunk fairy tale world featuring giant winged lizards, enormous mysterious sea beasts, and fantastical squid submarines, and is replete with allusions to canonical Gothic literature and culture. The *ASoUE* novels detail the persecution of the Baudelaire orphans – 14-year-old Violet, 12-year-old Klaus and their baby sister, Sunny – by their inheritance-seeking, despicable uncle, Count Olaf, and his hench-people, after the orphans lose their home and parents in a fire. Each novel places the children with a new guardian, all of whom betray the children in service of their own self interests. As the novel series progresses and the orphans mature, their search for a safe and loving home evolves into a search for the truth behind their parents' death and the fractured secret organisation, "VFD" (Voluntary Fire Department), to which their parents and the villainous Count Olaf, belong. From the show's opening title sequence, which entreats us to "look away" from the horrors that are about to unfold, the Netflix adaptation announces its fidelity to the dark and subversive play of the novels, offering an experience both discomforting and comical in ways that underscore alignments between edgily dark family content and the Netflix brand. This chapter examines the unstable discourses around family, children, and nostalgia resulting from Netflix's strategy of playful adaptation of the Snicket books, conventions which have become embedded across this genre cycle of Netflix Originals, creating a new, transformative territory for intergenerational viewing.

As the previous chapter highlighted, potential broadcasters thought *Stranger Things* needed to be less scary if it was going to be a show featuring children *for* children, or conversely, the emphasis on the child characters needed to be removed so the show could become darker and more explicitly positioned for adult audiences (Grow 2016). *ASoUE* both draws on and departs from this prototype. Star Neil Patrick Harris reflects,

> I think at times it's shockingly dark … Netflix was concerned that adults weren't going to be able to value it because it was skewing to a younger demographic … now that it's done, they want to make sure the kids still value it and its not gone too *Stranger Things*. (Quoted in Giroux 2016)

"Too *Stranger Things*" in this context is deliberate branding that positions *ASoUE* in relation to this prototype show while also emphasising how it is distinct via its more explicit child orientation. Netflix's evolving brand is thus narrativised in tandem with the developing dark family telefantasy genre strategy.

In a sign of the ongoing success and flagship status of the dark family telefantasy genre cycle, *ASoUE* was another ratings success for Netflix, being watched by 3.755 million adults 18–49 "over the average minute" (Maglio 2017). Reporting in January 2017, *The Wrap* led with the headline: "Netflix's 'Series of Unfortunate Events' Tops 'Luke Cage' in TV Ratings (Exclusive)" (Maglio 2017). This is despite the fact that the article goes on to clarify that while *ASoUE* rated higher than the high-profile superhero Netflix Original shows *Luke Cage* (2016–2018) and *Daredevil* (2015–2018), *ASoUE* sits behind family sitcom *Fuller House* in terms of three-day viewership numbers. This is a sign of the public and journalistic interest that dark family telefantasy attracts by comparison to family sitcoms like *Fuller House*. While this 'wholesome' family sitcom is the more popular show by the article's metrics, the headline instead appeals to readers by focussing on Netflix's gritter content, pitting *ASoUE* against more adult-oriented (and hotly anticipated) superhero shows. Similar to the superhero film and television serials, *ASoUE* is a project designed to "connect with passionate fan bases" according to Brian Wright, VP of Family Content for Netflix (quoted in Tiffany 2017). As such, *ASoUE* illustrates the distinctive nature of the dark family telefantasy programs under the "Family Watch Together TV" label as shows designed to solicit shared intergenerational viewing, the process of which involves linking outwards to more adult content. This combination of adult, fan, child, and family appeal enables these programs to move across markets, a slippiness further enabled and encouraged by Netflix's use of "altgenres" to classify its content (Madrigal 2014).

In contrast to linear television's use of program classifications or scheduling, Netflix's family television not only moves across markets, but enjoys a simultaneous existence across multi-genres and age-based classifications. Constructed through a plethora of tags assigned to content by teams of trained watchers, alt-genres are central to Netflix's subscriber recruitment and retention strategy (Madrigal 2014). The "menu of intertexts" (Gray 2010: 141) constituted by these tags as well as interface imagery such as tiles, thumbnails, and banners varies across profiles and according to the viewing histories and age of the subscriber. Accordingly, as well as being tagged under "genres" as "Family Watch Together TV", *ASoUE* is also tagged with "Kids' TV Shows" and "TV Shows Based on Books", but this does not restrict the program from appearing under other categories not overtly listed on its descriptive tile on the interface. *ASoUE* also appears in searches for "Gothic Movies & TV Shows" despite the absence of this label among the program's various genre tags, where it sits with vastly different titles on child and adult user profiles: it is aligned with comedic Gothic family films such as *Hotel Transylvania* (Genndy Tartakovsky 2012) and *The Addams Family* (Barry Sonnenfeld 1991) on the one hand, and TV-MA or R 18+ rated materials on the other, such as *Crimson Peak* (del Toro, 2015) and *The Devil All The Time* (Campos, 2020) (Figure 3.1).

Figure 3.1 Netflix desktop interface showing *ASoUE* appearing in a search for "Gothic Movies & TV Shows" among TV-MA (in Australia MA15+ and R18+) content as of July 2022 on an adult profile. Screenshot by authors.

While this fluid catalogue placement and content categorisation strategy raises *ASoUE*'s profile across markets, it also underscores how the series is ambivalently and variously positioned in relation to adult tastes and viewing histories. This is reflected in the differing thumbnails across user profiles and alt-genres which feature a range of images that capture the varying tonal elements and influences of the show. A few examples of the *ASoUE* thumbnails include a dark, Gothic-infused image of the frightened villainess, Esmé Squalor (Lucy Punch), clinging to her adopted daughter, Camelia Spats (Kitana Turnbull); an image of hench-man, "Hooky" (Usman Ally) holding a 19th-century diving helmet, a reference to the steampunk aesthetic of the show; an image of the baby character, Sunny Baudelaire (Tara Strong), looking cheekily and knowingly at the viewer; and an image of a sugar bowl, an Easter egg for the novel's fans who will know it as the mysterious object fought over by the secret VFD society. Chandrashekar et al (2017) on Netflix's technology blog explain that this varied approach to the artwork in its thumbnails is tied to the platform's "personalized recommendation system". They explicate the need to "get the right titles in front of each of our members at the right time":

> If the artwork representing a title captures something compelling to you, then it acts as a gateway into that title and gives you some visual 'evidence' for why the title might be good for you. (Chandrashekar et al, 2017)

Netflix reported that multiple versions of the artwork tailored to individual subscribers "significantly raised view share of the titles" as well as "aggregate streaming hours" (Netflix Technology Blog: 2016).

The variety of thumbnails artwork – as entryway paratexts (Gray 2010) – speak to an intergenerational audience defined by a range of different demographics across various different fan "niches" rather than a broadly defined "family audience". The location of *ASoUE* amongst TV-MA and R 18+ titles as part of this fluctuating catalogue placement strategy highlights Netflix's intention of producing dark telefantasy content that attracts a family audience, but which does not alienate its adult subscriber base, particularly adults without children (Giroux 2016).

Dive in: Netflix Family Viewing and Serial Anachronisms

The promise of "prestige, plenitude, and participation to its subscribers, through a mix of technological and aesthetic appeals" (Tryon 2015) persists across this cycle of dark family telefantasy programs. In *ASoUE* the appeal to participation and prestige follows a complex multi-layered world building strategy based on an approach to adaptation as play. Madeleine Hunter defines adaptation itself as a form of play in relation to Eckart Voigts-Virchow's concept of "meta-adaptation", which foregrounds the mediality of the adaptation: "both the mediality of the text being adapted and of the medium in which the adaptation takes place" (2018: 274). *ASoUE* engages with the adaptation process in ways that emphasise the show's complex "mediality", in a simultaneous play with the show's literary source material and its fans, the affordances of Netflix's platform and algorithmic distribution strategy, Netflix's edgy Original content strategy, and the Netflix brand. Thus, playful adaptation in this context constructs an interface between this particular show, Netflix's brand identity, and the SVOD's evolving approach to family television production and distribution. *ASoUE* thereby builds upon the success of *Stranger Things* to position the dark family telefantasy cycle as a key site of the reinvention of family television in the SVOD era.

The multigenerational marketing of *ASoUE*, as a targeted appeal to not just family audiences but adult subscribers (particularly the lucrative 18–49-year-old market), is evident in the promotional video for *ASoUE* released on New Year's Day 2018 for Season 2. The villain, Count Olaf (Neil Patrick Harris), leans in from the left side of the frame and taps the lens with his large knife (the subject of a visual gag in the first season referencing Peter Faiman's 1987 *Crocodile Dundee*), hailing the viewer: "Hey you! Yes, you – the one who very clearly seems to have burned the midnight oil. I am so sorry to disturb your 'recovery', but it's time for us to get this New Year's Day binge started". The multigenerational appeal of *ASoUE* is referenced in this hail to the audience as Olaf addresses viewers young enough to be condescended to and, it would seem, old enough to be out partying late on New Year's Eve. Stepping back so his whole body is in frame, Olaf's begrudging sarcastic tone lifts to one of a light-hearted arrogant address, as he invites viewers to "dive on in" (2018). Rather than the distracted glance historically associated with broadcast television (Ellis 1982: 161–162), here Olaf promotes Netflix's preferred binge-viewing model, offering an immersive, all-encompassing, and protracted viewing experience for its holiday family content, signified by Olaf's idiom "dive".

ASoUE's unconventional compendium structure nonetheless refashions family viewing in ways that sit between much older legacy models and its own binge viewing model. While full seasons were delivered as a bundle on Netflix as is typical of the company's "all at once", non-linear release strategy, each of the adapted novels is divided into two episodes, labelled "Part One" and "Part Two", which are approximately 60 minutes each in length. The first episode always ends on a cliff-hanger, whereas the second episode offers a conclusion to the plot of that particular novel, even though the plight of the orphans remains unresolved so that a long-form serial structure overarches the season as a whole. Rather than encouraging binge-watching the whole series, this distinctive two-part compendium structure offers clear breaks between the two-episode bundles. As such, the program both reflects Jason Mittell's observation that contemporary television programs frequently employ "episodic forms under *the influence of serial narration*" (2015b: 18, emphasis in original), while also idiosyncratically reflecting the program's status as a literary adaptation in two-episode bundles per novel. The Netflix program thereby plays with the content and the form of its literary source material.

While Olaf encourages the bingeing "dive", by contrast the compendium structure invites a slower paced consumption, potentially more suitable for a younger or family audience. As such, the full season drop combined with the two-part compendium, along with the paratextual advertising, encourage two *different* modes of family viewing: the binge-viewing model for which Netflix is best known, and a more slowly paced one novel/two episode compendium structure more closely aligned to its 2014 "Watch Together" family movie night campaign (Brouwer 2014) which, as we noted in Chapter 1, immediately preceded its "Family Watch Together TV" interface tag and the dark family telefantasy cycle. The compendium structure equally appeals to the novel's fans, as it facilitates a readerly pace and fosters appreciation of the adaptation's visual "aesthetics of expense" (Baker 2017: 43, 45) via giving "plenty of time for all the little references that readers wanted to see onscreen" (Eloise 2019). Thus, while an innovative television episodic/serial narrative structure well-suited to on-demand viewing is sustained, the structure of the novels is also clearly and self-reflexively built into the show in ways that play with different modes of family viewing.

Notably, while the compendium structure makes use of Netflix's on-demand affordances in ways that emphasise its ongoing commitment to disruptive innovation, the serial structure of *ASoUE* also continues the dark family telefantasy cycle's distinctive (and at times disjunctive) combination of *nostalgia* with such narrative structural innovation tied to algorithmic distribution strategies. As well as the literary source material, the series achieves this via connections with a very distant moving image antecedent,

Hollywood film serials produced between 1929 and 1956. Overt references to the old serials thereby become part of the adaptation's network of playful anachronisms. Serials, otherwise known as B grade Saturday matinee movies, were primarily known for being targeted at a children's audience but aimed to appeal to both children and adults (Barefoot 2011: 181). Guy Barefoot notes that "serials could be exploited as juvenile entertainment, but also as a form of old-time melodrama, or as a form of action-based entertainment that had a cross-generational appeal" (2011: 181). Accordingly, one exhibitor noted in the press book for William Witney's *The Perils of Nyoka* in 1942: "I can't tell whether the adults are bringing the kids to see this serial, or whether the kids are bringing the adults ..." (quoted in Barefoot 2011: 182). The paratextual discourse around cinema serials therefore circulated around the same audience slippage and uncertainty demonstrated by Netflix's dark family telefantasy cycle.

This cinema serial heritage is playfully acknowledged within the show, but notably also playfully repudiated, in the first season episode "The Reptile Room" (Mark Palansky 2017). In this episode, a preference for Netflix's mode of domestic family television viewing is gestured to over the communal theatrical experience of Hollywood movies (and movie serials), when Olaf is forced to join the children and their current guardian in an evening at the cinema watching a serial melodrama film. Olaf protests, "I prefer long-form television to the movies. It's so much more convenient to consume entertainment from the comfort of your own home". Olaf then turns to share the joke with the audience, staring directly into the camera with a knowing smile – praising the audience for enjoying the promotional pitch. Nonetheless, it is Olaf as arch villain who is praising the quality of long-form television, and thus implicitly Netflix, and the episode does not contrast streaming with feature films, broadcast television, or cable, but rather (and anachronistically) with old black-and-white cinema serials. In the episode, the Baudelaires' new guardian Dr. Montgomery Montgomery ("Uncle Monty", Aasif Mandvi) ostensibly celebrates his new-found family members by taking them to the cinema, in an instance of what at first appears to be a ritual of intergenerational bonding via media consumption. As well as criticising the format, Olaf rolls his eyes at the thought of having to sit through the commercials, which notably Netflix (thus far) does not include. While the children are initially excited, once at the cinema theatre, it becomes clear that Monty's purpose is to watch a poorly made, melodramatic serial called *Zombies in Snow*, made by the secret VFD society in order to send him a secret message via the subtitles. Although the message is ultimately intended to help the Baudelaires, the cinematic experience itself does not turn out to be one of intergenerational bonding, with Monty largely ignoring the children and their baffled dismay at the poorly acted serial. Olaf's direct address to the streaming audience and the debacle at the cinema, where not only are the children *not* entertained, but also left abandoned when Monty is kidnapped from the theatre, frames streaming spectatorship as the natural home of comfortable shared family viewing, even as it makes a ridiculously anachronistic comparison to make its point.

Furthermore, despite this playful dismissal of the virtues of the format, the melodramatic and anachronistic excesses of cinema serials that "The Reptile Room" parodies are themselves frequently and playfully employed by *ASoUE*. The Hollywood serials were 10–15 chapter-long "action-orientated cliff-hangers", encompassing a range of genres including Westerns, jungle serials, aviation, and sci-fi serials. Later serials were seen as nostalgic fare for adults, with the press book for Ray Taylor's 1933 remake of *The Perils of Pauline* stating it would "bring back fond memories to our parents, who remember the motion picture in its infancy, and will bring new, modern thrills to the new generation" (Barefoot 2011: 182). *ASoUE* echoes the original 1914 *Perils of Pauline* in particular, in which Pauline (Pearl White) is left a substantial inheritance that is sought by her dastardly guardian Koerner (Paul Panzer), who tries to dispose of her to get her fortune. Pauline is subsequently menaced by a wide range of villains – from pirates to gypsies and Native Americans (Harmon & Glut 1973 : 6) – in a vast array of locations, in situations that look sure to result in her imminent death. However, the end of each instalment shows how she is rescued or otherwise escapes the danger. Final title cards for each episode destabilise this happy ending, reading (firstly) "The End" (and secondly) "?" implying that the story will continue. In *ASoUE*, every episode similarly features the Baudelaire's inventive means of escape from Count Olaf or his hench-people in a wide and excessively diverse range of settings that underscore the show's generic hybridity while reverberating with serials like the *Perils of Pauline*. These myriad settings include a Gothic mansion and 19th-century theatrical stage; a mansion infused with the jungles of South America and its reptile inhabitants; the timber mills of the Gilded Age; a boarding school that recalls the 1857 novel *Tom Brown's School Days* by Thomas Hughes; the New York High Society of the 1930s; the frontier town of the Western; a 1930s hospital evoking film melodramas; turn of the century carnivals; the fantastical deep seas of Jules Verne; and the desert islands of Daniel Defoe's 1719 novel *Robinson Crusoe*.

As a result, antiquated media approaches to family viewing are self-reflexively built into the show's narrative structure, in so doing positioning play as a dynamic that structures the character interactions and format of the show as a whole. To return to Hunter's analysis of how play operates in the adaptation process in *The Lego Movie* (Lord and Miller, 2014), play functions as "an act of imaginative (re)production – one which thrives on the deferral of resolution in its attempts to test the limits of both the player and the conditions under which the play unfolds" (building on Henricks 2018; Hunter 2018: 275). Hunter also articulates how play operates as an interplay between "creativity and control" (2018: 275), which is also a key structuring device across *ASoUE*'s narrative. As we outline later in this chapter, *ASoUE* includes Gothic horror within its generically hybrid mix as is typical of the dark family telefantasy genre, however the emphasis on play throughout the show spans its multiple genres, serving to mitigate these darker generic elements in ways that emphasise child friendliness. This playful dynamic is thus key to how the show engages with a family audience and cultivates an intergenerational dynamic as part of this engagement. The complex serial structure of *ASoUE* offers a particularly extreme and ridiculous "deferral of resolution" that tests both the protagonists' and viewer's limits, deploying the adaptation process to invite playful participation with Netflix's flexible episode release strategies via mediated nostalgia both for the literary source material (which had similarly excessive, limit-testing resolution deferrals), and for the Hollywood serial.

Such emphasis on play is particularly evident in the text in moments when playful dynamics between characters code and structure the narrative events. For instance, the often implausible and seemingly fruitless undercover activities and heroic actions of the members of the secret VFD organisation, relayed through tones of heightened melodrama that align with Hollywood's cinema serials, encourages a reading of this plotline in particular as a state of play fighting. In the episode "The Austere Academy: Part Two" (Barry Sonnenfeld 2018), Olaf and his newly acquired accomplice, the obnoxious, spoilt, 12-year-old, student, Carmelia Spats, have captured the unassuming, faithful VFD member, Larry (Patrick Breen), while on his mission to help the Badelaires, locking him in a freezer to freeze to his death. As Larry paces the freezer in despair reciting Jack London passages, with ice shards dangling from his face, a tall buff, backlit shadowy figure karate kicks down the door. In a cut to an extreme close-up of a stripe of light across the mysterious figure's determined eyes, and with a riff of the *Mission Impossible* musical motif playing in the background, the figure declares, "Snicket! Jacques Snicket! Did somebody call for a taxi?" Cradling a frozen, vulnerable Larry in his arms, the tall, broad chested, Jacques (Nathan Fillion) is stopped by the diminutive, Shirley Temple-styled Carmelita, who has delighted in bullying Larry prior to locking him in the freezer. Whereas Larry had been kicked in the shins for invoking his authority as an adult in addressing Carmelita as, "little girl", Jacques confronts Carmelita as a worthy adversary. Displaying his nobility as a hero, Jacques challenges: "this man here is my friend, and I don't appreciate anyone mistreating my friends – no matter what age they are". Jacques' declaration is accompanied by the strains of violins playing tense, ominous music on the non-diegetic soundtrack as he looks down and fixes Carmelita with a contemptuous stare. Jacques does not assume the authority of an adult in his response: instead, in instructing Carmelita that Larry is his friend – a status Carmelita has neither possessed nor laid claim to – Jacques acts like a protective older brother of a bullied sibling while dismissing assumed child-adult power hierarchies, a common feature of the dark family telefantasy genre cycle. As he walks past Carmelita, Jacques turns and delivers his withering blow, "Oh and by the way, I believe that it takes one to know one, cake sniffer". Larry is surprised by this encounter and gratefully declares, "You stood up for me!" In a hero-like monotone, Jacque explains, "Going back to school can be traumatic for anyone – that's why I keep a trauma blanket in my cab". A relieved and overwhelmed Larry, still cradled in Jacques' arms, gushes, "My hero!" – a direct reference to the rescued damsels in distress of Hollywood's serial melodramas. This scene is both satirical and poignant, troubling the line between expected adult and child behaviour in ways that, in line with Hunter's above-cited description, test categorical limits and fluctuate between creativity and control, and "imaginatively (re)produce" the codes of Hollywood serial melodramas, in tandem with the original books the show is based on. Play is thus deployed in *ASoUE* to dismantle clear divisions between adult and children's cultures in ways that refract the broader aims of Netflix's dark family telefantasy content.

The adaptation of the novels into a Netflix series is thus itself enacted as a meta-textual, meta-medial form of play (Hunter 2018, Harmon & Glut 1973: 274), but in a way that also highlights playful engagement with family viewing histories that emphasise the story's transition into the audio-visual realm. The array of nostalgic and anachronistic references encourage interaction between adult audiences who can make sense of this for younger viewers. For instance, as will be further detailed later in the chapter, our seven-year-old interview participant Dean saw the complex references throughout the show as simply part of an amalgamated and undifferentiated "olden days" – yet he nevertheless enjoyed this aesthetic and saw it as part of the show's "quality". As such, the program invites adult guardians to unpack its playful adaptation and playful intertextuality for younger viewers. In turn, the structuring emphasis on play invites adult viewers into childhood worlds and experiential frames. *ASoUE* thus positions Netflix's dark family telefantasy cycle as a complex curator of family viewing traditions past and present, remediating obsolete family viewing traditions like the Hollywood film serial in ways that serve to highlight Netflix's own narrative innovations in relation to family viewing.

Through its play with the audience and its assemblage of imagery from the past, the Netflix adaptation extends the novel's knowing wink between narrator Lemony Snicket (Patrick Warburton) and the reader, to a wink to Netflix's audience, continually extending the playful direct address to the reader in both the program and its paratexts. For instance, at the start of the second season in the episode "The Austere Academy: Part One" (Barry Sonnenfeld 2018), the combined family/fan audience is directly referenced when the banker Mr. Poe (K. Todd Freeman), who is responsible for the welfare of the orphans, updates his boss on the story of the orphans, stating, "it's delightful and educational and it's appropriate for families, a phrase which here means 'delightful and educational ...'". The humour of this declaration rests on the audience's knowledge of Mr Poe's persistent obliviousness to the fact that since their parents' murder, the lives of the

Baudelaire children have been constantly threatened and are anything but delightful. This joke reinforces *ASOUE*'s – and Netflix's – self-reflexive play with the frontiers of "delightful and educational" content "appropriate for families", while also playing down the horror of the Baudelaire's situation via humour.

The Promise of Prestige for Adults and Families Who Watch Together

The selection of key creatives is central to the playful adaptation at the centre of *ASoUE*'s world building and narrative structure. This strategy works in parallel with the fluid dynamics of the show's interface and catalogue positioning, used to speak to not just child or family audiences, but also an adult demographic. Handler's involvement as author of the novels and writer on the show has been positioned by himself and others in relation to appeal to the fans "who remember every word in every volume of the novels", and the parents watching with their children. As Handler himself has stated, for instance:

> as a parent myself, I know that I get very tired of family entertainment that is only for my child. It's really tiresome for me and I don't like to sneak out of the living room when the TV is playing to go mix myself a second Manhattan. (Quoted in McHenry 2017)

Handler, using his pen name Lemony Snicket, playfully commented on the shift in Netflix's branding from adult to family Original content, noting: "After years of providing top-quality entertainment on demand, Netflix is risking its reputation and its success by associating itself with my dismaying and upsetting books" (quoted in Andreeva 2014). This dark unsettling content was, of course, entirely the point: the choice of *ASoUE* strategically seeks to appeal to the target adult audiences of its gritty Originals as well as child and family demographics.

The choice of Barry Sonnenfeld as producer and director for *ASoUE* reflects the show's status as a flagship family product for Netflix via its alignment with edgy family *and* adult content. The program's highly stylised, Gothic other-worldy look has its roots in Sonnenfeld's work on the dark family films *Addams Family* (Sonnenfeld 1991) and *Addams Family Values* (Sonnenfeld 1993), as well as playful sci-fi-horror generic hybrids *Men in Black* (Sonnenfeld 1997) and *Wild Wild West* (Sonnenfeld 1997), the latter of which has an odd steampunk aesthetic aligned with *ASoUE* but within a sci-fi-inflected Western. The show also has notable aesthetic and thematic links with Sonnenfeld's Emmy Award-winning adult-oriented dark fantasy, comedy-drama show *Pushing Daisies* (2007–2009). *Pushing Daisies* featured very dark comedy with a misleadingly bright colour palette disjunctive with its macabre, unsettling themes, a style replicated in *ASoUE*. As the acerbic voice-over narrator informs us in the first episode of *Pushing Daisies*, "Pie-Lette" (Sonnenfeld 2008), the show is the story of a boy beset by the "unfortunate" side effects of his ability to bring people and animals back to life. Namely, whenever he uses this ability someone else must die in place of the resurrected, and if he touches the resurrected again, they too will return to death. Sonnenfeld brings the quality association with this adult fantasy series to *ASoUE*, which shares the dark yet quirky sensibility, overt stylisation and wordplay of *Pushing Daisies* (Gartenberg 2017). Sonnenfeld was key to the show's paratextual positioning via interviews emphasising his unconventional and painstaking creative efforts, in which he explains how he "went to Netflix and said, 'I want to shoot this show entirely on the stage; I want everything to be controlled, from the skies, to the colors, to the water' … I love to create specific worlds" (quoted in Lloyd 2019). Further reinforcing Sonnenfeld's auteur status, he makes brief cameos in the show, a device made famous by the archetypal auteur figure, Alfred Hitchcock. Critical commentary around the show picks up on this "prestige" quality and discourse via Sonnenfeld, often in ways that omit or downplay the show's family status: in an article for the *LA Times*, for instance, Robert Lloyd (2019) describes *ASoUE* as "one of the great works of television art – yes, art", and remarks that while the previous film version starring Jim Carrey in 2004 was "disappointing", it has become clear "the series was just waiting for the age of streaming television … most important" to this success and quality, he explains, is "Barry Sonnenfeld".

ASoUE enhances its set with CGI flourishes that inject a fantastical otherworldliness into the anachronistic, theatrical materiality of the production design. This approach produces a very high level of aesthetic detail, intrigue and immersion that persistently draws attention to the quality and prestige of the show. As Mark Wolf notes of world-building strategies, "an important part of the audience's experience" comes from "the excess detail and descriptive richness" around the construction of fictional worlds (2012: 29; see also Jenkins 2006: 114). The complex aesthetics of *ASoUE* combine such aesthetic richness with play with adult-child generic boundaries. In "The Vile Village: Part One" (Barry Sonnenfeld 2018), for instance, when Mr. Poe brings the children to the hinterland, the village buildings are covered in digitally duplicated crows, visually recalling Hitchcock's horror film *The Birds* (1963). The village sits unnaturally low on the horizon with a noticeably artificial sky and is home to a steampunk-styled hot air balloon-home. Whereas *Stranger Things* curates a specific 1980s experience as an alternate dimension rather than a real historical past, *ASoUE* creates an assemblage of anachronistic historical markers that leaves its world in fantastical steampunk indeterminacy. This is an immersive nostalgic world compiled of a dizzying array of reference points. Sonnenfeld notes:

> We make whole towns and water and carnivals and a city block. We create this world where you don't really know what year it takes place.

> The cars are all over the place, from the 1940s to a brand new Fiat 500. There are no electronics, no computers, no cell phones. Yet I wouldn't call this a period piece. (Feldman 2018)

The Netflix adaptation thereby extends the historical indeterminacy of the books – in which the children use Morse Code to send messages from a store that also paradoxically stocks fiber optics in *The Horrible Hospital* (2001) – and combines it with Sonnenfeld's signature use of visually complex yet artificially constructed worlds.

The promotional strategy for *ASoUE* playfully addresses the fans of the books in tandem with children and families, adapting the mock warnings made through the book covers and throughout the novels, where narrator (and faux author) Lemony Snicket entreats the potential reader to "put down" the books, as surely "nobody in their right mind" would read them (*The Vile Village* 2001). The announcement for the second season of *ASoUE* extends this play from its literary origins to Netflix, directing fans to a farcical website (www.vastlyfrighteningdecision.com), "A Very Unfortunate Announcement" created by Netflix. The only thing on the site was a letter ostensibly written by Lemony Snicket (2018) stating:

> It has come to my attention that, despite my repeated warnings, you have viewed the Netflix adaptation of my distressing work, known collectively as *A Series of Unfortunate Events*. Some of you have even binged, a word which here means "watched several episodes in a row, despite having much better things to do with your time". To my horror, Netflix has been encouraged by this and funnelled their ill-gotten gains toward a second season of this unhappy and unnerving series .... I hope you are happy. Because you won't be. Ever again.

In this address, even the act of Netflix's preferred mode of binge-watching – watching "several episodes in a row, despite having much better things to do with your time" – is reframed through the conventions of play, which aims to provoke "a feeling of tension, joy, and consciousness that it is 'different' from 'ordinary life'" (Huizinga 1949: 28). The promotion asserts the simultaneous threat and promise of a playful but "shockingly dark" program (Harris in Giroux 2016). In *ASoUE*, the playful tone is key to its delivery of the Gothic horror genericity discussed below, and thus the inherent darkness of this mode is tempered via playful textual and paratextual dynamics. Yet, self-reflexively sedimenting the conventions of Netflix's dark family telefantasy cycle, this playfulness nevertheless serves to *ironically emphasise* how subversive it is for Netflix's family television strategy to centre on such "unhappy" and "unnerving" genres, and positions this subversiveness as central to the show's edgy, "quality" status.

This carnivalesque play with rich anachronistic imagery is also central to the prevailing discourses of the show's quality, repeatedly linked to the authorial figures of both Handler and Sonnenfeld. However, the child viewer will likely lack this screen and literary auteur framework and precise recognition of different temporal markers. In our semi-structured interviews, seven-year-old Dean asserted that *ASoUE* was set in the olden days, because of the old-style houses and the fact that "at the start … it's black and white", a reference to the title sequence in which a teaser for upcoming events is shown in a compilation black and white flashforward. Dean was ultimately unsure what decade the show had been made or was set in, suggesting that the "olden days" might possibly be the 1970s or 1980s. Dean also suggested that the actor who played Count Olaf (who Dean's father could identify as Neil Patrick Harris, but Dean himself could not) was a "good actor" in part because he, too, was "from the olden days". Instead, Dean, who was too young for the recommended 10+ reading age market category of the novels, approached this generalised sense of oldness as a curiosity and marker of quality, rather than as derived from a complex authorial intent. Dean's response contrasts with the media and social commentary around the pleasure adult viewers have taken in noticing the precise anachronistic details in both Sonnenfeld and Handler's carefully constructed worlds. The "gorgeous and weird" (2017) sets which Kathlyn Tiffany notes as a marker of authorial creativity and quality are pivotal to the show's fidelity for fans of the novels who have professed a love for the Netflix adaptation because it, "perfectly portrayed what happened in the books" (amritnitnrniininitninini 2020) and more particularly, "the show gives me the same feeling the book gave me when I originally read it" (Kintaku 2020). These reactions indicate the different levels of naïve and knowing engagements with the worlds created by dark family telefantasy programs such as *ASoUE*.

The teaser trailer for the first season self-reflexively positions Netflix at the centre of this world building, situating the streaming service as the primary creative authority over the show, albeit a seemingly unwise one, uniting the subversive risk-taking of the Netflix and *ASoUE* brands. The trailer emphasises the "unwiseness" and riskiness of the SVOD's creative choices in producing such a dark family show, implying that Netflix is initiating new frontiers for family viewing. An onscreen Lemony Snicket explains:

> Under ordinary circumstances this room would be buzzing with excitement and activity as directors, designers, stagehands, and indentured servants prepare for a dazzling season of top-notch entertainment. But the story of the Baudelaire orphans is so upsetting and so utterly unnerving, that the entire crew is suffering from low morale – a phrase which here means currently under medical observation for melancholia, ennui, and acute wistfulness. … So please, don't make the same mistake that Netflix has and look away before this dire tale is even filmed and avoid the cruel whimsy and the whimsical cruelty of what's to come. (Netflix 2016a)

The playful nature of the *ASoUE* promo invokes the transauthorial nature of *ASoUE*'s imaginary world – and the wider imaginary world of dark fantasy in which it resides – to satirise how audiences participate in the content selection and binge-watching experience on Netflix. The teaser draws attention to Netflix's personalised algorithmic distribution model by deflecting the moral responsibility for the suffering associated with watching *ASoUE* back onto the viewer. In reminding its viewers of the affordances of choice associated with SVOD, this promo is a subtle reminder that Netflix is a portal, not a linear television provider, and is thereby freed from the scheduling, content restrictions, and regulatory responsibilities that govern the relationship between these legacy media formats and their family audiences. In the promo, Snicket appears to be both an object within this world and its creator; however, he defers his role as creator to Netflix. This ironically obscures the reality that Daniel Handler is the primary creator of *ASoUE*, and instead situates the streaming service as the true auteur. The teaser thereby makes fun of the markers of authorial quality that Netflix itself employs elsewhere to promote the program, as canvassed previously. This tongue-in-cheek approach not only builds on the irony of the novels, but for millennial viewers also recalls the poorly received Brad Silberling 2004 feature film of *ASoUE*. Whereas the film kept Snicket off screen, the Netflix series not only puts him on screen but also puts him to work in self-reflexively warning *against* watching the series in the teaser, intertextually constructing an appeal to its subscribers as edgy, knowing and subversive viewers. In place of the individualisation associated with Netflix's algorithmic personalisation, dark family telefantasy content invites families to come together to watch TV – even as it playfully and ironically warns against doing so.

The title theme song for the Netflix adaptation, sung by Harris as Count Olaf, similarly playfully entreats the viewer to "look away" from the upcoming "horror", safe in the knowledge that this only makes the show more enticing. The title song operates like a warning, insisting the viewer should "look away" because their day, and even their life, will be completely ruined by the show. The urgency of the melodramatic, excessive claim of these lyrics is impelled by the driving 6/8 time. "Look away" falls on the two bigger beats in each measure, but as the beats diminish so does the validity of this assertion. In contrast to the lyrics, the intricate images of the title sequence entice us to look more closely. Like the interface tags and thumbnail images previously discussed, television titles are a form of paratext (Abbott 2015: 112; Gray 2010) that "initiate a set of expectations" about a program (Baker 2018: 111; Ellis 1992: 119–120; Schwichtenberg 1987: 130). Although they may seem redundant on streaming services where the thumbnail images are the first point of access (and where they can easily be skipped via the "skip intro" button), as Baker notes, title sequences "nonetheless continue to contribute to quality branding" even in the SVOD era (2017: 44). In the case of *ASoUE*, quick edits provide fleeting glimpses of images by threads and pins on an evidence board, inviting the audience to study every minute detail for clues to the mystery. Whereas a repeat viewer might normally be tempted to skip the titles, every episode has a teaser narrated by constantly updated song lyrics sung by Harris as Olaf. The high production values and Harris' profile as a Broadway musical star provide markers of quality that jostle with the absurdly melodramatic lyrics that are humorous even as they promise the show will be full of bleak "horror". The playful tension in the opening credits (look/don't look, bleak Gothic horror/comedy) introduces the ambivalence that codes the Netflix adaptation with a similar degree of category crisis as that previously noted of *Stranger Things*; however, in this show, this play with the frontiers of family and child-appropriate viewing is explicitly stitched into the themes of the show via such direct address in the text and paratexts.

This playful tension between horror and humour responds to and ultimately reworks the ambivalent "happy" Gothic tendencies of the novels. The novels construct a dystopian fantasy realm that challenges the expectation that children's literature should impart "lessons of conduct and morality" (Piatti-Farnell 2018: 95), contain "concrete images of villains and monsters on which to project undirected anxieties and fears, so that they might be contained and dispatched" (Coats 2007: 78, quoted in Piatti-Farnell 2018: 95), and achieve a happy ending (Tanderup Linkis 2020: 60), facilitated by the restoration of the social order. The repudiation of these conventions is a conspirative source of humour shared between Lemony and his young readers. Noting this humour and *ASoUE*'s "characteristically Gothic plot" (Spooner 2017: 54), Catherine Spooner identifies *ASoUE* as belonging to a wider trend of the late 1990s, the rise of the "happy Gothic" – the infusion of the Gothic, including its terror and trauma, with "a range of positively inclined emotions or moods" (2017: 3). Spooner argues that this happy Gothic aesthetic infused culture industries including music, fashion, children and adult's literature and family films, citing *Hotel Transylvania* as an example of this last category. However, Spooner points out that the "the mordant irony" (Spooner 2017: 191) of the *ASoUE* novels, and its "characteristically Gothic plot" (Spooner 2017: 54) troubles the happy Gothic's "celebratory politics of difference and inclusion" (Spooner 2017: 191). Instead, Spooner argues that the *ASoUE* novels tip the "happy" Gothic into darker, more fully Gothic territory, harnessing the Gothic's power to provoke, critique and disturb (2017: 11). Netflix's television adaptation both celebrates and tempers this categorical ambivalence, reformulating the playful challenge to children's literature into a playful challenge to legacy media's model of family viewing.

Tempering the Happy Gothic Horror through Nostalgic Fantasy Fulfilment

ASoUE's play with the adaptation and audience positioning process is tied in with this ambivalently Gothic style, as can be seen in how the eclectically assembled dark fantasy world of the novels is reimagined in the show through a tumbling array of nostalgic and anachronistic objects. This excessive and polyphonic approach to nostalgia resonates with strategies employed in *Stranger Things*. Richards argues that in its homage to "primarily eighties popular American cinema", *Stranger Things* critiques the allure of nostalgia as a return to a romanticised past, "to show that there is no way to go back" (Richards 2021: 40, 64–65). Indeed, as we highlighted in Chapter 2, the nostalgic dynamics of *Stranger Things* are complex and self-reflexively worked through via the construction of the 1980s as not the historical past but a nostalgic "alternate dimension". In contrast to the empowered childhoods of the 1980s depicted in *Stranger Things*, the *ASoUE* novels construct childhood as an experience of "being young, correct, and punished", in a world where "sometimes there really are no answers" (Nedd 2019), raising the question: why would you want to go back? Netflix's adaptation, by contrast, plays with a desire for a restorative nostalgia, which Svetlana Boym influentially defines as a longing to "rebuild the lost home" of the past in a way that covers over the gaps and troubling fragments of memory (2001: 41). Such restorative nostalgia is constructed in the show through its eclectic compilation of historical, cultural, and media references interwoven with those of the novels, to offer not only the appeal of a return to multiple pasts but also a fairy tale ending denied by the novels.

The Netflix adaptation carefully tempers the darkest elements of the source materials in their quest to position the show for family and child audiences. Daniel Handler has stated that his family's chaotic experience of fleeing Nazi Germany in the late 1930s had a "huge effect" on *ASoUE*, particularly, "the notion that terrible things can happen at any reason and not – they're not punishments for bad behavior, just as good things happening are not rewards for good behavior" (quoted in Gross 2017). Whereas the *ASoUE* novels have been critically applauded because they "do not sugarcoat difficult topics" (Roth 2018), the Netflix adaptation attempts to lighten the disquieting menace of the novels through theatrical moments of slapstick comedy and musical numbers that meld the dark telefantasy with comedy, and in so doing lighten the overall tone of the program through generic hybridity, a hybridity typical of the dark family telefantasy cycle explored throughout this book. Hybridising horror and comedy is a strategy often used to modulate the horror in children's horror television: for instance, as Balanzategui points out in her analysis of the children's horror program *Goosebumps* (YTV Canada/Fox Kids, 1995–1998), comedy is deployed to create "a rollercoaster effect in which the horror is inflated to a point of peak tension that is abruptly deflated via comedy" (2018a: 216). In *ASoUE*, comedy is used not just to modulate horror's generic focus on inciting dread and terror, but to play down – and play *with* – very dark themes.

The first six books of the *ASoUE* series repeat a narrative structure in which the Baudelaire orphans are taken by the banker, Mr. Poe, to live with a new guardian after each guardian and each home fails to nurture the children or keep them safe from Count Olaf. Through this uncanny repetition, the moral order signified by a return to a safe and secure home is continually promised but deferred, confirming the unsettling suggestion that 'home' can never be restored for the children. As Lemony states in the first novel, *A Very Bad Beginning*, "the Baudelaires could not go home knowing the moral of the story, for the simple reason that they could not go home at all" (1997: 211–212). The Netflix adaptation, by contrast, adopts a more conventional approach to children's literature and to fairy tales in particular, where a happy ending is guaranteed (Tanderup Linkis 2020: 60). This happy ending is facilitated by restoration of the moral order by the end of the final season, signified by Count Olaf's failure and the orphans building a happy home on their own terms. Even more significantly, as previously noted, in the Netflix adaptation, Lemony appears on screen as a character attempting to help the orphans, as well as the embodied narrator.

In the novels, writer Handler inserts a parodic version of his own authorial voice into the text not only by using Lemony Snicket as his pen name, but also by using Snicket as the narrator who directly addresses the child reader as he tells the tale of the Baudelaire orphans (Magnusson 2012). Lemony is revealed to be a character tangentially involved in the Baudelaire's story itself and a member of the secret VFD society, thus he simultaneously functions as a character, potentially unreliable narrator, and the (fictional) author. Lemony commandeers his power as author/narrator to elicit his reader's allegiance and sympathy as he blends his heartbreak over the loss of his true love, Beatrice, with the story of the attractive, White, wealthy, well-educated and highly intelligent Baudelaire orphans. In the final book it is revealed that the Baudelaires are Beatrice's children. In the Netflix version, Lemony is the ultimate source of a watchful parental gaze – in each episode his commentary narrates the scrapbook of the children's lives posted on his walls and chartered through pictures connected with string, as appears at the start of each episode. Lemony eventually achieves social reintegration through his newfound relationship with his young niece, Beatrice, in the final episode "The End" (Bo Welch 2019). In the novels, Beatrice is born in the final book, *The End* (2006), and her attempts as a child to find her uncle are told in a separate, parallel book of letters and telegrams, *The Beatrice Letters* (2006), in which it is strongly implied, though not confirmed, that the two meet. Overtly showing Lemony and Beatrice reconciled as a family on screen at the very end of the Netflix adaptation is one of many strategies employed to ensure that the "disturbing narratives of alienation, entrapment, illicit desires, and perversions" (Piatti-Farnell 2018: 95) of 19th-century fairy tales, and late 18th and early 19th-century Gothic novels – on which the *ASoUE* novels are grounded – is mitigated for Netflix's family audience. This shift reflects the interplay between the rejection and celebration of safe and sanitised family content traditions discernible as a convention across Netflix's dark family telefantasy cycle, as darker elements are at once strategically emphasised while also being tempered for child and family audiences. Ironically, the Netflix adaptation of *ASoUE* is at its most ideologically troubling as a result of its attempt to mitigate the darkness and moral ambiguity of the novels, as the program still exposes the family audience to themes of child abuse, sexual threats, paedophilic intentions, and other deeply shocking narrative events from the novels, but also displaces robust interrogation of such themes via the comedic overtone. This tempering is further evident in the reconstruction of Count Olaf from the menacing villain of the books to a musical and often pitiable buffoon.

The Gothic horror of *ASoUE* addresses the powerlessness of a child's experience while also intertextually referencing a Gothic tradition that its older readers and viewers may recognise. Anna Jackson suggests contemporary "children's Gothic may in fact pull in opposite directions: the often ironic and playful use of Gothic *motifs* may not produce at all a Gothic, or uncanny, *effect*" but rather highlights a knowingness on the part of both the young reader and young protagonist about "the conventions of the genre they are in" (2017: 9). In the first episode, "The Bad Beginning: Part One" (Barry Sonnenfeld 2017), the orphaned Baudelaire children are delivered to the dubious care of Count Olaf, who is their only living relative, who soon reveals himself to be a harsh guardian, forcing them to cook and clean. Utilising Neil Patrick Harris's Broadway background, the Count and his hench-people break into a song and dance number about how wonderful he is, proclaiming that the "n" in his name stands for "knowledge". After this moment of levity, however, comes a shocking interruption of violence as he slaps 12-year-old Klaus (Louis Hynes) forcefully across the face and endangers the safety of baby Sunny (Presley Smith) by holding her high in the air with one hand. In the second episode, "The Bad Beginning: Part Two" (Barry Sonnenfeld 2017), the Count reveals that despite declaring himself the children's father, he plans to marry the under-age Violet (Malina Weissman) to get his hands on their fortune more quickly, and locks Sunny in a birdcage in a tower to force their compliance. In the novels, Olaf reveals his paedophilic desire and delight in menacing Violet, asking, as he strokes her chin, "Would it be so terrible to be my bride, to live in my house for the rest of your life? You're such a lovely girl, after the marriage I wouldn't dispose of you like your brother and sister" (Snicket 1999: 109).[1] In the Netflix adaptation, Olaf's attack on Klaus and threat to Violet unsettles the performative construction of Olaf as merely a singing-and-dancing pantomime villain, as he disconcertingly transforms into the unsettling embodiment of what James Kincaid in his assessment of depictions in popular culture of child predators has defined as a "gothic monster" (Kincaid 1992: 25). A significant aspect of this horror is the divesting of Violet's agency, as she is transformed by Olaf's desire from a reassuring nurturing figure into the epitome of eroticised childhood 'innocence' (Kincaid 1992: 10–16). As Ailise Bulfin notes (2021: 31), this sexual threat is heightened in the Netflix adaptation when Olaf puts his head on Violet's shoulder and says, "I'll touch whatever I want". Part of the horror of this perverse relationship between Olaf and the children lies in the fact that it is the most enduring and formative intergenerational relationship in the series, ending only with Olaf's death in the final episode.

Olaf's nefarious scheme to marry Violet recalls the trope of virgins in danger and themes of incest and entrapment found in late 18th and early 19th-century Gothic novels (Bulfin 2021: 27; DiPlacidi 2018; Hugie 2017: 36–37). The imaginary worlds of Gothic horror, particularly those intended for young readers or viewers, "challenge the idyllic myths that still hold sway … in our culture's representation of children" by revealing, if in heightened terms, that the world is a dangerous place, through tropes such as kidnapping, entrapment and the threat of abuse, and by reconceptualising the home as a site of horror (McCort 2016: 141). *ASoUE* highlights its Gothic lineage by invoking writer Edgar Allan Poe through the character of Mr. Poe and his sons, Edgar and Albert. In "A Bad Beginning: Part One", Edgar and Albert argue over whether their meal is crow or raven, a reference to Poe's poem "The Raven" (1845), a reference returned to in "The Vile Village: Part One" (Barry Sonnenfeld 2018) with the "Nevermore tree" in the Village of Fowl Devotees. The name of the children alludes to poet Charles Baudelaire who was influenced by Poe (Hugie 2017: 40). The intelligence and resourcefulness of the Baudelaires provide them with agency that helps to mitigate the despair of Poe's Gothic stories (Hugie 2017: 37), such as "The Pit and the Pendulum" (1842) or "The Premature Burial" (1844) in which victims may survive at the last moment, but not through their own actions. In *ASoUE*, the arrival of Mr. Poe tends to be a harbinger of imminent death, yet he is also simultaneously a "bumbling" buffoon, completely incapable of protecting the children (Hugie 2017: 40). The *ASoUE* books and the Netflix series address an adult audience who may know the references to Poe while mitigating through playful dynamics Poe's tone of dread and existential despair for younger readers and viewers. The show thereby rewards the literate viewer and through its intertextual references provides an opportunity for intergenerational sharing.

In the novels Count Olaf is an archetypal "Gothic tyrant" (Buckley 2018: 2), but he is simultaneously comic in his vanity, ignorance, and, in the Netflix adaptation, his musical numbers. It is an ongoing joke shared between Lemony and his reader that Olaf's obvious and ridiculous disguises fool all the adults even as the children see right through them. It is an ironic challenge to the perception that children are naïve and vulnerable, a gag that works to their best advantage in the adaptation given the benefit of being shown on screen. The Netflix adaptation adds references to Harris' prior career just for the adults, for example, joking about his role in *How I Met Your Mother* (2005–2014) in "The Carnivorous Carnival: Part One" (Loni Peristere 2018), in which he mentions that he tried having his own show in the city "for nine years", the duration of the CBS program. "Look where it got me", he laments. This direct comic address hence tempers and plays with his status as the series arch villain.

Indeed, more broadly, Count Olaf's asides and frequent direct addresses to the viewer in the Netflix adaptation encourage a level of empathetic engagement missing in the novels, which, along with his musical prowess and comedy schtick, divests his character of a significant amount of its menace. His hench-people are similarly amusing, innocuous, and cartoonish rather than monstrous. For instance, the Henchperson of Indeterminate Gender also known as Orlando is introduced in the first novel, *Bad Beginning*: "there was a person who was extremely fat, and who looked like neither a man nor a woman" (1999: 47–48). They are later dehumanised as a creaturely figure of horror, as the "enormous creature looked at Violet with its blank white eyes and shook its head" (1999: 114). Lemony shares the children's harsh moral judgement, describing them as a "despicable creature" (*Wide Window* 2000: 143), after Klaus has deemed this character to be "the scariest" of all of Olaf's Hench people (*Wide Window* 2000: 136). In contrast, played by Matty Cardarople in the Netflix adaptation, this character becomes comedically likeable and inclusively engaged, with an often-overlooked moral compass and an agency neglected as much as the orphans.

The playful nature of Olaf's villainy is also established from the moment the orphans meet him, at which point he swiftly leads them through a comical tour of his ludicrously unkempt and dilapidated mansion, ending with the previously wealthy and indulged children being inundated with an excessive list of chores. This satirical reference to *Cinderella* disenchants the concept of noble suffering embodied by the passive and feminine stepchild figure at the centre of the Grimms fairy tale. While Klaus bitterly complains about the unreasonable nature of the tasks assigned to them, Violet assumes a Mary Poppins-like optimistic pragmatism to the point of putting together an impromptu dinner party for Count Olaf's troupe. The Netflix adaptation invests Violet's character with a cheery resilience and adaptability typically associated with the heroines of Disney's family films, recoding the darkness of the novels, in which the dinner party ends with "Klaus in the bed, Violet on the floor, Sunny on her little cushion of curtains", all three "crying quietly all night long" (*Bad Beginning* 1999: 55). The disturbing nature of the orphan's predicament is further mitigated through an ensemble musical number that Olaf performs with his hench-people in which they literally sing his praise – coming at the beginning of the series, this number immediately establishes Olaf as an arrogant, comical buffoon rather than a figure to fear, whilst evoking Harris' previous performance as the inept and horrible musical villain, Dr Horrible, in the 2008 *Dr. Horrible's Sing-Along Blog*. Thus, beyond the ridiculous Mr. Poe, *ASoUE* adds ironic and intertextual humour to its world of Gothic horror.

The Unexpected Horror: Playing with Intergenerational Relationships

ASoUE continues the intergenerational dynamic central to Netflix's dark family telefantasy cycle. The failure of intergenerational relationships is a prevalent theme in the *ASOUE* novels that is announced from the very beginning when Lemony describes the story as the mystery of the Baudelaire orphans, a designation imposed on the children that signifies their otherness. However, through various forms of play with the adaptation process, intertextuality, and genres, the Netflix Original re-engineers the story with a focus on intergenerational connections in a parallel with *Stranger Things*. This textual valuing of intergenerational bonds onscreen – and its extension, via paratextual positioning, to the audience dynamics offscreen – thus celebrate engaged child-rearing strategies in ways that inherently value them as "investing in the future" (Hendrick 2003: 15–16). In the *ASoUE* novels, the orphans are perplexed and consistently disappointed by the strange behaviour of the adults. Unlike the books, the Netflix adaptation teases the possibility of a loving parent-child relationship through the reframing of adult characters as actively watching over the orphans. The dark family telefantasy cycle is populated by adult care-givers, like *Stranger Things*' Joyce and Hopper, whose willingness to endure physical and psychological extremes as acts of love and loyalty to their children is important in enhancing the audience's sympathetic identification with the characters (Vaage 2015: 40). This model of intergenerational relationships is stifled in the *ASoUE* novels by the self-obsessed adults who do not listen to the children or who are murdered before a meaningful relationship can be established, and the melodramatic excess with which acts of adult heroism are depicted, which blocks sympathetic identification. By contrast, the Netflix adaptation includes positive adult guardian figures to gesture to the hope of a secure intergenerational bond, indicating that intergenerational ties remain key to the show's underlying values, as in *Stranger Things*.

In addition to the ever-watchful Lemony Snicket himself, the inclusion of a loving intergenerational relationship is most significant in the first season in the subplot line that traces the journey of an unnamed and kidnapped 'mother' and 'father'. These parents are introduced at the end of the first episode "A Bad Beginning", after a sequence depicting the orphans lying in bed, dejected after Klaus has been slapped and Violet has been threatened. As the orphans stare blankly at the ceiling, the camera pans down to Lemony in the tunnels under the house, where he directly addresses the viewer to explain the orphan's dedication to getting out of this situation and his own dedication to telling this story. Lemony's narration is accompanied by images of Justice Strauss (Joan Cusack), a well-meaning but absurdly pedantic high court judge reading up on adoption law; Lemony walking through the tunnels; and then a cut to a prison van where a highly skilled, refined couple dressed in evening wear are introduced uttering their shared concern for their children and their commitment to saving them so that they can return home. At this point it is not clear who the couple are, but their listing in the credits as "mother" and "father" fuels the false hope that the Baudelaire's parents are still alive and that a fairy-tale narrative closure based on family reunification is possible. The devoted parents undertake heroic efforts to break out of jail, defeat a bar filled with adversaries, charter a biplane through a storm, survive its crash and cross the jungles of South America to be reunited with their children (exploits that once again recall the ridiculous deeds of old cinema serials).

For the former child fans of the novels who are now the adult viewers of Netflix's adaptation, this subplot seems designed to satisfy a wish fulfillment, shared with the Baudelaire orphans, that their parents really *did not* die in the fire and would eventually return and rescue them. The climatic emotional intensity of a long-awaited reunification is intentionally set up as a source of heartbreak and bitter disappointment at the conclusion of "The Miserable Mill: Part 1" (2017) through a match on action between shots of the parents ready to be reunited with their children, and the Baudelaire children waiting to be greeted. This time the heartbreak is for the viewer, rather than the orphans. At the end of Season One, it is revealed that "mother" and "father" are the parents of the Quagmire triplets, another set of orphans the Baudelaires befriend at Prufrock Prep, and not the Baudelaires. Contrary to narrative convention, their successful reunification concludes with the parents' murder as the family home is burnt down. This twist elicits a complex intergenerational and nostalgic response from its viewers, as exemplified by Marniie's comments in a YouTube video review of the show:

> I broke down when they revealed the parent twist! I knew that their parents were dead in the book, but it brought me so much comfort knowing that these parents were trying so hard to get back to them only to reveal that the Baudelaires (sic) were truly alone. It was so well done despite leaving me quite broken-hearted. (2018)

TV reviewer Zack Handlen similarly describes this plot twist as "a genuinely upsetting climax" (2019). Such responses point to viewers' imaginative empathetic (Vaage 2015) engagement with these parental figures, even with their scant screen time. The "horror" that the title sequence warns against is that the longed-for ideal of family and home is constantly thwarted as potential guardians, like the Baudelaire parents before them, seldom survive. This play with audience expectations upholds the desire for intergenerational bonds onscreen and functions as an appeal to audiences offscreen to treasure and nourish their own intergenerational connections.

Ironically, the introduction of these sympathetic and helpful adults who are absent from the novels diminishes the orphans' agency, and in so doing introduces a new level of misery into the series. As such, the caring adult figures of the adaptation unwittingly engage in a subtler form of adultism, "the oppression children experience at the hands of adults" (Flasher 1978: 31). The program introduces a new character not in the novels, Mr. Poe's assistant Jacquelyn Scieszka (Sara Canning), installed in Mr. Poe's office by their parents to watch over their children in the event of their death. She is the antithesis of Mr. Poe, ever watchful and present. Jacquelyn models the healthy intergenerational relationship between female caregivers and children idealised across the dark family telefantasy cycle. Jacquelyn instructs the children as to how to stay safe and arranges assistance for them at each of their known locations, her disappearance in the third season bizarrely explained as a decision to take up a position as Duchess of Winnipeg. In *The Carnivorous Carnival* novel (2002), Madame Lulu tells the nefarious Count Olaf the location of the Baudelaire children, however, in the Netflix adaptation, Madame Lulu (Sara Rue) actually helps the Baudelaires, even sacrificing herself to the lions (literally) to save them. In the Netflix adaptation, in the "Wide Window: Part Two" (Barry Sonnenfeld 2017), Larry (Patrick Breen), the waiter, devises a plan to trigger an allergic reaction in the orphans as a means of escape from Count Olaf. A comical scene ensues as Larry, posing as a waiter, covertly tries to convey the plan and convince the orphans to go along with it without attracting Olaf's attention. In contrast, in the *Wide Window* novel, it is *Violet* who devises the plan and orders her siblings to eat the peppermints given to them by Mr. Poe, because she knows that the ensuing allergic reaction will buy them time to form an escape plan. The inclusion of this plotline resituates the figure of the child within a protective intergenerational relationship, where adult protection becomes a form of play in which the orphans are unwitting participants rather than active agents.

The Netflix adaptation is similarly hesitant to impugn the orphans with morally bankrupt behaviour. In the novel, *The Slippery Slope* (Snickett 2003), when Sunny is kidnapped by the villains, her siblings plan to trap Olaf's girlfriend, Esmé Squalor, in a pit to force a hostage exchange. In the novel Klaus invokes Count Olaf's moral relativism, justifying the plan with, "We'll fight fire with fire" (2003: 252). Quigley Quagmire (Dylan Kingwell) challenges Klaus, declaring "throwing people into pits isn't the greater good! … It's villainous treachery!" (2003: 277). In the Netflix adaptation, Esmé accidentally stumbles into the pit and Quigley suggests using Esmé as a bargaining tool to get Sunny back, and utters the justification, "fight fire with fire". Klaus questions, "do you really want to be like Count Olaf?", a position which Violet defends. As Hanlen protests, "we're supposed to be worried about the moral quandary the children are in, and instead, I was just trying to figure out if Violet had forgotten the spying plot, or if Klaus just didn't care" (2019). By divesting the orphans of their moral ambiguity, the Netflix adaptation invests the orphans with a vulnerability, naivety, and innocence that demands adult oversight and intervention, inadvertently downplaying the self-sufficiency employed by the novels.

ASoUE ultimately depicts the transition through childhood to adolescence – and babyhood to toddlerhood – not as a time of joyful and teleologically productive growth (Edelman 2004), but as a series of repetitive sequences of losses of family homes and idealised parents. Despite this, *ASoUE* still implicitly idealises family and intergenerational connections, but by mourning their absence. The series of events endured by the children across the books is explicitly framed as a pastiche of *Forza del Destino*, an opera with themes of tortured love, fractured friendships, disguise, and betrayal. In the novel, *The Penultimate Peril*, Lemony Snicket notes that the opera contains a gun that "goes off accidentally and kills someone in an incident eerily similar to one that happens in chapter nine of this very book" (2005: 17), thereby inviting the reader to see the two stories as mirrors of one another. In the adaptation, the accidental death of Count Olaf's father is shown in flashback as the music swells dramatically, towards the end of the final season, in the series' second last episode (Season 3, episode 6) "The Penultimate Peril: Part Two" (Barry Sonnenfeld 2019). Thus, the reveal of Olaf's father's death is positioned in the series as a climatically revealing moment for the show as a whole. Viewers familiar with Handler's novels and the Verdi opera will realise the death of Olaf's father occurs precisely when the central protagonist, Alvaro, fatally wounds the Marquis, the father of his true love, Leonora by accident, forcing the couple to flee. The opera thereby musically narrates the key incident that sends Olaf on his journey towards revenge and villainy – his father's accidental death by falling down the stairs at the opera – and creates a schism among the members of the secretive VFD society at the heart of the Baudelaire mystery. As previously outlined, the melodramatic performance style and music seemingly reduces the activities of the VFD to the level of play fighting, ostensibly "a safe place to learn things like survival skills, social rules, and creativity" (Schubart 2018: 3). However, despite this playful dynamic which situates the dramatic conflicts of the narrative within an ironic frame, in both the novels and the Netflix adaptation all of Lemony's family and friends die playing the game. The orphaned children, forced into the adult's game as unskilled players, pay the price through their loss of family and the constant inability to establish a new, safe home with secure intergenerational attachments. The sight of Olaf's father falling down the stairs at the opera in the Netflix adaptation functions as a key originating moment to the story of Olaf and the Baudelaires, who, as it turns out, share the trauma of being orphaned. In the adaptation, this is foreshadowed by the uncanny repetition of murder via the recurring visual motif of shock and falling throughout the series – backwards into a pond, a lake, a lion's den, and the floor of a salon, for instance. The death of Olaf's father is revealed to be the original intergenerational trauma that is revisited upon the Baudelaires in the series' climactic sequence.

In his dying breath, in both the novel and the Netflix adaptation, Count Olaf explains his villainy by reciting the Phillip Larkin 1971 poem, *This Be The Verse*. Larkin defines the parent-child relationship as an unavoidable cycle of intergenerational trauma, that "deepens like a coastal shelf" whichcan only be resolved by not having children. This is declared by the concluding advice that Olaf sneers in both the book and the program: "Get out as early as you can./And don't have any kids yourself" (quoted in *The*

End 2006: 253, "The End" Bo Welch 2019). Olaf recites this poem to his true love, Kit Snicket, as he lies dying, using its intent as the justification for his villainy. Olaf's invocation of the Larkin poem darkly suggests that becoming a villain is inevitable, as in the transition to adulthood one becomes that which one despises, rejecting the value of the family. This philosophy is particularly disquieting in the novels as the Baudelaire orphans increasingly carry out villainous acts, becoming fire starters and kidnappers themselves, acts which reaffirm the dystopian moral universe of the books, as the children continue the intergenerational trauma cycle. Lemony Snicket in *The Penultimate Peril* clarifies, "it is very difficult to make one's way in this world without being wicked at one time or another, when the world's way is so wicked to begin with" (2005: 316) – a broader consequence of this cycle of intergenerational violence. Relinquishing the role of the victim, the orphans adopt a philosophy of moral relativism to justify undertaking Count Olaf's strategies of disguise and deception, and eventually contemplate murdering Count Olaf – a desire that places them both literally and figuratively in the same boat as Count Olaf.

The Netflix adaptation, in contrast to the books, offers its intergenerational audience redemption through the successful intergenerational collaboration that saves both the orphans and the world. In the books, Lemony suggests it is a rite of passage to enter into morally grey territory, a position the adaptation rejects. Lemony comments:

> In any case, a moral compass appears to be a delicate device, and as people grow older and venture out into the world, it often becomes more and more difficult to figure out which direction one's moral compass is pointing, so it is harder and harder to figure out the proper thing to do. (*The End* 2006: 18–19)

However, when reciting Larkins poem *This Be The Verse*, in both the novel and Netflix adaptation, the dying Olaf chooses to omit the first line in the Larkin poem, "They fuck you up, your mum and dad./They may not mean to, but they do" – the only line in the poem that offers redemption.[2] In the Netflix adaptation, the adults do not "fuck up" the next generation, instead they ultimately save them. As a result, the orphans maintain a morally uncompromised status – very much unlike their counterparts in the novels. As such, the Netflix adaptation mitigates the intergenerational trauma inherent in the text in a similar manner to *Stranger Things*, where the dysfunctional relationships between children, teens, and parents are worked through in climactic moments in which they learn how to communicate across and between their age-based frames of experience to save each other's lives and to save the town of Hawkins. This structuring conceit continues to escalate until intergenerational traumas have apocalyptic consequences by Seasons Three and Four, with the path to overcoming such traumas established again by the rebuilding of connections between family and friends.

The Netflix adaptation of *ASoUE* thereby models a dystopian intergenerational dynamic as a playful invitation to its audiences to distance themselves from the characterisation of adulthood on screen, and to celebrate and cherish alternative models which respect children and the intergenerational bonds between children and adults. As one parent noted in their review on *Common Sense Media*, "I really like that the intelligence is given to the kids rather than the adults" (Asouelover888 2019). Another *Common Sense Media* parent echoed this sentiment, noting that *ASoUE* "makes fun of societies [sic] adult group think with the young siblings trying to tell the adults what is really going on – while the adults largely ignore them" (KCK 2020). This playful Gothic horror, in which negligent parental figures prosper and caring adults are brutally disposed of, mocks intergenerational bonds yet highlights their importance – horror is the absence of those bonds.

Conclusion

In the *ASoUE* novels, there truly are no happy endings and the fate of the orphans is at the end unknown, leaving Lemony to assume that they drowned at sea. In contrast, the Netflix adaptation perpetuates the 'happy ending' denoted by the reunified family that recurs as both a narrative climax and a visual motif across Seasons One to Four of *Stranger Things* and is also key to the final season of *Lost in Space*, explored in the next chapter. Although the family home as a site of horror is a theme common across the dark family telefantasy cycle, the Netflix adaptation of *ASoUE* most clearly reflects this cycle's reliance on well-meaning adult guardians on and offscreen to mitigate the darkness of these shows for onscreen child characters and offscreen child viewers. Whereas the novels end with Lemony declaring that he does not know what becomes of the orphans, the Netflix adaptation ends on a scene in which Lemony meets up with his tween-aged niece, Beatrice, in a soda shop, finally uniting with him over a root beer soda at a diner and regaling him with stories about the adventurous life with the orphans over the past decade or so. Lemony has been on the run since taking the blame for Olaf's father's murder, and thus throughout the series he has appeared in tunnels and transitory spaces, removed from his glamorous life with his friends and family as members of the wealthy elite due to being on the run from the law. The swell of the uplifting non-diegetic score and Lemony's relaxed appearance in public suggest his union with his niece means that he has finally come "home": the mystery of the orphans has been solved and Lemony can come out of hiding and live a comfortable life once again with his remaining family. This closing sequence thus facilitates a happy ending aligned with family film and television conventions. In this context, memory and nostalgia are again positioned as key to the show's themes and structure, and to the intergenerational dynamic the show constructs, in ways that celebrate how they operate as access points to understanding and connection between generations. Beatrice's trauma is reframed in this conversation with Lemony as a resilience building series of adventures that can be looked upon with some level of appreciation – maybe even nostalgic fondness – from the safe vantage point of warm and secure intergenerational bonds. In turn, it is Beatrice's unification with Lemony as an adult who listens to children which facilitates the cathartic narrative closure of the series. This alteration of the dystopian repetitive cycle that informs the moral universe in the novels via a more forgiving and inclusive portrayal of this key adult character creates a different interplay of shock, humour, and despair in the Netflix adaptation.

As the first flagship dark family telefantasy show to be foregrounded consistently in association with Netflix's "Family Watch Together TV" tag, *ASoUE* plays particularly self-reflexively with the emerging conventions of this complex genre cycle. Throughout, the show invites the audience's investment in the securing of the Baudelaires' intergenerational bonds, reinforcing the value of such a dynamic by persistently deferring the possibility of such connections in absurdly macabre ways. The continual direct address to the audience throughout the show works together with the nostalgia of the diegesis and aesthetics to play with the acceptable limits of child-appropriate family content – this show being much more clearly positioned for children than the ambiguously defined *Stranger Things*. However at the same time, through celebrating intergenerational dynamics onscreen by underscoring the traumas that emerge from their absence, and inviting adult caregivers to decode for their children a complex nostalgic aesthetic assembled from a diverse array of past texts, genres, media forms, and viewing practices, *ASoUE* also invites family audiences to both cherish and find comfort in their own intergenerational connections. The show even offers audiences an opportunity to improve these connections by encouraging adult viewers to reject the grotesque "adultist" modes of communication displayed by a number of key characters in favour of actively listening to their children, as is modelled in the final endearing scene between Beatrice and Lemony.

Notes

1 Daniel Handler notes that the *ASOUE* novels were banned in a school district in Decatur, Georgia, in the US in response to this plotline (Gross 2017).
2 In this case, the constraints of YA fiction and Netflix's family programming work in the author's favour, facilitating the inclusion of the poem for its altered meaning.

4 Affective Contagion

Lost in Space's Old Fans and Young Viewers

In June 2016, Netflix announced that it would be commissioning "a 10-episode first season of the one-hour sci-fi drama, from Legendary TV, based on the beloved 1960s sci-fi classic from Irwin Allen", *Lost in Space* (1965–1968). While *Stranger Things* harks back to horror and dark fantasy films of the 1980s and *A Series of Unfortunate Events* adapts a Gothic book series published from 1999 to 2006, by contrast *Lost in Space* reaches even further back to reboot a program from the childhood of adults who are now Baby Boomers, given the original *Lost in Space* ran from 1965 to 1968. Netflix asserted that all three shows were part of a strategy to produce high-quality family programming (Wright in Tiffany 2017), emphasising the way that Netflix frames its dark family telefantasy as a distinct cycle used to appeal to the family audience. *Lost in Space* continues Netflix's reliance on telefantasy with a pre-sold component, but its distinct status as a reboot complicates both its intergenerational dynamic and how this intersects with fan address. Cindy Holland, Netflix vice president of original content, emphasised Netflix's expectation that the program would attract cross-generational interest: "The current creative team's reimagining of the series for Netflix is sure to appeal to both fans who fondly remember the original and to create a new generation of enthusiasts around the world" (quoted in Netflix 2016c).

In remaking *Lost in Space*, Netflix sought to activate affections for a "dormant fan object" (Williams 2015: 29). Netflix's *Lost in Space* (2018–2021) reboots a family show from the past to ostensibly invite nostalgia among adults, including (but of course not restricted to) parents, grandparents, and other guardians. However, unlike *Stranger Things* and *A Series of Unfortunate Events* (*ASoUE*), this is not enacted through nostalgic *stylistic* choices, but rather through *narrative* call backs to the original show – and a plethora of other science fiction texts – as well as a revamped version of the family values that underpinned the 1960s show. Thus, *Lost in Space* aligns with Holland's comments cited in Chapter 2 about Netflix's aim to provide parents with "the evolution" of older fan favourites by offering contemporary versions (quoted in Koblin 2016), but along different axes, given Holland's comments related specifically to the 1980s nostalgia of

DOI: 10.4324/9781003223498-4

Stranger Things. *Lost in Space*, like *Stranger Things* and *ASoUE*, offers not just a nostalgic return, but rather functions as a reboot that seeks to showcase Netflix innovation while providing nostalgic access points to certain segments of the intergenerational audience. Under the top-down logic of Netflix's microgenre system as a "persuasive component" of the interface (Lawrence 2015: 358), the "Family Watch Together TV" tag – to which *Lost in Space*, like *ASoUE*, is consistently anchored – then encourages adults to introduce the reboot program to their children, while being built on the hope that existing adult fans will be invested in watching it *with* them. To encourage family viewing, the *Lost in Space* reboot keeps the wholesome family focus of the original, yet reconfigures what family means in the present and future, depicting an aspirational, futuristic onscreen family to address an imagined offscreen family.

This chapter uses *Lost in Space* to examine how Netflix positions its "Family Watch Together" telefantasy genre cycle through an intergenerational dynamic not just between family members, but also between older *fans* and younger *viewers* as future subscribers, a dynamic particular to the rebooting of a dormant fan object. In this way, as outlined in Chapter 2, we continue to focus on how intergenerationality cultivates "relations between discrete age cohorts" (Johnson 2019: 4), a focus that Derek Johnson rejects in his own work in favour of the *trans*generational, but which is key to understanding the dynamics of Netflix's dark family telefantasy cycle. While this is a dynamic common to reboot logic more broadly, it finds specific articulation in the SVOD era – and in Netflix's dark family telefantasy cycle – which, as this chapter illuminates, in turn must be nuanced when dealing with a *very* dormant fan object.

Reboots, Regenrification, and Paratexts

The original *Lost in Space* was a science fiction program created and produced by Irwen Allen and broadcast on CBS, based broadly on Johann David Wyss' 1812 novel *The Swiss Family Robinson*. The novel was in turn an adaptation of Daniel Dafoe's *Robinson Crusoe* of 1719 rewritten for child readers, one in a long line of "Robinsonades" (Axelrod 2018: 316; Mayer 2010; Seelye 1990: 4), and even further back, of Shakespeare's *The Tempest* of 1610 (Axelrod 2018: 316). *The Swiss Family Robinson* became an ongoing tale, with Barronne Isabelle de Montolieu publishing five new volumes between 1824 and 1826 (Sánchez-Eppler 2011: 433). As such, even the "original" *Lost in Space* television program was itself steeped in nostalgia from the outset, being part of adaptation culture that evokes the cultural aura of earlier texts even in the absence of direct textual memory (Leitch 2002: 44). In this case, this process of adaptation culture entered into generically hybrid terrain. In turn, Netflix's subsequent *Lost in Space* reboot continues this process of regenrification in the context of its cycle of dark family telefantasy. William Proctor argues that a reboot takes a serialised storyworld and restarts it afresh with a new serialised story, "untethered from the pre-established continuum" (Proctor 2013). This is distinct from the remake, which involves the creation of new singular versions of a prior stand-alone text, though as with all typologies there will be texts that blur these boundaries, and the terms are often used interchangeably in the press (Gil 2012; Proctor 2012: 4). Indeed, given that the *Swiss Family Robinson* story became serialised across several novels, even the original television series of *Lost in Space* can be considered both an adaptation and a reboot, as well as a "regenrification" (Altman 1999: 71, 78–9) of the story into science fiction.

At the beginning of the 1960s, the story of a marooned family was back in the public consciousness thanks to the critical and box office success of Disney's *Swiss Family Robinson* in 1960. Writing for *The New York Times,* Howard Thompson (1960) declared,

> it's hard to imagine how the picture could be better as a rousing, humorous and gentle-hearted tale of family love amid primitive isolation and dangers … any parent who denies it to the kids deserves to be ship-wrecked on a remote island.

On television, *Gilligan's Island* (1964–1967) continued the shipwrecked theme, while a concurrent interest in the Space Race led to several space-aged versions of the *Swiss Family Robinson* story being pitched for TV in the mid-1960s (Macek III 2013a).[1] *Lost in Space* depicted the adventures of the Robinson family, who embark on a journey to a new colony on another planet to escape an overpopulated Earth in 1997. Their trip becomes waylaid due to sabotage by foreign agent Dr Zachary Smith (Jonathan Harris), who becomes an inadvertent stowaway.

In its first season in 1965, *Lost in Space* was listed in the *TV Guide* schedule as "adventure", a label it would use subsequently to describe Allen's *Time Tunnel* (1966–1967) and even *Star Trek* (1966–1969) (Baker 2018: 55). This might at first come as a surprise to contemporary viewers and scholars, for whom such shows are remembered primarily as science fiction (Baker 2018: 55). As Rick Altman notes, genre labels change in use over time, both within the screen industry and retrospectively among scholars, in a constant process of "regenrification" (1999: 71, 78–9). In the contemporary streaming era, the "Family Watch Together TV" label on Netflix is itself an example of regenrification, as is the way that its dark family telefantasy draws on the popularity of gritty adult Quality Telefantasy but refashions it for a family audience. Jason Mittell notes how television genres are "cultural products, constituted by media practices" that include "marketing techniques … schedule listings … editorials and commentaries" and are "subject to ongoing change and redefinition" (2004: 1, 24). Mittell suggests, "it is up to the genre critic to hunt these out and incorporate an array of these sites to create a broad and rich genealogy of generic operation around any specific example" (Mittell 2004: 25). In paratextually labelling

Lost in Space as "adventure", *TV Guide* situates the program with adventure-based space operas of the 1950s and 1960s that were primarily pitched at children, in contrast with anthology science fiction dramas of the era aimed at a more adult audience (Baker 2018: 47). The enormous, if controversial, success of *Captain Video and His Video Rangers* (1949–1955) had established an association between space-faring shows and the child audience (Baker 2020: 124). Reviews reveal that this assumed association persisted well into the 1960s (Baker 2020: 124). For its part, *Lost in Space* soon garnered support as a show suitable for the whole family. The program initially aired at Wednesday 6:30 pm before moving to 7:30–8:30 pm, amongst CBS's comedy line-up (Cohn 2011: 265) at a time that had been long established in the industry as a key cross-over between peak child and adult viewing (Baker 2020: 123). In his review of *Lost in Space*, *TV Guide*'s Cleveland Amory laments that this time slot was almost always slanted in the child's favour:

> Between the dark and the daylight, when night is beginning to lower, comes a pause in the adult viewing, which is known as the children's glower. And most shows designed primarily for children are not only written for them but also apparently – so it seems – by them. (Amory 1966: 1)

Nonetheless, Amory (1966: 1) suggests *Lost in Space* is able to rise above the banality of its wholesome family due to the wide appeal of its B-9 Robot (Bob May and Dick Tufeld) and its "marvellous villain" Dr. Smith, making the show "something remarkable" and suitable for all ages, adults included.

If the perceived audience for *Lost in Space* quickly changed from children to the whole family, contemporary reviewers also noted the program's shifting genre terrain from adventurous science fiction fantasy to camp comedy (Sontag 1967), demonstrating the long history of family telefantasy "regenrification" that Netflix continues in the current era. Writing in 1964, Susan Sontag explains that camp celebrates "artifice and exaggeration" and disregards "ordinary aesthetic judgment" (Sontag 1967: 275, 286). In reviews from the 1960s, the comedic appeal of the original *Lost in Space* program overshadowed both its "adventure" genre label and the domestic family at the heart of the show. Dwight Whitney (1966: 13) asserts the "tooth-gnashing" excesses of Dr. Smith and his comedic animosity with the robot provide the audience with camp pleasures, a reading supported by Harris hamming it up for the press, declaring of his character: "I am deliciously wicked … I am selfish, self-pitying, pompous, pretentious, peremptory, conniving, unctuous, scornful, greedy, unscrupulous, cruel, cowardly, egotistical and absolutely delightful" (Harris quoted in Whitney 1966: 12). Indeed, *Variety* even considered the show a "spoof" of science fiction (Cohn 2011: 265). In contrast to the camp delights of Dr. Smith, Whitney implies the family itself had little to offer, given the mother Dr. Maureen Robinson (June Lockhart) "seemed mostly concerned with getting out the space laundry", while the father Professor John Robinson (Guy Williams) "was reduced to the status of good-looking traffic cop" (Whitney 1966: 13). This was not lost on Guy Williams, who was publicly vocal about too much screen time being devoted to "the bad cop" (Fesser Jr. 1966: 24). After complaining to Allen, Williams was able to get some more "tough guy" episodes (Abbott 2006: 121, 122), such as "Hunter's Moon" (Don Ricardson 1967), in which John finds himself the prey of an alien undertaking a competitive game. This periodically brought the series back to the adventure emphasis it had originally been tagged with. The original *Lost in Space* program was, therefore, generically and tonally fluid, even as over time it leaned more heavily into its camp comedy in the final two seasons, as part of a bigger trend exemplified by *Batman* (1966–1968) (Abbott 2006: 147, 154; Torres 1999: 340).

Faced with this hybridic original, the Netflix reboot, by contrast, leaned more heavily into *Lost in Space*'s family and adventure components in both the text and its promotion to align with the dark family telefantasy cycle within "Family Watch Together TV". Whereas the Robinson family at the heart of the original show was frequently downplayed or even derided in the press at the time of the show's initial broadcast, by contrast Netflix (2016c) declared their rebooted version of the show would be "equal parts family drama and sci-fi adventure". Netflix's Cindy Holland says, "The original series so deftly captured both drama and comedy, and that made it very appealing to a broad audience" (Netflix 2016c). The press release was notable in moving away from the tendency in high-budget telefantasy reboots of the 2000s to *downplay* the family audience of original programs. Michael Z. Newman and Elana Levine suggest that part of the process of legitimating television in the first decade of the 21st century was to contrast with "a delegitimated 'other' TV" (2012: 13). As Andrew Lynch notes, this tendency could be seen in the way that director Michael Rymer described the rebooted *Battlestar Galactica* (2004–2009) as "not your parents' *Battlestar Galactica*, this is an adult show for grown ups" (quoted in Lynch 2022: 37, see also Baker 2018: 4, Urbanski 2013: 7). This rhetoric reflected the "childish" and "immature" cultural connotations previously associated with telefantasy (Baker 2018: 40, 44–5; Barker 2009: 286; Bourdaa 2014: 23; Hassler-Forest 2014: 191; Lynch 2022: 2). As Lynch argues, Rymer's clarification sought to reposition telefantasy via the discourses of Quality TV, addressing valuable demographics by stressing "challenging entertainment" that is distinctly adult (Lynch 2022: 37; Schlütz 2016: 101). Indeed, Lynch and Alexa Scarlata (2023) note that SVODs such as Netflix have overwhelmingly commissioned "violent, gritty and sexually charged" science fiction programs with high production values that can participate in the prestige market. *Lost in Space* aligns in some ways with this trend as it is a high-budget special-effects laden reboot, but as a show that is "equal parts family drama and sci-fi adventure" (Netflix 2016c), it does not otherwise fit into the adult-oriented trend outlined by Lynch and Scarlata.

Lost in Space was greenlit before *Stranger Things* and was released later in 2016, which, as we noted in Chapter 2, would go on to successfully attract an intergenerational audience. As Wallin asserts, genre cycles are informed not only by production schedules but also by release and promotion strategies that help shape public perception (2019: 2). The promotion and reception of *Lost in Space* was heavily influenced by *Stranger Things*, leading Danny Vena (2018) to ask, "is Netflix's *Lost in Space* the next *Stranger Things*?" By 2018 when *Lost in Space* premiered, "science fiction and fantasy" had become the most popular genre of Netflix Originals (Houghton 2018; Lynch 2018). This was a trend that Ampere Analysis argues the streaming service was able to "anticipate" through its famous algorithms and analytics (Houghton 2018). Ampere found an increase in both the audience appetite for science fiction and fantasy, and in the quantity of telefantasy titles being commissioned by rival streaming services (O'Halloran 2018). Continuing the success of the dark family telefantasy genre cycle, *Lost in Space* picked up 6.3 million viewers in the United States in the first three days, with heavy binging (McCreesh 2018). In the first season release of *Lost in Space*, only the second season of *Stranger Things* rated higher on Netflix according to Nielsen (Graham 2018). The third season topped the Nielsen U.S. streaming charts, with "1.018 billion minutes of viewing" in the week of 6 to 12 December 2021 (Stanley 2022), and became the number one Netflix show (Tassi 2021). Netflix was therefore successful in continuing its dark family telefantasy strategy of soliciting both families and adults (with and without children).

This appeal to adults, including parents and grandparents who are encouraged to share the program with their families through the "Family Watch Together TV" tag, is evident in the way the program is paratextually presented by Netflix on its interface by highlighting the prestige of star Parker Posey. On the authors' profiles on 19 November 2019, the thumbnail image for the show proclaimed: "Starring Golden Globe nominee Parker Posey", invoking the discourses of taste and value discourses around awards designed to have traction with an adult audience. Diane Negra (2005: 71) argues actors such as Posey, "while perhaps not fully meeting the criteria for stardom in the conventional sense, nevertheless generate personae that operate as legible, functional trademarks". In Posey's specific case, her brand image functions as the "queen of the indies ... associated with *quality* material" (Negra 2005: 71, 74–5). Thus, *Rolling Stone*'s Noel Murray (2018) notes that *Lost in Space* takes "indie film queen Parker Posey" and "*Deadwood* [2004–2006] and *House of Cards* [2013–2018] star [Molly] Parker". As Craig Haslop (2021: 38) notes, stars are used to strategically legitimate Quality TV, a strategy that has now extended in the 21st century to what he calls "mainstream cult telefantasy", or what Lynch calls "Quality Telefantasy" (2022). Just as Winona Ryder brought her "Hollywood cult fame" to *Stranger Things* and her authentic connections to the 1980s when her stardom first emerged (Haslop 2021: 46), in turn Posey and Parker are positioned as bringing the legitimacy of their prior careers to *Lost in Space,* a casting and branding approach that appeals primarily to adult audience members.

Posey's performance style and star persona informs the public discourse around her character Dr. Smith as antagonist to the Robinson family. Writing in 2005, Negra suggests that mainstream "action/adventure and family film categories" have not been able to accommodate Posey's "tartly ironic presence" (2005: 83), yet *Hollywood Reporter*'s Daniel Fienberg (2018) asserts her "her familiar flat and wry line-readings" as Dr. Smith in *Lost in Space* are "perfectly pitched for a character who's never supposed to be trustworthy". This reading relies upon knowledge of Posey's star persona and previous work that might not be familiar to a younger audience. The "Watch Together" tag invites adults to share this cultural knowledge with children to help understand Posey's performance style as Dr. Smith along ironic lines. For example, in the second episode "Diamonds in the Sky" (Neil Marshall 2018), Smith comments to Don West: "You put on a good show of being completely self-interested. But I know you're a good person. Look how you saved this chicken". Although ostensibly straight-faced, Darren Franich (2018) notes Posey's flat delivery turns the banal line into a joke. The statement is also ironic, given Smith is pretending to be a good person but is actually completely self-interested. Netflix's choice to promote *Lost in Space* through highlighting Posey on the interface thumbnail seeks to harness the "aesthetic and status economy" (Negra 2005: 71) associated with Posey's niche indie persona for an adult audience (who, in the case of Gen X, have aged alongside her), as she takes on an iconic role in the series.[2]

Murray (2018) notes that *Lost in Space* takes these well-regarded actors and puts them in "the dazzling backdrops of a high-end prestige streaming service show", harnessing the associations of quality around large budget productions (McCabe and Akass 2007: 43) and more specifically Netflix's assertion at this time that "family content can be great content" (Wright in Tiffany 2017). Indeed, Brian Wright, VP of Family Content for Netflix, made a direct connection between *Stranger Things*, *A Series of Unfortunate Events*, and *Lost in Space*, as programs that demonstrate this strategy (Wright in Tiffany 2017). Wright thereby narrativises its key dark family telefantasy programs as a cycle built around both the family *and* discourses of quality. As Amanda Ann Klein argues, "cycles are a direct result of their immediate financial viability as well as the public discourses circulating around them" (2011: 4). By 2 December 2019, *Lost in Space* was described on the thumbnail as "slick, suspenseful, alien sci-fi" (Figure 4.1), phrasing that also suggests the broader discourses of adult Quality Telefantasy (Lynch 2022), promising to present its science fiction story with an "aesthetics of expense" associated with contemporary prestige television (Baker 2017: 43). The Netflix streaming interface thus becomes the site of a "tacit" genre "contract" (Schatz 1981: 16). The thumbnail tags seek to activate genre "expectation and hypothesis" (Neale 2012: 179) around its specific

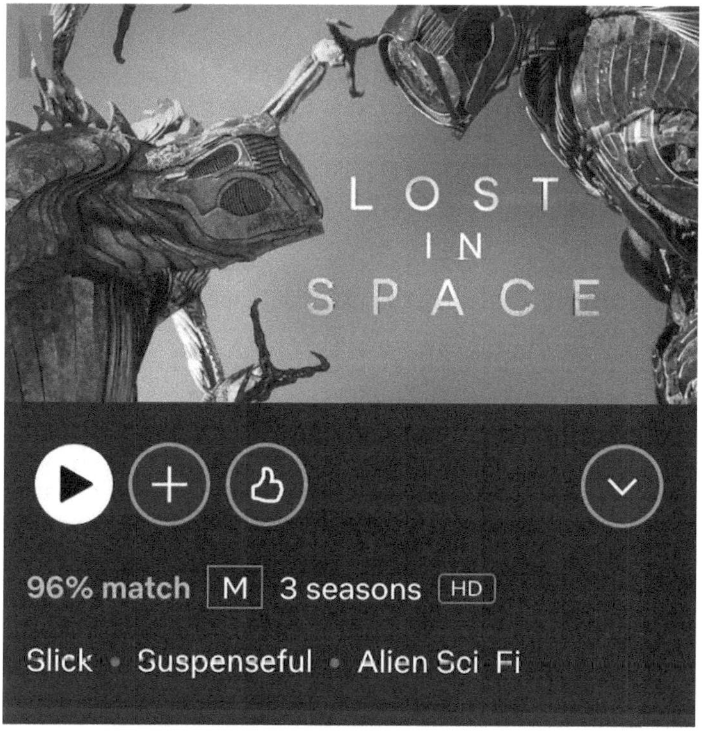

Figure 4.1 Thumbnail for *Lost in Space* on adult profile (Australian classification). Screenshot by authors.

prestige articulation of science fiction designed to harness click-through viewing, but more specifically, the larger promotional framework both on and beyond the interface reframe its discourse of quality around "Family Watch Together TV" that is "just as good" as adult Quality Telefantasy, and also "just as good" as its dark family telefantasy programs *Stranger Things* and *A Series of Unfortunate Events* (Wright in Tiffany 2017).

By situating the program under the "Family Watch Together TV" label, Netflix positions the show paratextually for a combined intergenerational audience. As noted in our introduction, our survey revealed that even among adults and families without children, the Netflix "Family Watch Together TV" label was primarily understood as both a viewing practice involving parents and children, and as content specifically designed with that audience in mind. In other words, even families who watched Netflix together but did not have children in their household still overwhelmingly thought the "Family Watch Together TV" microgenre tag was designed with both children and adults in mind. This perception in the case of *Lost in Space* was emphasised in promotional interviews upon the launch of the show. Showrunner Zack Estrin, who previously worked on *Prison Break* (2005–2017), said of receiving the script:

> I have two kids, ages 14 and 11, and they haven't been able to watch anything I've done. When I pitched them this show, they basically signed the contract for me … I think that there's a stereotype that all remakes have to be dark and edgy. We didn't want to do that with this show. Our family dynamic is one that loves each other, they have problems just like every family has. (Quoted in Burton 2018)

By 2019, Estrin was delighted to report that at the San Diego Comic-Con:

> we had so many people come up to us to say thank you for the fact that the 2nd season is releasing at the holidays. It's the time when families are together. So many people watching the show have been waiting for the weekends, so that parents could watch it with their kids, with no homework or other activities getting in the way … one of the huge appeals of the show is families watching it together. (Quoted in Combemale 2019)

The "Family Watch Together TV" tag on the Netflix interface works within the larger network of promotional materials such as press releases and interviews to affirm the family-friendly status of *Lost in Space*, providing product differentiation in the context of a genre cycle (Grindon 2012) of otherwise gritty contemporary science fiction and fantasy programming on SVODs (Lynch 2022; Lynch and Scarlata 2023). More explicitly than the examples discussed so far in our book, Netflix set out to present *Lost in Space* in the public discourse in direct relation to prior adult "dark and edgy" Quality Telefantasy to highlight how this genre can be reframed for the family audience: not only can family programming be "just as good" as adult Quality Telefantasy, with an emphasis on discourses of quality, in turn "dark and edgy" Quality Telefantasy can be turned into wholesome viewing, with an emphasis on family.

"Fantastically Super-Duper Settings": Quality Family Viewing

Netflix's vision of what constitutes family viewing had understandably shifted from CBS' vision in the 1960s. The first season of the original show was more suspense-filled but was considered too "dark" for families (Britt 2021). Actor Bill Mumy recalls, "CBS told Iwrin Allen it was too scary. Our show aired during the family hour. So, the message was to 'lighten it up'" (quoted in Britt 2021). Rather than constituting something entirely new, the original series actors Mumy and Cartwright see the Netflix reboot as a *return* to the "darker, edgier" first season of *Lost in Space* (Britt 2021). This is despite producer Estrin proclaiming they did *not* intend to go "dark and edgy" in the manner of most contemporary remakes (quoted in Burton 2018). In other words, a tense survival format that seemed too dark and edgy for families in the 1960s had instead become core family content with intergenerational appeal by 2018, particularly when compared to contemporary science fiction made exclusively for an *adult* audience.

The formula of "equal parts family drama and sci-fi adventure" (Netflix 2016c) was reflected in the disparate reception of the program along both lines, where the "sci-fi adventure" component is frequently situated in relation to discourses of contemporary Quality TV. Although the reboot is more serious than the camp humour of seasons two and three of the original, reviews stress *either* its return to the darker vision of dangerous space of the first season, or conversely, its return to a *less* serious adventure format for which the show is better known (Britt 2021; Burcham 2020; Nathan 2018; Seibold 2018). Ian Nathan (2018) suggests,

> What gives Netflix's high-end reboot of Irwin Allen's sixties TV romp … such innocent, head-on pleasure is the fact it is hardly a reboot at all … rather than labouring over the kind of twisty-turny, self-important report on the human condition that demarcates big telly, they have simply reopened the old playbook – a shipwrecked family escape an endless medley of perils in paradise.

While Nathan makes a distinction between the rebooted *Lost in Space* and "big telly" of the current era, the show does position itself within at least some of the prevailing public discourses around Quality TV that help to distinguish the show from the retrospective perception of the original as silly camp fun.

Indeed, Witney Seibold (2018) suggests "the scenarios and cheap sets and dated costumes and hairdos" of the original *Lost in Space* "put it well beyond *Star Trek* and *Space 1999* [1975–1977] in terms of it being distinctly of its time". In other words, the *look* of the original show, with its "kaleidoscope of Carnaby Street colors" (Abbott 2006: 116), is seen to both date it and provide a point of contrast with the reboot. This is, however, a retrospective assessment of the look of the show. Upon the program's release, it was praised in the *New York Times* for its "fantastically super-duper settings" (Gould 1965: 93). Indeed, J. P. Telotte asserts that Irwin Allens' programs had "slightly larger budgets" and his "use of filmlike special effects … brought a big-screen look to SFTV" (2008: 13–4). The contrast between this assessment and the popular perception of the original *Lost in Space* program today is at least in part a result of differences between the first and subsequent seasons. As Jon Abbott notes,

> the first season was filmed in crisp, clear monochrome like such classic shows as *The Twilight Zone* [1959–1964] and *The Outer Limits* [1963–1965], whereas the second season looks much more garish

> because it was CBS' first year of color. Unfortunately, many of the props and planet backgrounds look much less convincing when painted in bold primary colors. The second season also looks flatter and more studio bound, as the close of the first year also brought the end of such luxuries as the debut season's highly effective crane shots and location filming. (2006: 120)

The original show is now predominantly remembered for its garish (if amusing) poor quality look, but the first season in particular was seen as relatively high end for the science fiction genre in its time. In 1965, the program was described as a "tour de force of versatile hardware" featuring the "superb ... trick photography of L.B. Abbott and Howard Lydecker", making it suitable for both younger and older viewers (Gould 1965: 93). Given the show was *also* seen by *Variety* as a sci-fi "spoof" in the context of a cycle of family-based comedic telefantasy programs of the mid-1960s (Spigel 2001), Cohn suggests "*Lost in Space* thus began as a deeply polysemic text, with at least two dominant readings: one of the show as a serious sf action adventure, and one of the show as making fun of this genre" (2011: 265). Despite Netflix's overt strategy to stress quality markers, this mixed reception can also be seen in the reception of the reboot as being both "a high-end prestige streaming service show" content suitable for adults (Murray 2018) and *not* "big telly" but rather simple family fun (Nathan 2018). As Dan Gentile (2021) asserts, "in a landscape of hard sci-fi like *Foundation* and *The Expanse* with Herculean amounts of world-building, it's refreshing for a show with all the spectacular VFX dressings to have a premise as simple as the Robinsons finding their way home". The mixed interpretation of the show can be seen as reflecting Netflix's strategy to target *both* prestige and family markets simultaneously in its "Family Watch Together" telefantasy genre cycle.

This dynamic between family suitability and quality was evident in our semi-structured interview with 15-year-old Jack. His family watched *Lost in Space* when he was 11 after a supervised scroll through Netflix on the hunt for family appropriate content. He explains that his Mum and Dad decided they "didn't want me just watching YouTube and just kind of like content without much story. And so it was: 'go browse Netflix', and then I just scrolled through until I found this show that seemed interesting. And we watched it". Jack singled out *Lost in Space* along with *Stranger Things* as his favourite shows on Netflix, because "I really like the visual effects": the quality of the production values is thus acknowledged here as a central reason why these two shows, both key works of the dark family telefantasy cycle, felt distinct from others to Jack. Indeed, Jack felt *Lost in Space* was a stepping-stone to subsequently watch *Stranger Things* as a family when he was a little older, aligning the two programs within the genre cycle.

While Netflix promoted the hard sci-fi NASA credibility of the new *Lost in Space*, it simultaneously acknowledged it is, at its core, family fantasy

(Burton 2018; Weintraub 2021). As such, the creators acknowledge the reboot series "space fantasy" is only "partially rooted in real science" (Longo 2019), For the original series, Irwin Allen initially collaborated with NASA, who hoped the program would be "TV's first prime time space opera" to help promote their brand (Cohn 2011: 269). This relationship soon broke down, however, as Allen preferred a science fiction flying saucer design for the *Jupiter II* over the stream-lined linearity of the missile-like NASA spaceships (Cohn 2011: 269). The audience also seemed to prefer fantasy to reality, flooding CBS with complaints when the show was replaced by live footage of *Gemini 8*, when real astronauts were "in danger of losing their lives" (Warwick 1968: 30). Although the reboot retained this saucer design as a nod to the original, for the reboot producer Zack Estrin also worked with NASA, telling them,

> we didn't want ideas for things they were *hoping* to achieve, we wanted to know what they could actually deliver ... In one of our storylines, the Robinson family is able to convert the waste of a creature into usable fuel ... That's something that NASA is working on right now. (Quoted in Burton 2018)

At the same time, writer Sharpless admits the program is primarily a "space opera" fantasy "family show" acknowledging that "the robot race is not science and it's okay that it isn't. It's a big swing sci-fi concept" (quoted in Weintraub 2021). The creators thereby seek to balance publicity around the program's sci-fi credentials and its family fantasy narrative, both distinguishing it from and aligning itself with the original show. This is a means of managing the cultural legacy of a 1960s program that is both loved and made fun of, to legitimate the remake while retaining the family associations of the original.

Space Family Robinson

The paratextual materials around the rebooted *Lost in Space*, from press releases to interviews with key creatives, stayed on message by stressing the show would be "equal parts family drama and sci-fi adventure" (Netflix 2016c). The "family drama" component provides the narrative arc to the reboot as a whole, updating yet retaining the original program's core family values and family audience. The family focus of the series is emphasised in the opening titles to the show, which, much like the title sequence to *Star Trek: Enterprise* (2001–2005), presents a montage of real space missions from Earth history and segues into the imagined science-fiction future (Baker 2018: 125). The difference with the rebooted *Lost in Space* titles is that every image of this space history and future contains either families or children. The future of space exploration, and children as ideological symbols of the future of humanity (Edelman 2004: 4), thus become narrativised in tandem. Producer Estrin claimed in early promotion when the first teaser was released, "there aren't a lot of family shows that *everybody can watch for themselves.* There are very few things ... that adults and kids can *enjoy together*" (quoted in Hibberd 2018, emphasis added).

In other words, the program aimed to solicit different audience sectors individually and intergenerationally, both through promotional paratexts and in the program itself. Writer/producer Burk Sharpless asserts the show was pitched to Netflix as "a giant sort of movie" (quoted in Weintraub 2021; Monji 2018), with each season functioning as act one, two, and three in which the younger characters could be shown to come of age by the end (Weintraub 2021). This idea was extended from the children *onscreen* to the children *offscreen*. Just as the Robinson children grow up, Estrin notes the younger viewers who watched the first season would also be getting older, so they wrote the show "so that they feel like they're growing up with Will or ... Penny" (quoted in Longo 2019). This was reflected in our interview with mother-of-three Breanna, who noted her family watched the program together from the time her youngest son, Dylan, was five years old, and he has "grown up with it". Dylan "used to hide under the doona a bit" if he got too scared by the robots, and Dylan added he would "even block [his] ears because there might be ... scary sound effects". He thought watching the program with his family also helped and was "much better than watching it alone". As he got older, Dylan, now eight years old, asserted that *Lost in Space* "got scarier and scarier" each season. Breanna also ascribed this to Dylan growing up "because he understands more ... as an 8 year old" than he did when he started watching. As such, Dylan's experiences of "growing up" with *Lost in Space* echo the intentions of the writer/producer and showrunner around crafting a coming-of-age tale to align with a key, intended segment of the audience. Indeed, Estrin cites the coming-of-age film *Stand By Me* (Rob Reiner 1986) as an inspiration for separating the children from the adults in season one so that they can have an adventure of their own (Burton 2018).[3] This is replicated on a larger scale at the beginning of season three, when *all* the *Resolute* children are stranded on a planet and separated from their families, with the sole adult being Dr. Smith ("Three Little Birds" Frederick E.O. Toye 2021). This creates two different worlds for the children and adults, respectively, literally separating the generations onscreen for the dual audience offscreen, but, like *Stranger Things*, ultimately bringing them back together to overcome adversity as a shared intergenerational endeavour.

As the estranged John and Maureen try to put their marriage and family back together in the first season, the difficult family dynamics are positioned as points of identification for adults and children albeit in different ways. Toby Stephens, who plays John Robinson, notes, "this family isn't perfect, but they are trying to be better. It's aspirant TV ... it's couched in reality ... that grown-ups watching it with their kids can identify with" (quoted in Combemale 2019). When the children become separated from their parents and their fate is unknown ("Three Little Birds" 2021), Maureen feels she has nothing, and even John is not sufficient to make up for her no longer being able to function as a mother. This emphasises the importance the series places on family as a point of continuity from the original show.

The focus on "family drama" was highlighted in Netflix's promotions (2016c) and within the show itself, as it harnesses associations with the original 1960s program in ways that emphasise how this legacy has been reworked for the 21st century, both today and in 2058 when the reboot is set. As Edelman (2004: 4) suggests, children embody futurity in largely conservative ways. *Lost in Space* maintains the centrality of reproductive futurism while presenting it as progressive within a matriarchal structure. Thus, producer Estrin notes the Robinson family, and the addition of other colonist families, are "very diverse" to reflect changing values around race and gender since the original show (quoted in Burton 2018). The rebooted vision of the Robinsons is a blended family that includes the biracial Judy, Maureen's daughter from an earlier relationship. Women of colour occupy several key leadership roles, including the captain of the *Resolute* itself, Captain Kamal (*House of Cards* actor Sakina Jaffrey), while at the same time, this progressive revisionism is tempered by the fact that apart from Judy, people of colour remain in secondary roles. The writer's room for the show was equally comprised of men and women (Combemale 2019). As Molly Parker notes, she was attracted to the role of Maureen because she is the head of the family, and while John is concerned for the emotional well-being of the family; "Maureen is looking at the problems she can fix" (quoted in Combemale 2019). This contrasts with many shows where "what an actress does a lot of the time is play the feeling center of the story, while the man is the active center of the story" (quoted in Combemale 2019). The original show is steadfastly White and patriarchal (Axelrod 2018: 317), and when John and Don need to leave their base, they leave young Will in charge rather than Maureen. While only Maureen, Judy, and Penny are shown doing domestic duties in the original show, such as cooking and laundry (de Los Santos 2009: 32), the first season women are not without spine. When John looks set to drift out into space, it is Maureen who suits up to save him ("The Derelict" Alexander Singer 1965). Similarly, when John is stuck down a crevasse, it's Judy who grabs a rope to save him ("Island in the Sky" Anton Leader 1965). This theme is replicated in the reboot in "Run" when John is injured in a well and Judy rushes to save him with medical equipment. A fleeting moment from the original is expanded in the reboot as the basis of an entire episode to explore the stepfather/daughter bond between John and Judy. Beyond the Robinsons, family bonds are extended in a kinship network where it is up to every member to save one another, and in this network matriarchal figures are key.

Maureen's status as an exceptional mother, scientist, and leader is contextualised as a shared status amongst the women of the *Resolute* who all enact a womanhood characterised by self-determination and "economic capacity" (McRobbie 2007: 722). This is exemplified in "Unknown" (Jabbar Raisani 2019) when Maureen stages a mutiny and takes control of the *Resolute* in an attempt to save the friends and family about to be abandoned on the planet below. Maureen's plan is born from a maternal instinct to protect family, and a prioritisation of kinship structures. The failure of the mutinous plan similarly results from this motivation. It is revealed that Maureen previously entered into an illicit deal with Intelligence Officer Alastair Hastings (Douglas Hodge) after Will failed the tests to join the colonists. Hastings doctors Will's test scores to allow him to join his family, in exchange for critical mission passcodes from Maureen. Maureen's coup is foiled by Hastings, who uses the passcodes to override Maureen's control of the ship. While Hastings has the same ultimate goal – to get his people to Alpha Centauri – his pragmatism is taken to an extreme, such that he is willing to sacrifice anyone to reach the new colony. The Robinsons, headed by Maureen, represent the alternative and ultimately favoured world view that values the kinship ties of all colonists.

Within this matriarchal culture of scientific leaders in *Lost in Space*, the role of the father is reconfigured. John Robinson functions as a key site of disruption to "the naïve nostalgia for the gendered 'story' that is America" (Jeffords 1989: 78). Within this myth, ideal masculinity is defined by the physically punishing and aggressive pursuits of "laborer, marksman, boxer, soldier", in which child rearing is "a world for the most part kept from men" (Webb quoted in Jeffords 1989: 106). Indeed, Toby Stephens notes his interest in the role was specifically because John was not simply a one-dimensional tough guy (Combemale 2019). The first season introduces John Robinson in the process of reintegration with his family after leaving them to take up a high-risk military position. John is an ex-navy SEAL who utilises his technical and survival skills to prove his worth on his wife's mission and to enable a nurturing connection with his family, rather than attempting to take on a role in military leadership. In "Unknown" (Jabbar Raisani 2019), John tells Dr. Smith that his parents sent him away to military school because they were unable to keep him out of trouble. The military family succeeded where his biological family failed. Nonetheless, on joining Maureen's mission, John rejects the paternal military family to take up his role as father to his own children. Similarly, Ben Adler eventually rejects his military role in favour of being a paternal role model for twin boys he will never see again.

Thus, in *Lost in Space*, redemption comes from making sacrifices that prioritise family, kinship, and community, a moral thematic emphasis that extends from the nuclear family and outwards even across species. This extension of family inclusion is ultimately true even of Dr. Smith. Parker Posey situates Dr. Smith's story as someone from a broken family who joins the Robinsons and "wants to be a part of the family, yet is not part of the family" (quoted in Longo 2019).[4] Indeed, Dr. Smith ironically introduces herself as "family" in "Echoes", knowing it to be far from the truth. In

"Contact", Dr. Smith tells Penny Robinson (Mina Sundwall), "not everyone can have parents like John and Maureen Robinson". Her character arc nonetheless suggests that like the robots in the series, even humans can change the programming of their makers. By the end of the series in "Trust", the Robinson family table includes the Robot, Don, and Debbie the chicken, extending beyond blood ties to a broader sense of kinship. Maureen invites Dr. Smith to get in touch with her when she gets out of prison, effectively bringing her into the fold as well, suggesting a future Robinson dinner when Dr. Smith might be included. The matriarch has spoken. The *Lost in Space* reboot thus retains the focus on the wholesome family and community bonds from the original show, even as it reconfigures what family might mean, presenting an aspirational onscreen family to address an imagined offscreen family.

However, Netflix had to manage an instance of where their onscreen construction of motherhood clashed with their expectations around the offscreen audience. While the official paratextual materials stayed on brand, social media erupted in April 2018 with comments on the Robot as a hot sex symbol, shifting the discourse into more adult terrain (News.com.au 2018). Netflix was late to acknowledge this trend because it did not fit with the family-friendly image they had constructed for the show, particularly as it was picked up by James Corden for *The Late Late Show* (2015–2022) where he declared, "I would let him get lost in my space any day" (2018). Netflix eventually responded with a humorous tweet titled "Y'all need Jesus", specifically around the unexpected response from "mom" viewers (Netflix 2018a). This included framing a shot of Maureen and the Robot together in a rosy halo, such that the Robot as a potential replacement father figure for Will becomes reimagined as a replacement partner for Maureen as well. *Lost in Space* as "Family Watch Together" telefantasy may overtly address and solicit an intergenerational audience in both its paratexts and texts, yet ultimately cannot contain textual meaning, as demonstrated by its "mom" fans, even as characterising them as "moms" attempts to contain even this unexpected expression of fandom within the discourse of family. This is an unforeseen challenge of targeting the intergenerational audience, as seeking to address personalised viewing pleasures while still trying to maintain a family-friendly image and accessibility carries with it possibilities of tensions between these two aims.

Netflix's triadic pitch of *Lost in Space* to an adult/child/family audience also faced limitations through variations in international ratings systems. At the TV-PG rating assigned to the program in the United States, the recommendation is that "parents might want to watch it with their younger children" (TV Guidelines 2021). However, here in Australia where the authors reside, the program is rated M, deemed "not recommended for children under the age of 15", in contrast to the Australian PG, "not recommended for viewing by people under the age of 15 without guidance from parents, teachers or guardians" (Commonwealth of Australia 2022).

Although the M rating is advisory only (with the recommendation that "parents, teachers and guardians may need to find out more about the specific content"), it meant that if Australian parents had set their children's profiles with restrictions on anything above PG, then *Lost in Space* would not appear in children's own feeds. Netflix's "Family Watch Together TV" tag addresses these adult gatekeepers through the interface in encouraging them to share *Lost in Space* with the whole family, even when the classification suggests otherwise. Thus, again this content label and its flagship genre cycle become a means by which Netflix is able to showcase and emphasise its internet-enabled "over-the-top" operations, which enable disregard for the regional classification and regulatory structures that govern linear television.

Reviving Dormant Fan Objects

The adult address of *Lost in Space* itself spans more than one generation. Whereas Lizardi suggests contemporary media companies tend to target Gen X and older Millennials by harking back to the late 1970s and particularly the 1980s (2017: 2–5), by contrast *Lost in Space* addresses Baby Boomer subscribers who watched the original broadcasts and Gen X subscribers who watched the reruns, while simultaneously suggesting they "Watch Together" with their families. Parker Posey, who plays the new Dr. Smith, represents this latter demographic, asserting she "was such a fan of the show", having grown up watching the syndicated reruns on morning TV (Brockington 2018). Netflix released the first trailer for the rebooted show on 6 March 2018, the 50th anniversary of the final episode of the original show (Seibold 2018). As Lizardi posits, it is "economically advantageous to appeal directly to a dual audience" across generations with remakes that target "two age demographics" (2017: 20). Remakes aim "to be readily intelligible to an audience that has never even heard of their originals, but ideally they provide additional enjoyment to audiences who recognize their borrowings from their sources" (Leitch 2002: 41). For an older property such as *Lost in Space*, this recognition may in fact stretch back to the third, original broadcast generation. *Variety*'s Oriana Schwindt (2016) notes that Netflix has been pushing back further in time in its nostalgic content to appeal to different demographics across different genres, harking back to the 2000s (*Gilmore Girls* 2000–2007, *Gilmore Girls: A Year in the Life* (2016), the 1990s (*The Baby-Sitters Club* 1995, 2020–2021), the 1980s (*Full House* 1987–1995, *Fuller House* 2016–2020, and *Stranger Things* 2016–), the 1970s (*One Day at a Time* 1975–1984, 2017–2020, *The Get Down* 2016), and 1960s (*Lost in Space*, 1966–1968, 2018–2021). This list contains sequels that continue the same story in revivals; reboots that remake the same story afresh; and new stories set back in time. Lizardi (2017: 113) calls this "transgenerational magnet programming", to attract a wide age range of subscribers and offset risk by offering a range of shows that appeal to different age groups with both contemporary and nostalgic content. The constant recirculation of old texts may foster familiarity among several generations (Butler 2016), but recognition will be greatest for *Lost in Space*'s original and rerun generation, who Netflix leaned into as key to facilitating intergenerational sharing under the auspices of the "Family Watch Together TV" recommendation. When *Lost in Space* was commissioned, this older demographic was identified as key to expanding the subscription base. Schwindt (2016) reports,

> Streaming service penetration decreases slightly, to 68%, for those aged 35–44, but drops precipitously to 57% for those ages 45–54. And there's a very real question about the value the majority of Gen X – and late Boomers that are also a still-untapped customer reservoir – might ascribe to the service. Namely: Is something like a "One Day at a Time" remake, or a "Lost in Space" reboot, enough to make them try it out?

The strong Nielsen ratings among 50–64 year olds (29%) indicates that *Lost in Space* did find this key audience (Graham 2018). However, as Mark Graham (2018) notes, the program also performed well with younger viewers, suggesting "a lot of parents who grew up when the original *Lost In Space* was on the air (or in syndication) passed along their love for the program to their children". On the review site *Common Sense Media*, one parent writes, "My boys are 9 & 11 and we watched it together with my parents. All three generations give it Thumbs Up!" (MommaFino 2020). This rhetoric is repeated in the official promotions, with actor Maxwell Jenkins who plays Will Robinson saying, "I'm going to watch it with my grandparents, my sister and my mom and my dad", in an article encouraging intergenerational viewing of *Lost in Space* over Christmas (Keveney 2019). While Lizardi is ultimately critical of nostalgic reboot strategies as a cynical marketing strategy that appeals to the "arrested tastes" of older generations, while disenfranchising the younger generation from cultivating their own original taste cultures (2017: 1), by contrast Djoymi Baker argues corporate expediency around targeting fans does not in itself exclude meaningful fan engagement (2018: 147; Hills 2002: 3–19). As such, Netflix's strategy to harness a "Family Watch Together" audience for a reboot of a 1960s show is *both* an economically canny move to capture a key sector of existing (and potential) adult subscribers *and* an opportunity for families to experience intergenerational exchange.

Although reviving a "dormant fan object" (Williams 2015: 29) through a reboot takes advantage of existing intellectual property, its ability to harness an associated fan base is uncertain, given that some maintain their fandom once a television program has ended, while for others it might become "peripheral" (Williams 2015: 29–30, 41). Fans may nonetheless choose to pass down their love of a show to the next generation. For example, Matt Hills reflects upon becoming a fan of *Doctor Who* (BBC 1963–1989, 2005–)

through his father's enthusiasm for the program, calling it a type of "associative contagion" (2002: 58). This associative contagion can result in exchanges of fandom between family members both within and across genders (Yodovich 2022: 58). By rebooting a series like *Lost in Space*, Netflix actively courts such "associative contagion", inviting affective connections between nostalgic older viewers (both Baby Boomers and Gen-X) and younger viewers. Rebooting *Lost in Space* means starting the story afresh with a 21st Century vision of the future in direct contrast with an abandoned "retro-future" (Bukatman 1991: 59–60). Nonetheless, reboots exist in relation to earlier versions that continue both as artefacts and as cultural and personal memories of viewers (Ndalianis 2009: 282). Whereas *Stranger Things* as a homage presents an alternate 1980s based on filmic references (Chapter 2), and *ASoUE* as a direct adaptation invites comparison with its source books and provides an anachronistic bricolage of references including old cinema serials (Chapter 3), *Lost in Space* is the only reboot in the dark family telefantasy cycle, addressing multiple generations of fans with an attachment to a dormant object that is started afresh along new lines.

Some short-lived (and in some cases controversial) attempts at reviving and rebooting *Lost in Space* prior to the Netflix program means that *Lost in Space* was not solely attached to the original Baby Boomer broadcast audience, but rather was periodically brought back into the public consciousness, if not always in ways that were critically or commercially successful. *Lost in Space* was momentarily continued as a 1973 Hanna-Barbera animated TV movie sequel featuring Jonathan Harris (Dr. Zachary Smith) as the only original cast member, which was intended as a pilot for a new series that never eventuated. In 1991, Bill Mumy, who had played Will Robinson on the original show, wrote a sequel comic *Lost in Space* by Innovation Comics, which was criticised for showing adult Judy and Penny in revealing clothing (or no clothing at all) (Macek III 2013b). A 1998 feature film reboot directed by Stephen Hopkins removed *Titanic* (James Cameron 1997) from the top spot at the box office (*New York Times* 1998: 3), yet was slammed by the critics, with Roger Ebert proclaiming, "what can be said except that William Hurt, Gary Oldman and Mimi Rogers deserve medals for remaining standing?" (1998). Irwin Allen's widow was unhappy with what she perceived as the dark treatment of the story, which is when the Netflix reboot's producers Kevin Burns and Jon Jashni secured the rights (Britt 2019). In the early 2000s, Burns and Jashni pitched a concept to NBC for a show in which a new crew would meet up with the original characters, conveniently in cryogenic suspension, but the concept was not picked up (Britt 2019). In 2004, they made a pilot for *The Robinsons: Lost in Space,* directed by John Woo, for WB network, which omitted Dr. Smith among other departures, but again it was not greenlit (Jeffery 2018; Terrace 2013: 251). Burns acknowledges that this patchy post-1960s history made the public "perception of *Lost in Space*" somewhat "schizophrenic" by the time it came for their third attempt, this time with

Netflix (Britt 2019). Netflix's assertion that the rebooted new show would appeal to existing fans "who fondly remember the *original*" is an attempt to revive the dormant fan object while simultaneously negating its messier subsequent history (Netflix 2016c, emphasis added).

The maintenance of the original program's core family values, albeit updated, combined with the reboot's adherence to contemporary Quality TV production values – that both meet viewer expectations and contrast with the retrospective perception of the original – can be seen as strategies that negotiate the simultaneous difficulty and appeal of legacy. Referencing the old *Lost in Space* program alongside science-fiction icons with higher recognition factor is another method by which the reboot both leans into and away from its original, in order to address and attract the fan, the new viewer, and the family (which are not, of course, mutually exclusive categories). The reboot must negotiate between fan nostalgia for a camp favourite on the one hand and the prestige branding strategies of Netflix's contemporary dark family telefantasy cycle on the other, while making it just dark enough for adults but not too dark for "Family Watch Together TV", a juggling act the entire cycle struggles with, albeit in different ways.

The Intergenerational Science Fiction Intertext

Lost in Space revives its dormant fan object by assembling a bricolage of science fiction intertextual references from the past, but typically these references have higher profiles and thus more cross-generational recognition than the original show itself. In this way, it can reward science fiction viewers and fans, even if they are not very familiar with the 1960s *Lost in Space*. Writer Burk Sharpless notes they pitched the show to Netflix as being "James Cameroney" and "Ambliny" (quoted in Weintraub 2021), the latter being a reference to Steven Spielberg's Amblin Entertainment production company, which, as noted in Chapter 2, is particularly associated with a shift in child-appropriate content in the mid-1980s and that *Stranger Things* draws upon extensively. In turn, *Lost in Space* harks back to science fiction and horror-inflected fantasy of the 1970s, 1980s, and 1990s to appeal to adult and parent subscribers who are encouraged to share this knowledge with their children through the "Family Watch Together TV" recommendation. For example, in the second season episode "Run" (Jon East 2019), Penny Robinson suspects Dr. Smith of hatching yet another nefarious plan, and takes her friend Vijay (Ajay Friese) into the trash compactor of the *Resolute* colony ship to find clues in Dr. Smith's garbage. In an homage to *Star Wars* (George Lucas 1977), the trash compacter gets turned on with the teenagers inside it. Cori Burcham (2020) suggests the original scene in *Star Wars* is ultimately lighter in tone, because once Luke Skywalker (Mark Hamill), Han Solo (Harrison Ford), Princess Leia (Carrie Fisher), and Chewbacca (Peter Mayhew) are saved from imminent death in the compactor, C3P0 (Anthony Daniels) mistakes their cries of joy for the cries of death, thereby ending the sequence with a comedic misunderstanding. By contrast, when Penny gets stuck in the rubbish, Vijay leaves. Although he turns off the machine and saves her life, this information is initially withheld, and it is clear that Penny thinks Vijay is saving himself and deserting her. Burcham (2020) suggests, "Penny's panic and distrust of Vijay" in the *Lost in Space* trash compactor scene is both "a clever maneuver to attract fans of the sci-fi genre" while also demonstrating "how the reboot is exchanging its comedic roots to explore more dire themes of morality in the face of danger". This seemingly contradicts Showrunner Zack Estrin's assertion that they didn't want the remake "to be dark and edgy" (quoted in Burton 2018), but this seriousness is partly undercut by the fact that Penny and Vijay are clearly foolish for getting into the trash compactor in the first place, an apparent indicator that by 2046 young people are no longer watching the original *Star Wars* film. Similarly, in "Echoes" (Leslie Hope 2019) the famous kitchen hunting scene from *Jurassic Park* (Steven Spielberg 1993), in which siblings Lex (Ariana Richards), and Tim Murphy (Joseph Mazzello) try to hide from two velociraptors, is referenced when another brother and sister team, this time Penny and Will Robinson (Maxwell Jenkins), hide in the dining hall of the Resolute space vessel as they are hunted by a robot adversary. Knowing these references is not necessary for comprehending the narrative, but rather provides "an optional bonus pleasure" (Leitch 2002: 42), one potentially accessible to multiple generations who can note tonal variations. *Lost in Space* thereby mediates its dark moments through the framework of both family drama *and* intertextual references, both of which solicit intergenerational engagement. The program's "teachable moments" are not merely around family values but also the intergenerational cultural heritage fostered by nostalgic "Family Watch Together TV" that, in this instance, ties the Netflix brand to the longevity of the *Star Wars* franchise. As has been seen with *Stranger Things* and *ASoUE*, this strategy of nostalgic brand alignment is key to the dark family telefantasy cycle as a whole.

Lost in Space very carefully curates its intertextual references not only to harness audience recognition of high-profile science fiction, horror, and fantasy, but also more specifically to use these references to frame its family drama around the key interspecies relationship between Will and the Robot, in ways that push the dark territory of the genre cycle and reconfigure what is meant by family. Early in the first season, as Will starts to bond with his "potentially deadly" (Wainio 2019) Robot, the program evokes several prior screen robot/child pairs, such as the relationship between a young John Connor (Edward Furlong) with his cyborg protector (Arnold Schwarzenegger) in *Terminator 2: Judgment Day* (James Cameron 1991). As actor Maxwell Jenkins (Will Robinson) points out in promotional interviews, it also suggests the friendship between Hogarth (Eli Marienthal) and The Iron Giant (Vin Diesel in *The Iron Giant* Brad Bird 1999), Elliott (Henry Thomas) and his alien visitor in *E.T. The Extra-Terrestrial* (Steven Spielberg

1982), and, of course, between Will and the Robot in the original series of *Lost in Space* (Keveney 2019), albeit along more dramatically fraught lines that align with the dark family telefantasy cycle.

In the Netflix episode "Diamonds in the Sky", Will teaches the Robot to play catch with a baseball. Their game is disrupted when Will and the Robot share a sudden psychic link, allowing Will to see the Robot's memories of killing humans during an earlier robot attack on the *Resolute*. This scene of "mass slaughter" by a previously trusted character was cited by one parent on review site *Common Sense Media* as a key reason they considered the program to have "too much violence" (cZalyun 2021). Although Will is understandably shaken by this experience, the Robot appears not to recall its earlier deeds. By the season one finale, "Danger, Will Robinson" (David Nutter 2018), Will has been manipulated by Dr. Smith to be so concerned that the Robot might pose a serious danger to his family and the other colonists that he orders the Robot to walk off a cliff. Parents on *Common Sense Media* identified this scene as traumatic for both parents and children, being akin to a "child asking his best human friend to kill himself" (AndamanOz 2018; JAinVA 2021). The shared psychic connection between Will and the Robot elevates their friendship *beyond* that of just friends, echoing the connection between Elliott and E.T. as a shared realm where each exists as an extension of the other. As Marshall Sahlins notes, the "mutuality of being" derived from the "enigmatic effects of kinship bonds" means that "what one person does or suffers also happens to others" (2011: 1). When E.T. drinks beer, Elliott slips drunkenly from his desk at school and when E.T. is dying, Elliott too falls gravely ill. In *Lost in Space*, the revived Robot makes cave drawings of his experiences with Will, but also includes images from Will's memories when he was apart from the Robot, indicating they retain a two-way psychic bond ("Severed" Tim Southam 2019). The fact that the Robot can also care deeply for the horse Gypsy and his fellow robot Scarecrow indicates that this empathic bond is not simply a fluke. In the program's narrative arc, psychic and empathic connections between robots and humans will be essential to ending hostilities between the species ("Trust"), foreshadowed by the intertextual references to *T2* and *E.T.*

As discussed in Chapter 2, in *Stranger Things*, Will's shared memories with a monster threaten his sense of self and the safety of his community, whereas shared memories with family and friends help forge life-saving connections. By contrast, for *Lost in Space*'s Will, psychic connection and shared memories with the interspecies 'other' is necessary for the survival of the human species and expands his family unit to include the Robot. *Lost in Space* draws upon its nostalgic cinematic references to cultivate and extend the intergenerational dynamic key to the dark family telefantasy cycle, in ways that challenge suitable family viewing (offscreen) and rethink what family might mean (onscreen) via not just intergenerational but *interspecies* dynamics between characters. Throughout *Lost in Space*, references to older science fiction from the 1970s, 1980s, and 1990s address multiple generations, including many young viewers, who may be familiar with *Star Wars*, *E.T.*, and *Jurassic Park* as family science fiction viewing, but also invites adults to either introduce these texts to their children or explain how these references are operating, as the intergenerational dynamic extends to Netflix in concert with adult guardians acting as “cultural curators” for younger viewers.

Lost in Space stresses the importance of onscreen family connections and solicits offscreen sharing of cultural heritage even as it pushes at the boundaries of acceptable family viewing through including some very adult references in its nostalgic reworking of science fiction, fantasy, and horror. For example, “Echoes” also evokes *Aliens* (James Cameron 1998), a film with a US rating of R. This makes it unlikely that younger children watching *Lost in Space* will recognise the predicament the Robinsons discover on the *Resolute* colony ship where the colonists have all fled from “monsters” according to a lone young girl, Samantha (Nevis Unipan), who is left behind. In keeping with the episode name, this “echoes” the abandoned colony on LV-426 in *Aliens*, where Ellen Ripley (Sigourney Weaver) finds a lone survivor, Rebecca “Newt” Jordan (Carrie Henn) (Burcham 2020). Where the film presents Ripley’s “maternal heroism” (Bundtzen 1987: 14) to protect Newt from the alien mother (Creed 1993: 51) in decidedly visceral terms that align with the film’s science fiction/horror/action genre hybrid, by contrast *Lost in Space* builds the tension of immanent confrontation with the enemy robot, only for John and Maureen to work together to contain it and save their children without bloodshed.

The series as a whole nonetheless has a significant onscreen body count, as well as fleetingly bloody moments. In the first episode “Impact” (Neil Marshall 2018), Maureen is injured after crash landing on an alien planet, and Penny has to cut into her leg under the remote guidance of her older sister Judy, which one parent on *Common Sense Media* described as “gross and not appropriate to expose children to” (Malina87 2021). In the episode “Infestation” (Tim Southam 2018), Dr. Smith cuts an identity chip out of her sister’s wrists in a scene that many parents similarly cited as inappropriate for family viewing (Lisa 2018; nika 2018; Sandra 2018). Families that work together are contrasted with families that do not, communicated not only through narrative but also these moments of fleeting bloodiness that push at the boundaries of “Family Watch Together TV”. Netflix provides a warning that the program contains “blood and gore” in the upper left-hand side of the screen at the beginning of episodes, but this assessment seems relative to expectations around a family show. In the context of the program as a whole, therefore, situating *Lost in Space* with a reference to *Aliens* serves to draw comparison with the shared tone of constant threat, yet simultaneously highlights the contrast between the onscreen violence of the referenced film and the program. The suspense and violence suggested by the nostalgic *Aliens* reference are harnessed in *Lost in Space* to the service of family values, both with the onscreen Robinson family and offscreen with the invitation to "Watch Together" and share heritage texts in the process. Much as the dark family telefantasy prototype *Stranger Things* provides fantastical contexts in which different generations need to work together, so too *Lost in Space* provides fantastical scenarios – often in the form of interspecies connections – for families to thrive (or fail).

While the Netflix reboot uses intertextual references to prior science fiction for intergenerational appeal, the original *Lost in Space* was also understood in the 1960s as show that would appeal across age groups (Gould 1965: 93) in part because it also harked back to earlier sci-fi and adventure films and television, although its pragmatic economic considerations contrast markedly with Netflix's big-budget appeal to quality. The original show re-used the music from *The Day the Earth Stood Still* (Robert Wise 1951) in the pilot (Clark 1985: 27) and subsequent episodes such as "The Dream Monster" (Don Richardson 1966). It used Robby the Robot from *Forbidden Planet* (Fred M. Wilcox 1956) in "War of the Robots" (Sobey Martin 1966), and "The Condemned of Space" (Nathan Juran 1967). The Robinsons discovered an underground civilisation in "The Lost Civilization" (Don Richardson 1966) that harks backs to science fiction movie serials such as *Flash Gordon's Trip to Mars* (Ford Beebe et al 1938) or *The Phantom Empire* (Otto Brower and B. Reeves Eason 1935) (Abbott 2006: 122, 151, 158, 169, 180), but this was recycling as a matter of frugal expediency, given that the underground world used the set of Irwin Allen's 1964–1968 show *Voyage to the Bottom of the Sea* (Abbott 2006: 158). The original program delves back into the science fiction past because it is cheap and efficient, prompting continued comparison in the press around the "expense" of Netflix's "family-friendly" reboot (Royal 2018; Yeoman 2018). What in the original series was merely pragmatic is instead highly strategic for the Netflix reboot, aligned with its stated objective to attract an intergenerational audience and reconstitute family viewing practices adapted for the streaming era.

The original program was received in the popular press as suitable for family viewing in part because of the way it borrowed tropes from earlier science fiction, even as it was not overtly marketed along these lines in the manner of the Netflix reboot. *New York Times*' Jack Gould asserted the original show "is a surefire winner for young viewers and probably will amuse senior devotees of science fiction" due to its mix of the old and the new (1965: 93). In its first season, *Lost in Space* overtly borrowed the cliff-hanger serial format used in earlier science fiction television such as *Captain Video* (Abbott 2006: 113). At the end of the first broadcast episode, "The Reluctant Stowaway" (Anton Leader 1965), John Robinson becomes untethered from the ship while trying to make repairs during a spacewalk. His startled face within a space suit is frozen into a still image, while bold onscreen text proclaims: "to be continued next week! Same time, same channel". As with the earlier *Captain Video*, at the beginning of the next episode ("The Derelict" Alex Singer 1965), a male narrator provides a recap on the previous episode's events as a voice at the beginning. The press in turn directly related this cliff-hanger format to even earlier cinema serials, including the action-adventure *The Perils of Pauline* (Louis J. Gasnier and Donald MacKenzie 1914) (Gould 1965: 93), and the science fiction *Flash Gordon* (Frederick Stephani and Ray Taylor 1936) (Whitney 1966: 12). Indeed, even after the series had abandoned the serial format in the second season in favour of self-contained episodes, *TV Guide* compared the high camp antics of Dr. Smith with the *Flash Gordon* villain Ming (Whitney 1966: 12). Creator Irwin Allen asserted that *Lost in Space* reflected the fact that "I have been a science-fiction fan all my life" (Clark 1985: 26). Although the original show was seen as appealing to adult sci-fi fans in part because of its use of old genre formulas and specific intertextual references, it was not as overtly or intensively marketed along those lines as we find in the contemporary era. The status of Netflix's *Lost in Space* as a reboot situates it more specifically in direct dialogue with its predecessor and means that it can address and court the intergenerational fan base overtly, and encourage the passing on of that fandom through its "Family Watch Together TV" recommendation on the interface.

Addressing the *Lost in Space* Fan

While Netflix pitches its references to other science fiction to both young and older viewers, in turn more specific Easter Eggs are provided for *Lost in Space* fans. In effect, then, there are *two* dual addresses: adult and child, fan and non-fan. *Lost in Space* thereby extends the intergenerational address inherent in Netflix's dark family telefantasy and its discourse of combining quality with family to also seek fan legitimation as well, a difficult task when fans may be resistant to rebooting their beloved storyworld (Proctor 2017). Whereas revivals provide a "substantive bridge" of continuity between the past and the present (Hills 2014: 105), by contrast reboots ostensibly "delete established memory to begin again" (Proctor 2017: 230), yet simultaneously harness "the iconographic memory of the cultural product" (Proctor 2012: 5; Ndalianis 2009: 282). As Leitch argues in the case of remakes, it is prudent to reference the original text to provide moments of pleasurable recognition for fans without relying upon them for crucial plot points that might confuse or alienate other viewers (2002: 41). The dual address to both fans and other viewers can be seen as part of the mainstreaming of fandom more broadly (Jenkins and Scott 2013: vxii) since the era of the original series. Bill Mumy, who played Will Robinson in the original show, appears in a cameo as the "real" Dr. Smith, whose identity is stolen by June Harris ("Impact" Neil Marshall 2018 and "Echoes"). In turn, June's name combined that of actors June Lockhart, who played the original Maureen Robinson, and Jonathan Harris, who played the original Dr. Smith. "Echoes" also features a cameo from Angela Cartwright, the previous Penny Robinson, as June's mother Stella. While many viewers may recognise elements of John Williams' theme tune from the original show embedded into Christopher Lennertz' otherwise original score for the reboot, and repeated in the end credits each episode (Melrose 2018), by contrast the brief screen time devoted to Mumy and Cartwright function as fleeting moments of recognition likely only among fans, and even more so with June Lockhart (the original Maureen) featuring as the voice of Alpha Control in the third season episode ("Contingencies on contingencies"), likely only recognisable by noting the credits or keeping up with promotional interviews (Weintraub 2021).

Beyond bringing back original cast members in new roles, more broadly creator Matt Sazama was inspired by the more serious serialised episodes from Season One, a move which aligns both with the quality branding around Netflix's dark family telefantasy and with rewarding the "knowledgeable fan" (Hills 2002: 37) by respectful deference to the original. This situates Netflix within the historical continuum as a curator of *Lost in Space* even as it reboots it. Season One of the original program focused on the family's survival strategies after they crash land on an alien planet. Sazama notes,

> The first five or six episodes of the original *Lost in Space* were in black and white, and they're beloved by the hardcore fans, and they actually have a tone that's a little different from the campy brightly colored ones that are also fun, but are remembered by most … I think people who loved the show from the 1960s will recognize that we draw upon the first five or six episodes in Easter egg ways. (Quoted in Schwerdtfeger 2018)

Indeed, the credits for the Netflix reboot specifically note that it is "based on *Lost in Space* 'No Place to Hide'", the unaired first pilot that did not feature the Robot or Dr Smith.[5] The black and white first season was featured only infrequently in reruns in favour of the later colour seasons, and as such is less widely remembered by a general audience (Abbott 2006: 116). The largely serious tone of the reboot led commentators such as Seibold (2018) to suggest "this is not a series that seems to be paying distant Olympian homage to the original (like *Star Wars*) or milking audiences with nostalgia imagery (almost all reboots)". The reboot nonetheless returns to the earliest episodes that are less prominent in the cultural consciousness except among "hardcore fans", to thereby reward niche fan knowledge and position Netflix as the curator of television history.

Thus, despite rebooting the story anew, the Netflix show returns to the rugged survivalism of the first season original and replays several of its key narrative scenarios. In the pilot for the Netflix reboot, "Impact" (Neil Marshall 2018), the Robinsons crash land on an inhospitable planet, as occurs in the original third episode "Island in the Sky" (Tony Leader 1965). As with "There were giants in the sky" (Leo Penn 1965), the temperature then drops to dangerous levels. In Netflix's "Shipwrecked" (Alex Graves 2019), the Robinsons become marooned on yet another planet, and must turn the *Jupiter II* spaceship into a sailing boat, much as in the original series

"The Hungry Sea" (Sobey Martin 1965), in which the Chariot land vehicle was similarly turned into a boat. The adventure-based survivalism of these early episodes[6] along with specific set pieces, are carried over into the new series, aligning with the dark family telefantasy cycle but also in an active address to the knowledgeable fan across, potentially, several generations.

Although Dr. Smith continues to be self-centred and troublesome throughout the original series, his character arc in the first five episodes informs the rebooted Smith's arc across all three seasons of the reboot. In the 1965 episode "The Hungry Sea", Dr. Smith realises the temperature is about to rebound and become deadly hot, and after some deliberation, decides to save everyone's lives by sending the Robot to the rescue. Smith's decision is a turning point for the character given he starts the series planning to murder the entire crew ("The Reluctant Stowaway") and is shown in subsequent episodes to be lazy and self-serving ("There were giants in the sky"), trying to get out of doing work and thinking of ways to get home to Earth instead of going to the new colony on Alpha Centauri. The reboot Dr. Smith is similarly manipulative and murderous, initially stealing the identity of her sister Jennifer (Selma Blair) and leaving her to an uncertain fate on a dying Earth ("Infestation" Tim Southam 2018). Later, she jettisons Jennifer's lover into space on the *Resolute* space vessel so that he will not expose her to the authorities ("Infestation"). Unlike the original, here an actual murder, while bloodless, occurs onscreen. Despite her ruthless self-preservation, Smith is clearly shaken when she meets the man's daughter ("Echoes"), indicating she is not entirely without remorse or empathy. By the series finale "Trust" (Jabbar Raisani 2021), the Robot convinces Smith not to murder another man who can identify her (Captain Radic, played by Shaun Parkes). She then puts her own life in danger to pilot a ship so that Will can attempt to broker a peace with the other robots, before turning herself in to authorities. The Netflix reboot thereby echoes the original season one story arc of redemption around Dr. Smith, expanding upon it across its three seasons and positioning Netflix as a curator of the show's more serious legacy for avid fans.

The original Robot similarly has a bumpy trajectory in the original series, yet is eventually brought into the family fold, an interspecies family bond replicated in the reboot in which he operates as a surrogate father figure to Will, who initially has difficulties accepting his estranged biological father. The Robot is reprogrammed by Dr. Smith in the first episode of the original series to kill everyone on board and destroy the *Jupiter II* ("The Reluctant Stowaway"). Indeed, because it is continually reprogrammed by Dr. Smith for nefarious ends, neither John nor their pilot Don West (Mark Goddard) trust the Robot, and Don even opens fire on it when it comes to warn them of the impending deadly heat wave in "The Hungry Sea". However, Will is sympathetic to the Robot, arguing with his father about trying to fix him. Although the Robot is from Earth, Will is the first human to encounter an alien in "The Derelict" (Alex Singer 1965), and is the only person to seriously attempt communication (the adult males make things worse by shooting at it instead). The Netflix reboot combines these two strands in "Impact", in which Will discovers an alien Robot (Brian Steele). Will saves the Robot from a fire, after which the Robot in turn saves Will and then his half-sister Judy (Taylor Russell). Here the motivation belongs to the Robot itself, yet the Robot similarly functions as an ongoing figure of unease for the adults in the reboot, particularly as other robots continually threaten their lives. The interspecies bond between child and Robot is thereby extended from the original program even as it constantly suggests potentially deadly consequences, in ways that reward fan knowledge while simultaneously pushing at the edges of prevailing notions of family.

Whereas in the original series, the Robinsons must decide whether their robot is merely a replaceable tool or a friend, in the reboot the bond that the Robot has established with Will puts him in direct conflict with his own family and species. A major narrative arc in the reboot that leads to a war between humans and the robots, as well as between robots, is an expansion on the first season episode from the original series, "War of the Robots" (Sobey Martin 1965). As with the reboot, it is Will who discovers the alien Robotoid (Eldon Hanson), and it is Will who reactivates it (in the original episode, this is despite the warnings of his own Robot). Robotoid is in fact Robby the Robot from *Forbidden Planet*, also designed by Bob Kinoshita (Abbott 2006: 151). The Robinson's Robot perceives Robotoid to be a threat primarily because it can exercise free will, but as Abbott notes (2006: 150), this is ironic given this episode is where we see the Robinson's Robot itself assert free will and start to develop a personality with emotions ("I am not jealous" it protests out loud to itself, "it is a human emotion"). In turn, the family is initially pleased to have the more advanced Robotoid, but they come to feel bad about their own Robot being made effectively redundant. The Robot eventually foils Robotoid's plans to hand the family over to alien captors. By the end of the episode, the family and crew acknowledge that the Robot is more than mere programming, but rather their friend. In the reboot, robots develop free will and exterminate their creators, perceiving them as oppressors. Indeed, they want to "kill all masters" ("Final Transmission" Julian Holmes 2021), including humans. This is not unfounded. The *Resolute* space vessel relies on an enslaved and tortured robot called Scarecrow, who crash landed on Earth (as revealed in "Final Transmission"). Thus, rather than idealising the past media text (Lizardi 2014), the Netflix reboot expands upon its darker strands and questions its underlying ethics.

In the original series, the crew envy the stellar maps and guidance systems of aliens in "The Derelict", yet are nonetheless quick to open fire on them. In the reboot episode "Diamonds in the Sky", John and Maureen similarly find the robot's stellar map, but more broadly the ruthless opportunism and cruelty of forcing Scarecrow to be a pilot on the *Resolute* has its foundation in the violence of the original towards the non-human. In the 1960s show, this approach is questioned only by Will. Indeed, Will's kindness and willingness to forge connections with alien others is frequently dismissed by the adults as the foolishness of youth. These adult concerns are usually shown to be correct, justifying their world view. Nonetheless, to 21st century eyes Will is the unacknowledged moral core of the early episodes. The reboot mirrors this, in that Scarecrow becomes an ally due in large part to the kindness shown by the children. As such, the Netflix version privileges the child's point of view to extend the intergenerational dynamic at the heart of the whole dark family telefantasy cycle to include interspecies bonds. In turn, Deputy Director of Advance Systems on the *Resolute*, Ben Adler (JJ Field), once one of the captors of *Scarecrow*, joins the children in freeing it ("Shell Game"), and even sacrifices his own life to save it ("Ninety-seven"). He thanks Will for reminding him of who he used to be (by implication, a good person, a father, and – once – a child with the same innocent worldview as Will). When Penny shows compassion to a dying enemy robot on the battlefield of their own final war of the robots in "Trust", lifting off the debris that has it pinned down, she expects it to kill her. Instead, her act of kindness transforms the robot, its faceplate changing from aggressive red to the blue screen that their own Robot has. Empathy has enabled freedom from programming. The original *Lost in Space* depicts the family gradually coming to the realisation that their Robot is more than a mechanical tool, acknowledging their bond of friendship that is most strongly articulated by Will. The Netflix reboot builds on this interspecies bond to make it central to the entire three season arc, in which it is not only the survival of the (newly extended) family that is at stake but also the entire species.

In the denouement of the reboot finale, the Robot is shown sitting at a Robinson family dinner, indicating its inclusion in the family, even as the other robots, now also freed from their programming, depart the planet. The series ends with Will and Robot together on the "First Human-Robot Exploratory Group". The reboot thereby expands upon the ethical dimension of the encounter with the alien and robot "other" in the original, ethical dilemmas that are only fleetingly voiced by Will only to be continually overruled by adults. The reboot makes the children more overtly the ethical core of the show, and it is only through their continued acts of kindness towards alien and even overtly enemy "others" that they make the allies that will ensure the survival of humanity itself.

While some of the more overt references to the original *Lost in Space* are humorous, such as the alien chimp-like being Debbie the Bloop (introduced in "Island in the Sky") becoming Don's companion Debbie the chicken, the reboot pulls out more sombre strands from the early episodes to expand upon, such as its survival scenarios, robot ontology, and the aggression of its adult characters outlined above. Its creator notes that only (adult) fans will be able to notice these narrative and thematic connections (Schwerdtfeger 2018). In turn, by bringing these connections to the attention of viewers in promotional interviews, *Lost in Space*'s creator Sazama implicitly invites even new viewers and a new generation to revisit the original, to become new fans of both versions (albeit not the episodes the original is best known for), and in so doing remodel its otherwise patchy cultural legacy under the auspices of Netflix's quality-branded reboot. In keeping with the dark family telefantasy cycle, an intergenerational dynamic is established onscreen and encouraged offscreen, but in this case specifically around the show's status as a reboot.

Conclusion

Netflix first announced its reboot of *Lost in Space* as "equal parts family drama and sci-fi adventure" (Netflix 2016c), remaining remarkably on point in promotional interviews with cast and crew across its three seasons from 2018 to 2021 in addressing both the family audience and the science fiction fan. Paratexts such as thumbnail tags on the interface, interviews with the press and reviews help shape the genre expectations and "menu of inter-texts" audiences are invited to think about (Gray 2010: 141). *Lost in Space* producer Estrin asserts, "Yes, there's adventure. Yes, there are great visual effects. But the whole thing hangs from this family" (quoted in Longo 2019). As Estrin notes, it was important to stress this core idea, given

> for *new* fans of the show, there's a certain baggage associated with the title – 'Oh, that's that campy show from the '60s,' or, 'That's that movie from the '90s that was … what it was.' We are taking that core of an idea – the Robinson family is striving to hold together and survive in this incredible circumstance … we think it's going to have a broad appeal beyond genre fans. (Quoted in Hibberd 2018, emphasis added)

Lost in Space is a telefantasy program with constant peril and a high body count that was nonetheless pitched as family viewing both to adults and families with children, fans, and non-fans (of the original show, of science fiction more broadly), moving across *two* dual forms of address. This chapter has demonstrated how, both within the text and across its paratexts, *Lost in Space* harnesses an intergenerational dynamic between older *fans* and younger *viewers* to revive a *very* dormant fan object, and in the process remodel what family might mean by stressing and expanding the interspecies bonds from the original program. The "Family Watch Together TV" label on the Netflix interface works within the larger network of promotional paratexts to assert the family-friendly status of *Lost in Space*, positioned alongside its credentials as science fiction and Quality TV. This provides Netflix's own cycle of "Family Watch Together" telefantasy with its point of product differentiation from grittier adult science fiction and fantasy of the Quality Telefantasy era.

Notes

1 This resulted in some overlapping iterations, with Gold Key Comics 1962–1982 *Space Family Robinson*, but as the company was already working with Allen on

other properties such as *Voyage to the Bottom of the Sea*, they decided against suing and instead changed the comic book title to *Space Family Robinson: Lost in Space* from issue #15 (January 1966) onwards as cross-promotional move (Wells and Dallas 2014: 137). In cinemas, the castaway space-faring theme emerged in *Robinson Crusoe on Mars* (Byron Haskin 1964). Indeed, the screenwriter for that film, Ib Melchior, claims CBS stole his concept for what would become *Lost in Space* (Weaver 2014: 282).

2 This said, Posey's Golden Globe nomination was for one of her lesser-known roles, in Ed Gernon's 2002 *The Battle of Mary Kay*. Indeed, Negra suggests this role in a made-for-TV movie was a sign of Posey's declining cultural capital at this time (2005: 87), from which she appears to have subsequently recovered.

3 As noted in Chapter 2, this film is also a reference point for *Stranger Things*, suggesting a developing repertoire of familiar family intertexts.

4 Negra even suggests this is part of Posey's profile, with her "body of work consistently plac[ing] her as a member of a dysfunctional family (either literal or symbolic)" (2005: 83).

5 This footage was then incorporated into the first four broadcast episodes instead (Abbott 2006: 116).

6 Allen would build on this survivalist approach for his disaster films in the 1970s when he became known as the "master of disaster" (Santas et al 2014: 488).

5 The Haunted Nostalgia of *The Dark Crystal: Age of Resistance*

Like *Stranger Things*, *A Series of Unfortunate Events (ASoUE)*, and *Lost in Space* before it, the Netflix Original puppet-animated series *The Dark Crystal: Age of Resistance* (2019) revolves around a carefully crafted intergenerational dynamic to cultivate a Netflix-specific approach to family television. This chapter argues that key to this process in *Age of Resistance* is a self-reflexive challenge to traditional notions of "family content" associated with linear television, specifically via the show's activation of a confronting "haunted nostalgia". In this way, *Age of Resistance* exemplifies Netflix's negotiation of dark telefantasy for a family audience. The series, a prequel to Jim Henson and Frank Oz's cult 1982 puppet-animated dark fantasy film *The Dark Crystal*, sparked fervent commentary among popular culture reporters for its dark and complex appeal to both adult nostalgia and childish wonder. Media commentators' descriptions of the show focused on ambiguity surrounding its intended audience: writing for *Vox*, Aja Romano (2019) deems the show "more brutal than its forebear, which is itself frequently criticized for being too grim for kids", and suggested that the puppetry paradoxically served to lend the show "moments of real horror" and "a disturbing sense of the uncanny valley". Similarly, in an article for *Salon*, Melanie McFarland (2019) writes:

> When someone recently asked me whether *Age of Resistance* was good, I could only answer with a series of questions: Who will be watching? Is that person easily frightened by scary-looking characters? How do you feel about oozing snot and dripping pustules? Are you OK with brutal, gory puppet-on-puppet violence? These are all real concerns.

Crystallising the perceived contradictions and ambiguities surrounding its intended target audience, a number of commentators characterised *Age of Resistance* as "*Game of Thrones* with Puppets" (Asarch 2019; Duncan 2019; Fullerton 2019a; Trenholm 2019; Wired 2019). These comparisons to the notoriously dark, violent, and decidedly *adult*-oriented HBO Quality telefantasy series playfully highlight the disjuncture between *Age of Resistance*'s

DOI: 10.4324/9781003223498-5

seemingly child-oriented format and aesthetics – as is incarnated by the show's puppets – and its adult themes and somewhat gruesome, grotesque style.

In tying the show to *Game of Thrones*, such commentary also registers both the *dark* and the *Quality* status of *Age of Resistance*'s family telefantasy. Characteristic of such commentary, Griffiths in *Metro UK* writes, "few would have expected *Game of Thrones* to be out-done by a bunch of puppets, but that's just what happened when Netflix dropped *The Dark Crystal: Age of Resistance*" (2019). Similarly, Shager, writing for *The Daily Beast*, praises this "rich, expansive, imaginative fantasy epic cast in a *Game of Thrones* mold that stands as a triumph for Netflix" while straddling "the line between playful kids' adventure and grim adult drama" (2019). Implicit within the public commentary around *Age of Resistance* is a recognition that the plural audience address exhibited by the show is distinctive from the audience engagement strategies expected or typical of the "family film" or "family television".

In this chapter, we examine how *Age of Resistance* advances Netflix's strategy around dark telefantasy for intergenerational audiences by positioning its challenge to legacy media paradigms of child appropriateness as key to its appeal. Resonating with other dark telefantasy Netflix Original series categorised under the "Family Watch Together TV" tag, *Age of Resistance* harnesses personal and collective nostalgia for a beloved text from the 1980s. Yet notably, cultural nostalgia for *The Dark Crystal* is grounded in the film's notoriety for frightening child audiences. This *haunted nostalgia* is a core theme of the media commentary surrounding the Netflix show, indicating that it is key to the show's allure, and, as we articulate in this chapter, the show's intergenerational dynamic. As discussed in Chapter 2, Balanzategui has elsewhere examined how nostalgia, typically associated with a warm and comforting (albeit melancholy) relationship with the past, can also foment uncanny dread (2016: 241), as, just like the uncanny, nostalgia operates as an agent of both the familiar and the foreign (243). Indeed, Balanzategui argues that certain media aesthetics, like the nostalgia-soaked horror film *Sinister* (Derrikson, 2012) and electronic music movement Hauntology, invoke

> the uncanniness inherent in nostalgia, exposing how our crafting of warm fictions out of the ever-etiolating flakes of our former selves entails the simultaneous intensification of, and attempt to conceal, the splitting and dividing of the self-wrought by the unrelenting progression of time. (2016: 244)

Age of Resistance also hinges on nostalgia's uncanny potentialities, in this case by invoking a combination of adult nostalgia for and troubling memories of a cult film renowned for unsettling a generation of children. That *Age of Resistance* seeks to recreate this experience in the present for a new generation of children intensifies and draws to the surface the "haunting" nature of the nostalgia it cultivates.

In addition, via its painstaking replication of the aesthetics and style of the original film in service of a new narrative that sets up the story of the 1980s film, the show operates like an uncanny double for *The Dark Crystal*, and by extension invites an uncanny doubling of the adult viewer's past experiences with the original text. Such doubling of perceptions operates at the interface of familiarity and unfamiliarity, and thus aligns with the definition of the uncanny so influentially established by Freud (1919). As Nicholas Royle articulates of the intersection between *déjà vu* and the uncanny: "*Déjà vu* is the experience of the double *par excellence*: it is the experience of experience *as* double. There can be no uncanny, perhaps, without some experience of this duplicity" (2003: 183). *Age of Resistance* thus constructs haunted nostalgia in a related but different type of engagement with the aesthetic, ontological, and phenomenological relationships between nostalgia and the uncanny previously examined by Balanzategui and also Dylan Trigg (2006). Among adults, the show invites nostalgia for an unnerving viewing experience from the past – doubling yet simultaneously defamiliarising this past in the process by recreating it with the cutting-edge production and on-demand algorithmic distribution technologies of the present. Yet among child audiences, the show presents an opportunity for "fresh contact" (Mannheim 1997: 171) with unsettling content, "fresh contact" that may eerily double their parents' own past experiences with the original film. Further deepening this interplay of past and present generational media experiences, *Age of Resistance* raises the possibility of *future* nostalgia in adulthood among these current child viewers, as this once troubling viewing experience may be warmly remembered in hindsight. Indeed, it is upon this very constellation of intergenerational exchanges that the show's marketing, appeal, and ambivalently positioned "family-friendliness" and "child appropriateness" are built. The intergenerational dynamic in *Age of Resistance* thus is particularly tangled and layered in ways that illuminate the distinctiveness of the *dark* in Netflix's dark family telefantasy genre cycle.

This chapter combines analysis of the discourse surrounding *Age of Resistance* with consideration of the original film's own challenge to paradigms of child appropriateness in order to illuminate how Netflix deploys haunted nostalgia to spark an intergenerational dynamic. Like *Lost in Space*, *Age of Resistance* seeks to appeal to what Rebecca Williams calls "post-object" fandom, for it motivates new affective attachments to a "dormant fan object" (2015: 29) in the form of the original film, *The Dark Crystal*. This film was also made available on Netflix at the time of the series' release, in an example of Netflix using its back catalogue as a platform for the creation of new material, and in turn creating a process of selective cultural curation. Unlike *Lost in Space*, the haunted nostalgia invited by *Age of Resistance* encourages adult subscribers to introduce a new generation to a frightening and even unpleasant viewing experience, a pleasure in displeasure akin to that offered by *ASoUE* that unsettles the family viewing model while reshaping it for the SVOD era.

Family Films and Family Television

As we highlighted in Chapter 2, Netflix's initiation of paradigmatic shifts to longstanding industry and cultural practices around "family"-oriented television echo the rise of the dark or subversive family film of the 1980s. Like *Stranger Things*, *Age of Resistance* self-reflexively constructs a parallel with these challenging 80s family films in a way that brands Netflix as aligned with them. While fantastic genres have a long history of pushing the boundaries of acceptable family fare, as we highlighted in the chapter on *Stranger Things*, Netflix is unique among contemporary SVODs for the way that it has positioned dark and subversive family telefantasy with intergenerational appeal as key to its brand identity and narrative at a moment of maturity for the SVOD sector and for Netflix itself. *Age of Resistance* is an intriguing metonym for these tectonic shifts, because in similar but more explicit ways than *Stranger Things*, the show troubles both the mass cultural and child suitability of the "family" mode via its direct interaction with the wave of subversive family films of the 1980s. While *Stranger Things* is inconsistently and ambivalently positioned in relation to family tags on Netflix, *Age of Resistance* is positioned more explicitly as a child-appropriate family-oriented show in that it is consistently tagged as "Family Watch Together TV" (usually alongside the "Fantasy TV Shows" tag and the not particularly family-friendly tag of "Political TV Shows"; see Figure 5.1). It was also awarded the

Figure 5.1 Netflix desktop interface for *Age of Resistance*, as of July 2022, indicating Netflix's genre tags for the program. Screenshot by authors.

Figure 5.2 Netflix desktop interface showing *Age of Resistance* alongside other "Family Watch Together TV" content, April 2020. Screenshot by authors.

2020 Emmy for Most Outstanding Children's Show. Nonetheless, key to the show's appeal is its *challenge* to conventional paradigms of child appropriateness (Figure 5.2).

Like many Netflix Originals tagged as "Family Watch Together TV", *Age of Resistance* engages with past media traditions in multilayered ways to invite interaction between adult audiences and young family members. *Stranger Things* achieves this through operating as a nostalgic pastiche of 1980s popular culture. By contrast, rather than exhibiting a bricolage of 80s texts and styles, *Age of Resistance* is a prequel to a specific 1980s film now revered as a cult classic. In our audience research, 15-year-old Jack explained in a semi-structured interview that his interest in the show was sparked by a previous family movie night in which his father introduced him to *The Dark Crystal.* He explains that he later saw the trailer for the prequel show on YouTube, and said "hey Dad, Netflix's doing a reboot of that film you showed us". Subsequently, Jack, his ten-year-old brother, and his father watched it together when it came out. Jack also explained that while he wasn't necessarily scared of the show, "my brother was a bit scared", which he attributed to "how good the effects and puppets are. You know, to get that scared reaction that's like something obviously more like a horror show like *Stranger Things*". Jack said that *Stranger Things* and *Age of Resistance* are "the two shows I would consider scary". It is notable and in alignment with the operations of Netflix's dark family telefantasy cycle that Jack connected these two shows via how frightening they were. Also, in this case, while the parent introduced the original film to his children, it then became a nostalgic access point to the Netflix series via *the child,* with Jack acting as the "media broker" (Katz 2010) for his family. As Van den Bulck et al. explain of this process, "sometimes families become aware of new developments – such as new genres – because a child discovered it first" (2016: 32). It was parental intergenerational sharing of nostalgia that sparked Jack's interest in the show, but it was Jack who subsequently discovered the series and introduced it to his family, highlighting the reciprocal rather than top-down workings of the intergenerational dynamic.

Notably the original film *The Dark Crystal* was received ambivalently upon its initial release, as it also unsettled expectations around child-oriented content and family viewing in its time. The film has since come to be culturally treasured as metonymic of a cycle of "dark" children's films in the 1980s (Dovey 2010; Maesar 2022) and is thus now recognised as a cult film – even more so after the release of *Age of Resistance*. For instance, a major, multi-day 40th-anniversary celebration for the film was held at the Jim Henson Lot in Los Angeles in November 2022 which featured memorabilia and props from both the series and the film (Miller 2022). *The Dark Crystal* is thus nostalgically remembered on a cultural level as symptomatic of the supposedly more permissible and unconstrained children's culture of the 1980s: a period of imagined liberation and freedom that is celebrated in contemporary screen media like *Stranger Things*.

As a result, *Age of Resistance* plays with legacy media approaches to family audiences in quite direct and self-aware ways. Like *Stranger Things,* the show performatively challenges established modes of producing, distributing, categorising, and classifying children's and family content, and in so doing highlights the "over-the-top" capabilities of Netflix that enable the SVOD to operate without attentive regard to regional classification frameworks and with complete disregard for television scheduling. Indeed, while the show is rated TV-PG in the US, in Australia it is rated M: for mature audiences 15 years and over because such content contains "material that is considered to be potentially harmful or disturbing to those under 15 years" (ABC 2020). Although it is categorised as "Family Watch Together TV" in Australia, this M rating – which Netflix relates to the show's "blood and gore, violence, fantasy themes" – thus sits in tension with the explicitly signalled family orientation. This defiance of legacy media modes of family viewing is enacted through the show's commemoration and direct continuation of a period of children's entertainment culturally celebrated as particularly open and daring. Indeed, the cultural commentary surrounding the show often playfully suggests that the film is notorious for leaving emotional scars on the adults who grew up during this period, a point to which we will return later in this chapter. It is in this way that *Age of Resistance* deploys a "haunted" form of nostalgia – a nostalgia not associated with warm, cosy, and comfortable memories but with childhood discomfort and fear that from the hindsight of adulthood is remembered as a valuable and perhaps even a formative and treasured experience.

This haunted nostalgia celebrates family content and viewing while rejecting "safe" family screen traditions like the family sitcom or Jim Henson's family-friendly television and films centred around *The Muppets*, including the show that remains paradigmatic of educational children's television, *Sesame Street* (1969-) and the more family-focused *The Muppet Show* (1976–1981). Notably, one of Netflix's key competitors, Disney+, has foregrounded new and exclusive Muppets content such as the mockumentary series *Muppets Now* (2020) as a key ingredient of their child and family-focused strategy. Instead, *Age of Resistance* is positioned as a renaissance of a specific, lost period of spooky and challenging children's films which operate as the dark underside to *Sesame Street*/*The Muppet Show*.

The haunted nostalgia conjured by *Age of Resistance* thus operates on both personal and cultural levels. In reviving the cultural relevance of *The Dark Crystal*, Netflix locates itself as in a unique position to "bring back" the "lost" era of subversive children's films in televisual form in the 21st century, while in tandem playing upon personal adult memories of an unsettling film viewing experience and inviting parents to facilitate a similar experience for their own children. As in previously explored examples – in particular *Stranger Things* and *ASoUE* – this haunted nostalgia thus invites an inter-generational dynamic that constructs "Netflixified" family viewing as "edgy" by comparison to more sanitised traditional models.

Legacy Media's "Safe" Family Viewing Traditions

To illuminate how *Age of Resistance* invites such an "edgy" family viewing dynamic, it is important at this juncture to consider how the show and the film that it is based on performatively contrast with "safe" family viewing traditions that have shaped the very concept of family content in the cultural consciousness. This association of family content with safe and sanitised content was refracted in our audience research: for instance, in a semi-structured interview, Brian, the father of two boys, one 12 and one 15, explained that "in terms of our kids' viewing habits anything with the word 'family' in it as a category is aimed at primary school kids or younger. And our kids are beyond that". Brian went on to describe family content on the Australian public broadcaster, the ABC (Australia's primary destination for children's television) as "very conservative", and his 12-year-old child Grady explained that he associates family content with "family movies" for "little kids aged 5–7". This definition of "family" viewing and content was refracted in our survey, where adults overwhelmingly associated "Family Watch Together TV" primarily with programs designed for co-viewing among parents and children, rather than other kinds of families, despite the fact that only half of our respondents had children themselves. It is just such associations that Netflix's dark family telefantasy cycle seeks to combat and subvert with its appeals to prestige via dark themes and content, and notably Brian and Grady's family had enjoyed watching *Stranger Things* together, and they did not align it with the type of "conservative" content they associated with family viewing. In other words, there are cultural associations around what family viewing means that do not necessarily align with how and what families actually watch together.

The entrenched assumption that "family content" equates to safe, sanitised, and conservative content relates to foundational legacy media approaches to family content, which were typically underpinned by the quest to appeal and cater to a broad but unified audience via suitability for all age demographics. As noted in Chapter 1, in his research on the development of Hollywood films targeting the nebulously defined family audience, Noel Brown articulates how the "so-called 'family audience' symbolised respectability, profitability and mass cultural acceptance" (2013: 1). Brown highlights that Hollywood's commitment to "family entertainment" from the 1930s onwards – in part due to commercial imperatives, and in part due to the influence of the Hays Code on production practices – was represented largely through screen texts designed to be suitable for, appealing, and palatable to all audience segments within the nuclear family. Based on extensive archival research, Brown's article traces how both political and commercial pressures led to the solidification of the family-oriented film, including a "strategic programme of prestigious literary adaptations explicitly targeting 'family' audiences" (2013: 2). Indeed, Hays himself once remarked:

> Not only the cornerstone but the foundation of the success of the American motion picture enterprise may be summed up in the phrase, "one program for one audience". Here, pictures are not rated for showing to children or adults, theatres are not graded and films are not made for different classifications of audiences. (quoted in Brown 2013: 7)

Brown underscores the importance of family films such as *Little Women* (Cukor, 1933) in re-establishing "Hollywood's increasingly endangered identity as a 'family'-oriented cultural institution" (2013: 2).

As a result, ideas about the family audience were clarified and popularised in the Hays Code era (1930–1968) in ways that came to underpin Hollywood production policy and strategies. The construct of the family audience thus became a core facet of Hollywood business models, resulting in a distinctive "'family-oriented' aesthetic" that by the late 1930s constituted the bulk of Hollywood output (Brown 2013: 16). Due in part to changes to the classification system in the US highlighted in Chapter 2, the family film of the 1980s was characterised by a self-reflexive manoeuvre *away* from the family films of the classical Hollywood era. Thriving after the wave of New Hollywood films of the late 1960s and 1970s – adult-oriented films including *Easy Rider* (Hopper, 1970) and *The Graduate* (Nichols, 1967) that challenged classical Hollywood's conservative moral codes – dark and morally complex family-oriented films such as *The Dark Crystal* similarly subverted the aesthetic and themes of classical Hollywood, but in the domain of children's and family content.

While ideas about the family audience and templates for family-oriented entertainment were established in the classical Hollywood era, broadcast television further sedimented this Hollywood-initiated, unified family demographic. As a mode and medium form that enters the domestic space and thus the ritualistic rhythms and ebbs and flows of the family's everyday lives, television has long been positioned as a primary site for family entertainment, even during the 1980s when approaches to the family audience and aesthetic were changing in Hollywood film. In particular, the family sitcom – such as *The Donna Reed Show* (1958–1966), *The Brady Bunch* (1969–1974), *Family Ties* (1982–1988), and *Growing Pains* (1985–1992) – is responsible for positioning broadcast television as synonymous with "wholesome", scheduled family viewing. As Sally Steenland details in a 1985 report into children's representation on family television, there are three distinctive family styles at the centre of the family sitcom: kids in charge, in which child characters run the show with adults peripheral; family as democracy; and the 'traditional' nuclear family where parents are in charge, which she notes was most common in the 1980s (1985; also cited in Cantor 1991: 213). In all three types of family sitcom, the intention is to deliver content suitable for all members in a nuclear family, from young children to parents, in ways that Muriel Cantor argues function as parables or morality plays about appropriate and inappropriate family dynamics. Similarly, in her book on the 1980s family sitcom, Alice Leppert argues that "the largely fantasy scenarios of 1980s sitcoms offered pedagogical models for organizing family life at a time when familial ideals [during the Reagan era] were up for debate" (2019: 1). In the 1980s, television remained a key site of conservative family-oriented entertainment. This is indicated even by Steenland's (1985) claim that the most popular family sitcoms of the 1980s centred on a traditional nuclear family dynamic, with examples including *The Cosby Show* (1984–1992) and *Family Ties*.

The family sitcom has remained one of the most fundamental mainstays of linear television since the 1980s. As Maria San Filippo suggests, "seventy years since its carryover from radio made it one of television's first successful genres, the sitcom remains a programming stalwart and the family sitcom its prototype" (2016: 305). Similarly, Dalton and Linder point out that while journalistic reportage around the turn of the century predicted the impending death of the family sitcom, by the end of the first decade of the 21st century, the sitcom was still thriving (often with some format renovations) on linear television (2016: 319–320). As we have previously outlined, it was to the family sitcom that Netflix initially turned when it sought to reposition the SVOD as catering to a family audience, with the release of family sitcom revival *Fuller House*. While the work of Dalton and Linder, and the many contributors to their *Sitcom Reader: Second Edition*, highlights how televisual approaches to the family demographic on linear television have certainly not been static over time, at the same time the collection points to the remarkable resilience of core features of the family sitcom on American television. As the authors summarise in the conclusion, despite tweaks and twists that have resuscitated tired formats, contemporary family sitcoms often retain many elements familiar to archetypal family sitcoms of the 1950s and 60s (2016: 319–320). This consistency and the genre's cultivation of scheduled family viewing have in turn been a key part of television's status and cultural identity as a domestic medium. Netflix's ventures into family television territory, initially via the family sitcom, thus negotiate such cultural understandings of television's role in domestic family life just as it seeks to rewrite them.

As we previously outlined, Netflix pivoted away from the family sitcom after *Fuller House* failed to sustain positive and engaged cultural buzz, and by contrast the subsequent flagship cycle of dark telefantasy programs establish the Quality and prestige of "Family Watch Together TV" in part by *defying* such traditional televisual attempts to engage a family demographic. The alignment with the "dark" side of family entertainment in the 1980s crafted by *Age of Resistance* underpins this appeal to Quality via a darker and edgier interaction with the family. Released in 1982, *The Dark Crystal* appeared during a juncture in which dark fantasy and horror film releases for child and family audiences were becoming increasingly popular and were shifting the frontiers of children's screen culture. As we flagged in Chapter 2, horror and fantasy film releases in the early 1980s, ostensibly intended for families, eventually provoked a reconsideration of the PG classification in the US. A pivotal film in this shift was the 1982 film *Poltergeist*, directed by Tobe Hooper (best known for *The Texas Chainsaw Massacre* from 1974) and produced by Steven Spielberg. This particularly influential family horror-fantasy film was initially released under an R rating "for terror" because the ratings board believed that the film was too frightening for children, despite the family-oriented themes and lack of explicit violence (Vaughn 2005: 114–115). A successful appeal was launched to re-classify *Poltergeist* as PG, a change that sparked controversy and subsequently played a role in motivating the new PG-13 rating (Afra 2016: 46; Antunes 2013: 19; Vaughn 2005: 115). The controversy around the children's horror film *Gremlins* (Joe Dante, 1984) ultimately sparked the classification change: as Lester charts, this film had "content perceived by parents and critics as too violent for its PG rating" which "led directly to the creation of the PG-13 rating", in turn opening up a liminal space for "new possibilities for late-1980s children's horror films" (Lester 2021: 17). The PG-13 rating was introduced in July 1984, with the advisory: "Parents Are Strongly Cautioned to Give Special Guidance for Attendance of Children Under 13 – Some Material May Be Inappropriate for Young Children".

While *Gremlins* was a direct influence on the introduction of PG-13, as the example of *Poltergeist* indicates, this liminal space was being carved across a number of films in the early 1980s. Another film released in 1982 and ambivalently positioned for younger audiences was the muscle-bound fantasy *Conan the Barbarian* (John Milius). In his review of the film, influential critic Roger Ebert (1982) declared

> Not since Bambi's mother was killed has there been a cannier movie for kids than *Conan the Barbarian.* It's not supposed to be just a kids' movie, of course, and I imagine a lot of other moviegoers will like it.

The mid- to late 1980s subsequently saw a wave of children's horror films that capitalised on the new PG-13 rating, introducing approaches to family audiences via the draw of horror and dark fantasy that could scintillate and unnerve not just younger viewers but perhaps also their adult guardians. Aside from *Gremlins*, such films include *Return to Oz* (Walter Murch, 1985),

The Gate (Tibor Takács, 1987), *The Monster Squad* (Fred Dekker, 1987), and *Beetlejuice* (Tim Burton, 1988). These films mark a sharp contrast with classical Hollywood approaches to family audiences outlined by Brown, in which suitability for all age groups in the nuclear family is constructed via moral conservatism and themes and subject matter deemed appropriate and "safe" for younger viewers. Instead, all of these films push the boundaries of child appropriateness through dark themes and/or onscreen violence, and a resistance to the sanitised child-friendliness associated with family sitcoms or Disney films. In many of these films, this playful and subversive challenge to child appropriateness is underpinned by aesthetics and narratives that venture into the generic territory of horror.

The Dark Crystal

Even among these other films ambiguously or controversially positioned for family audiences in the early 1980s, *The Dark Crystal* – rated PG and released in 1982, the same year as *Poltergeist* and two years prior to the introduction of PG-13 – received a particularly ambivalent critical reception upon its initial release because critics were uncertain as to the film's intended demographic. Indeed, it is productive to examine the reception and production contexts of the original film *The Dark Crystal* because of the way they parallel Netflix's approach to the prequel series in 2019. Ebert gave the film a firm thumbs-down due to confusion over the intended audience on his review program *At The Movies* (1982), and in *The New York Times* Vincent Canby (1982) described the film as a "solemn fairy tale" in which dark themes and puppetry coalesce in strange and off-putting ways:

> In the way that great comic actors are supposed to long to play Hamlet, Jim Henson, who created *The Muppets*, and Frank Oz, his longtime associate, have apparently dreamed of creating mechanical marvels more significant and timeless than the irrepressible Miss Piggy and her pals. The result is *The Dark Crystal,* which aims, I think, to be a sort of Muppet *Paradise Lost*.

Andrea Wright positions *The Dark Crystal* as a particularly challenging contribution to a wave of dark screen fairy tales in the 1980s, films that she suggests "stand out as an identifiable group of fantasy films distinct from their closest generic neighbours, horror and science fiction" (2005: 256). These dark fantasy films also include *Legend* (Ridley Scott, 1984), *The Company of Wolves* (Neil Jordan, 1984), *The NeverEnding Story* (Wolfgang Peterson, 1984), *The Black Cauldron* (Richard Rich and Ted Burman, 1985), *Ladyhawke* (Richar Donner, 1985), *Labyrinth* (Jim Henson, 1986), *The Princess Bride* (Rob Reiner, 1987), and *Willow* (Ron Howard, 1988). As Wright's characterisation suggests, these dark fairy tale films nonetheless incorporate elements of horror and sci-fi that challenge the boundaries of child appropriateness. Such fantasy films flourished adjacent to the new wave of children's horror films of the period.

A number of media commentators have reflected on *The Dark Crystal*'s cult status and poor critical reception upon initial release in their reviews of the Netflix prequel series (McFarland 2019; Romano 2019). As Melanie McFarland's (2019) writing for *Salon* puts it:

> what seemed to confuse Ebert and his contemporaries was that, in their estimation, puppets are kid's stuff. *The Dark Crystal* is not outwardly child-friendly … . But it nevertheless raises the question of who, exactly, is this story's target audience. The answer may seem obvious except for, well … puppetry.

Similarly, Aja Romano (2019) for *Vox* writes:

> Probably because it was brought to us by Jim Henson, creator of the lovable, bright, and happy Muppets and Fraggles, the original film's dystopian tone, with its barren population and scorched world, is a concept that critics just couldn't seem to get over. Even as late as 2009, the film was widely framed as "surprisingly dark (despite the hint right there in the title) for a children's film". Many critics of *The Dark Crystal* were dismissive, often negatively contrasting the film to the Muppets and panning Henson's attempt to create a fully immersive universe – a world that transcended the genre constraints of what "children's" storytelling might do, while enhancing the fantasy capable through the wonder of puppetry. (Romano 2019)

Such popular commentary suggests that in the 37-year interval between the release of the film and the Netflix series, contemporary critics – many of whom were child audiences themselves at the time of the release of these films – see the film differently through the lens of nostalgia. The disturbing object of 1982 has become, by contrast, revered precisely because of the trauma and unsettling confusion it once raised (now viewed in hindsight from the safe vantage of adulthood), and celebrated on a cultural level for how the film challenged "safe" and conservative notions of family viewing.

Notably, *The Dark Crystal* represented Jim Henson's attempt to move in a different creative direction to the explicitly child- and family-oriented puppet-based fare such as *The Muppet Show* (1976–1981) and *Sesame Street* (1969-). Instead, *The Dark Crystal* sought to use puppetry as a technical showcase for elaborate special effects in a dark, high fantasy film. Thus, as Wright points out, Henson and his team intended for the puppetry in the original *The Dark Crystal* film to operate as "an elaborate industry demonstration of film design and the possibilities offered by sophisticated animatronics" (2005: 261). Indeed, the film's technology was displayed at a number of science fiction and technical conventions in Paris, the US, and London. As Wright suggests,

> it appears that the film, at a time when the future dominance of CGI would have been unknown, was used as a 'calling card', an experiment to promote the skills of the Henson Company and to present the effects of new animatronics to a competitive market. (2005: 263)

Thus, the puppetry wasn't necessarily a signal that this was a film intended only or "merely" for children, but was designed to function as a spellbinding technical showcase for both younger and older audiences and also for film and special effects practitioners.

The Dark Crystal's ambiguously defined target audience can also be related to the rise of what Filipa Antunes has called the "pre-teen" demographic in the 1980s, which she sees as bound up with the introduction of the PG-13 film rating in 1984 (2017: 216). Antunes argues that the new PG-13 rating clearly signposts "new ideas about children and the structure of childhood as a concept" (217). *The Dark Crystal* thus exemplifies Antunes' (2017: 39) and Lester's (2021: 15) claim that the dark and frightening family films of this period engaged with new ideas about childhood via pushing the boundaries of acceptable childhood experiences with screen content in the context of feature films. Nearly four decades later, Netflix's *Age of Resistance* transfers this period of shifting cinematic boundaries to streaming television content as part of Netflix's wider transformational (but nostalgic) renegotiation of family viewing under "Family Watch Together TV".

Age of Resistance and Haunted Nostalgia for *The Dark Crystal*

Age of Resistance targets both younger viewers and their adult guardians by harnessing the troubled nostalgia for its source text, *The Dark Crystal.* The show does not feature child characters or deliver parables about appropriate family dynamics to signal its family-friendliness (common devices of the family sitcom and other more unambiguously family-oriented media traditions), instead being set in the fantastical world of Thra and focusing on the complex political and social tensions between the various fantastical (and often grotesque) species that inhabit this world. The series explores the violent and often gruesome clash between the tyrannical and frightening Skeksis – creatures that look like scaly, reptilian vultures – and the rest of the inhabitants of Thra, primarily the lively, innocent Gelflings, whose peaceful existence on Thra is threatened by the Skeksis. The "*Game of Thrones* with Puppets" moniker used by many popular media commentators in reviews points to not just the show's focus on violently warring clans, but the geographic, political, and thematic complexity of the world of Thra which underpins the show's narrative, as the various beings use different methods to uncover the truth and depths of the corruption of the ruling Skeksis' class. The Skeksis hold dominion over the lands of Thra and seek to harness the power of the mystical Dark Crystal, which drains the life-force of other species, to cement their tyrannical rule of Thra's more peaceful species and unnaturally extend their own lives. Three key characters from different Gelfling clans, Rian, Deet, and Brea, embark on a quest to unite the various Gelfling clans to resist and rise against the Skeksis. While the Gelflings are the central focus, the various oppressed species of Thra use different methods to attempt to investigate the Skeksis' misdeeds: in the case of the Gelflings, "dreamfasting" is used to share memories through physical contact, a method which combats the lies and propaganda that drive the Skeksis' political machinations. The focus on interspecies collaboration and conflict recalls *Lost in Space* and, as in that show, has deep resonances with the construction of an intergenerational dynamic: connections are solicited *offscreen* between audiences across different ages and generational groups in ways that parallel the interspecies connections so privileged in the narrative dynamics and aesthetics *onscreen*. These themes related to interspecies collaboration to overcome the oppression of a monstrous ruling class are underpinned in *The Dark Crystal* by allegories regarding the intersections between racism and the inherent exploitation and oppression of neo-liberal capitalist political structures. The critical importance placed on the Gelflings' ability to "dreamfast" also recalls the key themes of *Stranger Things*, in which the sharing of memories bolsters the key characters, solidifies intergenerational connections, and allows the characters to defeat the alternate-dimensional evil of the Upside Down. Thus, as is typical of the dark family telefantasy cycle, in *Age of Resistance* the sharing of memories is elevated to the status of heroism, which serves to encourage and celebrate memory sharing between audience members offscreen.

At key climactic moments, the political turmoil in the show is embodied and personified by complex shifts in character allegiances with rich moral underpinnings in similar ways to *Game of Thrones*. Griffiths' (2019) opinion piece for instance compares two similar characters across the two shows, Seladon and Daenerys Targaryen, both of whom have long, blonde braided hair, full lips, and elfin features, and both of whom are seemingly fragile and delicate but are revealed at dramatic moments to be very powerful women. Griffiths' article presents the argument that Seladon in *Age of Resistance* has a parallel but more convincing downfall character arc than *Game of Thrones*' Daenerys Targaryen. Reinforcing this link, as a number of articles point out, three of the main stars of *Game of Thrones* voice key characters in *Age of Resistance* (Lena Headey, Natalie Dormer, and Nathalie Emmanuel), a casting strategy that draws further attention to the connections between these shows (Harris 2018; Renfro 2019). Indeed, if it were not for the show's puppet-animated aesthetic and placement under the "Family Watch Together TV" tag on Netflix, the show's intended audience would not be at all clear.

As a prequel series, *Age of Resistance* details the events that led to the dystopian scenario of *The Dark Crystal*, facilitating a haunted nostalgia that is key to its targeting of both young viewers and their adult guardians. Even when it comes to the nostalgic narrative thrust of the show, viewers familiar with the original film enter the prequel show with the awareness that things will not go at all well for the innocent and virtuous species the Gelflings, Podlings, and Mystics across the course of the series. In *The Dark Crystal*, the Skeksis have been successful in their quest to exploit and control the crystal's power, and the film thus focuses on the post-apocalyptic ramifications of their actions, with Thra and its species in ruins and disarray (including the almost total genocide of the Gelflings) and the Skeksis on the brink of eternal rule. Thus, viewers familiar with the film will be aware from the opening moments of *Age of Resistance* that the heroic Gelflings will not succeed in their attempts to thwart the Skeksis' evil. The series shares the film's dark fantasy aesthetic, and thus the grim and dramatic narrative and themes combined with the unsettling aesthetic promise to disturb contemporary child audiences in a similar manner to the notorious original film. As *Age of Resistance* voice actor Shazad Latif put it, "I remember, when I was young, being really scared of the movie – and I think there'll be a whole new generation scared by this show" (quoted in Fullerton 2019c). The show's director, Louis Leterrier – who had previously made adult-oriented fantasy films *Now You See Me* (2013), *Clash of the Titans* (2010), and *Incredible Hulk* (2008) – had been interested in developing a reboot or revival project around the film for some time after becoming obsessed with the original film, which he says left him "traumatized" (quoted in Zakarin 2019). Leterrier has also detailed how the film had "a tremendous effect on me" (quoted in Escobar 2020) and was "the first movie to scar me ... but in a good way!" (quoted in Fear 2019). The affectual potency of Leterrier's childhood experience with the film is consistent with the collective memories which have come to define *The Dark Crystal* in the cultural consciousness, and aligns with what Ernest Mathijs and Jamie Sexton (2011: 194) describe as the "phenomenal experience" conjured by the heightened, norm-defying emotional, aesthetic, and collective experience associated with cult film. As they explain, this "phenomenal experience" is characterised by "a commonality of congregation that sees itself at odds with normalised culture", an experience which "is a shared one, even when the actual perception occurs individually" (Mathijs and Sexton 2011: 19–20). In the case of *Age of Resistance*, the director's "phenomenal experience" with the cult film *The Dark Crystal* inspires his attempt to cultivate a similar experience for audiences of the revival.

In explaining the careful balance the creative team struck between unsettling, gruesome content and child appropriateness, Halle Stanford, President of Television for the Jim Henson Company, points to the mid-1980s period of dark family films as a justification and model for this approach: "there are some moments that were like, 'do we push the line?'

But when I was a child, I watched faces melt on *Raiders of the Lost Ark*" (quoted in Gillibrand 2019). Notably, a key factor in the introduction of the PG-13 rating in 1984 was parents' protests around the heart-gouging scene in the subsequent Indiana Jones film, *Indiana Jones and the Temple of Doom* (Spielberg, 1984) (Afra 2016: 45), so Stanford's reference to this 80s period of film culture places *Age of Resistance* in dialogue with these classification-shifting texts. Lisa Henson, CEO of the Henson Company, adds that "even if the show is scary or thrilling, we want to still keep it in the family viewing zone", with Stanford continuing: "I think children are very sophisticated and are used to the fairy-tale darkness. … Let it be a conversation starter to let them talk to their children like 'what do we do when especially little people like the Gelfling aren't being treated well?' Let's get some meaningful conversations going" (quoted in Gillibrand 2019). Here, Stanford justifies the dark and confronting tone of *Age of Resistance* via reference to its intended offscreen intergenerational dynamic.

The haunted nostalgia of *Age of Resistance* thus buttresses its complicated intergenerational dynamic. As the paratextual positioning of the show repeatedly points to, the show cultivates nostalgia for a "traumatizing" film, to return to the director's words. This is not a nostalgia built on warm and comforting memories, but on memories spawned from troubling encounters with media content. More specifically, this type of nostalgia is associated with how this unsettling media encounter extended the previous limits of one's childhood viewing experiences and tastes. Thus, this haunted nostalgia, as in the show's director Leterrier's case, is associated with "fresh contact": an experience of formative novelty which can lead to a "striking transformation of the consciousness of the individual … a change, not merely in the content of experience, but in the individual's mental and spiritual adjustment to it" (Mannheim 1997: 171). In their own research on generational identities and media, Göran Bolin and Eli Skogerbø build upon Mannheim's concept to articulate how "media technologies and content one encounters during the formative years of youth can be expected to be the media that will also form all subsequent media experiences" (2013: 9) – referring here to the significant structural influences of fresh contact and first impressions with new experiences outlined by Mannheim. It this process that undergirds the formation of what Bolin calls "media generations" (2016a). These generational collectives are shaped by their affective links with their phenomenological perceptions of media within specific technological, cultural, and social settings (Bolin and Skogerbø 2013: 9).

The Dark Crystal is metonymic of a period of challenging and dark children's films that provided a generation of children with "fresh contact" with exhilarating but frightening – maybe even traumatic – media experiences. Thus, in this case, nostalgia is entwined on personal and cultural levels with the difficult but potentially identity-forming memories ignited by childhood "fresh contact". Indeed, as above, Leterrier describes his experience of seeing *The Dark Crystal* in a movie theatre as a young child as both traumatising *and* tremendous, and he details that when preparing to shoot the show he sought to recapture this powerful phenomenological encounter with the film by locating a 70-mm print: he describes watching it as "like rediscovering it all over again. It's almost like the theatrical experience. Almost like an out-of-body experience" (quoted in Escobar 2020). A key step in Leterrier's process was thus to attempt to recreate the experience which fomented his haunted nostalgia for the original text – to restage his "fresh contact" with it – and this dynamic is subsequently built into the prequel series. This "haunted" nostalgia is related to but distinct from the deeply uncanny model previously established by Balanzategui (2016; 2020) in which nostalgia can be unsettling in its negotiation of different versions of self that emerge and fade with the passage of time. In the case of *Age of Resistance*, while a troubling experience that may have been emotionally all-encompassing as a child haunts the adult, from the retrospective vantage of adulthood this nostalgically cherished experience is tied to foundational shifts in identity that can be gratefully and fondly reflected on, and perhaps considered anew. In *Age of Resistance*, haunted nostalgia cultivates such pleasure out of displeasure, which as in Leterrier's, Henson's, Stanford's, and Latif's comments, is constructed as a productive tension.

Puppetry and Prestige Nostalgic Aesthetics

The puppet-based materiality of *Age of Resistance*'s elaborate production design is a key aesthetic driver of this haunted nostalgia. The weird, uncanny, and grotesque creatures of Thra foreground a distinctively material aesthetic approach to family entertainment, one that does not foreground CGI and digital animation. This materiality is frequently emphasised in media commentary as a feature which taps into adult nostalgia for a lost period of childhood entertainment (Fullerton 2019a; Marshall 2019; Phillips 2019). For instance, in his review and interview with Brian and Wendy Froud – conceptual and costume designers who worked on the puppets in both the film and prequel series – Fullerton (2019b) states that:

> The finished effect is striking, visually arresting and lush, and is sure to stand the test of time better than most modern CGI blockbusters. In practice, *Age of Resistance* is the ancient art of puppetry on turbo mode, filled with countless creatures, characters, action scenes and wide vistas bound to make you wonder "How did they do that?" … the new *Dark Crystal* is a purely hand-crafted fantasy world following on from the 1980s original, eschewing modern CGI techniques in favour of the charming, impressive world of puppetry.

In fact, as Fullerton goes on to point out, some CGI was used in *Age of Resistance*, primarily to hide the puppeteers and enrich the backgrounds and physical sets. Yet the creators repeatedly underscore the decision to rely on puppetry rather than pixels, playing into the discourse around the show's nostalgically material aesthetic. Emphasising the materiality and texture of the puppetry over CGI, Brian Froud states

> It's a whole world that's realised, and you feel like you're in it. You feel like the characters belong in it, and you're engaged with it because it's tactile. The textures are real, and they're not made up of pixels, which aren't real. (quoted in Fullerton 2019b)

Thus, the tactile materiality of the puppetry is a core element of the show's uncannily nostalgic aesthetic. Notably, in his review of the show – titled "*The Dark Crystal* prequel is a horror about evil billionaires that will scare kids: and that's the point" – Zakarin emphasises "how striking it was to watch … innocent puppet[s] be tormented and mutilated" and the show's "fanciful creatures" serve only "to make the dark parts even scarier" (2019). In a passage that is tellingly tangled in its paradoxes, Zakarain points to the tension inherent in the fact that the very aesthetics that position the show in alignment with children's content traditions are what underscores its uncanny and unsettling effects: "you almost forget that *Dark Crystal* is ostensibly a children's show, except for the fact that these are puppets being thrown off cliffs and stabbed. In fact, the fact that these are puppets makes it somehow more horrifying". That haunted nostalgia is a core theme of the media commentary surrounding *Age of Resistance* indicates that the expensive gambit to use puppet animation was at least partially successful for Netflix, as it suggests that this strangely disconcerting nostalgia for the original is indeed key to the appeal of, and captured in, the show.

While the evil Skeksis are particularly grotesque in their materiality with their oozing pustules, leathery wrinkled skin, beady shiny eyes, and clapping beaks, even the heroic and most human-like species to inhabit Thra, the Gelflings, have a deeply uncanny appearance. Indeed, the uncanny's unsettling "feeling of unreality" created by "the familiar and the unfamiliar" (Windsor 2019: 51, 54–55) is often associated with puppets. As Kenneth Gross notes, puppets are frequently associated with this uncanny effect, due to their "materiality" and the way they appear to give "life to the unliving" in a way that creates a "fundamental strangeness" (2011: 4). In *The Age of Resistance*, there is a very sharp contrast between the Gelflings' large, soulful eyes and inert lower facial composition that renders the region around their mouths and noses eerily stiff and devoid of expression. The puppets also have wide, glassy eyes surrounded by impressive animatronic brows and lids that convey expression; however, the eyes vacillate between being remarkably soulful and lifelike to unnervingly mechanical. Thus, while there are downright unsettling scenes throughout the show, such as multiple scenes in which the evil Skeksis use the crystal to drain the Gelflings of their "vital essence" – the creatures are tied to a chair as the crystal's purple beams drain their life-force, leaving them dead or catatonic – even when the Gelfling characters are having pleasant interactions with other characters, an eerily uncanny undertone inflects their way of being in their strange world of Thra. A range of other strange and eerie creatures inhabit Thra, such as the hobbit-like Podlings – often used for comic relief but in some scenes represented as the victims of Skeksis torture, such as when two Podling slaves appear with their mouths' stitched shut – and the towering, lumbering Mystics, all of which are manifested via puppetry and animatronics that emphasise their materiality and thus their otherworldly, unnatural physiognomy. Unlike hand-drawn or digital animation, these strange creatures must operate according to the laws of gravity and physics. In harking back to *The Dark Crystal* by nostalgically revisiting its uncanny aesthetic, the tactile materiality of the puppets in *Age of Resistance* thus conjure the uncanny on multiple levels, offering fresh contact with this unsettling experience to children and haunted nostalgia that brings back adult memories of such fresh contact for adult viewers.

The nostalgia for physical effects and puppetry in the age of digital animation and CGI thus undergirds *Age of Resistance*'s unsettling haunted nostalgia, refracting Boym's articulation of the phenomenon whereby "nostalgic manifestations are side effects of the teleology of progress" (2001: 10). As Christina Hodge points out in her exploration of the intersections between materiality and nostalgia:

> Definitions of nostalgia from all periods resonate strongly with ideas of materiality … Nostalgia may be especially "felt", especially visceral and material, because: (1) it has persistently been associated with somatic perceptions and senses of bodily displacement; and (2) it is multidimensional and can be activated through places and things. (2009: 493–494)

Nostalgia's "bodily displacement" is particularly strongly felt when an adult is reflecting upon the sensations, emotions, and environments of childhood. Furthermore, the authors of this chapter can attest to the phenomenon whereby the strange puppet objects at the centre of *Age of Resistance* evoke a nostalgia for screen images that *feels like* nostalgia for material things rooted in a particular time and place. The tactile, material quality of *Age of Resistance*'s characters and sets thus engage a specific type of nostalgia for a distinctively material type of children's screen culture: not just the original film *The Dark Crystal*, but other puppet-based fantasy films and television series of the 1970s, 1980s, and 1990s, a period before CGI and digital animation became commonplace in children's screen texts. Examples include other Henson creations *Labyrinth* (1986), *The Muppet Show* (1976–1981), *Sesame Street* (1969–present), *Fraggle Rock* (1983–1987), and *Bear in the Big Blue House* (1997–2006). Nostalgia for the materiality of puppet-based animation thus also connects *Age of Resistance* with nostalgia for past material trends in children's screen culture more broadly, and by extension to what Amy Holdsworth describes as television's function "as part of both a material network of memory and a system of everyday memory-making within and in relation to the home and the family" (2011: 3).

Despite being frequently associated with warmth and comfort – albeit warmth and comfort laced with melancholy – nostalgia has a closer relationship with feelings of discomfort and the uncanny than is often recognised. Nostalgia is often characterised as an inherently conservative phenomenon, as in the influential work of Fredric Jameson (1992) and Zygmunt Bauman (2017), for the way it lovingly reconstructs the past from the vantage of the present. Nonetheless, Boym suggests that nostalgia is always laced with the bittersweet tinge of that which is lost and can never fully be recovered (2018). In reconstructing the past through the lens of the present, nostalgia creates a doubled, *troubled* recreation of pastness that is inherently tinged with both the familiar and unfamiliar. Thus, while nostalgia is always to some extent "haunted", Boym suggests two different types of nostalgia: "restorative nostalgia", which seeks to recover a perceived truth of the past but is in fact strategically selective (2018: 234, 241), and "reflective nostalgia", a "meditation on history and passage of time" that can be "ironic and humorous" (2018: 241, 242). Boym tempers this typology by acknowledging nostalgia may operate in a grey zone somewhere in between. Thomas Leitch suggests that Hollywood family movies frequently (though not exclusively) employ restorative nostalgia to construct an ideal image of childhood by returning to older stories (2018: 9). By contrast, *Age of Resistance* plays upon a nostalgia for a *disquieting* childhood experience that is nonetheless looked upon fondly – perhaps even recognised as a formative, fortitude building moment – via the optic of adult memory.

As a result of this haunted nostalgia, *Age of Resistance* intentionally negotiates a specific type of "post-object" fandom (Williams 2015) explored in Chapter 4 in relation to *Lost in Space*. *Age of Resistance* motivates renewed affective attachment to the film as a "dormant fan object" (Williams 2015: 29): texts or artefacts that have long been out of mainstream circulation and distribution. Though not as dormant as *Lost in Space*, the dormancy of *The Dark Crystal* is raised in media commentary surrounding the release of *Age of Resistance*. As Huw Fullerton (2019a) puts it in a piece for *Radio Times*:

> It is a truth universally acknowledged that the ideal time for a movie sequel isn't a couple of years later, or even on the 10th anniversary, or the 25th. No, it's obvious that the ideal time for a follow-up to an iconic movie is exactly 37 years after it came out, at a point where all your original child audience are middle-aged, your unique selling point has largely vanished from film and TV and you might assume that everyone had moved on.

Such an appeal to post-object fandom via nostalgia has become an oft-used strategy for Netflix. Older texts dormant from mainstream circulation are often picked up for or rejuvenated on the SVOD,[1] their dormancy making licences and rights more straightforward or affordable to acquire. Through nostalgically motivated reboot and revival series, Netflix harnesses dormant films such as *The Dark Crystal* and creates new reasons for audiences to recognise and articulate their post-object fandom for them, and the updated puppet and animatronic technologies in the show – mixed with state of the art but understated CGI which serves to support rather than distract from the show's material aesthetic – injects this nostalgic approach with prestige and appeals to "Quality". This post-object fandom is registered in the media commentary surrounding the new series, with the series used as a platform for Gen Y and X authors to articulate their ambivalent attachments to – and haunted nostalgia for – the original film. For instance, in his review of the series, Hugh Montgomery's (2019) writing for *BBC Culture* suggests that *The Dark Crystal* looms large in the collective memory in part because "for each generation of adults, there's something particularly indelible about those cultural works that first gave us nightmares". *Age of Resistance* thus illuminates how fostering new affective threads between dormant and new releases is key to Netflix's content strategies for the family demographic, promoting a mode of fandom that travels in precise ways between child viewers being introduced to the content for the first time and their nostalgic adult guardians.

Age of Resistance and Reconsidering the "Child" in Family Viewing

Through its self-reflexive cultural alignment with *The Dark Crystal*, *Age of Resistance* invites retrospective reconsideration of the cultural role the original film played in re-situating the boundaries between family, child, and adult-oriented content. The series encourages cultural celebration and reflection on the personal role of the film in the childhood psyches and perhaps trauma-inflected memories of a generation of now adult viewers. While cementing in the popular imaginary the original film's subversively productive contribution to children's screen cultures of the 1980s, the Netflix release has seen the original film take on new meanings as a film treasured in large part *because* it was troubling to a generation of children. In so doing, the Netflix prequel series builds upon and strengthens a cultural narrative around the film: that it was a formative childhood text for many current young to middle-aged adults. Kathleen Loock contends that reviving "dead" – or to return to Williams' terminology, "dormant" – films or TV series through reboot or revival series has become pivotal to Netflix's strategy to capitalise on viewer nostalgia (2018: 366). The centrality of nostalgia to the business models of Netflix and other SVODs has thus become a key part of what Katharina Niemeyer has dubbed the contemporary nostalgia wave that operates at the interface of television and the internet (2014: 2). Yet *Age of Resistance* highlights how, when it comes to

Netflix's flagship dark family telefantasy cycle, this nostalgia operates in a complex, multilayered, and ambivalent rather than straightforwardly "rosy" or conservative way.

Notably, a key part of the haunted nostalgia conjured by *Age of Resistance* is how it *celebrates* emotionally confronting childhood experiences with frightening content, which productively aligns with Netflix's quest to construct an "edgy" brand around its family television. For instance, Beth Elderkin (2019) reviewing *Age of Resistance* for *Kotaku*, writes:

> Characters are maimed, tortured, even killed. That thing you might remember the Skeksis doing to Podlings and Gelfling, yeah, there's even more of it. There is no shortage of death and tragedy here – along with the grim reality of what's to come in the future. That doesn't mean this show isn't for children … Sure it's dark, but it's healthy to introduce complex stories like this to children, just as they were introduced to us when we were growing up.

Elderkin concludes by emphasising how "healthy" such "dark" and "complex" stories are for children, pointing to how such experiences benefited her own generation. Williams emphasises that shifting personal and cultural relationships between a treasured dormant text and the fan community's narratives of selfhood are central to post-object fandom, as transitions through various life stages inflect and transform fans' affective attachments to the text (2015: 29). As Balanzategui has argued elsewhere of post-object fandom around the Australian children's TV show *Round the Twist* (1989–2001),

> such transitions are particularly important when it comes to children's texts, as a text that was a key part of someone's processes of identity development while growing up is reflected on afresh in adulthood, particularly when childhood fans have children themselves. (2022: 81)

Netflix's dark family television provokes this process particularly intentionally and self-reflexively in its encouragement of an offscreen intergenerational dynamic, as adult viewers are compelled to articulate and share their own shifting attachments to troubling texts like *The Dark Crystal* with their children in tandem with encouraging their children's "fresh contact" with the same challenging emotions via shows such as *Age of Resistance*. In tandem with this personal and intergenerational function, as Bolin articulates, media texts shape collective notions about how one generation's cultural experiences and surrounding mediascapes compare and contrast with others, thus operating as "formative components" of generational identity construction (2016a: 4). The *Age of Resistance* think-pieces analysed throughout this chapter reflect on how "fresh contact" with and subsequent haunted nostalgia for troubling media experiences contributes to generational identity formation: the show is framed as introducing a new generation to the nightmare fuelling, emotionally scarring – yet resilience building – effects of the 1982 film (Dovey 2010; Gillibrand 2019; Maesar 2022).

In think pieces on *Age of Resistance*, the "fresh contact" offered by the show to a new generation of child viewers is thus paralleled with the now fondly remembered, exhilarating fresh contact adult audiences experienced with the original film. In this way, the release of *Age of Resistance* was registered as a moment to reconsider the cultural and personal impacts of *The Dark Crystal*, reinforcing Netflix's socio-cultural role as a content curator not just for individual families but as a cultural curator for its vast collective of subscribers. *The Dark Crystal* was "rediscovered" as a film that sparked potent, resonant emotional attachments among former child viewers. In this way, *Age of Resistance* created an opportunity for *The Dark Crystal* to be *culturally* remembered as a moment of "fresh contact" that extended the limits of a generation of children's generic tastes and comfort zones around disturbing screen content. The recharged post-object fandom of *The Dark Crystal* in light of the new series highlights Netflix's potential to harness nostalgia in ways that propel productive retrospective reflection across and between generations, on both personal and collective scales. In this way, Netflix positions itself as not *just* a streaming service, but as a cultural curator and meaning-maker in the manner of television's previous status as a cultural "glue" (Holdsworth 2011).

Conclusion

When Netflix first announced *Age of Resistance*, it described it as a "horrifying" prequel to "a beloved classic from the 80s" and "fan favorite" (Netflix 2017b). The glowing terms around fandom mirror the announcements made for the adaptation *A Series of Unfortunate Events* and reboot *Lost in Space* earlier in the dark family telefantasy cycle under its "Family Watch Together TV" interface tag. Yet by hinting at the "horrifying secret" at the heart of the new show, the promotion was clearly intending *Age of Resistance* to revive and benefit from conversation around *The Dark Crystal* as delightfully traumatic and on the edges of suitable family viewing.

While *Age of Resistance* effectively capitalised on haunted nostalgia to spark a cycle of media commentary, the show ultimately did not get renewed for a second season. This announcement was made by Netflix and the show's creative team mere days after the series was awarded the 2020 Emmy for Outstanding Children's Program (Thorne 2020). Another cycle of reportage emerged around this "upsetting" (Warner 2020) cancelation, with commentators using the opportunity to dwell on the disjuncture between the show's visibility on social media and in media reportage and Netflix's tightly guarded data around a show's success or lack thereof (Burton 2020; Fullerton 2020; Stuewe 2020). Our previously cited interview participant who introduced his family to the show, 15-year-old Jack, expressed dismay around the cancellation in line with this commentary, explaining that it left him "very confused" because he thought it "performed well" and they "left it open in the air at the end of the season" in ways that, in his opinion, cleverly tied-in to the original film. Jack related the show's cancellation to concern around Netflix's broader habit of cancelling quality shows before their time: "I was just confused that they were choosing to, I guess, fund these other shows that I didn't think were good and then neglect an original and really good one".

As Matt Kamen (2020) points out, Netflix's data are tied to the minutiae of viewers' habits and behaviours around a program, including whether a show is binge-watched, finished within a 28-day window, or dropped by viewers mid-season or even mid-episode. The metrics by which dark family telefantasy programs are assessed on Netflix thus differ markedly from the ratings and publicity based metrics of linear television. While *Age of Resistance* did indeed succeed in the apparent aim to spark nostalgia-fuelled public and social media discourse upon first release, and was critically acclaimed, this was not enough to garner a series renewal. The cancellation however, is not necessarily inconsistent with the "cult" reputation of *The Dark Crystal*. Ultimately, the "phenomenal experience" (Mathijs and Sexton 2011) of cult texts is not predicated on traditional metrics of success.

While the ambiguous positioning of *Age of Resistance* between both (happily traumatised) nostalgic adult viewers and their children effectively sparked public discourse, perhaps when it came to viewers sticking with the season for its duration this ambiguity became an obstacle. While haunted nostalgia clearly propelled cultural interest in the show upon its release, it is possible this situated the program in the public consciousness as a source of short-term intrigue and quirky novelty for family audiences, rather than translating into sustained interest in a family-oriented show with extremely dense, dark, and complicated themes around the greed, corruption, and exploitative machinations of the ruling classes. It has been suggested that the impact of COVID-19 on production strategies and budgets might also have influenced Netflix's controversial decision to cancel the costly series (Fullerton 2020). As Alec Bojalad (2020) notes, the cancellation of the show indicates that Netflix's famous algorithms cannot always predict commercial success. The Emmy success of the series nonetheless helped contribute to the Quality branding around the streaming service's pivot to family content. Ultimately, *Age of Resistance* illuminates Netflix's experimental strategies around dark and subversive family content, and the show was likely one of Netflix's most expensive experiments with dark family content to date. Indeed, an insider described the series as an "expensive disappointment" that possibly was in part behind a shake-up of Netflix's executive team in 2020 (Cruz 2020; Goldberg et al 2020). Nonetheless, Matt Hills notes how cancellation can drive rather than limit the cult status of a television text, noting that "indeed, cult TV can be defined by its 'post-object fandom' as dedicated fan cultures continue to develop their relationships with cult texts long after television cancellation" (2018: 310). In other words, the cancellation of the *Age of Resistance* does not preclude and could even enhance its potential for "cult" status.

Netflix's strategy with *Age of Resistance* was to cultivate post-object fandom via haunted nostalgia, and thus new affective attachments to the 1982 film for adult viewers. While perhaps not the sustained ratings hit that the company had hoped for, the new affective attachments to older content underpinning interest in *Age of Resistance* was a clear part of a strategy started with *Stranger Things* to spark conversations and the sharing of experiences between nostalgic adult viewers, and between adults and their children. Thus, *Age of Resistance* continues the dark family telefantasy cycle's commitment to an intergenerational dynamic, a dynamic tied to edgy defiance of "traditional" or conservative modes of family viewing. This process involves the exchange of "fresh contact" between adults and children: while contemporary child audiences encountered the frightening but wondrous world of Thra for the first time, their adult guardians were likely fondly recalling the impact of their own prior fresh contact with the film on which the series is based during their own childhoods.

Note

1 Other examples include *Lost in Space* (2018–present), *Fuller House* (2016–2020), *Nurse Ratched* (2020–present), and *Cobra Kai* (2018–present).

6 *Raising Dion*

Paratexts, Genre Creep, and the Horror Next Door

The "Family Watch Together TV" tag is a recommendation for content Netflix believes the whole family will enjoy, but also implicitly infers a need for parental oversight more aligned with the TV-PG rating. Netflix's Original science fiction superhero program *Raising Dion* (2019–2022) illustrates this tension, targeting viewers across multiple points of attraction for its dark family telefantasy cycle that push at the edges of perceived notions of inclusive family viewing. This chapter will examine these tensions through a focus on the paratextual discourses around *Raising Dion* both on and off the Netflix portal. *Raising Dion* was praised for its diversity of casting that made it distinct from its forerunner *Stranger Things*, but *Raising Dion* was nonetheless criticised by parents for becoming increasingly violent and too "creepy" throughout the series (JMPakele 2019), despite featuring a seven-year-old protagonist and a Netflix US rating of TV-G. Indeed, parents on review sites such as US-based review website *Common Sense Media* frequently disagree with Netflix's classifications for its controversial dark family telefantasy under "Family Watch Together TV". The tonal variations in Netflix's own paratexts around *Raising Dion*, the reviews that paratextually circulate around the program, and finally the telefantasy paratexts that *Raising Dion* sits next to in the catalogue, together speak to a larger uncertainty around what can really be considered "Family Watch Together TV" in the age of SVODs.

As noted throughout this book, the genre organisation of the Netflix interface is a key paratextual element in informing viewers' engagement with its content (Chamberlain 2011: 233; Johnson 2019: 111), even as it is highly changeable (Johnson 2017: 122). While the alt-genre tag "Family Watch Together TV" overtly encourages intergenerational viewing, the algorithm also catalogues *Raising Dion* along more conventional genre lines. Other telefantasy programs frequently sit next to *Raising Dion* in the interface feed: *Chilling Adventures of Sabrina* (2018–2020, TV-14), *See You Yesterday* (2019, TV-MA), *Rim of the World* (2019, TV-14), and *Locke & Key* (2020–2022, TV-14), each feature young protagonists yet have drawn controversy around perceived inappropriate content. Netflix's classification and cataloguing of youth-led telefantasy, and the parental social media response, indicate a tension between the child *on* the screen and the child *watching* the

DOI: 10.4324/9781003223498-6

screen that has long haunted these genres. This tension finds new expression in the streaming era, in which something even creepier is often found right next door to "Family Watch Together TV".

Raising Dion

Raising Dion is a Netflix superhero sci-fi fantasy program based on the one-issue comic book (2015) of the same name by Dennis Liu. It features African American widowed single mom Nicole (Alisha Wainwright, known for *Shadowhunters: The Mortal Instruments*, 2017–2019), and her seven-year-old son Dion (Ja'Siah Young), both grieving the loss of Dion's father Mark (Michael B. Jordan). Dion starts to manifest strange abilities, including invisibility, teleportation, and telekinesis – the ability to move objects using only thought. Taiwanese American writer Liu wanted a minority superhero and a strong female character, aiming "to tell a story through the eyes of a parent because a common trope in superhero stories is that the parents die" (quoted in Gajanan 2015). *Raising Dion* was attractive to Netflix for two reasons: it would help extend and promote the racial diversity of its family offerings, and it would hopefully harness some of the success of the tele-fantasy program *Stranger Things* (2016–)(Goldberg 2017). Industry buzz started circulating about *Raising Dion* in 2016 when, as previously noted, Netflix publicly announced it was going to focus on family-oriented Originals (Baker et al 2020; Goldberg 2017; Littleton 2017). At this time, children and teens were primarily watching broadcast and cable television, and as such represented an untapped market through which to gain parent subscribers (Lindsey 2016: 181). The success of *Stranger Things* meant that by 2016, Netflix was looking to intergenerational audiences and telefantasy Originals to drive subscriptions and branding (Flint 2016; Littleton 2017; Tiffany 2017). The production of *Raising Dion* was nonetheless met with delays, redevelopment, and staffing changes (Goldberg 2017). Although Netflix wanted to build on the popularity of *Stranger Things*, they were also cautious to make sure that *Raising Dion* was sufficiently distinct, given that both programs featured a "kid-with-powers", a shady government agency, and a terrifying creature manifesting in the sky (Goldberg 2017). As a result, Netflix sent the concept back to the writers' room (Goldberg 2017). Carol Barbee came on board as showrunner, while Michael B. Jordan, best known at that time for his critically acclaimed performance in *Creed* (Ryan Coogler 2015) and pegged as a "Black star rising", joined as executive producer and guest stars as Dion's deceased father (Goldberg 2017). By April 2018 when filming started on *Raising Dion* (FTIA 2018), Jordan had become a household name thanks to his role as Erik Killmonger in *Black Panther* (Ryan Coogler 2018). In the meantime, strong ratings for *A Series of Unfortunate Events* in 2017 (see Maglio 2017) and *Lost in Space* in 2018 (Graham 2018; Spangler 2018b; Stanley 2022; Tassi 2020) helped maintain the new family profile of the platform through Original dark telefantasy content.

Netflix nonetheless remained dominated by adult content in 2018 as filming commenced on *Raising Dion*, with 61% of Netflix Originals classified TV-MA. Of the remaining Originals,

> only 16% of programming [was] for families – nearly half of that is TV-PG [7% of Originals], which means parents are to be advised over some content … Other companies like Disney and Apple are threatening to be major competition for Netflix, especially since both have claimed to produce content that's more family friendly. (Cobb 2018; Farrand 2018)

By April of 2019, surveys suggested that Netflix would be due for a major hit once Disney+ became available due to the difference in original content: "Parents were more than twice as likely to cancel Netflix in favor of the family-friendly Disney platform, with 23% of households with children age [sic] 15 and younger saying that they may cancel Netflix when Disney+ becomes available" (Ellingson 2019).

As such, Ben Travers (2019) suggests the timing of *Raising Dion*'s release on 4 October 2019, a little over a month before the Disney+ launch on 12 November 2019, was highly strategic:

> With Disney+ looming, Netflix needs more star power ("Hey, Killmonger is in this!"), franchises ("This is a lot like 'Stranger Things' …"), and family-friendly content. ("I guess Disney doesn't have *every* show my kids and I want to watch.")

By the end of 2019, Netflix publicised the fact that *Raising Dion* was its number one rating "Kids & Family Series" of the year (Netflix Family 2019), making it an important family tentpole series in a newly competitive market and a key program through which it sought to pre-emptively get ahead of Disney+ in particular.

"Recommended for You": Challenging Classifications

Netflix's self-applied classification, parental advisory website recommendations, and parental feedback around *Raising Dion* reveal its contested status as a family program, and the unsettling of this category in the SVOD era more broadly. As parents on *Common Sense Media* indicate, many families watched *Raising Dion* together (GLHoover 2019; Jessascroggs 2019; Kellywelly 2019; kelschandler 2020; KPhilogone 2020; TheycallmeMaaaaaaa 2020). However, considerable debate emerged around its suitability for younger children. One father proclaimed "I loved it. However, the fact that this is available to my 8 year old on his Netflix login is deeply not OK. Can't wait til Disney's streaming service, Netflix is not to be trusted with my kids" Simon R. 2019). Netflix's classification of *Raising Dion* as TV-G, which means it is included in

Netflix Kids unless parents specifically block the title, was challenged by several parents on the review website *Common Sense Media*:

> Netflix shows a TV-G Rating - Terribly Incorrect
>
> I mistakenly watched this thinking it was safe due to the Netflix TV-G rating. Perhaps I don't understand ratings, but I always thought a G rating meant it was for General audiences which would include small children … The show itself was very entertaining and I would have had no problem with it had it been rated PG-13 or at a minimum PG. I trusted Netflix's TV-G rating and got broadsided with the adult content within the show. (Cpamario 2020; see also AutisticYoungAdult 2019; imska 2019)

Rather than a review etiquette around avoiding spoilers (Grandinetti 2017: 22), by contrast parental advisory websites operate under user assumptions of full disclosure of information deemed relevant to making decisions around family viewing that is more detailed than information from providers such as Netflix. While parents criticised Netflix's classifications, in turn several parents challenged *Common Sense Media*'s own reviewer over what they considered significant omissions in "what parents need to know" about *Raising Dion*, including sexual references, alcohol consumption, scariness, and stalking, all of which impacted upon parents' own assessment of whether the program was family viewing and for what age of child (Appledaddy 2019; AutisticYoungAdult 2019; Lena 2019).

Disagreement over *Raising Dion* in the *Common Sense Media* posts primarily revolved around its "creepy" and "scary" telefantasy elements, that were giving children "nightmares" (Aussie Dad of 2 2020; JMPakele 2019; Momoftwoboys123 2022; Srspashly 2019), despite having a protagonist who is seven years old at the beginning of the first season (and ten years old in Season Two). In part, these responses were relative to children's prior exposure to superhero content. *Raising Dion*'s episodes are numbered as "Issues", and the program is labelled as "TV Shows Based on Comics" (albeit only one issue), hinting at its superhero story even as it does not overtly use the "superhero" label on the interface. In our parent interviews, Felicity, parent of two boys, commented that *Raising Dion* was a suitable stepping-stone for superhero content at an age at which she felt they were not yet ready for Marvel films such as *Black Panther*. Parents on *Common Sense Media* varied in this assessment, with most asserting it was suitable for those *already* watching superhero films (Cyntheak 2022; Susan 2019), while others suggested that depicting a trusted family friend turn into a villain made it *more* scary for their children than superhero films (Denver Dad 2022). At the end of the first episode (#101 Seith Mann 2019), what seem to be ghosts appear in a thunderstorm including Dion's father, Mark, and a large, ominous figure seemingly constituted of lightning. Dion names this figure "The Crooked Man", evoking horror for much older viewers by using the same name as the supernatural antagonist in James Wan's 2016 horror film *The Conjuring 2*, rated R by the MPAA for "terror and horror violence". The Crooked Man is revealed in *Raising Dion* #105 (Seith Mann 2019) to have killed Mark, lifting him into the sky with a lightning bolt as he grimaces in pain and his companion screams in terror. In Issue #108 "You Won't Like Him When He's Angry" (Neema Barnette 2019), Dion's godfather Pat (Jason Ritter) starts to stalk Nicole. When their friend Charlotte confronts him about his behaviour, Pat reveals himself to be the murderous Crooked Man himself, despite having previously been an ostensibly jovial and trusted adult figure in Dion's life. Up until this point, Pat has been a mentor to Dion, spending significant time at his home and guiding his development through references to superhero comic books. This twist, and the nature of the murders committed by Pat/Crooked Man, upset many children and their parents (Cpamario 2020; Denver Dad 2022), a reaction relative to the TV-G rating and its placement in Netflix Kids.

In Season 1, meteorites are identified as the origin of the superhuman abilities in *Raising Dion*, providing the tagline for Season 2, "energy never dies, it just takes a different form" (@RaisingDion 2022). However, this science fiction framing shifts into horror in Season 2, as the Crooked Man's energy passes on to a child, Brayden Mills (Griffin Robert Faulkner), and they create an army of zombie-like plant people by using infectious parasitic spores that cause pustules over their bodies ("Issue #203: Monster Problem" Dennis A. Liu 2022). The character of Brayden invokes the horror trope of "children as innocent victims of demonic possession … illustrating a clear delineation between the body usurped by evil forces and the soul of the victimized, powerless child trapped inside" (Balanzategui 2018c: 11). Although the Season 2 arc is ultimately sympathetic to the plight of the orphaned Brayden, on *Common Sense Media*, this development drew negative reactions from parents, with Faith (2022) proclaiming: "It's a Kids Horror show, and I think those two words should never be together" (see also Gwenmeyers 2022). As Lester (2016, 2021) has demonstrated in the case of film and Balanzategui (2018a) in the case of television, horror is frequently seen in these terms as an "impossible" and irreconcilable genre for children and families. In the case of *Raising Dion*, the genre slippage between superheroes, science fiction, and horror created difficulties for the reception of the show particularly into its second season. This creates particularly fraught territory for family viewing, where Netflix's "Family Watch Together TV" label functions as an implicit social contract in which the slippage between science fiction and fantasy on the one hand, and horror on the other, is frequently seen as a violation. This is further exacerbated for telefantasy, which, as we noted in Chapter 1, is subject to slippage between elements of science fiction, fantasy, and horror and as a result lacks a clearly defined genre social contract (Johnson 2005: 2).

Beyond parental ambivalence around *Raising Dion*'s darker telefantasy elements, more broadly the *Common Sense Media* responses to the program reveal disparities in how parents conceptualise family viewing itself. Justin Grandinetti interprets the interplay between professional and nonprofessional reviewers online as an example of Gerard A. Hauser's "vernacular rhetoric" (Grandinetti 2017: 23),

> dialogue in which an active society critiques, negotiates, associates, and ultimately constitutes its interests and opinions on the issues confronting them. Each contribution speaks the claims of differences and affiliations that allow us to recognize, discriminate, and interpret meanings within the socially negotiated limits that define social membership. (Hauser 1999: 91)

This power dynamic is inherent in the organisational logic of *Common Sense Media*, which leads with its official reviews and back-ends its parent and child reviews. A similar dynamic was also revealed in our semi-structured interviews. Father-of-two Brian noted he used the official reviews provided on the website to help choose family viewing, but not the parents' own reviews given the disparity of different opinions. The role of advisory websites in negotiating a public discourse around family viewing, in both their official and parent reviews, is complicated by the fact that "under the Netflix model, entertainment correspondents are given the same release [date] as viewers (or at least only given access to a few episodes a day or two before the full season is released)" (Grandinetti 2017: 17). As Grandinetti notes, this tightens the review window (2017: 17) meaning Netflix's own recommendations around what content is suitable for family viewing under labels such as "Family Watch Together TV" will appear in profiles before full seasons have been reviewed.

In a feature that commenced in 2018 (Spangler 2018a), Netflix momentarily displays a rationale for their classification of *Raising Dion* on the upper left-hand corner of the screen, indicating *Raising Dion* contains "mild themes, mild violence, scary scenes". The level of detailed parental controls introduced by Netflix between 2018 and 2020 to block specific titles and thumbnails in Netflix Kids (Sattelberg 2020; Spangler 2018a) presuppose a very attentive oversight in a catalogue that is constantly changing. Parents have to keep up as the Netflix algorithm keeps making new recommendations. Netflix's narrowcasting approach uses constantly refined "data algorithms, which analyze user behaviour in an effort to make specific content recommendations" (Novak 2017: 163). This is based on comparisons with other customers with comparable viewing habits, particularly around genre (Novak 2017: 163, 165). However, parent feedback suggests not only that tone is just as important as genre, but also that targeting children's feed around a *child's* viewing habits may not accord with what *parents* would want to appear. As parent JMPakele (2019) cautions of *Raising Dion*,

> Don't be fooled when it comes up as a match on Netflix for your kiddo.
>
> So, this came up as a 99% match for my kid on Netflix. We've only watched the first episode and I was freaked out! I won't allow my 9 year old to continue it because to me, it's creepy!

Here, the debate among parents for and against the suitability of *Raising Dion* is articulated partly as a mismatch by the Netflix algorithm itself, as not being aligned with the parent's perspective of their child's viewing habits and family intergenerational viewing. As our interview participant Breanna explained, family television for her in the streaming era equates to "challenge" as it is very difficult to choose content that all three boys in her family like, aged 8, 13, and 15. To choose content appropriate for her youngest and entertaining for her eldest, she turns to reviews rather than the Netflix recommendations:

> I don't think I use [Netflix recommendations] very much as I wouldn't trust it … I think what I do when I see something and think oooh that could be quite good is immediately look at reviews online rather than trust Netflix. I don't think I've ever trusted them.

Father-of-two Brian similarly expressed distrust in the algorithm for choosing family content. Sarah Arnold notes that while Netflix's personalisation and recommendations system (PRS) "does not draw from user demographics, such demographics are built into its design and its system of tagging genres … Netflix simply shifts such demographic markers to genre tags" (2016: 56). As we have noted previously, Arnold suggests the algorithm necessarily "makes reductive claims about its users" (2016: 57). By extension, this reductive tendency is amplified in the case of family viewing, where Netflix only knows through which profile a program is being watched, not who is in the room, nor the dynamics between the child viewer and the adult guardian potentially acting as gatekeeper. Parents want to trust the rhetoric around Netflix's distinction from broadcast and cable TV in being able to provide personalised recommendations, however family viewing presents a challenge for this system both functionally (in terms of what the algorithm does and does not know, and the messy distinctions between individual profiles) and culturally.

The "You" in "Recommended for You" is programmed to address the profile made up of "the cumulative set of choices made by the viewer" and comparisons "with a group of strangers who all happened to have made similar choices" (Alexander 2016: 84, 86, 93), a logic that also underpins *Common Sense Media* parent reviews. The adult guardian interrupts and complicates Netflix's address to "You" in the case of a child viewer in ways that the algorithm cannot track. Given the implied plural address of the alt-genre "Family Watch Together TV", "You" may in many cases be plural, a family whose collective viewing practices and dynamics are only imperfectly captured by the algorithm. In her semi-structured interview, Breanna's eight-year-old son Dylan noted that when their family watches Netflix together, "we don't have a group profile … it's just the first one to get to the remote, gets to go in their profile". As Breanna observes, this has "muddled" the children's profiles with content and recommendations she would prefer to reserve for watching together. She suggests "we would be better off having an icon for family". However, this option is limited by the fact that Netflix only allows five profiles on a single Netflix account.

Parental control works against the central logic of Netflix, which strongly encourages viewers to cede to its recommendations, a strategy which Netflix claims has been successful given according to their metrics, users stay within the recommendations 75–80% of the time (Hallinan and Ted 2016: 130; Johnson 2019: 116). More specifically, our survey indicated that 65% subscribers sometimes selected *family* viewing based on the recommendations appearing in their profile, but were most likely to pay attention to good reviews outside the platform when making decisions about family content, a finding also supported by Frey (2021: 133, 170, 210, 213). Arnold suggests in the Netflix model, "human agency … is posited as an encumbrance, something best surrendered so that the user is not overwhelmed with uncertainty and, in the worst case, indecision" (2016: 59). Parental desire for greater oversight goes against this central operating logic. If parents restrict children's profiles and programs quite tightly and conservatively but are still on the lookout for material to watch together, this complicates Netflix's emphasis on recommendation and requires that family material targets parents as much as, or even more than, children.

The Netflix Family Market & Diversity

Just as original family content has quickly become a key sector in the SVOD landscape (Johnson 2018b), Netflix has also been keen to develop and promote its diversity, both across the platform and in family viewing more specifically. *Raising Dion* premiered at a time when Netflix was overtly trying to both address and publicise its commitment to diversity. Netflix famously added "inclusion" to its "Netflix Culture" manifesto in 2017 (Smith 2020). As we have noted throughout this book, "family", "family viewing", and "family television" are all culturally contingent, discursive categories. This raises the issue of how Netflix conceives of and strategically targets the family at the heart of its "Family Watch Together TV" micro-genre tag. For *Raising Dion*, this meant stressing its genre connections with the intergenerational hit *Stranger Things*, while being distinguished by its Black leading characters and younger protagonist.

As such, *Raising Dion* appears not only in Netflix's alt-genre tag "Family Watch Together TV" but also "Black Stories" (Figure 6.1), "Black Stories for Families", and "Strong Black Lead". In particular, "Strong Black Lead" was an initiative "spearheaded by a group of black executives at Netflix" in

Figure 6.1 The "Black Stories" alt-genre tag on adult's profile as of July 2022. Screenshot by authors.

2018 (Anderson 2018; Smith 2020). As Catherine Johnson notes, descriptive text and images on SVOD interfaces function as paratexts in Jonathan Gray's terms, shaping the viewer's expectations around a text (Gray 2010: 26; Johnson 2019: 111). Further, interface paratexts also situate the user within broader ideological discourses (Van Esler 2020: 3–4). The "Strong Black Lead" initiative became particularly important in the light of Netflix's controversial "Artwork personalisation" algorithm launched in the same year, that used viewer data to create thumbnail posters presenting minority actors as lead characters even when they were only in very minor support roles (Iqbal 2018). The "Strong Black Lead" tag for *Raising Dion* is, therefore, more than simply descriptive, but rather serves to reassert the brand's commitment to diversity in Original content in the face of paratextual controversy. Adriana Obertova and Caitlin Reder (2019) identify a 34% increase in casting people of colour in Netflix exclusives from 2012 to 2018, while also noting their continued under-representation in many Netflix exclusives and unevenness between lead and supporting roles.

In 2019, Netflix claimed the increasing diversity of its products and its audience was reflected in its revamped animated logo, or ident, released on 1st February. It still featured the "Netflix sound", but the capital N logo "breaks out into an array of colors – which is inspired by the spectrum of stories, emotions, languages, fans and creators that collectively make up who we are as a brand" (Netflix 2019b). As such, Van Esler suggests an image of "multiculturalism" becomes bound up with selling an idea of "user choice, and content abundance" which might nonetheless still be somewhat misleading (2020: 7). Illustrating Van Esler's contention, Netflix's own productions and commissioned Originals have been predominantly White across its two dominant family genres, the family sitcom and dark family telefantasy. *Raising Dion*'s creator Liu responded to the monoculture by strategically producing a single-issue comic book and a trailer as part of his pitch to Netflix (Gajanan 2015; Smail 2019). Liu asserts that putting out content first was a necessary change in approach to the challenging pitch process, "when you're the only person in the room who's Asian … because no one else in the room can see their former self in you" (quoted in Tan 2019). The trailer Liu made to pitch *Raising Dion* to Netflix went viral on YouTube, a fact that Netflix used in its promotion of the subsequent series (Netflix 2017a).

In the case of the family sitcom, the Netflix-commissioned Black sitcom *All About the Washingtons* (Amblin Television, ABC Signature Studios 2018) was cancelled after one season, while the Cuban-American sitcom *One Day at a Time* (2017–2019) was cut after three, and was subsequently continued by Pop in 2020. Netflix VP of Content Cindy Holland explained, "We wouldn't have renewed that show on a viewing-to-cost basis. We also look at, is it reaching different audiences? Is it gaining critical acclaim? Is it doing something for us as a business that we like?" (quoted in Mehmedova 2019). Netflix addressed the subsequent gap in diverse family sitcoms with its own productions *Family Reunion* (2019–2022) and the multi-racial *Alexa & Katie* (2018–2020).

In its focus on black lives, *Raising Dion* is distinctive within the dark family telefantasy cycle under the "Family Watch Together TV" label, an address to the blindcasting discernible across the other telefantasy shows in this category. Kristen Warner suggests that the act of divorcing characters of colour from cultural specificities through colourblind casting frequently, if inadvertently, still upholds "normative whiteness" (Warner 2010: 119). In more specific genre terms, Ebony Elizabeth Thomas asserts that "when people of color seek passageways into the fantastic, we have often discovered that the doors are barred" (Thomas 2019: 2). *Stranger Things* was criticised for only having one character of colour in a regular lead role, Lucas Sinclair (played by Caleb McLaughlin) (Solin 2016). While *Lost in Space* (2018–2021) features a blended family, including bi-racial teen daughter Judy Robinson (Taylor Russell), it otherwise features people of colour in secondary roles. As Charles Mudede suggests, by initially presenting Judy's parentage as a puzzle even among onscreen characters such as Don, the program "says something that almost all other science fiction movies and TV shows refuse to admit: The future is *not* post-racial" (2018, emphasis added).

In *ASoUE*, the decision to introduce diversity into the Netflix adaptation was limited to taking characters drawn as White in the novel illustrations and casting them as people of colour. While the novels depict a dystopian world filled with Anglo-European characters, in which adults are inept or selfish or worse, the adaptation notably introduces new sympathetic guardian figures as outlined in Chapter 3, all of whom are White. *ASoUE* focuses on a White family with diverse actors only in supporting roles, the most prominent being the recurring Black character Mr Arthur Poe

(K. Tood Freeman), a cheery but incompetent banker who inadvertently puts the Baudelaire children in harm's way. In the Netflix adaptation (as opposed to the novels), he knowingly leaves the children to burn at the stake in "The Vile Village: Part Two" (Barry Sonnenfeld 2018). As such, the program's blindcasting frequently has seemingly unintended effects (Warner 2010: 75, 120), leading parent-reviewer, Geoffrey Vee, to declare that the show "has too many racist undertones ... This is not the type of show I want my children exposed to!" (2020).

Finally, although it depicts a world of puppets, *The Dark Crystal: Age of Resistance*, examined in Chapter 5, came out during the same diversity drive as *Raising Dion*, and was promoted by Lisa Henson, CEO and President of The Jim Henson Company, for using "blind casting as best we could for voices. There are several cases where people were playing siblings where the actors themselves are of different ethnicities. Our goal was to cast the right people with the right timbre of voice" (Lisa Henson, quoted in Holden 2019).[1]

The colourblind voice casting is thereby intended to, and overtly marketed as, signifying diversity *within* each fantasy race in the *Age of Resistance* story world, even as simultaneously, there is a limited range of onscreen skin colours among the heroic Gelflings.

Liu's commentary on the pitching process for *Raising Dion* becomes pertinent here, in that it is not simply a matter of conceptualising the contemporary Netflix family, but rather more precisely of adult executives drawing on their memories of "their former self" as a child to picture what family might mean (Liu in Tan 2019). Reflecting on Netflix's more recent "Black Lives Matter" collection, Ben Smith notes an increasing diversity in the Netflix pitching room, while also suggesting "Netflix's stories offer a glimpse of how the industry is and isn't changing" (2020). This can be seen across other areas of diversity in casting and onscreen representation as well. *Stranger Things* was praised for casting Gaten Matarazzo (as Dustin Henderson), whose rare condition of cleidocranial dysplasia was written into the show "but ... never defines his character" (Active Rehab 2016; McNamara 2016). Yet the program had no LGBTQIA+ characters until Robin Buckey (Maya Hawke) was introduced in Season 3.[2] The program has continued to attract criticisms around casting and its Black representation (Radillo 2022; Shunyata 2022). Equally, when Netflix made its own series YouTube trailer for *Raising Dion*, it attracted criticisms of "colorism" given the role of Dion's mother had been recast with a lighter-skinned actor, Alisha Wainwright (Keahey 2019; Richardson 2018). This made strategic sense for Netflix to the extent that Wainwright is known for the telefantasy program *Shadowhunters* and could potentially draw teen and adult fans over to the new show. Her casting and the response are nonetheless indicative of an ambivalent "bittersweet" sentiment around the way Netflix's moves towards greater diversity are still hampered by prevailing and conservative racial norms they are still employing (Keahey 2019).

Liu's original promotional trailer presents the challenges of raising a child with special (superhuman) abilities as analogous to those facing parents of minority children who are under-represented in popular culture. As noted in Chapter 4, paratexts "ensure the text's presence in the world, its 'reception' and consumption" (Genette 1997: 1). Developing Gérard Genette's work for screen media, Gray argues that "entryway paratexts" such as trailers introduce a potential audience to the premise of a text, including its genre and characters (2010: 73, 141). In Liu's trailer, Dion's mother Nicole (Upenda Morton) narrates, thereby situating the young boy's story through a parental lens. As Dion (Nyri Haywood) practices his telekinesis, Dion's mother Nicole worries about how to give her son "a normal childhood". Unnamed agents in dark suits and sunglasses are implied to be as much a threat to this normalcy as Dion's abilities. Nicole comments, "The right children's books won't exist. So, you need to get creative. I drew a rule book called *When do I use my powers?*" In this context, the address to "you" is not the child or even family audience (Baker 2020: 117), but rather more specifically to the parent who finds their child under- un- or misrepresented in children's popular culture. Emphasis is thereby placed on the *Raising* part of *Raising Dion*, with a direct address to other parents.

Indeed, the trailer overtly posits that there are two superheroes in this story – both mother and son. Liu presents his YouTube trailer by saying:

> Imagine Superman, but from Martha Kent's point of view. Or imagine Spiderman, but from Aunt May's point of view. This is a superhero story, but from the parent's point of view. But unlike her son, she doesn't have any powers. (Liu 2015)

Nonetheless, by the end of the trailer, Nicole asserts, "the most important thing about raising a superhero is learning how to become one first". Stacia L. Brown (2015) suggests that the "the popular comparison of single mothers to superheroes" is a cliché that "comes with the unintended implication that we're impervious", an association she argues Liu's trailer overtly challenges by showing Nicole's frustration and exhaustion alongside her fortitude. As Nicole declares herself to be a superhero too, Dion lifts his mother's camera up into the sky using his powers, transforming a selfie into an aerial shot, and the music by Pakk Hui rises along with it. The trailer's ending is literally and figuratively uplifting, highlighting Nicole's belief in her ability to be a superhero mother for Dion.

The subsequent Netflix program itself showcases what *The Black Cape* magazine (Davis 2019) calls a "wealth" of "black excellence": Dion's father is a scientist, his mother a dancer and designer, and his aunt a doctor, while other Black leaders in the community include Nicole's boss, who is a dance company owner, and Dion's school teacher (see also Jackson 2019). In turn, the young Dion actor Ja'Siah Young overtly links his character to Black Panther and Miles Morales, situating Dion within a wider pantheon of superheroes of colour (YayOMG 2019). Nonetheless, this is not a utopian fantasy where race ceases to matter. At school, Dion momentarily loses control and uses his powers to push over his White classmate Jonathan (Gavin Munn) for stealing his father's watch. Even though Jonathan still has the watch on him when the pair are confronted by their White school principal, only Dion is punished. The cultural ideal of childhood innocence is exposed here as raced, in that "*some children are more innocent than others, and Black children are not innocent at all*" (Thomas 2019: 56, italics in original; Cunningham 2020). The incident leads Nicole to have "the talk" about racism with her son. This provoked strong reactions online, with Kristi Smedley initially proclaiming, "I didn't want this topic to appear in children's fiction", but after her niece had a similar incident with a teacher, Smeldey updated her post, realising her niece could "watch Dion's plight and feel a little less lonely" (2019). On *Common Sense Media*, parents asserted "the talk" onscreen could be mirrored by a similar talk with their own children offscreen: "we can have important talks about the social issues it brings (ableism, racism, etc) while watching them play out for kids that are my son's exact age" (Susan 2019). The intergenerational dynamic onscreen is thereby paratextually linked to intergenerational dynamics among offscreen families as well. *Raising Dion* prompted conservative backlash that the show was racist against White characters (FeliciaRH 2019; u/iamzaizen 2019), a frequent claim made against Netflix which included a #BoycottNetflix campaign for *Dear White People* (2017–2021) (Ugwu 2018). The hostility towards *Raising Dion* conveniently ignored the fact that Dion has a positive White role model in Charlotte (Deirdre Lovejoy), who is similarly endowed with special powers and helps to train Dion, before making the ultimate sacrifice of giving her life to protect him.

While Dion suffers discrimination, he is shown to have some preconceptions of his own about best friend Esperanza (Sammi Haney), who in the show and in real life is in a wheelchair due to brittle bone disease (osteogenesis imperfecta type III). Notably, Epseranza's role in Dion's "Triangle of Justice" superhero group works in opposition to M. Night Shyamalan's 2000 film *Unbreakable*, in which brittle bone disease forms the origin story to the emergence of supervillain Elijah Price (Samuel L. Jackson), an ableist narrative that is challenged in *Raising Dion*. In episode 8, Dion uses his powers to raise Esperanza into the air and move her legs without her consent, making the assumption that she would enjoy the experience. Esperanza, however, is incensed. Charlotte points out that what Dion imagines he would want if he were in a wheelchair is clearly not what Esperanza wants. Charlotte's conversation with Dion creates another "teachable moment" identified by parents watching the show that can be mirrored offscreen (Kellywelly 2019; Susan 2019). Dion may be well meaning, but his ableism momentarily threatens his closest friendship. In the next episode, Dion apologises "for trying to fix you, when you aren't broken". Showrunner Carol Barbee cast the character of Esperanza authentically, earning the program The Ruderman Seal of

Approval for Authentic Representation (Drury 2019; Ruderman Family Foundation 2019). A 2018 study indicated that despite 25% US adults having a disability, onscreen television representation for recurring characters was only 2.1% (Sullivan 2020) and 95% of those were played by able-bodied actors (Berman 2018). Netflix has publicised its increased all-abilities characters, including "Family Watch Together TV" content such as *One Day at a Time* (2017–2019) and *The Healing Powers of Dude* (2020), albeit not always with authentic casting across all its content. Dion's lesson about consent and projection is given a darker mirror in his godfather Pat, whose character arc takes him from hero's mentor to nemesis, in which his hidden superpowers become a tool of toxic masculinity and entitlement. Dion, with the benefit of adult guidance, corrects his assumption that others either think like him or ought to. By contrast, Pat's refusal to do likewise has horrific and deadly consequences. The representation of racism, ableism, and consent issues in *Raising Dion* within a TV-G program implicitly presuppose a PG viewing environment under the auspices of "Family Watch Together TV", whereby parents or other adult guardians are assumed to be present and capable of discussing and unpacking these teachable moments with their children.

Finally, *Raising Dion*'s diverse construction of community includes queer characters where queerness is neither a plot point nor a special issue-of-the-episode, but rather is positively framed as an integral part of Dion's family and community. Nicole's boss at the dance studio (Kwame, played by J. Harrison Ghee) is played as queer, while Nicole's sister Kat (Jazmyn Simon) is a lesbian. The narrative issue around Kat's relationship is not one of orientation but rather work ethics, as her girlfriend Danielle (Erica Tazel) is her superior at the hospital where Kat is a surgical resident. Kat brings Dion to the hospital when he suffers an extremely high fever in her care, dismissing Nicole's earlier accounts of his strange new abilities. However, upon witnessing him levitating, Kat deletes Dion's medical records. When caught by Danielle, she refuses to disclose her reasons, and is not only fired as a result, but also loses Danielle in the process. Some conservative parents felt the relationship between Kat and Danielle, who cuddle and share one kiss in episode #107, was inappropriate for a TV-G show (Cpamario 2020; Funkyrake 2019; Lena 2019), while conversely for other parents this was another teachable moment to discuss with their children offscreen (hao 2019; KPhilogone 2020; Mom of two kiddos 2019). Commenting on this intergenerational dynamic, parent KPhilogone [sic] suggests, "You just have to be there to answer any question that may arise" (2020), a function shifted from the official Netflix classification to the "Family Watch Together TV" tag, making it the responsibility of parents rather than Netflix per se.

The "Family Watch Together TV" alt-genre suggests that a perceived expectation around the family television model persists even as its temporality is being reframed and its White, heteronormative foundation reworked. Broadcast television schedules "assume that its domestic audience takes the form of families … a powerful cultural construct" (Ellis 1982: 113).

This most often accords with a "heteronormative logic" both on and off the screen (Needham 2008: 156). Normative family temporality has in turn been disrupted by streaming services, such that Maria San Filippo questions whether Needham would still be correct today in saying television "imagines that the family audience is the ideological glue that holds it together" (Needham 2008: 145; San Fillippo 2017: 77). Commenting on "recommended family viewing" in the United Kingdom's television magazine *Radio Times*, Gary Needham suggests:

> The need for this additional signage for the family audience is indicative of an inconsistency in the familial imaginary since this surely is the point of the watershed and safe harbour ... This gesture also implies the need to protect the family from what must be imagined as potentially unsafe programming. (2008: 146)

In other words, there is a pre-existing anxiety around the family and television that is accentuated in streaming, which does away with the temporality of family-based schedules altogether. This places added pressure upon classifications, alt-genre tags, and recommendations, both on and outside the platforms, to manage expectations around what the slippery and contentious domain of family viewing might mean in the streaming era. Netflix's attempts to actively promote the diversity of its onscreen families occurs at a time when it is simultaneously trying to both shift and manage how family viewing works, mediating the intergenerational dynamics of the family both on and offscreen.

A Family-Friendly *Stranger Things*

When it was taken on by Netflix, *Raising Dion* maintained Liu's focus on minority parenting but changed the tone to better capitalise on the success of *Stranger Things* (discussed in Chapter 2). Nelson (2019) notes, "*Raising Dion* is clearly trying to mimic *Stranger Things* with its intergenerational conflicts and focus on how relationships grow and change in the face of the unknown". The program acknowledges the legacy of Netflix's dark family telefantasy prototype by featuring the *Stranger Things* theme as Pat's ringtone. Netflix's strategy was ultimately successful, with *Raising Dion* widely received in the media as a "family friendly *Stranger Things*" (Painter 2019; Salfen 2019; Travers 2019).

The shift from Liu's original trailer for *Raising Dion* to Netflix's recast and revamped official YouTube trailer is illustrative of the Netflix branding process, and highlights how, following the success of the genre cycle's prototype, *Stranger Things*, Netflix sought to curate a slate of family telefantasy tonally linked to its flagship show. As Gray suggests, "the high trade in trailers and promos over YouTube ... puts ever more power into studios' hands to pre-purpose and repurpose films and television shows" (2010: 72).

While trailers have always drawn upon "market research" to select "elements … they feel will capture and maximize their (imaginary) audience" (Kernan 2004: 38), Netflix can use its extensive customer data to help further refine this process. The YouTube trailer release is an important part of its marketing to potential new subscribers. The Netflix YouTube trailer for *Raising Dion* begins with Dion's mother, Nicole Warren (recast with Alisha Wainwright), showing her son Dion (Ja'Siah Young) footage of his deceased father Mark (Michael B. Jordan), while the soundtrack holds a single synth note for 12 seconds. Already, this is a more sombre opening than Liu's trailer. As musician Bryce Miller notes, "the first half of trailers … [is] Where they're floating and you have to find ways to move the tension, move the emotion" (in Vehling 2019). Nicole is again the narrator, but her address shifts from fellow adult parents to the child: "You're such a special kid. You're charming, smart, very handsome". Nicole's narration is revealed as a diegetic conversation directed at Dion himself. In both trailers, there is an address to "you", but whereas in Liu's trailer that address is to other parents, here it is from Nicole to her son, and perhaps by extension, to children in the audience, emphasising the family pitch. When Dion is nearly struck by a car, he spontaneously teleports to the safety of his mother's arms in front of Pat. At this point, the slow and sparse background melody fills out and becomes dominant in the sound mix, revealing itself to be a synth rendition of the lyrical theme in D-flat major from the first movement of Tchaikovsky's Piano Concerto No. 1. In an increasingly rapid montage, the trailer shows Dion pursued, abducted by a high-tech government agency, and attacked by a colossal figure made of lightning. The montage sequence ends with a shot of Nicole holding her son's face and desperately telling him, "It's you and me. You and me". This emphasises the onscreen intergenerational bond between mother and child, rather than the address from an onscreen parent to offscreen parents in Liu's original trailer.

The title card wraps up the trailer and the music trails once more to slow, single notes. Nicole's shaking and earnest assertion to her son emphasises the intergenerational dynamics of the program and showcases her grit, but gives greater prominence to her distress at the continuing threat they face together. The Netflix trailer creates a more menacing fantasy world that contains none of the humour of Liu's original trailer, in which Dion wonders why he can turn invisible but his "poop" does not. This is despite the fact that in the Netflix version, Dion's feisty friend Esperanza and the initially nerdy Pat both provide moments of comic relief in the program itself. The strategic shift to an overall darker tone in the promotion of the series aligns with Netflix's strategy around its flagship dark family telefantasy programs offered under "Family Watch Together TV".

Although Nicole addresses her own child rather than other parents in the audience, the non-diegetic music in the Netflix trailer is aimed at adult sensibilities and intertextual references. Classical music has high cultural capital in Pierre Bourdieu's terms, being associated with "highbrow" educated tastes

(Bourdieu 1979/2013; Lizardo and Skiles 2008, 493). However, Lizardo and Skiles note "the capacity to display 'omnivore' taste" across traditional high/low, fine art/popular art binaries has become more highly prized "in contemporary post-industrial societies" (2008: 494). Miller's synth arrangement of Tchaikovsky for a family streaming program straddles these high/low distinctions. The "harmonic language" (Lehman 2018: 16) and "lyrical melodies of Tchaikovsky" have been particularly influential in the development of "neo-classical scores" for the screen, particularly the work of John Williams, and their aural associations with wonder (Audissino 2017: 221; Barone 2017; Orosz 2015: 300, 316). This wonderment can be briefly seen in the *Raising Dion* trailer in Dion's awe as he levitates toy LEGO bricks, and in Nicole's pleasurable astonishment upon realising he can produce floating particles of light.

Tchaikovsky aurally connects *Dion* with high culture associations and a broader romantic soundtrack tradition, but more specifically the piece was famously used in Rob Reiner's 1990 adaptation of Stephen King's *Misery*, a horror thriller. As Gray argues, paratexts serve to influence the "menu of intertexts" audiences are encouraged to connect with a new film or television program (Gray 2010: 141). *Misery* uses the first movement of Tchaikovsky's Piano Concerto No. 1 during a montage sequence in which writer Paul Sheldon (James Caan) is forced to write a new novel day and night while imprisoned by fan Annie Wilkes (Kathy Bates). The music is punctuated by the sound of his typewriter and culminates with the arrival of a lightning storm. In the *Raising Dion* trailer, the same music, albeit synthesised, plays over a lightning storm that manifests as a creature. The intertextual connection of the Tchaikovsky concerto inflects even the fleeting shots of wonderment in the *Raising Dion* trailer with a sinister edge. The Netflix YouTube trailer for *Raising Dion* provides a subtle intertextual cue for adults, thereby aurally aligning the program with adult horror.

On the Netflix platform itself, *Raising Dion* was pitched to address potential adult and child viewers along different lines. As discussed throughout the book, promotional paratexts have been reworked in the SVOD era and are key to Netflix's external and internal address to audiences. The Netflix Cinematch algorithm determines what programs are featured in any given profile – and in what way – and as such Mareike Jenner suggests it ultimately restricts "choice by highlighting programmes it determines relevant to the viewer" (2018: 110). This is shaped by the user's past viewing patterns; those of other users watching similar content; Netflix's metadata tagging shared features across works – its "altgenres" (Madrigal 2014) – and finally "Netflix's own agenda and commercial priorities" (Alexander 2016: 90). Indeed, the latter would seem to frequently trump all other factors given the Netflix interface prioritises its original content by placing it at the top, frequently with autoplay trailers, and larger images (Van Esler 2020: 3, 11).

For this chapter, we assesed our own family feeds in 2019 and 2020, primarily on desktops and laptops. This provides broad indicators of the way the algorithm presented its "Family Watch Together TV" titles such as *Raising Dion* in the Netflix catalogue in this period, even as it needs to be acknowledged that the exact feed will vary between specific user profiles and shifts over time. As Johnson and Mike Van Esler point out, interfaces are ephemeral by nature (Johnson 2017: 123; Van Esler 2020: 2–3). This makes studying their role in managing the SVOD experience challenging but necessary (Van Esler 2020: 2, 13). One approach has been for scholars to use their own account feeds in SVOD platforms as case studies, while acknowledging the partiality of this sample and the wider structural issues that inform them (Johnson 2017: 125; Van Esler 2020: 11). For Netflix's family content, cataloguing and taglines for *Raising Dion* have varied between our adult and child feeds. On 28 November 2019, the thumbnail for *Raising Dion* shown on children's profiles used the keywords "Twists and Turns, Growing Pains, Sci-Fi". By contrast, over on our adult profiles, the program was described in terms of being "Heartfelt, Exciting, Action". In these examples, the overt genre reference to sci-fi was absent in the adult catalogues, as were the coming-of-age associations of "Growing Pains". These differences suggest the algorithm had determined adults and children would find different aspects of the program appealing based on their viewing patterns. Nonetheless, the overt genre descriptors were the same for both adults and children: "Kids' TV Shows, TV Shows Based on Comics, Family Watch Together TV".

These Netflix tags are often in flux even after a season begins. By 4 September 2020, "TV Dramas" appeared in *Raising Dion*'s genre list on both our adult and child profiles, and by 9 September 2020, "TV Action & Adventure", although not all of these alt-genres were displayed on all devices. On the children's profiles, "Family friendly" (20 October 2019) changed to "Family Watch Together TV" (19 November 2019). Similarly, "Growing Pains" (20 October 2019) was swapped for "Nerds Rule" (19 November 2019). The continual refinement even after a title has been released is indicative of the Netflix algorithm's attempts to sell its Original content by emphasising different elements that might appeal to customers based on their viewing patterns (in comparison with an amalgamation of other subscribers), which may similarly shift over time.

The alt-genre tags displayed in the thumbnails work with the tile images and trailers to address the potential viewer. In each profile, a feature program has a larger image and autoplay trailer at the head, while underneath a horizontal row of titles is featured under headings such as "Popular on Netflix", "Trending Now", and "Netflix Originals" (the latter displayed with larger thumbnails), before moving on to both established genres and Netflix's alt-genres. In one of the smaller thumbnails on 27 November 2020 across both adult and child profiles, *Raising Dion* was represented by Dion himself, dressed in a casual hoodie, with his closed eyes and hands raised, from which emanates a purple, swirling light. The fluorescent lighting behind him indicates it is an interior but unspecified location. As Kevin M. Flanagan suggests of Netflix's earlier incarnation as an online DVD postal service, the Netflix menu images rework a function once served by VHS and DVD cover art in the video store, using a simplified visual language to flag genre to help "anchor … meaning" (2010: 11). Indeed, on a large widescreen television the thumbnail tile image is approximately the size of a DVD cover, also matching the portrait orientation. This display replicates the effect of browsing at a video store, something that younger viewers will not have experienced (Johnson 2019: 114; Van Esler 2020: 8). Dion's presence in the thumbnail indicates the central importance of a child character, while the mysterious gaseous lights emanating from Dion's hands iconographically locate the program within telefantasy in broad terms. The low key lighting along with his closed eyes and serious frowning expression suggest a dramatic tone.

By contrast, the larger thumbnail image that appeared under "Netflix Originals" in the same time period on adult and child profiles showed Dion looking in wonder at his floating breakfast cereal and milk. The cereal thumbnail does not connote the scarier elements of the program that might be problematic for younger viewers despite the TV-G rating. It is not clear that Dion is the source of the miraculous floating cereal, and his wide eyes and open mouth convey his astonishment. The brighter colour palette – with the multicoloured cereal, Dion's blue and yellow t-shirt and royal blue jacket – along with the high key lighting create a more playful tone that emphasises Dion's awe and youthfulness. While both images visually, if succinctly, suggest the telefantasy genre, they are tonally distinct. This emphasises how "the goal of promotion is to produce multiple avenues of access to the text … in order to maximize its audience" (Klinger 1989: 10). The thumbnails, as paratexts, offer different selling points and in turn different expectations around the programs (Gray 2010). Given the thumbnails are contradictory in tone, they thereby situate "Family Watch Together TV" as an unstable category, particularly within the dark family telefantasy cycle. An alternate small thumbnail for *Raising Dion* in the horizontal stack, which appeared only in the children's profiles at this time, depicts Dion and Esperanza goofing it up together in a medium shot, an image that emphasises their youthfulness, friendship and the show's comedic tone. There are no readily evident markers of telefantasy within *this* thumbnail image at all, displaced to other paratextual elements such as tags and trailers.

Similarly, for the second season, we found that in our adult profiles, *Raising Dion* was advertised with an image of Dion and Brayden facing off with their respective powers evident from glowing lights emerging from their hands, clearly identifying the program's telefantasy premise (Figure 6.2).

By contrast, over on a children's profile, it showed a young Dion sitting at his school desk, a location primarily associated with his more everyday youthful friendship dramas, with no evident markers in the image of telefantasy at all (Figure 6.3). As noted, thumbnail images will change over time and according to different profiles, which means they may sometimes match across adult and child profiles, yet often diverge based on how the "artwork

Figure 6.2 Netflix desktop interface for *Raising Dion* as of July 2022 on an adult profile. Screenshot by authors.

Figure 6.3 Netflix desktop interface for *Raising Dion* as of July 2022 on a child profile. Screenshot by authors.

personalisation" software assesses previous viewing histories (Iqbal 2018). For viewers – both children and adults alike – this multiplicity of paratexts means complex and shifting pathways through which expectations are formed around a program such as *Raising Dion*, emphasising its telefantasy content on the one hand, while omitting this in favour of its child-centred story on the other. While Netflix's alt-genre tags and thumbnail images can be seen as the latest example of how distribution and exhibition practices strongly frame audience understandings of genre (Altman 1999: 33; Smith-Rowsey 2016: 64), these paratextual framings are multifaceted. As Johannes Mahlknecht notes, the "variety and complexity" of paratexts means that they need to be understood in their "interrelationship" with one another (2015: 423).

In the case of the larger "Netflix Originals" tile, during Season 1, hovering over the thumbnail images automatically brought up the same trailer released on YouTube, however, in the case of the smaller thumbnail, an alternate trailer played that captures the tonal variations of *Raising Dion* in more detail. As Kernan notes, trailers negotiate this tension between "providing as well as withholding knowledge" (2004: 54). This tension is more fraught for "Family Watch Together TV" and family viewing more broadly, where feedback in the digital public sphere suggests parents lean towards greater information that would be considered annoying spoilers for other viewers. In other words, "the desire to know" (Kernan 2004: 55) that trailers rely upon operates according to different, age-specific criteria for family viewing. This would suggest an impetus for greater disclosure in trailers, which is what we get in the interface *Raising Dion* trailer. This trailer starts with the breakfast cereal sequence, with Nicole's voice-over from a phone conversation explaining that Dion is, indeed, the source of the strange levitation. This fact is emphasised when Dion levitates water and fish from a lake using his hands. Onscreen taglines during the trailer here amplify the selling points: "Super-powered sci-fi – with monumental stakes – kinetic action – full of heroic feats – a touching drama – about motherly love". This constitutes a mild version of what Mahlknecht in his work on movie poster taglines terms a "deliberate isotopic breach" (2015: 421). The initial taglines establish the sci-fi genre in rather grand terms ("super-powered", "monumental") and emphasise "action" and "feats", while the final two phrases instead pivot to interpersonal domestic ties and emotion rather than action. While this is not necessarily incompatible with sci-fi per se, it marks a distinct shift in tone. The trailer briefly references Dion's difficulties fitting into a new school, his blossoming friendship with Esperanza, and his family's grief at the loss of his father. As Daniel Hesford (2013) suggests, trailers function as "samples of a product", but the connotations of any given sample will vary. Unlike the YouTube trailer, the interface-only *Raising Dion* trailer more clearly introduces the two worlds that Dion negotiates: the ordinary world challenges of home and school, and a sci-fi "secondary" world of superhuman abilities and storm creatures (Wolf 2012: 25). Here the threatening secondary world is momentarily lightened in tone by Dion's more childish characteristics from the primary world, as he makes his own superhero costume and declares himself to be "The Mind Mover!" In yet another version of the autoplay trailer, the footage remains the same, but without the taglines, even as the edited sequences operate under the same sci-fi/melodrama duality.

The multiplicity of paratexts around *Raising Dion* on the Netflix platform provide a streaming manifestation of Klinger's point that promotional strategies aim to provide "multiple avenues" to bring in a range of potential audience members in different if related ways (1989: 10). *Raising Dion* features under a wide range of alt-genre headers, including, on 9 September 2020, "Superheroes", "Black Stories", "Black Stories for Families" and "Watch with the Family TV", a variation on "Family Watch Together TV". As noted in Chapter 1, the rationale for why a title might appear in any given person's feed might be overtly flagged by the alt-genre tags, or may, by contrast, remain hidden and untagged, "known" only to the algorithm (Madrigal 2014). Family viewing upsets this approach. What an individual watches alone might overlap with or differ completely from what they watch with the rest of the family, as we noted in the case of our interviews with Breanna and her son Dylan. The multiple paratextual appeals across text and image are designed to target different viewers in different ways, but who exactly they are appealing to for shared family viewing remains opaque. If the home page for a given profile is skewed most heavily towards individual viewing, a parent can still search for intergenerational family viewing by entering search terms that may yield varying results. In 2014, Netflix vice president of product innovation Todd Yellin noted the algorithm can sometimes forge unexpected connections: "These ghosts in the machine are always going to be a by-product of the complexity. And sometimes we call it a bug and sometimes we call it a feature" (quoted in Madrigal 2014). For example, in October 2020, searching "Black stories for families" in our adult profiles brought up *Raising Dion* as well as a range of other programs, genres, and classifications, including the Original Netflix telefantasy titles *See You Yesterday* (2019, TV-MA) and *Kipo and the age of the wonderbeasts* (2020, TV-Y7). The algorithm recommends a telefantasy title rated TV-MA that is, therefore, "intended to be viewed by mature, adult audiences and may be unsuitable for children under 17" (FCC 2019), highlighting the slippery construction of "families" on the platform and the difficulties of telefantasy featuring young protagonists, in which the age of the central character does not always align with the intended audience.

As Netflix re-classifies its content for other territories, "Family Watch Together TV" has spread into older classification ratings. Both *Lost in Space* (2018–, TV-PG, see Chapter 4) and *The Dark Crystal: Age of Resistance* (2019–, TV-PG, see Chapter 5) were rated at the more teen-oriented classification M in Australia where we reside, and will therefore not appear in children's profiles if ratings-based parental restrictions have been put in place on their account. Instead, these programs are targeted at parents through Netflix's alt-genres and thumbnail tags. Both programs frequently appear alongside *Raising Dion*, given they share the "Family Watch Together TV" tag and telefantasy connections.

These variations demonstrate how the Netflix algorithm "curates" the catalogue around *Raising Dion* in ways that vary widely, impacting the paratextual framing of the program itself as well as the type of program the viewer might watch next. Amanda Lotz suggests,

> Although selecting content is a key task of both channels and portals, nonlinear access distinguishes portals from their channel brethren by freeing them from the task of scheduling. Portals' primary task might be better regarded as that of curation ... portals are characterized by more than just their program content, but also by the features of their interface and capabilities they offer their viewers ... and the use experience of a single portal varies among viewers. (2017: location 243)

Lisa Perks conceptualises the movement through these curated portals or "gateways" as "entrance flow" (2014: xxiii, xxiv). Jenner suggests this flow is essential for Netflix's business model, in that the viewer is more likely to keep watching adjacent and recommended titles rather than cancelling a subscription after a particular show (2018: 127). We disagree with Jenner that it necessarily "guarantees viewers 'stay tuned'" (2018: 127), but the intention is certainly to encourage it.

The entrance flow is what makes the algorithmic curation of dark family telefantasy programs such as *Raising Dion* a site of conflict around family viewing. *Raising Dion* can appear alongside similarly tagged programs such as *See You Yesterday* ("Black stories for families" and "Exciting", TV-MA), *Locke & Key* ("TV Dramas" and "Fantasy TV Shows", TV-14), *Chilling Adventures of Sabrina* ("TV Shows Based on Comics", TV-14), *Rim of the World* ("Exciting" and "Sci-Fi", TV-14), and *Stranger Things* ("Exciting" and "Sci-Fi", TV-14). While the classifications would normally be key here in shaping family viewing choices, for SVODs such as Netflix, classifications jostle with the pull of entrance flow – including the influence of autoplay trailers and the tendency of most viewers to accept recommendations. These telefantasy programs frequently sitting next to *Raising Dion* each feature adolescent and teenage protagonists yet have drawn controversy around perceived inappropriate content.

The Program Next Door

The programs just next door to *Raising Dion* on the interface vary across Netflix's alt-genre tags and profiles at different times, such that entrance flow creates a number of potential encouraged pathways through the catalogue. This is a revised streaming manifestation of how older media paratexts encourage specific viewing journeys across texts (Baker 2018: 84). In the case of Netflix's Original telefantasy, characters' age becomes a key point of contention around the interface catalogue. Linda Sheldon has shown that children of all ages prefer television programs with characters either their own age or "a few years older" (1998: 85–6). *Common Sense Media* suggested *Raising Dion* was suited to viewers 11+, a good three years older than its protagonist. Parents on average recommended 11+ and children 10+ but the individual recommendations varied widely from 2+ to 18+ from parents and 5+ to 16+ from children. For many, then, there is a mismatch between the child on the screen and the child (or indeed adult) who should be watching. As discussed in Chapters 1 and 2, the debate around the suitability and viewing age of science fiction, fantasy, and (in particular) horror pre-dates the streaming era, but finds new articulation for SVODs given the combination of entrance flow, paratexts, and the visual interconnection of titles through the interface catalogue. While none of the programs discussed in this section are tagged as "Family Watch Together TV", their paratextual connections with *Raising Dion* on the Netflix interface encourage customers to draw links between them, and perhaps select them "next up" thanks to an intersecting range of tags that position them as recommended programs on the interface, or via auto-play.

See You Yesterday is paratextually linked in the Netflix algorithm to *Raising Dion* by virtue of being a science fiction story with young protagonists that is "exciting" and one of their "Black stories for families", but at the higher TV-MA classification. As Madrigal (2014) notes in her interview with Netflix's Todd Yellin, there may be other intersections that are tagged within the system but are not necessarily overtly displayed on the feed. Produced by Spike Lee and directed by his former student Stefon Bristola, the film follows two talented African American teens, CJ (Eden Duncan-Smith), and Sebastian (Dante Crichlow), as they develop a functioning time travel machine for a science project. At the beginning of the first YouTube trailer for *See You Yesterday* released on 22 April 2019, CJ speculates their science project will get them into "Stanford, Morehouse, Spelman" over the sounds of Tenor Saw's 1985 dancehall reggae hit "Ring the Alarm". At 30 seconds in, the tone suddenly shifts from this science fiction-inflected narrative of "goin' places". The Saw track abruptly stops as the NYPD pull over CJ's brother Calvin (Brian Astro Bradley). As Calvin pulls out his mobile phone, the police take aim, by implication mistakenly believing him to be armed. The gunshot is heard over footage of a coffin. This event provides a new motivation to get the time machine working: to prevent Calvin's murder. The taglines "go back – move forward – change the world" stress the way this personal motivation has larger cultural implications, which Netflix's content tagging – initially done by humans and then linked in the system by the computer algorithm – indicates is a pertinent talking point for families. Indeed, in this case the age of the high school juniors on screen in *See You Yesterday* (2019) approximately matches Netflix's recommended age for viewers.

As was the case with *Raising Dion*, the Netflix platform features the YouTube trailer but also an alternate version that autoplays when the thumbnail is selected for "more info", shifting the emphasis and integrating new intertextual connections. In this version, the trailer opens with Calvin's death, as a news reporter's voice over proclaims, "Thursday evening, a 19-year-old Black teen was allegedly shot and killed by a NYPD officer". Over a montage, the Priest (Samuel Smith) at Calvin's funeral asks, "Where is the justice for our sons and our daughters and our community?" As such, in this trailer the murder appears to be CJ's primary motivation for developing the time travel machine in the first place, rather than getting into a good college on her way to a successful science career. Indeed, the way the trailer is cut implies she only builds the machine after Calvin's death in order to prevent it. Saw's reggae track is absent, the soundtrack instead emphasising suspense from the outset. Just as the variations of *Raising Dion*'s thumbnail images recommend the show along different lines, marketing paratexts such as trailers similarly encourage audiences "decode" a program's "genre, style, tone" in a particular way (Gray 2010: 61–2). The interface trailer largely emphasises the grittier social justice issues, while the YouTube trailer balances this with the teen high school narrative.

However, an intertextual reference in the interface trailer complicates this reading and the perceived audience. For adults who recognise Michael J. Fox in a cameo appearance as the teens' teacher, the film trailer nostalgically harks back to the 1985 film *Back to the Future* (Robert Zemeckis), a comedy sci-fi film in which time travel threatens the existence of the protagonist himself. Fox's character in the 1980s film creates a temporal paradox during a time travel trip to 1955, when he inadvertently lets it slip that Black diner worker Goldie Wilson (Donald Fullilove) will become mayor in the future. This gives Goldie the idea in the first place. Although Goldie's boss Lou (Norman Alden) counters, "A colored mayor. That'll be the day", the audience has already seen this future fulfilled in 1985. In *See You Yesterday*, Fox's character can be seen reading Octavia E. Butler's book *Kindred* (1979), a time travel novel that confronts slavery in the Antebellum South, and narrativises the difficulties of forging a future that both acknowledges and moves on from that past. These intertextual references to time travel commentaries on race relations in the United States intersect with CJ's continued attempts to go back in time to save her unarmed brother Calvin from being shot by police. Controversially, the plot is never resolved. Alexis Jones suggests,

> CJ's struggle to change *her* past represents our struggle as a country to change *ours* – to change our history of racism, prejudice and violence … The entire movie, CJ and the audience are so focused on the past – on whether or not she'll be able to jump back in time and save her brother's life – that we ignore the possibility of the future. (2019)

The platform trailer has a more extensive range of taglines: "A poignant drama – about the power of loss – an intimate thriller – full of twists and turns – thought-provoking sci-fi – that is gritty and personal". Despite the "gritty" tagline, the presence of Michael J. Fox in the platform's trailer did lead some parents to assume that it would be a diverse take on *Back to the Future* more suitable for younger family viewing (Tamm12276 2019). This demonstrates how actors in paratexts – and as paratexts – impact the audience's expectations of a text (Hesford 2013; Klecker 2015: 405), in ways that may be inflected generationally.

This generational difference played out more forcefully in the case of *Chilling Adventures of Sabrina*, based around a 16-year-old half-witch whose character originated in the *Archie* comics back in 1962. *Chilling Adventures of Sabrina* is linked to *Raising Dion* in the Netflix catalogue via "TV Shows Based on Comics" and as such the two shows can appear alongside one another on the interface. *Sabrina* was an in-house Netflix production greenlit following CW's *Riverdale* (2017–), which Netflix distributes worldwide. Parents who fondly remember the earlier comedy animated *Sabrina* programs (*The Archie Show* 1968–69, *Sabrina the Teenage Witch* 1971–1974, *Sabrina The Animated Series* 1999–2000) and sitcom (*Sabrina, the Teenage Witch* 1996–2003) were frequently aghast at the Netflix program's horror gore content, satanism, and sexuality (Anastasiap7 2019; Jonathon Wilder 2020). This nostalgic shock highlights the way *Chilling Adventures* exposes and mediates the shift in family fantasy from broadcast television to SVODs such as Netflix. While child reviewers on *Common Sense Media* largely agreed with Netflix's TV-14 rating for *Chilling Adventures of Sabrina*, by contrast parents were split, many asserting it was 18+ but averaging out to 15+. As Sean Tiffee and Janie Filoteo note, "although *Chilling Adventures* is a reboot of a show aimed at a younger audience, it is still a horror story" (2020: 337). As noted earlier, horror intended for children is considered inherently culturally troubling (Balanzategui 2018a; Lester 2016; 2021), even at the higher age bracket than *Raising Dion*.

The trailer for Season 1 of *Chilling Adventures* struck a seemingly light tone that connected with the earlier programs even as it hints at horror content. Sabrina's (Kiernan Shipka) boyfriend Harvey (Ross Lynch) playfully proclaims "They're coming to get you, Barbara!" in a mock re-enactment of the famous line from zombie cult film *Night of the Living Dead* (George A. Romero 1968). Once inside her archetypally spooky house, Sabrina magically turns on Neil Sedaka's 1961 pop song "Happy Birthday Sweet Sixteen", referencing the character's comic book origins from the 1960s as she dances up the stairs. While the trailer depicts Sabrina resisting a "dark baptism", it ends by connecting horror back to humour via the pop song. Cousin Ambrose (Chance Perdomo) asks Sabrina's aunt Zelda Spellman (Miranda Otto) of the whereabouts of Aunt Hilda (Lucy Davis). Zelda responds, "She annoyed me. So, I killed her and buried her in the yard". The trailer cuts to night, as Hilda's arm is shown emerging from her grave to the upbeat xylophone at the end of the Sedaka pop song. Tonally, this gag seems far removed from Netflix's interface description of the show as "Chilling, Scary, Dark", and the rating clarification at the beginning of the program declaring it features "Strong Violence, Strong Blood and Gore, Strong Horror Themes". Instead, *Chilling* in the series name seems, in the trailer, to be linked to a parodic take on horror.

Nonetheless, the *Night of the Living Dead* reference ties to executive producer Roberto Aguirre Sacasa's desire to evoke not the earlier *Sabrina* programs but rather make "a dark horror version … like *The Exorcist* and *Rosemary's Baby* and all those great satanic horror movies from the 1960s and 1970s" (quoted in Tiffee and Filoteo 2020: 328; see also Henesy 2021: 1149–1150). In this specific case, parents must mentally assemble not only the "interrelationship" between various paratexts (Mahlknecht 2015: 423) around a show such as *Chilling Adventures*, including its trailer, tagging, and alignment with younger classified material such as *Raising Dion* in the Netflix interface, but also its intertextual references that are based less on generational nostalgia per se than fan genre knowledge that may cut across several age groups.

While the trailer for *Chilling Adventures* flags its intertextual genre intentions yet underplays the gore that appears in the show itself, the retro-inspired science fiction film *Rim of the World* drew the ire of parents for featuring 13-year-old protagonists yet omitting from the trailer the continual sexual references and profanity that would appear in the Netflix Original film. The film depicts the adventures of four young teens at a summer camp who end up in possession of a key to the satellite defence system that will help thwart an alien invasion, and set out on an apocalyptic road trip to get it to a NASA facility. The film is linked in the Netflix catalogue with the tags "Exciting" and "Sci-Fi". Further, like *Raising Dion*, the Netflix production casts more diversely with a Black, White, Latino, and Asian child. However, as reviewers pointed out, the characters in *Rim of the World* are played out in mostly disappointing stereotypes (Allen 2019). Although the film has a contemporary setting, it conspires to get the teens off their phones and on to Mongoose BMX bikes, such that it becomes reminiscent of 1980s youth films such as *E.T.* (Steven Spielberg 1982) or *Goonies* (Richard Donner 1985), as well as tapping into the retro 1980s trend in part initiated by *Stranger Things* that draws upon those same texts (Taurino 2019: 11, see Chapter 2). Similarly, the kitchen scene from *Jurassic Park* (Steven Spielberg 1993) is recreated with aliens in the place of dinosaurs, which notably was a scene recreated in the dark family telefantasy show explored in Chapter 3, *Lost in Space*. Thus, as is common in the dark family telefantasy cycle – with *The Dark Crystal: Age of Resistance* also remediating a specific mode of dark family fantasy film from the 1980s – *The Rim of The World* emphasises nostalgia for beloved family fantasy films from the 1980s and 1990s. Iconographically, the YouTube trailer for *Rim of the World* briefly depicts these nostalgic reference points, situating it within a science fiction pedigree. By contrast, the trailer omits the salty language in the film that 13-year-olds may well use but which made many *Common Sense Media* parents distinctly uncomfortable in family viewing. As Kernan suggests, "trailers generate promotional metanarratives that display assumptions about the implied audiences for the films they promote" (2004: 61).

Netflix rated *Rim of the World* TV-14 in the United States, and as such it "may be unsuitable for children under 14". The protagonists are one year younger than this (and often look younger on screen). As *Common Sense Media* reviewer Barbara Shulgasser-Parker notes, the tendency for children to like watching characters their own age or "a few years older" creates difficulties for *Rim of the World* in that "it's unlikely parents will want their 10-year-olds asking them for definitions of 'Lithuanian smoothie' or 'c--k block'" (Sheldon 1998: 85–6, Shulgasser-Parker 2019). Though not overtly tagged as family viewing by the Netflix algorithm in our feeds (in favour of "Coming-of-age, Teen Movies, Action & Adventure, Sci-Fi Fantasy"), it can (and often does) nonetheless appear alongside *Raising Dion* on the interface, and the age of the protagonists combined with its deliberate intertextual references to family sci-fi classics create a paratextual mismatch, troubling its use of nostalgia around family viewing.

Finally, *Locke & Key* features the adventures of the Locke children, elementary school age Bode Locke (Jackson Robert Scott) and high school siblings Kinsey (Emilia Jones) and Tyler (Connor Jessup), as the try to recover from the murder of their father and settle into the Gothic Locke ancestral home, Key House. This soon reveals itself to be the site of magical keys and a murderous, mysterious resident, the Well Lady. *Locke & Key* is linked to, and as a result can appear alongside, *Raising Dion* in our Netflix catalogue by the genre tags "TV Dramas" and "Fantasy TV Shows". As Madrigal (2014) notes, the placement of a program in a user's Netflix feed may have several points of connection with their previous viewing without necessarily being overtly flagged by the alt-genre tags. Like *Raising Dion*, the show features young protagonists and authentic casting of a disabled character, in this case double amputee Eric Graise as Tyler's acquaintance Logan Calloway. Also, like *Raising Dion*, *Locke & Key* is a comic book adaptation, being loosely based on the much grimmer set of IDW horror comic books written by Joe Hill, son of authors Stephen and Tabitha King. The casting of Jackson Robert Scott makes a further intertextual link with Stephen King, as the actor is best known for playing Georgie in Andy Muschietti's *It* (2017). Meredith Averill (*The Haunting of Hill House* 2018), Aaron Eli Coleite (*Heroes* 2006–2010) and Carlton Cuse (*Lost* 2004–2010, *Bates Motel* 2013–2017) came on board as showrunners for the Netflix production.

Despite this horror pedigree, the program's family orientation was criticised as being too derivative, "a specific kind of Netflix algorithm-based approach in some of the most glaring ways" (Greene 2020). As Emma Grey Ellis (2020) notes:

> The original *Locke & Key* is a horror comic. The Netflix show is more of an occasionally scary fantasy story … At many points throughout *Locke & Key*, you can feel Netflix trying to tweak the story to suit its

> successful show recipe: a hefty pinch of *The Haunting of Hill House* in its setting and family dysfunction, a dash of *Stranger Things* for whole-family appeal, a heaping tablespoon of *The Chilling Adventures of Sabrina* for supernatural teenage drama.

Similarly, Caroline Framke describes the program as an algorithmic combination of *A Series of Unfortunate Events* plus *Stranger Things* plus Netflix's CW teen shows, an approach that "comes as an unpleasant shock" to fans of the much creepier horror comic book (2020). In this instance, the YouTube trailer actually overplays the potential horror violence of *Locke & Key*, briefly showing Kinsey's face in dripping blood in what is revealed in the program to be food dye on set for a cheap horror film her friends are making. Season 1 deaths are notably bloodless, and it is only in Season 2 that there is any onscreen blood and gore at all, and even then it is relatively fleeting.

While the horror elements are clearly toned down for a family audience, particularly in Season 1, parents nonetheless cautioned, "don't let the fact that there is a little kid in this show trick you into thinking it's appropriate for viewers of that same age" (BinaryBlues 2020). Parents thought it may still be too scary for younger children in the family, in keeping with the TV-14 rating (Daddy 1975 [2020]). *Locke & Key* adds elements aimed at older teens, particularly a controversial sex scene in episode two featuring the Well Lady that starts with sexualised choking and ends with murder. One parent noted:

> I was confused what age demo the target audience is … I guess everyone has a different idea of what is considered 'family friendly' but for me, a girl telling a guy to choke her immediately disqualifies the show from that category. (AptlyNamed 2020)

Similarly, another parent commented, "it's very odd and feels like this show doesn't have an audience. Maybe it's trying to be both a *Stranger Things* and a *Goosebumps* at the same time" (BinaryBlues 2020). These commentaries around *Locke & Key* reveal a tension in the way that *Stranger Things* is situated as a contradictory touchstone, both in terms of "whole family appeal" (Ellis 2020) or conversely as a more adult alternative to the explicitly child-oriented *Goosebumps*, reinforcing the fluid and ambivalent way the dark family telefantasy genre cycle is positioned in relation to children and families. Just as has occurred with the release of each *Stranger Things* season, several parents on *Common Sense Media* expressed their confusion as to what the target age of the audience for *Locke & Key* was intended to be, being insufficiently scary for older viewers but sporadically too sexual for younger viewers. While a similar uncertainty around intended audience can be seen in the reception of *Raising Dion*, parents frequently mediate those concerns around its intergenerational teachable moments, a discourse not found in the case of *Locke & Key*, suggesting a hierarchy of concerns where discussion of sexual activity is deemed a step too far for family viewing.

Conclusion

While *Raising Dion* is tagged as "Family Watch Together TV" and *Locke & Key* is not, they appear together as "Fantasy TV Shows". Indeed, a search for *Locke & Key* in a classification-restricted child's profile frequently brings up instead … *Raising Dion*. This is also true of *See You Yesterday* and *Rim of the World*. Our combined Netflix feeds can only be broadly indicative of the way the Netflix algorithm works and the interface experience it produces. It is nonetheless important to analyse this changeable and ephemeral interface as a key paratextual frame to how Netflix customers are encouraged to conceptualise and connect its content before seeing the shows themselves. For telefantasy programs featuring young protagonists, a clear demarcation can occur on child feeds where they have classification-based parental restrictions in place. However, over on parents' feeds, "Family Watch Together TV" such as *Raising Dion* can lead to related telefantasy with young characters that is either sexier or creepier. The entrance flow of the interface creates moments of alarm for parents who have been at least partly trained both by the intergenerational success of *Stranger Things* and the design of the Netflix interface to pay more attention to alt-genre paratextual tags than aged-based classifications. In turn, as Netflix seeks to draw new subscribers through external paratexts such as YouTube trailers, tonal variations between the trailer and the program itself have created parental concern around what in the age of SVODs can really be considered "Family Watch Together TV".

Despite the fact that the first season of *Raising Dion* was Netflix's number one rating "Kids & Family Series" of 2019 (Netflix Family 2019), and its second season in 2022 went to number one across all categories in the United States and number two globally (McLaren 2022), the program was still cancelled. Season 2 left on a cliff-hanger with Pat willingly accepting back the Crooked Man energy as a set up for a third season (Leigh 2022). As Marc McLaren (2022) notes, as Netflix subscriptions fall,

> we heard earlier this week that Netflix spent a reported $30m per episode on *Stranger Things* season 4; that's $270m in total if true, which could possibly have impacted decisions on what other shows to cancel … leaving us with more questions than answers and increasingly wondering whether there's any point in watching a new series on Netflix.

As we noted in Chapter 1, a genre cycle is, by definition, produced during "a limited period of time" (Grindon 2012: 44) and functions as a form of company branding (Altman 1999: 120). The premature cancellation of otherwise ostensibly successful programs such as the award-winning *Age of Resistance* and the ratings-topping *Raising Dion* suggests Netflix's dark family telefantasy cycle may be either winding down or advancing in a new direction that increasingly does away with legacy media's frameworks and expectations around child appropriateness within the family demographic. As we will address in the final chapter of this book, it is notable that Netflix has concentrated funds amidst a post-lockdown subscription drop into *Stranger Things*, the flagship show of both the dark family telefantasy cycle and of Netflix as a whole, and the show which in large part prompted the cycle in the first place.

Notes

1 Henson also pointed out that the team of producers on the show were all women (Holden 2019).
2 Notably, in Season 4, it is strongly implied that central child-now-teen character Will may be gay.

7 New Frontiers in Family Viewing from *Stranger Things* to *Squid Game*

This book has presented the story of Netflix's "Family Watch Together TV" interface label and catalogue category – and, more specifically, the story of this category's flagship content type, the dark family telefantasy genre cycle. These high budget and high profile shows, released on the platform between 2016 and 2022, contributed to the reinvention of Netflix's brand identity at a moment when it was being repositioned as not *just* an online, on-demand, algorithmic screen distributor but also as a content creator and both a transnational and global TV network (Lobato 2019: 50). As we have outlined, a key but overlooked component of this period of transition has been Netflix's pivot to family television. This manoeuvre is a challenging one, because it involves harnessing nostalgia for content types and viewing modes associated with the very media forms the SVOD strategically supersedes – cable and broadcast television. However, in tension with such nostalgia is this genre cycle's performative dismissal of the distribution architectures and regulatory structures that traditionally buttress family content on linear television, including scheduling – which places family television at particular times of day and situates it alongside adjacent child and family-friendly programs – classifications, and child and family appropriate advertising. It is in this context that "Family Watch Together TV" operates as a *directive*: this interface label indicates how this content is designed to be viewed, even as the flagship shows within this category push the boundaries of acceptable family fare via dark sci-fi, fantasy, and horror.

This book has charted the development of the dark family telefantasy genre cycle in chronological order, from *Stranger Things* (2016-) to *Raising Dion* (2019–2022), as representative of a transformational juncture for Netflix and the broader SVOD ecology. While the shows themselves tend to be ambiguous in their demographic positioning, their association with the "Family Watch Together TV" tag – and their textual and paratextual commitment to an intergenerational dynamic – solicits a specific and nostalgic type of "family" viewing. Despite the family focus of this strategy, the cycle seeks to appeal to broad audiences, including adults without children, through prestige aesthetics and dark telefantasy content. Netflix's dark family telefantasy programs thus continue the trend of Quality Telefantasy

DOI: 10.4324/9781003223498-7

previously outlined by Lynch (2022), with influential examples including *Game of Thrones* and *The Walking Dead*. However, the dark family telefantasy genre cycle modulates and moderates such appeals to Quality to emphasise their child and family orientation. Such a balancing act between dark telefantasy, Quality, and family viewing amounts to a "Netflixification" of family television that reimagines intergenerational, communal television viewing for the SVOD era.

SVOD Family Television and the "Streaming Wars"

Netflix's experimentation with family television emerged at the precipice of a new period of maturity for the SVOD ecology, and children's and family television has become a key site of competition as the market becomes more crowded and household SVOD subscriptions increasingly commonplace. Derek Johnson (2018b) has outlined the significance of children's content to the strategy of Amazon Prime, one of Netflix's major competitors. Furthermore, in late 2019, Disney+ launched in the US, Canada, the Netherlands, Australia, New Zealand, and Puerto Rico, later expanding across Latin America, Europe, and Asia-Pacific. In keeping with Disney's well-established brand, the service was positioned as an SVOD especially for families – filling a distinct gap in the marketplace – with Disney CEO Bob Iger gesturing to Disney+'s laser focus on family-friendly material prior to the platform's launch (quoted in Littleton 2018). This point was subsequently reinforced by Disney executives at the company's bi-annual D23 expo months before the SVOD's launch: one representative explained that Disney+ would host *no* explicitly adult-oriented content as the catalogue "will all be PG-13 or softer" (quoted in Bonomolo 2019).

While at launch Disney+ hosted only family and child-oriented content, it did later include adult content, much of it organised under a separate content hub, "Star", launched in 2021. This enabled the SVOD to include the wealth of adult content that came with the conglomerate's acquisition of 20th/21st Century Fox. As Baker and Balanzategui have previously outlined, despite this development "Disney+'s catalogue organisation and interface aesthetics illuminate how the company is using its SVOD service to curate its brand identity around family content" (2022). Flagship Disney+ original programs such as *The Mandalorian* (2019-) indicate how elements of the Netflix dark family telefantasy approach is being emulated by Disney's SVOD. As we have previously argued (Baker et al 2020), *The Mandalorian* "encourages intergenerational modes of audience engagement in similar ways to the Netflix Originals" by harnessing nostalgia and fandom for both the *Star Wars* and Disney brands, in so doing encouraging adult guardians to introduce their children to a fantasy world that veers into more dark and violent territory than they otherwise might be comfortable with. As such, as in the Netflix shows analysed throughout our book, there has been "ambiguity and ambivalence" surrounding *The Mandalorian*'s family orientation

(Baker et al 2020). Like the Netflix Originals we have addressed, Disney+'s flagship show at launch – a dark telefantasy series with creative links to nostalgically beloved content and very high production values – facilitates prioritisation of the family audience balanced with broader appeal to adults without children.

Thus, while Disney+'s family orientation was clear-cut in the pre-launch framing by Disney executives and in the platform's design and catalogue at launch, *The Mandalorian* troubled straightforward alignments with family content in similar ways to Netflix's "Family Watch Together TV". Upon its release weeks after the platform's launch, *The Mandalorian* was positioned in the interface and in paratextual commentary as Disney+'s "headlining" show (Katz 2019). Yet comments on *Common Sense Media* from child and parent reviewers reflecting on its violent and scary elements (Baker et al 2020) highlight how *The Mandalorian* continues Netflix's successful strategy around "edgy" and dark family telefantasy that pushes the boundaries of child appropriateness. Notably, much of the journalistic commentary around the show picks up on this, describing the success of *The Mandalorian* in comparison to or competition with *Stranger Things*. For instance, Katz (2019) writes how "*The Mandalorian*'s surge has ended *Stranger Things*' 21-week reign as America's most in-demand digital exclusive series". Similarly, Knoop (2020) opens his article by asking "who would win in a fight? Eleven from *Stranger Things* or the adorable Baby Yoda from *The Mandalorian*? It looks like Mando has finally overtaken the kids of Hawkins". This "head-to-head" between these two flagship dark family telefantasy shows on competing SVODs is played out in different ways across a wide range of journalistic commentary (Chavez 2019; Clark 2019b; Comtois 2019; Snowden 2019). Thus, key to discourse around the "streaming wars" at this point in time between Netflix and Disney+ as major international players in the SVOD ecology was the battle between each SVOD's approach to dark family telefantasy content – discourse reflective of how crucial such shows are to the strategies and brand identities of each service. That the streaming wars were played out via dark family telefantasy further reinforces how such content has driven the period of transformational tension and transition represented by the mainstreaming of SVODs in global entertainment habits.

Thus, Netflix's dark family telefantasy cycle has navigated the cultural and industrial renegotiation of not just Netflix itself, but of SVOD platforms more broadly in the marketplace. Dark family telefantasy programs such as *Stranger Things* have contributed to a movement away from SVODs operating and being perceived as disruptive innovators offering algorithmically personalised content recommendations, and towards the era of SVODs functioning as mainstream content providers catering to family audiences. This period of transformative definitional tension has entered a new phase with the rise of family focused competitors like Disney+. In this context in which definitions of family television are in flux, even Disney+'s commitment to the family market has become increasingly ambivalent since the platform launched (see Baker and Balanzategui, 2022, for further detail). This indicates that after an initial period in which SVODs sought to prove their worth to families by offering intergenerational viewing pleasures, what it means to cater to families is evolving in distinctively SVOD-specific ways. In the remainder of this concluding chapter, we consider this next phase of Netflix's dark family telefantasy genre cycle.

Where to Next for "Family Watch Together TV": *Stranger Things 4*

As Grindon notes, a proprietary genre cycle operates for a "limited" time period (2012: 44). From 2016 to 2022, Netflix's dark family telefantasy was key to its branding of "Family Watch Together TV" and helped shape the public discourse around family telefantasy on its new rival Disney+. Nonetheless, Netflix lost subscribers for the first time in April 2022, not coincidentally also the same month when it cancelled *Raising Dion* after two seasons, a show that had been its top family program, and even at one point its top show of any genre (McLaren 2022; Pallotta 2022). Netflix cancelled a swathe of programs at this time, many of them after only one or two seasons (Spencer 2022). By August 2022, Disney+ as an individual streaming service still lagged behind Netflix (Iqbal 2022). Even though the Walt Disney company made headlines for ostensibly larger subscriptions, this was only when combining its different streaming services, namely Disney+, Hulu, and ESPN (Sweney 2022). Netflix responded to the rising fortunes of Disney+ by consolidating considerable funds into the program that initiated the dark family telefantasy cycle in the first place: *Stranger Things*. The fourth season of *Stranger Things* was widely hailed as stemming the loss of subscribers, with Netflix proclaiming: "In its first four weeks, *Stranger Things* season four generated 1.3 billion hours viewed, making it our biggest season of English [language] TV ever" (quoted in Pallotta 2022).

As such, in 2022, *Stranger Things* continues to operate as Netflix's flagship product, navigating the SVOD's identity shift post 2016 via deep connections between the show and Netflix's brands. For instance, for Season 4, the famous Netflix "N" logo and sonic pulsing "Tudum" accompaniment that one encounters whenever they open the app or watch Netflix Original content were amended to align with *Stranger Things*' diegetic world. Usually seen before a black background, the red "N" displayed at the beginning of each episode is surrounded by red crashing lightning and a sinister underlying juddering noise that crescendos into the monstrous screeching typical of *Stranger Things*' alternate-dimensional, "Upside Down" creatures. This logo customisation highlights the distinctive aesthetic similarities between the Upside Down, which is shrouded in red and black, and Netflix's own red and black branding, as seen in its interface design as well as the logo. Netflix and *Stranger Things* thereby become branded together.

This logo customisation strategy is also reminiscent of the customised logos that became prevalent in blockbusters of the 1990s and early 2000s (Grainge 2008: 70–71), including another influential family entertainment franchise: Harry Potter. As Noel Brown notes, the "'darkness' and moral ambiguity" of the later Potter films contributed to expanding the notion of a "family film" at the end of the first decade of the 21st century (2018: 56–57), while in turn Warner Bros. harnessed the popularity of the franchise by melding logos. In this case, an immersive version of the Warner Bros. logo was used before each Harry Potter film (with the exception of the first film, which used the traditional logo). Each "WB" logo was folded into the film's diegetic world and positioned as a portal into the narrative with a range of effects, from clouds, to fog, magic sparks, lightning, and rust, thus highlighting the evolving intersections between the Harry Potter and Warner Bros.' brands. Netflix's own customised logo positions *Stranger Things* as its tentpole series, and implicitly harks back to Harry Potter's dark family fantasy footsteps. As art and design commentator Daniel Piper notes, "Netflix isn't known for playing with its visual identity" (2022), its last big makeover being the rainbow treatment in 2019 in its diversity push, analysed in the previous chapter. Fans across social media read the latest title-specific *Stranger Things* logo customisation as evidence that such treatment "remains solely reserved for its biggest blockbuster" (Piper 2022). This development came as Netflix concentrated more of its funds into *Stranger Things*, streamlining its portfolio and simplifying its branding.

It is notable that Piper uses the cinematic term "blockbuster" to describe *Stranger Things 4*, which he picks up from the fan discourse he canvasses. Netflix has sought to situate both its binge model of spectatorship and its quality Original programs through ostensible similarities with both the novel and the film as markers of cultural prestige since the inception of these strategies (Baker 2017: 46). As several scholars have noted, the "cinematic TV" comparison is often used in popular discourse in quite simplistic terms to mean television that employs complex, high-cost visual strategies (Baker 2017: 45; Jaramillo 2013: 67; Lury 2005a: 14; Mills 2013: 64; Wheatley 2016: 4–5). This is despite television's own history of visual spectacle (Wheatley 2016: 5), particularly in recent years with the development of Quality Telefantasy (Lynch 2022: 29). Nonetheless, Netflix's huge expenditure on *Stranger Things 4* reignited the public comparisons with film, marking a return to an earlier branding discourse, while inviting overt comparisons with blockbusters in particular (Chaney 2022; Press 2022; Sharf 2022). *Stranger Things 4* reportedly cost $30 million per episode (Casale 2022) and accordingly had elaborate, high quality, and oft-used CGI that rivalled the quality of recent blockbuster movies. The show's high budget and production quality was frequently highlighted in paratextual commentary (Roman 2022; Stranger Universe 2022), especially as the total cost for the series, a reported US $270 million, puts the budget in line with major Hollywood blockbusters, the benchmark for which are films in the Marvel Cinematic

Universe (MCU): the budget of *Thor: Love and Thunder* (Waititi, 2022) for instance, was US $250 million. Most episodes in *Stranger Things 4* were between 70 and 90 minutes long, pushing them increasingly closer to cinematic runtime expectations, with the final episode running to two-and-a-half hours long – which also aligns with the lengthy runtimes of recent films from the MCU.

As well as positioning the Netflix Original show in relation to these culturally impactful blockbuster family film franchises, this episode composition strategy also works with and extends Netflix's binge-viewing and on-demand affordances: Netflix does not have to set tight limits around episode lengths as broadcast and cable television do to accord with scheduling and associated advertising requirements (Baker 2017: 41). Furthermore, the season title conventions – *Stranger Things 2*, *Stranger Things 3*, and *Stranger Things 4* – position each season as though it were a "sequel" in an evolving film franchise, connecting with long-form storytelling conventions of family franchise cinema such as the MCU, Star Wars, and Harry Potter. While we do not seek to repeat thoroughly worked through and problematic aesthetic hierarchies between cinema and television, as the dark family telefantasy cycle has developed it has increasingly pushed the definitional limits of both "family" and "television" in more dramatic and self-reflexive ways, in so doing foregrounding Netflix's functioning as a "hybrid TV-cinema-digital media distribution system" (Lobato 2019: 44–45).

In line with the dark family telefantasy genre cycle's movement away from the personalised "binge-viewing" model that Netflix itself popularised – which is sustained by a release strategy in which all episodes appear on the platform upon series launch – and in response to Covid production constraints (Lewis 2022), *Stranger Things 4* was released in two instalments on the platform, Volumes 1 and 2. Volume 2 included only the last two lengthy episodes, impelling subscribers to wait for the release of the dramatic climax and consume it as a separate package, rather than as part of a "bingeable" bundle with the earlier episodes. Netflix's approach with *Stranger Things 4* taps into – without fully submitting to – Disney+'s successful weekly episode release strategy with *The Mandalorian*, which has subsequently been used for the SVOD's other flagship series. Disney+'s drawn out, scheduled release strategy defies Netflix's "binge-watch" approach in ways that sustain what Balanzategui has previously called "digital water cooler moments" (2018b: 664–667): the social media buzz that positions these shows as central to the pop cultural consciousness and prolongs their high profiles. By referring to each part of the season as "Volumes", Netflix also recalls the sequel title conventions of one of the MCU's most popular and nostalgic franchises, *The Guardians of the Galaxy Volume 1* (Gunn, 2014) and *Volume 2* (Gunn, 2017), which occupies similar comedic but dark fantasy/sci-fi generic terrain to *Stranger Thing.* Notably, the Guardians films model this sequel naming convention on cassette mixtapes – often featured in the film franchise's paratextual promotional materials, including trailers – in reference to the cassette tapes beloved by the nostalgic main character, Quill (Chris Pratt). This approach resonates with the fixation with nostalgic media pervasive to *Stranger Things*, including the mixed cassette tape, which is a key narrative focus in Season 4, as key character Max (Sadie Sink) listens to a cassette tape on her Walkman to empower her escape from the Upside Down's monstrous Vecna, a major narrative thread underpinning some of the series' most climactic moments. Thus, *Stranger Things 4* continues the dark family telefantasy genre cycle's experimentation with different types of "family" viewing that draw on while transforming the legacies of both film and television, in so doing adjusting the on-demand Netflix binge model so it nostalgically reverberates with legacy media traditions.

Wang and Lobato point to the "many structural and experiential differences" (Wang and Lobato 2019: 358) between SVODs like Netflix and other online video platforms as well as the legacy media formats of film and television. *Stranger Things 4* highlights how the dark family telefantasy genre cycle continues to reposition such "structural and experiential" distinctions not just in relation to media forms on a macro level but also, and in tandem, in relation to distinctions between family and adult-oriented content. Season 4's spectacular aesthetics serve to accelerate and accentuate the program's gradual movement towards more explicit horror and violence that has played out across each season (or "sequel"). As we highlighted in Chapter 2, this gradual shift towards horror has been a structuring conceit of the narrative arc since the first season: as co-creator Matt Duffer explained, the aim was to get kids hooked, and then late in the season "scare the shit out of them. Then the parents can get mad" (quoted in Thrower 2016). Continuing this movement towards ever darker generic territory, Season 4 is distinctively and baroquely horror in its generic allegiances, with the supernatural slasher film franchise A Nightmare on Elm Street being a key reference point. In *Stranger Things 4*, the monstrous Vecna, overlord of the Upside Down, operates like a supernatural serial killer who, like supernatural child killer Freddy Krueger, is able to enter the minds of his victims and force them to endure unbearable traumas drawn from their own personal pain. Vecna's appearance is nostalgically modelled on Krueger's, his grotesquely burned, scarred, and sinuous visage constructed out of latex (Bojalad 2022) rather than the sophisticated CGI one would expect given the show's high production budget. The monster's long claws also resemble Krueger's iconic metal, gloved talons, and, like Kreuger's fingers, they are distinctly material and tactile in their physics and appearance. Notably, Freddy Krueger performer Robert Englund makes a cameo in the film as Victor Creel, an imprisoned man falsely committed of murders carried out by Vecna, who turns out to be Creel's son. Thus, the many nostalgic references in this season make clear that this season is more straightforwardly "horror" by contrast to the generic hybridity of *Stranger Things 1*, *2,* and *3*, further "darkening" the dark family telefantasy cycle by foregrounding the genre allegiance that sits most uncomfortably with cultural expectations around child appropriateness.

The season's high production values and special effects budget are showcased via grisly body horror aesthetics, and thus are also deployed to underscore the series' generic gearshift into more overtly horror territory that challenges the family audience the show has attracted. For instance, as each child or teen dies at the hands of Vecna, their bodies float into the air and levitate, eyes wide in fear or rolling back into their heads, before their bodies and faces monstrously contort and bend out of shape – jaws, limbs, ankles, and wrists bend, twist and eventually snap. Eventually, their eyes appear to melt into black liquid, before they drop back to the ground like a rag-doll, sucked of their life force. As the Duffers explained in an interview with *NME*, their biggest influences in this series alongside *A Nightmare on Elm Street* (Craven, 1984) and *A Nightmare on Elm Street 3: Dream Warriors* (Russell, 1987) were R-rated horror films *Hellraiser* (Barker, 1987) and *The Cell* (Singh, 2000) – a surreal horror film that explores the twisted psyche of a serial killer, a focus of the latter half of *Stranger Things 4* – and also the TV mini-series *IT* (ABC, 1990), an adaptation of the Stephen King novel (1986). The imagery of floating child bodies with blank eyes is a violent variation on a similar, more simply realised aesthetic device in *IT*, and Tim Curry's depiction of the evil, child-killing clown from this series is also a clear influence on the villainous Vecna. As Ross Duffer explains, *IT* was a key reference point because it "scarred us, maybe more than anything else, so we talked about that a lot and why that messed us up as much as it did" (quoted in Daly 2022).

The intention with Season 4 then is to finally bring the horror that has been lurking at the fringes of the series centre stage – to "scar" a generation of children the way the Duffers were scarred by *IT* – which is self-reflexively reinforced by the pastiche of genre tropes that constitute the series' aesthetic composition. For instance, the crux of the mysterious Upside Down this season is Vecna's childhood home, which is a theme park-esque rendition of a haunted Victorian mansion. In the mundane every day of Hawkins, it appears like a classic haunted house, complete with boarded up windows and cobwebs filling its dark and decrepit corners. In the alternate dimension of the Upside Down, the house becomes an even more excessive display of horror genericity, appearing akin to Dracula's Transylvanian manor combined with the vast and imposing Gothic splendour of the house in the various screen adaptations of Shirley Jackson's *The Haunting of Hill House* (1959), *The Haunting* (Wise, 1963), *The Haunting* (de Bont, 1999), and, notably, the acclaimed Netflix Original series *The Haunting of Hill House* (Flanagan, 2018). Huge, rabid bats circle the house in the Upside Down, and it is framed by a red sky and lightning, recalling the customised *Stranger Things* branded Netflix logo. Echoing the complex nostalgic strategy in Netflix's dark family telefantasy program *Dark Crystal: Age of Resistance* (Chapter 5), as part of this strident exhibition of horror genericity, the Duffer brothers overtly engage in haunted nostalgia for past media texts grounded on a paradoxically pleasurable childhood trauma that they hope to replicate for a current generation of young people.

Stranger Things 4 attracted the same rating, TV-14, as the previous three seasons, despite its more explicit horror genre identity, which has caused controversy. A report from the Parents Television and Media Council (PTMC), for instance, concluded that this rating is inaccurate (2022: 1) and that "parents shouldn't be so swept away by nostalgia that they allow themselves to be taken-in by a deceptive content rating" (1). The report, which was widely picked up in news media (Berthiaume 2022; Gruenwedel 2022; Samsel 2022; Whittmer 2022), argues that the frequency of profanity has increased by 217% since Season 1 and that frequency of violence had jumped by 307%, and concludes that the TV-14 rating indicates "a vastly different standard between streaming content and broadcast content – even if that content is similarly-rated" and that "if a TV-14 doesn't mean the same thing on Netflix as it does on CBS, it is of little to no value to parents" (PTMC 2022: 4). As we have noted throughout this book, programs in Netflix's dark family telefantasy cycle have frequently caused parental concern over classifications, a tendency that is accentuated with *Stranger Things 4*. Ultimately, the PTMC report questions whether Netflix is "acting in bad faith" (2022: 4), pointing also to the extensive marketing effort across TikTok and other social media platforms to attract child audiences. Indeed, there have been numerous child-focused *Stranger Things* marketing campaigns and merchandise tie-ins across *Stranger Things* seasons, such as official kids' clothing lines (including with major fashion brand Zara), toys, games, and an extensive array of other official merchandise via the Netflix shop. The PTMC report and journalistic reportage surrounding the "inaccurate" rating for the show highlight the ongoing cultural tensions that dark family telefantasy shows like *Stranger Things 4* provoke and navigate as they forge new expectations around "family viewing" for the SVOD era.

Notably, in our audience interviews, we found that parents and older siblings provided "safe" access points into the show for children too young to watch it, along with the paratextual materials criticised in the PTMC report like merchandise, YouTube videos, and toys. For these children, in alignment with Netflix's on-demand model, *Stranger Things 4* exists on the platform as "content in waiting". Harry, the ten-year-old son of one of our interview participants, exemplified this type of viewer. Felicity, Harry's mother, explained that her son self-identifies as a fan of the show even though he has not yet watched a full episode. As Felicity explained, "he's aware of what's happening in the story because he asks what's happening in the story. But he also knows it's scary. So he's not saying 'when can I watch it?'". She later reiterated that despite his passionate interest, at this stage he knows it is a "bit too scary" for him. It is notable that Harry has not been pressing to watch the show before he is ready, as he is aware it will be available to him on Netflix to consume in whatever way he wishes when the time is right. At this point, he is satisfied with the paratextual materials that have thus far constituted his experiences with *Stranger Things*. Despite not having seen it, Harry has a favourite character, Dustin, and he engages with the characters via his collection of Lego mini-figures. Felicity explained that he has also inherited the show's official tie-in graphic novelisations from his older brother, through which he has been following the narrative. Felicity explained that Harry also engages with the show via watching clips on YouTube, and his key access point has been the love he shares with the show's protagonists for Dungeons and Dragons, which he plays with his friends at school. As Felicity explains, Harry's older brother thus:

> managed to find on YouTube sort of like, you know fan compilations of all the Dungeons and Dragons scenes put together. And so I think for Harry, what's lovely for him is he looks at those scenes of those four boys playing D&D, and he goes, that's me and my friends on screen! ... So he doesn't want to see the spooky stuff, but he wants to see the group of kids because he has a group of friends [like that] at school. .... I think [it is] particularly because they have built the D&D experience into the script. The characters of Vecna and all that sort of stuff are kind of integrated into the narrative. So I didn't have a clue who Vecna was, but Harry knew who Vecna was, and he hadn't even watched it.

Felicity, Harry, and Jack's experiences with *Stranger Things* encapsulate the flexible ways families can watch Netflix's dark family telefantasy content "together", encouraged by the overt marketing of the program and its affiliated products to children and families, and, in some profiles, its appearance under the "Family Watch Together TV" label. A shared and reciprocal intergenerational experience of the show is enacted via play and paratexts even for young Harry who has not yet seen it – indeed, his own knowledge grounded in childhood play has helped to frame and deepen his mother's understanding of key characters. Harry's older brother, who has watched the show in full with his parents, has curated and passed down selections of content for his brother that enabled Harry to participate in the family's engagement with the show. Harry's experiences with age-appropriate paratexts allow him to feel part of the culture around *Stranger Things* through a different access point to the program's alternate fantasy dimension. In these ways, the family have communally built a shared experience of *Stranger Things* that is differentiated by age but rendered richer and more complex by these differences. In this context, "Family Watch Together TV" may not mean all members of the family literally watching the program together, but nonetheless operates as a shared – and thus intergenerational – family experience.

Squid Game as the New Family Television Frontier

Another high-profile, dark telefantasy Netflix Original show that has controversially invited children into its world via paratexts is *Squid Game* (2021-). *Squid Game*, the South Korean horror-thriller drama that quickly became

Netflix's most popular show ever (Flint and Chin 2021), is not explicitly positioned in the catalogue in relation to family and child/young viewer tags, such as "Family Watch Together TV" or "Watch with Older Children". This show, unlike *Stranger Things 4*, has the rating US TV-MA for mature audiences only, designating the show as "specifically designed to be viewed by adults and therefore may be unsuitable for children under 17". However, as Balanzategui (2021) has pointed out, the interface aesthetics and themes of the show certainly appeal to younger viewers in ways that intersect with Netflix's dark family telefantasies. The show focuses on a group of heavily indebted Koreans who are convinced to take part in a mysterious "challenge" which promises great riches for the winner. The participants are transported to a complex that is part theme park, part reality television set, and part concentration camp – under constant surveillance, the participants endure horrific living conditions and are forced to take part in a series of challenges staged in elaborately constructed, brightly coloured arenas. These games are exaggerated versions of beloved traditional children's games, from marbles to what is known as "Red Light, Green Light" in Korea and the US, and "Statues" or "What's the time Mr. Wolf" in other Western countries. Yet they turn out to be death matches, as it is revealed that only the sole survivor at the end of the "games" will take home the cash prize. Thus, each challenge ends with these brightly coloured, ostentatious simulations of children's playgrounds covered in blood and littered with corpses. The show's emphasis on elaborately staged, theme-parkified children's play spaces is foregrounded in the interface aesthetics on the platform. The tiles and banners feature costumed characters navigating brightly coloured arenas that appear like amusement park maze attractions, or eye-catching features from specific challenges, in particular the huge robotic doll that is central to the "Red Light, Blue Light" game in the first episode.

Notably, the design of one of the images frequently used across paratextual promotions for *Stranger Things 4* (Figure 7.1) is reminiscent of this maze-like imagery associated with *Squid Game* (Figure 7.2) – this *Stranger Things* image appears on the Netflix interface and was featured in posters and billboards (including at the Melbourne Central Station, a major city train station where this book's authors are based). It features the protagonists standing in different zones of a strikingly coloured arena-style space organised in a non-Euclidean maze-like constellation. The aesthetic and generic intersections between the two shows were registered by one of the major *Stranger Things* fan social media accounts, the twitter account @ StrangeNews11 (2021), when they tweeted a "mash-up" poster combining the aesthetics of both shows called "Stranger Game". Thus, in the case of *Squid Game*, it is the interface and marketing aesthetics that connect this show to Netflix's high-profile dark family telefantasy cycle, rather than explicit processes of tagging and labelling.

Figure 7.1 *Stranger Things 4* Twitter advertisement from the official *Stranger Things* account (@Stranger_Things, 27 May 2022). Screenshot by authors.

Figure 7.2 *Squid Game* maze thumbnail on the Netflix interface. Screenshot by authors.

Notably, as has occurred with *Stranger Things 4*, paratexts have been key to *Squid Game*'s positioning for and popularity with younger audiences. As Balanzategui (2021) points out,

> young children's awareness of the violent show more likely relates to its pervasive presence on social media, which has extended to viral content on TikTok and YouTube, popular with teenagers and children. The show is certainly a craze within children's digital culture.

Balanzategui points to successful channels on YouTube Kids (the version of the platform designed for viewers under 12) that have capitalised on the global *Squid Game* phenomenon, including videos teaching children how to draw the key characters and gameplay videos based around *Squid Game* "levels" on the online videogame platform Roblox, which is according to some metrics the most popular game with 5–12 year olds in the US (Hill 2021): the game has an aesthetic similar to Lego and Minecraft, and enables users to program games and share them with others. Very high-profile videos on the main version of the YouTube platform aimed at young people have also helped to cement the popularity of *Squid Game* among kids. For instance, two of the world's most famous gaming YouTubers, Jacksepticeye and Pewdiepie, released a playthrough video of the pair playing a Roblox "challenge" together, in which they chose not to betray each other at the end of the level, allowing both of them to win, in a playful defiance of the logic of the deathmatch challenges in the show. At the time of writing, this video, "We Won the Squid Game!", had 5.5 million views. This positive reframing within the context of Roblox realigns *Squid Game*'s content as appropriate for younger viewers, as the brutal and unsettling nature of the show's deadly games is disarmed and repositioned within the structures of collaborative play. Further consolidating such mutually beneficial interactions between Netflix and other digital platforms such as Roblox, TikTok, and YouTube, another young YouTuber very popular with children and tweens, Mr Beast,[1] re-enacted his own version of *Squid Game*: "$456,000 Squid Game in Real Life!" This 25-minute video has to date almost 280 million views. It painstakingly replicates all of the distinctive "arena" sets from the show, yet in restaging the games, Mr Beast goes to great lengths to emphasise the safety measures in place, replacing the horror of the original with a child-friendly, playful reality TV style and aesthetic. In the case of both of these exceedingly popular videos, YouTube operates as a site of imaginative reproduction of Netflix content that is not suitable for children (according to the official rating) and situates it within children's play cultures, extending the reach and limits of what may operate as "family television".

Reflecting this phenomenon, in our audience research, *Squid Game* came up as a tension point that challenged parents' understandings of the boundaries of child-appropriateness in relation to Netflix's "family" content. Madeline, for instance, talked about how her 12-year-old son watched *Squid Game* with her and his father. She explained that, while "it's quite horrific" to think Cole has watched *Squid Game*, she and her husband were watching it without Cole

> because we thought it wasn't appropriate and he happened to walk into the room during one of the scenes, and he told us exactly what's going to happen. And we still don't know where he knows all this information, but he knew every single game and every outcome before we did.

Madeline explains that she and her husband were quite "horrified" by Cole's extensive knowledge of the show, but decided immediately the best course of action was to allow Cole to watch it with them so they could talk about the events as they unfolded. She explains that while she never figured out how exactly Cole knew so much about the show without having watched it, she assumed it was influenced by "social media and friends". In particular, she recounted a camping trip in November 2021, when the show came out, "and all the kids that were [Cole's] age were all playing 'Squid Games' in the playground, so we were like, Wow! Well, we're not the only parents then to have a child that was aware of all of that!" Madeline's experience was one of shocked realisation that *Squid Game*, a show her and her husband had decided was thoroughly inappropriate for Cole, was well and truly a part of children's culture – spanning both traditional children's play in the playground to digital cultures – and thus it was included in the "family watch together" repertoire alongside *Stranger Things*. Breanna and eight-year-old Dylan also highlighted this phenomenon: although Dylan has not yet seen the show, he says he "knows the song" via playing games from the show in the school playground with his friends – the child is presumably referring to the repetitive nursery rhyme-esque song emitted by the robotic doll at the centre of the show's first challenge, the "Red Light, Green Light" game. When asked how he knew the song and games from the show, Breanna explained that she thinks the children have picked it up from older family members who had watched it, and also that it is "so much part of social media and it was on YouTube, so they will probably be picking up pieces of it from YouTube". Dylan jumped in to add that "one of my friends has watched it" (Breanna was quick to suggest the friend may just have been boasting and his claim had not been confirmed). Dylan said he "knew all the settings" (meaning the challenge arenas), and despite being frightened of even the tile and banner images of both *Stranger Things* and *Squid Game* in the Netflix interface – which, along with the sounds he has heard emanating down the hall when his older family members watch the show, have completely put him off *Stranger Things* – he is very curious to watch *Squid Game*.

In another instance of *Squid Game* reshaping family boundaries around content appropriate for children, in an interview with another family, Caren and Brian explained that their 12 and 15 year olds "figured out" they could watch *Squid Game* while their parents were sleeping on Saturday mornings, with the older child being the access point to the show for the 12 year old. As Theo the 15 year old explained, he was already talking about the show with friends and on social media, which is what piqued his interest. When asked how he would compare the scare-factor of *Stranger Things* – the family's favourite show to watch together – with *Squid Game*, 12-year-old Grady explained that he didn't really find one or the other scarier, just that *Stranger Things* had more "jump-scares" and *Squid Game* was "gorier". Grady explained that it was the "drama" and "way it was written" that he enjoyed about *Squid Game*. Grady explained he was more frightened of crime dramas like the two British shows *Vera* (ITV, 2011–2017) and *Shetland* (ITV, 2013–2016): his father explained he "was terrified of" these shows because they had depictions of death and violence grounded in a more realist mode.

Thus, while *Squid Game*'s popularity with children has been very controversial – primary schools in various countries even issued warning letters to parents instructing them not to let their children watch (Balanzategui 2021) – in our interviews it was not described as a source of fear or discomfort for the children who had watched it or encountered its paratexts. Indeed, as Grady and Brian implied, the fantasy mode made shows like *Squid Game* and *Stranger Things 4* accessible and relatively comfortable viewing for Grady – with, as is typical of this genre, the dark *fantasy* mode attenuating the gory and frightening elements.

Squid Game's popularity with children and its remediation in children's digital cultures, and the widespread concern it has sparked among parents, commentators, and educators, highlight how Netflix's Original dark telefantasies continue to resituate the boundaries of family television. Netflix announced in June 2022 that it had greenlit a reality show tie-in with *Squid Game*, *Squid Game: The Challenge* – which it claimed would "bring Squid Game to life" via "the biggest reality competition ever" (Netflix 2022). This show is clearly designed to capitalise on the success of this grisly show – and in particular, on the success of *remediations* of the games from the show in children's digital and playground cultures – by constructing a version more suitable for family audiences and the younger children that may be part of these families, like eight-year-old Dylan, who is not yet ready for the scares and violence of *Squid Game* but is very eager to learn more about its challenges and games. Continuing the dark family telefantasy cycle strategy in new directions, Netflix VP of Unscripted and Documentary Series Brandon Riegg explains of *The Challenge* that "fans of the drama series are in for a fascinating and unpredictable journey", yet the press release makes clear that in this version, while the "stakes are high … the worst fate is going home empty handed" (Netflix 2022). Netflix thus continues to experiment with new ways to encourage families to watch together by inviting play with the horror next door.

The End of a Cycle?

The Duffer brothers' pitch for *Stranger Things* was rejected between 15 and 20 times, yet they resisted advice to reorient the program for a solely adult or child audience, rather than an ambiguous mix of the two (Grow 2016). Despite the TV-14 rating, the program went on to become a family viewing success story, shaping the way that Netflix greenlit and promoted its cycle of dark family telefantasy, even as these programs continually created controversy and confusion over their perceived audience. *A Series of Unfortunate Events* adapted the popular book series into a Gothic steampunk blend of anachronisms, combining absurd musical interludes with abuse and paedophilia in ways that draw upon while mitigating the darkness of the original novels. *Lost in Space* rebooted a dormant fan program from the 1960s, inviting a shared audience across three generations while returning the story to its often forgotten, darker roots. *The Dark Crystal: Age of Resistance* was grounded on haunted nostalgia for a film notorious for traumatising its young audience. Finally, *Raising Dion* harnessed the popularity of the superhero while overtly addressing Netflix's move to brand its diversity at a time when Netflix was facing new competition in family streaming with the arrival of Disney+. While *ASoUE* and *Lost in Space* completed their intended story arc, the early cancellation of Emmy-award-winning *Age of Resistance* and top-rating *Raising Dion* indicate the financial challenges of the high-budget dark family telefantasy cycle through which Netflix most heavily promoted its pivot to "Family Watch Together TV". The controversial interest among children for *Squid Game* represents the continuing if confronting legacy of dark family telefantasy, and also the continuing success of Netflix's strategy to push the boundaries of family viewing through its content and paratextual marketing strategies.

Note

1 While pinning down audience demographics on the main YouTube platform is notoriously difficult, Mr Beast in 2022 was voted "Favourite Male Creator" at the 2022 Kids' Choice Awards, and was nominated for the related "Favourite Male Social Star" at the 2021 version of these awards, in which children vote for their favourite media personalities.

References

Abbott, J (2006) *Irwin Allen Television Productions 1964-1970: A Critical History*, Jefferson: McFarland.

Abbott, S (2015) "'I want to do bad things with you': The television horror title sequence", in Geraghty, L. (ed.), *Popular Media Cultures: Fans, Audiences and Paratexts*, New York: Palgrave Macmillan, 110–126.

ABC (2020) "TV Classifications: G, PG, M and MA15+ what do they mean and how are they used?" *ABC Help Centre*, https://help.abc.net.au/hc/en-us/articles/360001185556-TV-Classiications-G-PG-M-and-MA15-what-do-they-mean-and-how-are-they-used-#:~:text=Mature%20(M)%20Classification%20is%20recommended,classifiable%20elements%20may%20contain%20detail

Abril, D (2019) "Proposed Law Would Require YouTube and Netflix to Do More to Protect Kids Online", *Fortune*, 4 April, https://fortune.com/2019/04/04/proposed-law-would-require-youtube-and-netflix-to-do-more-to-protect-kids-online/

Active Rehab (2016) "Dustin from Stranger Things Talks About Disability and Representation", 1 December, https://activerehab.net.au/dustin-from-stranger-things-talks-about-disability-and-representation/

Addams Family Values (Barry Sonnenfeld, Film, 1993)

Afra, K (2016) "PG-13, Ratings Creep, and the Legacy of Screen Violence: The MPAA Responds to the FTC's 'Marketing Violent Entertainment to Children' (2000-2009)", *Cinema Journal*, 55 (3): 40–64.

Agard, C (2018) "*A Series of Unfortunate Events*: Inside season 2's amazing new sets", *Entertainment Weekly*, 29 March, https://ew.com/tv/2018/03/29/series-of-unfortunate-events-season-2-sets/

Alderslade, M (2022) "Watch Metallica jam with *Stranger Things* actor Joseph Quinn backstage at Lollapalooza", *Metal Hammer*, September 20, Accessed 15 November 2022, https://www.loudersound.com/news/watch-stranger-things-actor-joseph-quinn-jam-with-metallica-backstage-at-lollapalooza

Alexander, N (2016) "Catered to your future self: Netflix's 'predictive personalization' and the mathematization of taste", in McDonald, K and Daniel Smith-Rowsey, D (eds), *The Netflix Effect: Technology and Entertainment in the 21st Century*, New York: Bloomsbury, 81–97.

Alexa & Katie (TV, 2018-2020)

All About the Washingtons (TV, 2018)

Alfred Hitchcock Presents (TV, 1955-1965)
Aliens (James Cameron, Film, 1998)
All in the Family (TV, 1971-1979)
Allen, N (2019) "Rim of the world", 24 May, *Roger Ebert*, https://www.rogerebert.com/reviews/rim-of-the-world-2019
Allen, N (2020) "Netflix's The Letter for the King Written with Medieval Cliches", 23 March, *Roger Ebert*, https://www.rogerebert.com/streaming/netflixs-the-letter-for-the-king-written-with-medieval-cliches
Altman, R (1999) *Film/Genre*, London: BFI.
American Graffiti (George Lucas, Film, 1973)
amritnitnrniininitninini [sic] (2020) "Netflix series vs film: A Series Of Unfortunate Events - NitPix", *YouTube*, 20 January 2017, https://www.youtube.com/watch?v=rC83z9DXFfo
Amory, C (1966) "Review: Lost in Space", *TV Guide*, 5-11 February, 1.
AndamanOz [sic] (2018) "Lost in Space", *Common Sense Media*, https://www.commonsensemedia.org/tv-reviews/lost-in-space-0/user-reviews/adult
Anastasiap7 [sic] (2019) "Orgies, cannibalism, human sacrifice, and more", *Common Sense Media*, 20 June, https://www.commonsensemedia.org/tv-reviews/chilling-adventures-of-sabrina/user-reviews/adult
Anderson, T (2018) "Everything you need to know about that Netflix 'Strong Black Lead' spot you saw during the BET Awards", *Los Angeles Times*, 24 June, https://www.latimes.com/entertainment/movies/la-et-mn-strong-black-lead-netflix-bet-awards-20180624-story.html
Andreeva, N (2014) "Netflix Adapting Lemony Snicket's 'A Series Of Unfortunate Events' As Series", *Deadline* [Online]. 5 November. Available at: https://deadline.com/2014/11/a-series-of-unfortunate-events-tv-show-lemony-snicket-netflix-1201274454/
A Nightmare on Elm Street (Wes Craven, Film, 1984)
A Nightmare on Elm Street 3: Dream Warriors (Chuck Russell, Film, 1987)
Antunes, F (2013) "Children and Horror after PG-13: The Case of *The Gate*", *Networking Knowledge* 6(4), 10.31165/nk.2014.64.313
Antunes, F (2017) "Attachment anxiety: parenting culture, adolescence and the family film in the US", *Journal of Children and Media*, 11(2): 214–228
Appledaddy [sic] (2019) "Amazing Show", *Common Sense Media*, 21 November, https://www.commonsensemedia.org/tv-reviews/raising-dion/user-reviews/adult?page=1
AptlyNamed [sic] (2020) "An decently executed show for teens and adults, really confusing tone", *Common Sense Media*, 25 February, https://www.commonsensemedia.org/tv-reviews/locke-key/user-reviews/adult
Are You Afraid of the Dark? (TV, 1992-1996; 1999-2000)
Arnold, S (2016) "Netflix and the Myth of choice/participation/ autonomy", in McDonald, K and Smith-Rowsey, D (eds), *The Netflix Effect: Technology and Entertainment in the 21st Century*, New York: Bloomsbury Academic, 49–62.
Asarch, S (2019) "*The Dark Crystal: Age of Resistance* Review: The Muppets meets *Game of Thrones*", *Newsgeek*, 3 September, https://www.newsweek.com/netflix-dark-crystal-age-resistance-review-muppets-game-thrones-1457428
A Series of Unfortunate Events (TV, 2017-2019)

Asouelover888 [sic] (2019) "Mysterious, suspenseful, interesting", *Common Sense Media*, https://www.commonsensemedia.org/users/asouelover888

At The Movies (TV, 1982)

Audissino, E (2017) "John Williams and contemporary film music" in Coleman, L and Tillman, J (eds), *Contemporary Film Music: Investigating Cinema Narratives and Composition*, Palgrave MacMillan.

Aussie Dad of 2 [sic] (2020) "Raising Dion", *Common Sense Media*, https://www.commonsensemedia.org/tv-reviews/raising-dion/user-reviews/adult

Auster, A (2005) "HBO's approach *to generic transformation*", in Edgerton, G and Rose, B (eds), *Thinking Outside the Box: A Contemporary Television Genre Reader*, Lexington: University Press of Kentucky.

AutisticYoungAdult [sic] (2019) "Sweet but too scary to be PG", *Common Sense Media*, 24 October, https://www.commonsensemedia.org/tv-reviews/raising-dion/user-reviews/adult?page=2

Axelrod, JBC (2018) "Mutiny on the sofa: historical patterns of patriarchy and family structure in American science fiction, 1945–2018", *Pacific Coast Philology*, 53 (2): 308–334.

Baker, D (2017) "Terms of excess: Binge-viewing as epic-viewing in the Netflix Era", in Barker, C and Wiatrowski, M (eds), *The Age of Netflix: Critical Essays onStreaming Media, Digital Delivery and Instant Access*, Jefferson NC: McFarland, 31–54.

Baker, D (2018) *To Boldly Go: Marketing the Myth of Star Trek*, London: IB Tauris.

Baker, D (2020) "Child's play: Addressing the young Cold War audience in Captain Video and His Video Rangers (1949–1955)", *Critical Studies in Television*, 15 (2): 112–128.

Baker, D and Balanzategui, J (2022) "Heritage Child Stars on Disney+: Child Stardom in the SVOD Era", *Celebrity Studies*, 14 (2) https://doi-org.ezproxy.lib.rmit.edu.au/10.1080/19392397.2022.2109307.

Baker, D, Balanzategui, J and Sandars, D (2020) "'Family Watch Together TV': Netflix and the dark intergenerational fantasy", *CSTOnline*, 3 April, https://cstonline.net/family-watch-together-tv-netflix-and-the-dark-intergenerational-fantasy-by-djoymi-baker-jessica-balanzategui-and-diana-sandars/#_edn2

Baker, D, Balanzategui, J, McIntyre, J and Burke, L (2021) "Beyond Bluey: why adults love re-watching Australian kids' TV from their childhoods", *The Conversation*, https://theconversation.com/beyond-bluey-why-adults-love-re-watching-australian-kids-tv-from-their-childhoods-169727

Balanzategui, J (2016) "Haunted Nostalgia and the Aesthetics of Technological Decay: Hauntology and Super 8", *Sinister Horror Studies* 7 (2): 235–251.

Balanzategui, J (2018a) "Are you afraid of the dark? Children's horror anthology series in the 1990s", in Schober, A & Olson, D (eds), *Children, Youth and American Television*, New York and Oxfordshire: Routledge, 201–222.

Balanzategui, J (2018b) "The New Quality Crime Drama in the TVIV Era: *Hannibal*, *True Detective*, and Surrealism", *Quarterly Review of Film and Video*, 35 (6): 657–679.

Balanzategui, J (2018c) *The Uncanny Child in Transnational Cinema*, Amsterdam: Amsterdam University Press. 10.5117/9789462986510

Balanzategui, J (2019) "Creepypasta, 'Candle Cove', and the digital gothic", *The Journal of Visual Culture*, 18 (2): 187–208.

Balanzategui, J (2020a) "*The Shining*'s Uncanny Children and the Conflicted Nostalgia of *Doctor Sleep*", *Senses of Cinema*, https://www.sensesofcinema.com/2020/the-shining-at-40/uncanny-children-nostalgia-in-doctor-sleep/

Balanzategui, J (2020b) "Towards an Understanding of Children's Screen Genres in the Streaming Era", *NECSUS: European Journal of Media Studies*, Autumn Special Issue: Methods. https://necsus-ejms.org/towards-an-understanding-of-childrens-screen-genres-in-the-streaming-video-era-reflecting-on-shifting-intersections-between-digital-media-and-screen-studies/

Balanzategui, J (2021) "How the hyper-violent Squid Game has crept into digital content for young children", *The Conversation*, https://theconversation.com/how-the-hyper-violent-squid-game-has-crept-into-digital-content-targeting-young-children-170209

Balanzategui, J (2022) "TV horror-fantasy for children as transnational genre: *Round the Twist*, generic subversions, and quality Australian children's television", in Olson, D and Schober, A (eds), *Children, Youth, and International Television*, Abingdon: UK, 69–88.

Balanzategui, J, Burke L and Golding, D (2018) "Recommending a new system: An audience-based approach to film categorisation in the digital age", *Participations: Journal of Audience & Reception Studies*, 15 (2): 297–328.

Balanzategui, J, Guy, J and Kaufman, J (2018) "Understanding children's play in the digital age: toys, digital games and the digital-material dialectic", CODE: A Media Conference of Platforms, Devices and Screens, Melbourne, 19-20 November.

Balanzategui, J and Lynch, A (2022) "Shudder and the Aesthetics and Platform Logics of Genre-specific SVOD services", *Television and New Media*, Online First: 24 (2): 156–172. https://doi.org/10.1177/15274764221093602

Barefoot, G (2011) "Who watched that masked man? Hollywood's serial audiences in the 1930s", *Historical Journal of Film, Radio and Television*, 31 (2): 167–190.

Barker, C and Wiatrowski, M (2017) "Introduction", in Barker, C and Wiatrowski, M (eds), *The Age of Netflix: Critical Essays on Streaming Media, Digital Delivery and Instant Access*, Jefferson NC: McFarland, 1–18.

Barker, C and Wiatrowski, M (eds) (2017) *The Age of Netflix: Critical Essays on Streaming Media, Digital Delivery and Instant Access*, Jefferson NC: McFarland.

Barker, M (2009) "Fantasy audiences versus fantasy audiences", in Buckland, W (ed), *Film Theory and Contemporary Hollywood Movies*, New York and London: Routledge: 286–309.

Barnwell, J (2021) "Returning home: set design and visual storytelling in the cult world of *Stranger Things*", in Mollet and Scott (eds), *Investigating Stranger Things: Upside Down in the World of Mainstream Cult Entertainment*, Cham, Switzerland: Palgrave Macmillan, 149–166.

Barone, J (2017), "Hear the Music That Inspired 'Star Wars'", *New York Times*, 14 September, https://www.nytimes.com/2017/09/14/arts/music/star-wars-soundtrack-classical-music-new-york-philharmonic.html

Barthes, R (1981) *Camera Lucida; Reflections on Photography*, Trans Richard Howard, New York: Hill and Wang.

Bartlett, M (2017) "Rose-coloured rear-view: 'Stranger Things' and the lure of a false past", *Screen Education* (85): 16–25.

Bastow, C (2021) "'Something is Coming … ': the screenwriter as Dungeon master of stranger things", in Mollet and Scott (eds), *Investigating Stranger Things: Upside Down in the World of Mainstream Cult Entertainment*, Cham, Switzerland: Palgrave Macmillan, 87–110.

Bates Motel (TV, 2013-2017)

Batman (TV, 1966-1968)

Bauman, Z (2017) *Retrotopia*, Cambridge: Polity Press.

Beckett, S (2009) *Crossover Fiction: Global and Historical Perspectives*, New York: Routledge.

Beetlejuice (Tim Burton, Film, 1988)

Berthiaume, O (2022) "*Stranger Things* deserves TV-MA rating, says Parents Television Council", *Entertainment Premiere News*, July, https://premiere.news/stranger-things-deserves-tv-ma-rating-says-parents-television-council/

Berman, L (2018) "Disability and TV Review: 'Stranger Things' (2016)", *Medium*, 29 March, https://medium.com/@laurenberman17/tv-review-stranger-things-2016-ba6f251c3297

Beyens, I and Eggermont, S (2014) "Putting young children in front of the television: antecedents and outcomes of parents' use of television as a babysitter", *Communication Quarterly*, 62 (1): 57–74.

BinaryBlues [sic] (2020) "File under Stranger Things (but not as good)", *Common Sense Media*, 29 February, https://www.commonsensemedia.org/tv-reviews/locke-key/user-reviews/adult

Black Panther (Ryan Coogler, Film, 2018)

Blunt, A and Dowling, R (2006) *Home*, London: Routledge.

Bojalad, A (2022) "How Stranger Things created its iconic Vecna", *Den of Geek*, 1 July, https://www.denofgeek.com/tv/how-stranger-things-created-iconic-vecna/

Bolin, G (2016a) *Media Generations: Experience, Identity and Mediatised Social Change*, London: Routledge.

Bolin, G (2016b) "Passion and nostalgia in generational media experiences", *European Journal of Cultural Studies*, 19 (3): 250–264.

Bolin, G and Skogerbø, E (2013) "Age, generation and media", *Northern Lights*, 11: 3–14.

Bonomolo, C (2019) "Disney Confirms Disney+ Won't Host R-Rated Content", *Comicbook*, 26 August, https://comicbook.com/movies/news/disney-confirms-disney-plus-no-r-rated-content/

Boym, S (2001) *The Future of Nostalgia*, New York: Basic Books.

Boym, S (2018) "The future of nostalgia", in Vatulescu, C (ed), *The Svetlana Boym Reader*, New York: Bloomsbury, 217–276.

Bourdaa, M (2014) "This is not marketing. This is HBO: branding HBO with transmedia storytelling", *Networking Knowledge: Journal of the MeCCSA Postgraduate Network*, 7 (1): 18–25.

Bourdieu, P (1979/2013) *Distinction: A Social Critique of the Judgement of Taste*, New York & London: Routledge.

Brand New Cherry Flavor (TV, 2021)

Britt, R (2019) "*Lost in Space*: Why the Third Time's the Charm", *Den of Geek*, 26 December, https://www.denofgeek.com/tv/lost-in-space-why-the-third-times-the-charm/

Britt, R (2021) "How Lost in Space Went From Dark Drama to Camp Classic – And Back Again", *Den of Geek*, 22 September, https://www.denofgeek.com/tv/lost-in-space-book-bill-mumy-angela-cartwright/
Brockington, A (2018) "'Lost in Space' bosses, cast talk updating the robinson family in reboot", *Variety*, 10 April, https://variety.com/2018/scene/news/lost-in-space-netflix-reboot-premiere-1202748923/
Brouwer, B (2014). "Netflix's newest ad campaign highlights family movie nights", *Tube Filter*, 23 December. https://www.tubefilter.com/2014/12/23/netflix-watch-together-family-movie-night campaign/#:~:text=Netflix%20put%20out%20a%20series,nights%20inside%20real%20people's%20homes
Brown, N (2012) "The Evolution of the Hollywood Family Film", *I.B. Tauris Blog*, 2 October, https://theibtaurisblog.com/2012/10/02/the-evolution-of-the-hollywood-family-film/
Brown, N (2013) "'A New Movie-Going Public': 1930s Hollywood And The Emergence Of The 'Family' Film", *Historical Journal of Film, Radio and Television*, 33 (1): 1–23.
Brown, N (2018) *The Children's Film: Genre, Nation, and Narrative*, New York: Columbia University Press.
Brown, SL (2015) "'Raising Dion' turns the single-mother-as-superhero cliche upside down", *Washington Post*, 4 September, https://www.washingtonpost.com/news/act-four/wp/2015/09/03/raising-dion-turns-the-single-mother-as-superhero-cliche-upside-down/
Bryant, JA (2014) "Understanding the children's television community from an organizational network perspective", in Bryant JA (ed.), *The Children's Television Community*, New York: Routledge, 47–68.
Buckingham, D, Davies, H, Jones, K and Kelley, P (1999) *Children's Television in Britain*, London: British Film Institute.
Buckingham, D (1996) *Moving Images: Understanding Children's Emotional Responses to Television*, Manchester: Manchester University Press.
Bukatman, S (1991) "There's always a Tomorrowland: Disney and the hypercinematic experience", *October* 57 (Summer): 55–78.
Bulfin, A (2021) "'I'll touch whatever I want': Representing Child Sexual Abuse in Contemporary Children's and Young Adult Gothic", *Gothic Studies* 23 (1): 21–42.
Bundtzen, L (1987) "Monstrous mothers: Medusa, grendel, and now alien", *Film Quarterly*, 40 (3): 11–17.
Burcham, C (2020) "Lost In Space: Best Sci-Fi Movie References in Season 2", *Screen Rant*, 20 January, https://screenrant.com/lost-space-sci-fi-movie-references-season-2-best/
Burroughs, B (2019) "House of Netflix: Streaming media and digital lore", *Popular Communication: The International Journal of Media and Culture* 17 (1): 1–17.
Burton, B (2018) "The Inside Story of How 'Lost in Space' Got Off the Ground at Netflix", *Hollywood Reporter*. 23 April, https://www.hollywoodreporter.com/tv/tv-news/inside-story-how-lost-space-got-ground-at-netflix-1104751/
Burton, B (2020) "Netflix cancels *The Dark Crystal: Age of Resistance* after one season", *CNet*, 21 September, https://www.radiotimes.com/tv/fantasy/dark-crystal-netflix-cancelled/

Butler, B (2016) "Is Netflix doing nostalgia better than anyone else right now?", *Washington Post*, 22 November, https://www.washingtonpost.com/news/arts-and-entertainment/wp/2016/11/22/is-netflix-doing-nostalgia-better-than-anyone-else-right-now/

Butler, R (2021) "A nightmare on maple street: family dynamics and suburban horror in *Stranger Things*", in Mollet and Scott (eds), *Investigating Stranger Things: Upside Down in the World of Mainstream Cult Entertainment*, Cham, Switzerland: Palgrave Macmillan: 149–166.

Butt, B (2003) "'He's Behind You!' Reflections of repetition and predictability in Lemony Snicket's a series of unfortunate events", *Children's Literature in Education* 34 (4): 277–286.

Caillois (1962) *Man, Play and Games*. Translated from the French by Meyer Barash, London: Thames and Hudson.

Canby, V (1982) "Henson's *Crystal*", *New York Times*, 17 December, https://www.nytimes.com/1982/12/17/movies/henson-s-crystal.html

Cantor, M (1991) "The American Family on Television: From Molly Goldberg to Bill Cosby", *Journal of Comparative Family Studies*, 22 (2): 205–216.

Captain Video and his Video Rangers (TV, 1949-1955)

Casale, M (2022) "*Stranger Things* Season 4 reportedly costs $30 million per episode", *News.com.au*, 21 April, https://decider.com/2022/04/21/stranger-things-season-4-30-million-dollars-per-episode/

Castillo, M (2022) "Before the *Stranger Things* Finale, Netflix Wants you to Experience It In-Person", *Cheddar News*, 14 May, https://cheddar.com/media/before-the-stranger-things-finale-netflix-wants-you-to-experience-it-in-person

Chamberlain, D (2011) "Scripted spaces: Television interfaces and the non-places of asynchronous entertainment", in Bennett, J and Strange, N (eds), *Television as Digital Media*, Durham and London: Duke University Press, 230–254.

Chandrashekar, AFA, Basilico, J and Jebara, T (2017) "Artwork Personalization at Netflix", *Netflix Technology Blog*, 8 December, https://netflixtechblog.com/artwork-personalization-c589f074ad76

Chaney, J (2022) "Stranger Things 4 has big blockbuster energy", *Vulture*, 27 May. https://www.vulture.com/article/stranger-things-4-review.html#:~:text=According%20to%20the%20Wall%20Street,budget%20for%20Top%20Gun%3A%20Maverick

Chavez, P (2019) "*The Mandalorian* with 'baby Yoda' surpasses *Stranger Things* as most in-demand streaming series after 21 weeks on top for Netflix show", *Daily Mail Australia*, 27 November, https://www.dailymail.co.uk/tvshowbiz/article-7729569/The-Mandalorian-baby-Yoda-surpasses-Stranger-Things-demand-streaming-series.html

Childwise (2019) "Monitor Report 2019", *Childwise.co.uk*, https://www.childwise.co.uk/reports.html

Chilling Adventures of Sabrina (TV, 2018-2020)

Chinatown (Roman Polanski, Film, 1974)

Clark, M (1985) "Irwin Allen Remembers 'Lost in Space' Part One", *Starlog*, 9, (100): 25–29.

Clark, T (2019a) "Netflix has canceled 'Fuller House' after 5 seasons, but most viewers abandoned it after season one", *Business Insider*, 2 February. https://www.

businessinsider.com/why-netflix-fuller-house-was-canceled-analysis-of-viewership-2019-2?r=US&IR=T

Clark, T (2019b) "*The Mandalorian* dethroned *Stranger Things* as the top streaming TV showin the US, breaking its 5-month streak", *Business Insider*, November 26th, https://www.businessinsider.com/the-mandalorian-beats-stranger-things-as-top-streaming-show-us-2019-11

Cobb, K (2015) "Family TV is dying. Can Netflix's bet on 'Fuller House' save it?", *Decider*, 13 May, https://decider.com/2015/05/13/fuller-house-netflix-family-programming/

Cobb, K (2018) "9 Surprising Facts About Netflix's Internal Ratings You Didn't Know", *Decider*, 23 April, https://decider.com/2018/04/23/surprising-facts-about-netflixs-ratings/

Cohen, JJ (1996) "Monster culture (seven theses)", in Cohen (ed.), *Monster Theory: Reading Culture*. Minneapolis: University of Minnesota Press, 3–25.

Cohn, J (2011) "A bumbling bag of ball bearings: *Lost in Space* and the Space Race", in Neighbors, RC and Rankin, S (eds.), *The Galaxy is Rated G: Essays on Children's Science Fiction Film and Television*, Jefferson NC: McFarland, 262–278.

Coleman, L (2009) "A needle through the heart: Violence and tragedy as a narrative device", in Leach, J (ed), *Doctor Who*, Detroit: Wayne State University Press, 142–156.

Combemale, L (2019) "LOST IN SPACE: Producers and Cast Chat Story, Character and Gender Balance", *Alliance of Women Film Journalists*, 24 December, https://awfj.org/blog/2019/12/24/lost-in-space-producers-and-cast-chat-story-character-and-gender-balance-leslie-combemale-interviews/

Commonwealth of Australia (2022) "What do the ratings mean?" https://www.classification.gov.au/classification-ratings/what-do-ratings-mean

Comtois, J (2019) "*The Mandalorian* dethrones *Stranger Things* as most-watched original streaming series", *SyFy*, 25 November, https://www.syfy.com/syfy-wire/mandalorian-most-watched-series

Conan the Barbarian (John Milius , Film, 1982).

Cpamario [sic] (2020) "Netflix shows a TV-G Rating - Terribly Incorrect", *Common Sense Media*, 11 April, https://www.commonsensemedia.org/tv-reviews/raising-dion/user-reviews/adult?page=1

Creed (Ryan Coogler, Film, 2015)

Creed, B (1993) *The Monstrous-feminine: Film, Feminism, Psychoanalysis*, London: Routledge.

Crocodile Dundee (Peter Faiman, Film, 1987)

Cruz, R (2020) "*The Dark Crystal: Age of Resistance* canceled? An 'expensive disappointment'", Micky, 21 September, https://micky.com.au/the-dark-crystal-age-of-resistance-canceled-an-expensive-disappointment/#:~:text=According%20to%20The%20Hollywood%20Reporter,as%20a%20puppet%20animated%20series

Cunningham, H (2020) *Children and Childhood in Western Society Since 1500*, 3rd Edition, London: Routledge.

Cyntheak [sic] (2022) "Raising Dion", *Common Sense Media*, https://www.commonsensemedia.org/tv-reviews/raising-dion/user-reviews/adult

cZalyun [sic] (2021) "Lost in Space", *Common Sense Media*, https://www.commonsensemedia.org/tv-reviews/lost-in-space-0/user-reviews/adult

D'Addario, D (2016) "Review: *Stranger Things* is Nostalgia that Works", *Time*, https://time.com/4406854/review-stranger-things-is-nostalgia-that-works/

Daddy1975 [sic] (2020) "Magical drama", *Common Sense Media*, 13 February, https://www.commonsensemedia.org/tv-reviews/locke-key/user-reviews/adult

Daily Times (2019) "'Raising Dion' – a hero's journey chaperoned by mom", 5 October, https://dailytimes.com.pk/478706/raising-dion-a-heros-journey-chaperoned-by-mom/

Dalton, MM and Linder, LR (2016) "Conclusion: the evolving resilient sitcom", in Dalton, MM and Linder, LR (eds), *The Sitcom Reader, Second Edition: America Re-Viewed, Still Skewed*, New York: State University of New York Press, 319–323.

Daly, R (2022) "'Stranger Things' cast and creators on the 'massive' new season", *NME*, 19 May, https://www.nme.com/en_au/features/tv-interviews/stranger-things-interview-season-4-duffer-brothers-cast-3229220

Daredevil (TV, 2015-2018)

Dark Crystal: Age of Resistance (TV, 2019)

Davies, MM (2001) *"Dear BBC": Children, Television Storytelling, and the Public Sphere*, Cambridge: Cambridge University Press.

Davis, J (2019) "'Raising Dion' Proves Family TV can be Inclusive AND Entertaining", *The Black Cape*, 9 October, https://theblackcape.com/raising-dion-proves-family-tv-can-be-inclusive-and-entertaining/

Day of the Dead (George Romero, Film, 1985)

Dear White People (TV, 2017-2021)

della Quercia, J (2018) "Spielberg things: the nostalgic heart of *Stranger Things*", in Wetmore, KJ (eds), *Uncovering Stranger Things: Essays on Eighties Nostalgia, Cynicism and Innocence in the Series*, Jefferson, NC: McFarland, 112–125.

De Los Santos, O (2009) "Irwin Allen's recycled monsters and escapist voyages", in Geraghty, L (ed), *Channeling the Future: Essays on Science Fiction and Fantasy Television*, Scarecrow Press, 25–40.

Denver Dad [sic] (2022) "Raising Dion", *Common Sense Media*, https://www.commonsensemedia.org/tv-reviews/raising-dion/user-reviews/adult

Derby, K (2020) "Kathy Castor Introduces Kids Internet Design and Safety Act in the House", *Florida Daily*, 29 September, https://www.floridadaily.com/kathy-castor-introdces-kids-internet-design-and-safety-act-in-the-house/

Diff'rent Strokes (TV, 1978–1985)

Dika, V (2003) *Recycled Culture*, Cambridge: Cambridge University Press.

DiPlacidi, J (2018) *Gothic Incest Gender, Sexuality And Transgression*, Manchester: Manchester University Press.

Doctor Who (TV, 1963-1989, 1996, 2005-)

Dodd, K (2021) "Stranger networks: ancillary threats, cult nostalgia and techno-logical invasions", in Mollet, T and Scott, L (eds), *Investigating Stranger Things: Upside Down in the World of Mainstream Cult Entertainment*, Cham, Switzerland: Palgrave Macmillan, 133–148.

The Donna Reed Show (TV, 1958–1966)

Dovey, R (2010) "The 20 Creepiest Kids' Movies of All Time", *Paste Magazine*, 4 June, https://www.pastemagazine.com/movies/the-10-scariest-kids-movies-of-all-time/

Driscoll, C (2011) *Teen Film: A Critical Introduction*, Oxford: Berg.

Drury, S (2019) "Netflix's 'Tales of the City,' ABC's 'General Hospital' Among Ruderman Family Foundation Honorees (Exclusive)", *Hollywood Reporter*,

9 November, https://www.hollywoodreporter.com/news/netflix-s-tales-city-abc-s-general-hospital-ruderman-foundation-honorees-1253688
Duchovnay, G (2008) "From big screen to small box: adapting science fiction film for television", in Telotte JP (ed), *The Essential Science Fiction Television Reader*, Lexington, KY: University Press of Kentucky, 69–90.
Dumaraog, A (2020) "Fuller House: What A Full House Sequel Should've Been About", *Screen Rant*, 22 November, https://screenrant.com/fuller-house-sequel-story-dj-jesse-better-reason/
Duncan, A (2019) "*The Dark Crystal: Age of Resistance* is *Game of Thrones* with Puppets", *Pedestrian*, 31 August, https://www.pedestrian.tv/entertainment/dark-crystal-brian-froud-interview/
Easy Rider (Dennis Hopper , Film, 1970)
Ebert, R (1982) "Review: *Conan the Barbarian*", Ebert, Roger, 1 January, https://www.rogerebert.com/reviews/conan-the-barbarian-1982#:~:text=Not%20since%20Bambi's%20mother%20was,jerkins%20go%20a%20long%20way./
Ebert, R (1998) "Lost in Space," 3 April, https://www.rogerebert.com/reviews/lost-in-space-1998
Eco, U (2005) "Innovation & repetition: between modern & postmodern aesthetics", *Daedalus*, 134 (4): 191 -207.
Edelman, L (2004) *No Future: Queer Theory and the Death Drive*. Durham: Duke University.
Edward Scissorhands (Tim Burton, Film, 1990)
Egan, DR and Hawkes, G (2008) "Disavowal and foundation fantasies: A psycho-social exploration of the class, race and the social construction of the sexual child in the Anglophone West", *Sexualities*, 16 (5/6): 635–650.
Elderkin, B (2019) "*The Dark Crystal: Age of Resistance* is the Groundbreaking Fantasy Epic We've Been Waiting For", *Kotaku*, 23 August, https://www.kotaku.com.au/2019/08/the-dark-crystal-age-of-resistance-is-the-groundbreaking-fantasy-epic-weve-been-waiting-for/
Ellingson, A (2019) "9 million Netflix subscribers may ditch it for Disney+", *BizWoman*, 25 April, https://www.bizjournals.com/bizwomen/news/latest-news/2019/04/9-million-netflix-subscribers-may-ditch-it-for.html?page=all
Ellis, EG (2020) "Locke & Key Masters the Netflix Recipe – for Better or Worse", *Wired*, 7 February, https://www.wired.com/story/locke-and-key-netflix-review/
Ellis, J (1992) *Visible Fictions: Cinema, Television*, Radio, London: Routledge.
Eloise, M (2019) "Here's why A Series of Unfortunate Events' ending betrays the best thing about the books", *Digital Spy*, 7 January, https://www.digitalspy.com/tv/a25773647/a-series-of-unfortunate-events-netflix-ending/
Escobar, A (2020) "Looking Back on *The Dark Crystal: Age of Resistance* with Director Louis Leterrier", *Discussing Film*, 01 October. https://discussingfilm.net/2020/10/01/looking-back-on-the-dark-crystal-age-of-resistance-with-director-louis-leterrier/
E.T. The Extra-Terrestrial (Steven Spielberg, Film, 1982)
Faith [sic] (2022) "Raising Dion", *Common Sense Media*, https://www.commonsensemedia.org/tv-reviews/raising-dion/user-reviews/adult
Family Reunion (TV, 2019-2022)
Family Ties (TV, 1982-1988)
Fang, S (2022) "Australia Streaming Wars Q1 2022: Netflix, Prime Video, Disney+

Consolidates", *Streambly*, 23 April, https://streambly.com.au/news/20220423-australia-streaming-wars-q1-2022-netflix-prime-video-disney-consolidates-2214

Farrand, T (2018) "61% of Netflix Originals Have Mature Content – Few Are Family Friendly", *Movieguide*, https://www.movieguide.org/news-articles/61-of-netflix-originals-have-mature-content-few-are-family-friendly.html

Fashingbauer Cooper, G (2022) "*Stranger Things* stars now and then: Wow, they've really grown up", *CNET*, 26 May, https://www.cnet.com/pictures/stranger-things-stars-now-and-then-wow-theyve-really-grown-up/

Father Knows Best (TV, 1954-1960)

Faughnder, R (2021) "Netflix's subscriber growth has slowed dramatically. Blame competition and the pandemic", *LA Times*, 20 July, https://www.latimes.com/entertainment-arts/business/story/2021-07-20/netflixs-subscriber-growth-has-slowed-dramatically

Fayelle, M, Maurage, P, Di Lorenzo, KR, Vogele, C, Gainsbury, SM and Billieux, J (2020) "Binge-watching: what do we know so far? a first systematic review of the evidence", *Current Addiction Reports*, 7 (44): 44–60.

FCC (2019) "The V-Chip: Options to Restrict What Your Children Watch on TV", 10 December, *Federal Communications Commission*, https://www.fcc.gov/consumers/guides/v-chip-putting-restrictions-what-your-children-watch

Fear, D (2019) "The Long Journey of *The Dark Crystal: Age of Resistance*", *Rolling Stone*, 28 August, https://www.rollingstone.com/tv-movies/tv-movie-features/dark-crystal-age-of-resistance-henson-interview-873063/

Feldman, K (2018) "'*A Series of Unfortunate Events'* returns to Netflix as dark as ever in its second season", *Daily News*, 28 March, https://www.nydailynews.com/entertainment/tv/series-unfortunate-events-back-netflix-dark-article-1.3897888

FeliciaRH [sic] (2019) "Need a Season 2", *Common Sense Media*, 11 November, https://www.commonsensemedia.org/tv-reviews/raising-dion/user-reviews/adult

Fesser Jr., M (1966) "When Guy hisses at the villain, he means it: The hero of 'Lost in Space' always ends up second best", *TV Guide*, 24-30 September, p. 24–27.

Feuer, J (1984) "The MTM style", in Feuer, J, Keer, P and Vahimagi, T (eds), *MTM: Quality Television*, London: BFI, 16–32.

Field, E (2021) "Profile piece: Libbie Doherty, Head of Children's Content at the Australian Broadcasting Corporation (ABC)", *ACTF Blog*, 4 November, https://blog-actf.com.au/profile-piece-libbie-doherty-head-of-childrens-content-at-the-australian-broadcasting-corporation-abc/

Fienberg, D (2018) "Lost in Space: TV Review", Hollywood Reporter, 10 April, https://www.hollywoodreporter.com/tv/tv-reviews/lost-space-review-1100276/

Firestarter (Mark L. Lester, Film, 1984)

Flanagan, KM (2010) "Browsing for dissonance: paratexts, box-art iconography, and genre", *Media Fields Journal*, 1 (1), http://mediafieldsjournal.squarespace.com/browsing-for-dissonance/

Flasher, J (1978) "Adultism", *Adolescence*, 13 (51) Fall: 517–523.

Flash Gordon (Frederick Stephani and Ray Taylor, Film, 1936)

Flash Gordon's Trip to Mars (Ford Beebe, Robert F. Hill and Frederick Stephani, Film, 1938)

Flint, J (2016) "Netflix to Ramp Up Originals Targeting Kids", *The Wall Street Journal*, 17 January, https://www.wsj.com/articles/netflix-to-ramp-up-originals-targeting-kids-1453058812

Flint, J and Chin, K (2021) "Netflix reports jump in users, calls *Squid Game* Its most popular show ever", *The Wall Street Journal*, October 19th, https://www.wsj.com/articles/netflix-adds-more-users-than-it-predicted-boosted-by-squid-game-11634674211#:%7E:text=In%20its%20letter%20to%20investors,in%2094%20countries%2C%20it%20said

Fogg, B (2020) "Netflix Party lets you throw a movie marathon (from a safe distance)", *Reviews.org* [online], 3 December. Accessed 25 March 2022, Available online: https://www.reviews.org/au/entertainment/how-to-use-netflix-party-chrome-extension/

Forbidden Planet (Fred M. Wilcox, Film, 1956)

Fraggle Rock (TV, 1987-1988)

Framke, C (2020) "Locke and Key‘ review: Netflix's family friendly show plays it safe", *Montreal Gazette*, 7 February, https://montrealgazette.com/entertainment/television/locke-and-key-review-netflixs-family-friendly-show-plays-it-safe/wcm/71dc2bc1-a5fd-4504-98e8-c7974bc9b6e1

Franich, D (2018) "A salute to Parker Posey and Dr. Smith in *Lost in Space*", *EW*, 13 April, https://ew.com/tv/2018/04/13/lost-in-space-parker-posey/

Freud, S (1919) "The uncanny", in McLintock, David (Trans.), *The Uncanny*, New York: Penguin Books, 2003b. 121–176.

Frey, M (2019) "The internet suggests: film, recommender systems, and cultural mediation", *Journal of Cinema and Media Studies*, 59 (1): 163–169.

Frey, M (2021) *Netflix Recommends: Algorithms, Film Choice, and the History of Taste*, Berkeley: University of California Press.

FTIA (2018) "Filming in May: Michael B. Jordan to Star in Upcoming Series 'Raising Dion' to be Directed by Dennis Liu in Canada", *Film & Television Industry Alliance*, 14 May, https://productionlist.com/filming-may-michael-b-jordan-star-upcoming-series-raising-dion-directed-dennis-liu-canada/

Full House (TV, 1987-1995)

Fuller House (TV, 2016-2020)

Fullerton, H (2019a) "*The Dark Crystal: Age of Resistance* review – *Game of Thrones* on Strings", *Radio Times*, 23 August, https://www.radiotimes.com/tv/fantasy/the-dark-crystal-age-of-resistance-review/

Fullerton, H (2019b) "How much of *The Dark Crystal: Age of Resistance* is CGI?" *Radio Times*, 31 August, https://www.radiotimes.com/tv/fantasy/dark-crystal-age-of-resistance-puppets-or-cgi/

Fullerton, H (2019c) "Is The Dark Crystal: Age of Resistance too scary for kids?" *Radio Times*, 29 August, https://www.radiotimes.com/tv/fantasy/is-the-dark-crystal-age-of-resistance-too-scary-for-kids/

Fullerton, H,(2020) "Why *The Dark Crystal: Age of Resistance* was cancelled – and how it could be saved", *Radio Times*, 22 September, https://www.radiotimes.com/tv/fantasy/dark-crystal-netflix-cancelled/

Funkyrake [sic] (2019) "Not PG", *Common Sense Media*, 26 December, https://www.commonsensemedia.org/tv-reviews/raising-dion/user-reviews/adult?page=1

Gair (2018) "Top 10 Differences Between A Series of Unfortunate Events Books & TV Show", *YouTube Comments*, 28 Mar, https://www.youtube.com/watch?v=LkNSL1SoieI

Gajanan, M (2015) "Raising Dion: a diverse comic book that turns its back on superhero tropes", *The Guardian*, 2 September, https://www.theguardian.com/books/2015/sep/01/raising-dion-comic-book-diversity-dennis-liu

Game of Thrones (TV, 2011-2019)

Gartenberg, C (2017) "Netflix's A Series of Unfortunate Events gets right what the movie got wrong", *The Verge*, 10 January, https://www.theverge.com/2017/1/10/14228706/a-series-of-unfortunate-events-netflix-tv-show-review

Gauthier, P (2019) "Nostalgia as a Problematic Cultural Space: The Example of the Original Netflix Series *GLOW* (2017)", in Pallister, K (ed), *Netflix Nostalgia: Streaming the Past on Demand*, Maryland, Lanham: Lexington Books, 75–90.

Genette, G (1997) *Palimpsests: Literature in the Second Degree*, Lincoln: University of Nebraska Press.

Gentile, D (2021) "'Lost in Space' on Netflix looks like a sci-fi show, but that's just a disguise", *SFGate*, 7 December, https://www.sfgate.com/streaming/article/lost-in-space-season-3-review-16679370.php

Ghostbusters (Ivan Reitman, Film, 1984)

Gil, SJ (2012) "Telefantasy's conflicting verisimilitudes: Composite genre and the X-Files", *Networking Knowledge*, 5 (2): https://ojs.meccsa.org.uk/index.php/netknow/article/view/270

Gilbert, A (2012) "The Death of Film and the Hollywood Response", *Senses of Cinema*, 62, March, http://sensesofcinema.com/2012/feature-articles/the-death-of-film-and-the-hollywood-response

Gillibrand, A (2019) "*The Dark Crystal: Age of Resistance* could have been so much darker, according to Lisa Henson," *Metro UK*, 1 September, https://metro.co.uk/2019/09/01/the-dark-crystal-age-of-resistance-could-have-been-so-much-darker-according-to-lisa-henson-10625338/

Gilmore Girls (TV, 2000-2007)

Gilmore Girls: A Year in the Life (TV, 2016)

Giroux, J (2016) "Netflix's 'A Series Of Unfortunate Events' Is 'Shockingly Dark,' Says Neil Patrick Harris", *Slash Film*, 13 December, https://www.slashfilm.com/548187/a-series-of-unfortunate-events-show/

GLHoover [sic] (2019) "Raising Dion", *Common Sense Media*, https://www.commonsensemedia.org/tv-reviews/raising-dion/user-reviews/adult

Goldberg, A, Masters, K and Jarvey, N (2020) "Inside Netflix's Surprising TV Chief Shakeu-Up", *The Hollywood Reporter*, 10 September, https://www.theguardian.com/tv-and-radio/2020/oct/07/netflix-killing-off-series-too-soon-glow-dark-crystal

Goldberg, A, Masters, K and Jarvey, N (2020) "Inside Netflix's Surprising TV Chief Shakeu-Up", *The Hollywood Reporter*, 10 September, https://www.theguardian.com/tv-and-radio/2020/oct/07/netflix-killing-off-series-too-soon-glow-dark-crystal

Goldberg, L (2017) "Michael B. Jordan Superhero Family Drama 'Raising Dion' Set At Netflix", *Vibe*, 5 October, https://www.vibe.com/2017/10/michael-b-jordan-raising-dion-netflix

Golder, A (2018) "19 Netflix Recommendations You Can Watch With Your Family", *BuzzFeed*, 30 December, https://www.buzzfeed.com/andyneuenschwander/19-family-friendly-netflix-titles-to-watch-over-the

Gomez, J (2019) "Here's Everything You Need to Know about New Coke from *Stranger Things*", *Seventeen*, August 20, Accessed 15 November 2022, https://www.seventeen.com/celebrity/movies-tv/a28749451/new-coke-stranger-things/

Good Times (TV, 1974–1979)
Goonies (Richard Donner, Film, 1985)
Goosebumps (TV, 1995-1998)
Götz, M, Lemish, D and Holler, A (2019) *Fear in Front of the Screen: Children's Fears, Nightmares and Thrills from TV*, Lanham, Maryland: Rowman & Littlefield.
Gould, J (1965) "TV: Premieres go on: 'Lost in Space'", *The New York Times*, 16 September, p. 93.
Graham, M (2018) "'Lost In Space' Is The Second Biggest Netflix Series Premiere Of The Last Year, According To Newly Released Nielsen Data", *Decider*, 24 April, https://decider.com/2018/04/24/lost-in-space-nielsen-ratings/
Grainge, P (2008) *Brand Hollywood: Selling Entertainment in a Global Media Age*, London: Routledge.
Grandinetti, J (2017) "From primetime to anytime: streaming video, temporality and the future of communal television", in Barker, C and Wiatrowski, M (eds), *The Age of Netflix: Critical Essays on Streaming Media, Digital Delivery and Instant Access*, Jefferson, NC: McFarland, 11–30.
Gray, J (2010) *Show Sold Separately: Promos, Spoilers, and Other Media Paratexts*, New York: New York University Press.
Gray, J (2017) "Reviving audience studies", *Critical Studies in Media Communication*, 34 (1): 70–83.
Greene, J (2007) *Mixed Methods in Social Inquiry*, San Francisco: Jossey-Bass.
Greene, S (2020) "'Locke & Key' Shows the Problem with Trying to Make a Hit TV Show from an Algorithm", *Indie Wire*, 15 February, https://www.indiewire.com/2020/02/locke-and-key-netflix-twist-ending-1202211005/
Gremlins (Joe Dante, Film, 1984)
Griffiths, G (2019) "How Seladon in The Dark Crystal: Age of Resistance nails Daenerys Targaryen's eventual downfall better than Game of Thrones ever did", *Metro*, 4 September, https://metro.co.uk/2019/09/04/how-seladon-in-the-dark-crystal-age-of-resistance-nails-daenerys-targaryens-eventual-downfall-better-than-game-of-thrones-ever-did-10678359/
Grindon, L (2012) "Cycles and clusters: The shape of film genre history", in Grant, BK (ed), *Film Genre Reader IV*, Austin Texas: University of Texas Press, 42–59.
Gross, K (2011) *Puppet: An Essay on Uncanny Life*. Chicago: University of Chicago Press.
Gross, T (2017) "The Man Behind Lemony Snicket Talks About Writing For Kids And His Childhood Fears", *NPR*, 13 January, https://www.npr.org/2017/01/13/509587895/the-man-behind-lemony-snicket-talks-about-writing-for-kids-and-his-childhood-fears
Grow, K (2016) "'Stranger Things': How Two Brothers Created Summer's Biggest TV Hit", *Rolling Stone*, 03 August, https://www.rollingstone.com/tv/tv-features/stranger-things-how-two-brothers-created-summers-biggest-tv-hit-105527/
Growing Pains (TV, 1985–1992)
Gruenwedel, E (2022) "PTC Report finds major increase of explicit adult content in Netflix's *Stranger Things*", *Media Play News*, 7 July, https://www.mediaplaynews.com/ptc-report-finds-major-increase-of-explicit-adult-content-in-netflixs-stranger-things/

Gwenmeyers [sic] (2022) "Raising Dion", *Common Sense Media*, https://www.commonsensemedia.org/tv-reviews/raising-dion/user-reviews/adult

Habyts Blog (2019) "10 TV shows that will make you wary about giving your kids Netflix", *Habyts*, 19 September, https://habyts.com/10-tv-shows-wary-kids-netflix/

Hallinan, B and Ted, S (2016) "Recommended for you: The Netflix prize and the production of algorithmic culture", *New Media & Society*, 18 (1): 117–137.

Handlen, Z (2019) "On an icy Unfortunate Events, titles can also be metaphors", *AV Club*, I January, https://www.avclub.com/on-an-icy-unfortunate-events-titles-can-also-be-metaph-1831401554

hao [sic] (2019) "If your kid is sensitive this could be too much", *Common Sense Media*, 9 November, https://www.commonsensemedia.org/tv-reviews/raising-dion/user-reviews/adult

Haralovich, MB (1992) "Sit-coms and suburbs: Positioning the 1950s homemaker", in Spigel, L and Mann, D (eds), *Private Screenings: Television and the Female Consumer*, Minneapolis & London: University of Minnesota Press, 111–142.

Harmon, J and Glut DF (1973) *The Great Movie Serials: Their Sound and Fury*, London: Woburn Press.

Harris, D (2018) "*Game of Thrones* stars join cast of *The Dark Crystal: Age of Resistance*", Winteriscoming.net, https://winteriscoming.net/2018/12/18/netflix-reveals-first-photos-cast-list-dark-crystal-prequel-age-resistance/

Hartley, J and O'Regan, T (1992) "Quoting not science but sideboards", in Hartley, J (ed), *Tele- ology: Studies in Television*, London and New York: Routledge.

Hartley, J (ed) (1992) *Tele-ology: Studies in Television*, London and New York: Routledge.

Haslop, C (2021) "'Do you wanna come with me?': the role of the star image as brand for the commodification of cult in mainstream telefantasy", *Celebrity Studies*, 12 (1): 36–50.

Hassler-Forest, D (2014) "Game of thrones: quality television and the cultural logic of gentrification", in Hassler-Forrest, D and Nicklas, P (eds), *The Politics of Adaptation: Media Convergence and Ideology*, New York: Palgrave Macmillan, 187–200.

Hassler-Forest, D (2020) "'When you get there, you will already be there': *Stranger Things*, *Twin Peaks* and the nostalgia industry", *Science Fiction Film and Television* 13 (2): 175–197.

Hauser, GA (1999) *Vernacular Voices: The Rhetoric of Publics and Public Spheres*, South Carolina: University of South Carolina.

Heathers (Michael Lehmann, Film, 1990)

Hellraiser (Clive Barker, Film, 1987)

Helmore, E (2022) "Netflix shares fall more than 35% after streamer loses over 200,000 subscribers", *The Guardian*, 21 April, https://www.theguardian.com/media/2022/apr/20/netflix-shares-fall-losing-subscribers

Henesy, M (2021) "'Leaving my girlhood behind': woke witches and feminist liminality in *Chilling Adventures of Sabrina*", *Feminist Media Studies*, 21 (7): 1143–1157.

Henricks, TS (2018) "Theme and Variation: Arranging Play's Forms, Functions, and 'Colors'", *American Journal of Play* 10 (2): 133–167.

Henson, M (2017) "Over-the-Top or a Race to the Bottom: A Parent's Guide to Streaming Video", Parents Television Council, https://www.parentstv.org/images/pages/A-Parents-Guide-to-Streaming.pdf & https://www.parentstv.org/

Heroes (TV, 2006-2010)
Hesford, D (2013) " 'Action!... Suspense!... Emotion!' the Trailer as Cinematic Performance", *Frames Cinema Journal*, 3, http://framescinemajournal.com/article/action-suspense-emotion-the-trailer-as-cinematic-performance/
Heyer, P (2013) "Islands in the Screen: The Robinsonnade as Television Genre", *Fictions Télévisuelles: Approches Esthétiques*, 23 (2-3): 121–142.
Hibberd, J (2018) "Netflix reveals Lost in Space action-packed trailer – Exclusive", *EW*, 6 March, https://ew.com/tv/2018/03/06/netflix-lost-in-space-trailer/
Hill, S (2021) "What you need to know about Roblox - and why kids are obsessed", *Wired*, 15 March, https://www.wired.com/story/unpacking-roblox-and-its-popularity/
Hills, M (2002) *Fan Cultures*, London & New York: Routledge.
Hills, M (2005) *The Pleasures of Horror*, London: Bloomsbury Academic.
Hills, M (2014) "When *Doctor Who* enters its own timeline: the database aesthetics and hyperdiegesis of multi-doctor stories", *Critical Studies in Television*, 9 (1): 95–113.
Hills, M (2018) "Cult TV revival: generational seriality, recap culture, and the 'Brand Gap' of *Twin Peaks: The Return*", *Television and New Media*, 19 (4): 310–327.
Hills, M (2021) "From 1980s Intertextualities to (Un)Faithful 'Inter-textualities': *Stranger Things* and Audience-Created Relations Between Media Texts", in Mollet and Scott (eds), *Investigating Stranger Things: Upside Down in the World of Mainstream Cult Entertainment*, Cham, Switzerland: Palgrave Macmillan, 189–208.
Hindle, D (2020) "Hansel and Gretel: a complex tale of parent-child interactions", *Infant Observation*, 23(1/2): 84–98.
Hodge, C (2009) "Materialities of Nostalgia at the Old Homestead", *Archaeologies: Journal of the World Archaeological Congress*, 5 (3): 488–510.
Holden, ME (2019) "The Dark Crystal: Age of Resistance A Pillar of Inclusive Entertainment", *Geena Davis Institute on Gender in Media*, https://seejane.org/spotlight/the-dark-crystal-age-of-resistance-a-pillar-of-inclusive-entertainment/
Holdsworth, A (2011) *Television, Memory and Nostalgia*, London: Palgrave Macmillan.
Hotel Transylvania (Genndy Tartakovsky, Film, 2012)
Houghton, R (2018) "Netflix is bringing out more sci-fi and fantasy shows after success of *Stranger Things*", *Digital Spy*, 30 April, https://www.digitalspy.com/tv/ustv/a856012/netflix-series-shows-sci-fi-fantasy-stranger-things-season-3-success/
House of Cards (TV, 2013–2019)
Huddleston, T (2016) *Miss Peregrine's Home for Peculiar Children*, https://www.timeout.com/movies/miss-peregrines-home-for-peculiar-children
Hugie, A (2017) "Snicket and Poe: A Juvenile Mystery", *Criterion: A Journal of Literary Criticism*, 10 (2): 35–44.
Huizinga, J (1949) *Homo Ludens: A Study of the Play-element in Culture*, London: Routledge.
Hunter, M (2018) "Bric[k]olage: Adaptation as Play in The Lego Movie (2014)", *Adaptation: The Journal of Literature on Screen Studies*, 11 (3): 273–281.
Hutcheon, L (1986-1987) "The Politics of Postmodernism: Parody and History," *Cultural Critique* 5 (Winter), pp. 179–207.
Hymas, C (2019) "Netflix to introduce official age classifications on all its films and shows," *The Telegraph*, 28 October, https://www.telegraph.co.uk/news/2019/10/28/netflix-introduce-official-age-classifications-films-shows/

imska [sic] (2019) "Netflix needs to readjust its age rating", *Common Sense Media*, 13 November, https://www.commonsensemedia.org/tv-reviews/raising-dion/user-reviews/adult?page=2

Indiana Jones and the Temple of Doom (Steven Spielberg, Film, 1984)

Iqbal, N (2018) "Film fans see red over Netflix 'targeted' posters for black viewers", *The Guardian*, 21 October, https://www.theguardian.com/media/2018/oct/20/netflix-film-black-viewers-personalised-marketing-target

Iqbal, N (2022) "Netflix Revenue and Usage Statistics (2022)", *The Business of Apps*, 27 October, https://www.businessofapps.com/data/netflix-statistics/

IT (Tommy Lee Wallace, Film, 1990)

It (Andy Muschietti, Film, 2017)

Jackson, A (2017) "New Directions in Children's Gothic: Debatable Lands", in Jackson, A (ed), *New Directions in Children's Gothic: Debatable Lands*, New York: Routledge, 1–15.

Jackson, P (2019) "8 Very Black Reasons to Check Out Raising Dion on Netflix", *The Root*, 7 October, https://www.theroot.com/8-very-black-reasons-to-check-out-raising-dion-on-netfl-1838855216

Jacobson, A (2020) "Child's play: SVOD's integral role in growing up today", *Radio + Television Business Report*, 26 June, https://www.rbr.com/childs-play-svods-integral-role-in-growing-up-today/

JAinVA [sic] (2021) "Lost in Space", *Common Sense Media*, https://www.commonsensemedia.org/tv-reviews/lost-in-space-0/user-reviews/adult

Jameson, F (1991) *Postmodernism*, London: Verso.

Jameson, F (1992) *Nostalgia for the Present Or, the Cultural Logic of Late Capitalism*, Durham, NC: Duke University Press.

Jameson, F (2014) "Postmodernism and consumer society", in Wood, N and Lodge, D (eds), *Modern Criticism and Theory: A Reader*, New York: Routledge, 542–554

Jancovich, M and Johnson, D (2009) "Film and television in the 1950s", in Bould, M et al (eds), *The Routledge Companion to Science Fiction*, London and New York: Routledge.

Jaramillo, DL (2013) "Rescuing television from 'the cinematic': The perils of dismissing television style", in Jacobs, J and Peacock, S (eds), *Television Aesthetics and Style*, New York: Bloomsbury, 67–75.

Jeffery, M (2018) "The story of the Lost in Space revival that never happened", *Digial Spy*, 25 April, https://www.digitalspy.com/tv/ustv/a855578/lost-in-space-2018-movie-unmade-revival/

Jeffords, S (1989) *The Remasculinization of America: Gender and the Vietnam War*, Bloomington: Indiana University Press.

Jenkins, E (2013) "Another *Punctum*: animation, affect, and ideology", *Critical Inquiry* 39 (Spring): 575–591.

Jenkins, H (2013) "I was a (pre-)teenage monster", *Journal of Fandom Studies*, 1 (1): 87–100.

Jenkins, H (2006) *Convergence Culture: Where Old and New Media Collide*, New York: New York University Press.

Jenkins, H and Scott, S (2013) "Textual poachers twenty years later: a conversation between Henry Jenkins and Suzanne Scott", in H Jenkins (ed), *Textual Poachers: Television Fans and Participatory Culture*, New York: Routledge, vii–l.

Jenks, C (2005) *Childhood*, Second edn, New York: Routledge.

Jenner M (2016) "Is this TVIV? On Netflix, TVIII and binge-watching", *New Media and Society*. 18 (2): 257–273.

Jenner M (2018) *Netflix and the Re-Invention of Television*, London: Palgrave Macmillan.

Jenner M (2020) "Researching binge-watching", *Critical Studies in Television*, 15 (3): 267–279.

Jessascroggs (2019) "Raising Dion", *Common Sense Media*, https://www.commonsensemedia.org/tv-reviews/raising-dion/user-reviews/adult

JMPakele [sic] (2019) "Raising Dion: Parent of a 9-year-old", *Common Sense Media*, 21 October, https://www.commonsensemedia.org/tv-reviews/raising-dion/user-reviews/adult

Johnson, C (2005) *Telefantasy*, London: British Film Institute.

Johnson, C (2012) *Branding Television*, New York: Routledge.

Johnson, C (2015) "Telefantasy", in Creeber, G (ed), *The Television Genre Book*, London: Palgrave Macmillan, 56–60.

Johnson, C (2017) "Beyond catch-up: VOD interfaces, ITV hub and the re-positioning of television online", *Critical studies in television*, 12 (2), 121–138.

Johnson, C (2019) *Online TV*, London: Routledge.

Johnson, D (2018a) "Television guides and recommendations in a changing channel landscape", in Johnson, D (ed), *Networks to Netflix: A guide to Changing Channels*, New York: Routledge.

Johnson, D (2018b) "Reluctant retailing: amazon prime video and the non-merchandising of kids' television," *Film and Merchandise*, 42 (2): November, 10.3998/fc.13761232.0042.208

Johnson, D (2019) *Transgenerational Media Industries: Adults, Children, and the Reproduction of Culture*, Ann Arbor: University of Michigan Press.

Johnson-Smith, J (2012) *American Science Fiction TV: Star trek, Stargate and Beyond*, London: I. B. Tauris.

Jones, A (2019) "What Does 'See You Yesterday's Ending Mean? The Netflix Film Ended Abruptly", *Marie Claire*, 23 May, https://www.marieclaire.com/culture/a27572403/see-you-yesterday-ending-netflix/

Jowett, L and Abbott, S (2013) *TV Horror: Investigating the Darker Side of the Small Screen*, London: I.B. Tauris.

Julia (TV, 1969-71)

Jurassic Park (Steven Spielberg, Film, 1993)

K [sic], J (2020) "Netflix, let's talk about these micro genres", *Medium*, 13 January, https://medium.com/@jksarti/netflix-lets-talk-about-these-micro-genres-477a28326d52

Kamen, M (2020) "Cancel culture: is Netflix killing off series too soon?" *The Guardian*, 7 October, https://www.theguardian.com/tv-and-radio/2020/oct/07/netflix-killing-off-series-too-soon-glow-dark-crystal

Katz, B (2019) "Is Disney+'s *The Mandalorian* more popular than Netflix's *Stranger Things*?", *Observer*, 25 November, https://observer.com/2019/11/the-mandalorian-timeline-disney-plus-ratings-viewership-netflix/

Katz, VS (2010) "How children of immigrants use media to connect their families to the community", *Journal of Children and Media*, 4: 298–315.

KCK (2020) "Smart & Creative Series with 3 Siblings Working Together", *Common*

Sense Media, https://www.commonsensemedia.org/tv-reviews/a-series-of-unfortunate-events/user-reviews/adult

Keahey, A (2019) "Why the new trailer for Netflix's 'Raising Dion' feels bittersweet", *Black Youth Project*, 27 September, http://blackyouthproject.com/why-the-new-trailer-for-netflixs-raising-dion-feels-bittersweet/

Keck C (2021) "Netflix is shifting the way it ranks its most popular titles", *The Verge*, 19 October, https://www.theverge.com/2021/10/19/22735379/netflix-changing-ranking-metric-popular-titles-hours-viewed

Keck C (2021) "Netflix launches new website for reporting its Top 10 titles" *The Verge*, 16 November, https://www.theverge.com/2021/11/16/22785623/netflix-launches-top-10-titles-website

Kecskes, I (2017) "Cross-cultural and intercultural pragmatics", in Huang, Y (ed), *The Oxford Handbook of Pragmatics*, Oxford: Oxford University Press, Oxford Handbooks Online: 10.1093/oxfordhb/9780199697960.001.0001

Kelly, JP (2020) "'This title is no longer available': preserving television in the streaming age", *Television & New Media*, 9 June, https://doi-org.ezproxy.lib.rmit.edu.au/10.1177/1527476420928480

Kellywelly [sic] (2019) "Raising Dion", *Common Sense Media*, https://www.commonsensemedia.org/tv-reviews/raising-dion/user-reviews/adult

kelschandler [sic] (2020) "Raising Dion", *Common Sense Media*, https://www.commonsensemedia.org/tv-reviews/raising-dion/user-reviews/adult

Kelso, T (2008) "And now no word from our sponsor: How HBO puts the risk back into television", in Leverette, M, Ott, BL and Buckley, CL (eds), *It's Not TV: Watching HBO in the Post Television Era*, New York: Routledge, 46–64

Kennedy, JF (1962) "Rice University", 12 September 1962, www.jfklibrary.org/Asset-Viewer/MkATdOcdU06X5uNHbmqm1Q.aspx

Kernan, L (2004) *Coming Attractions: Reading American Movie Trailers*, Austin: University of Texas Press.

Keveney, B (2019) "'Lost in Space' stars embrace Season 2 holiday launch as perfect time for family viewing", *USA Today*, 24 December, https://www.usatoday.com/story/entertainment/tv/2019/12/24/lost-space-family-sticks-together-despite-hazards-outer-space/2708957001/

Kincaid, J (1992) *Child-Loving: The Erotic Child and Victorian Culture*, London: Routledge

Kincaid, J (1998) *Erotic Innocence: The Culture of Child Molesting*, Durham: Duke University Press.

King, G (2014) *Indie 2.0: Change and Continuity in Contemporary American Indie Film*, London: I. B. Tauris.

Kintaku (2020) "Netflix series vs film: A Series Of Unfortunate Events - NitPix", YouTube, 20 January 2017, https://www.youtube.com/watch?v=rC83z9DXFfo

Kipo and the age of the wonderbeasts (TV, 2020)

Klarer, M (2014) "Putting television 'Aside': novel narration in house of cards", *New Review of Film and Television Studies*, 12 (2): 203–220.

Klecker, C (2015) "The other kind of film frames: a research report on paratexts in film", *Word & Image*, 31: 402–413.

Klein, AA (2011) *American Film Cycles: Reframing Genres, Screening Social Problems, and Defining Subcultures*, Austin: University of Texas Press.

Klinger, B (1989) "Digressions at the cinema: reception and mass culture", *Cinema Journal*, 28 (4) (Summer): 3–19

Knewitz, S (2022) "Reimagining the cold war: capitalist realism, anti-communism and nostalgia in twenty-first-century TV and streaming services", *Journal of Popular Television* 10 (1): 79–94.

Knoop, J (2020) "*The Mandalorian* beats *Stranger Things* as the Most In-demand show", *IGN*, 22 August, https://www.ign.com/articles/2019/11/26/mandalorian-stranger-things-ratings-ranking-in-demand-most-watched-disney-plus-netflix

Koblin, J (2016) "Netflix aims for family friendly nostalgia with new slate", *New York Times*, 26 February, https://www.nytimes.com/2016/02/26/business/media/netflix-aims-for-family-friendly-nostalgia-with-new-slate.html

KPhilogone [sic] (2020) "Good series, full of subjects to discuss with your kids", *Common Sense Media*, 22 March, https://www.commonsensemedia.org/tv-reviews/raising-dion/user-reviews/adult

Kümmerling-Meibauer, B (2013) "Paratexts in Children's Films and the Concept of Meta-filmic Awareness", *Journal of Educational Media, Memory & Society*, 5 (2): 108–123.

Kutulas, J (2005) "Who Rules the Roost?: sitcom family dynamics from the Cleavers to the Osbournes," in Dalton, MM and Linder, LR (eds), *The Sitcom Reader: America Viewed and Skewed*, New York: State University of New York Press, 49–59.

Labyrinth (Jim Henson, Film, 1986)

Ladyhawke (Richar Donner, Film, 1985)

Landsberg, A (2004) *Prosthetic Memory: The Transformation of American Remembrance in the Age of Mass Culture*, New York: Columbia University Press.

Langbauer, L (2007) "The ethics and practice of lemony snicket: adolescence and Generation X", *PMLA* 122 (2): 502–521.

Lawrence, E (2015) "Everything is a recommendation: Netflix, altgenres and the construction of taste", *Knowledge Organization*, 42 (5): 358–364.

Lawson, M (2013) "Showdown: will on-demand kill the big TV get-together", *The Guardian*, 16 December, https://www.theguardian.com/tv-and-radio/2013/dec/16/tv-viewing-christmas-netflix-on-demand

Lawson, M (2016) "Nostalgic nightmares: how Netflix made *Stranger Things* a watercooler smash", *The Guardian*, 5 August, https://www.theguardian.com/tv-and-radio/2016/aug/05/netflix-hit-stranger-things-highlights-tvs-trend-for-nostalgia

Leave it to Beaver (TV, 1957-1963)

Leavy, P (2017) *Research Design: Quantitative, Qualitative, Mixed Methods, Arts-based, and Community-based Participatory Research Approaches*, New York: Guilford Press.

Legend (Ridley Scott, Film, 1984)

Lehman, F (2018) *Hollywood Harmony: Musical Wonder and the Sound of Cinema*, New York: Oxford University Press.

Leigh, JA (2022) "Raising Dion ending explained: How season 2 finale sets up an epic season 3", *Digital Spy*, 1 February, https://www.digitalspy.com/tv/ustv/a38925300/raising-dion-season-2-ending-explained/

Leitch, T (2002) "Twice-told tales: Disavowal and the rhetoric of the remake", in Forrest, J and Koos, LR (eds), *Dead Ringers; The Remake in Theory and Practice*, Albany NY: SUNY Press, 37–62.

Leitch, T (2018) "There's No Nostalgia Like Hollywood Nostalgia", *Humanities*, 7 (1): 1–13.

Lena S [sic] (2019) "Great story... unexpected details", *Common Sense Media*, 7 October, https://www.commonsensemedia.org/tv-reviews/raising-dion/user-reviews/adult

Leppert, A (2019) *TV Family Values: Gender, Domestic Labor, and 1980s Sitcoms*, New Brunswick, NJ: Rutgers University Press.

Lester, C (2016) "The Children's Horror Film: Characterizing an 'Impossible' Subgenre", *The Velvet Light Trap*, 78: 22–37.

Lester, C (2021) *Horror Films for Children: Fear and Pleasure in American Cinema*, London, UK: Bloomsbury Academic.

Lewis, I (2022) "Stranger Things season 4 could have been even longer without the pandemic", *The Independent*, 20 July, https://www.independent.co.uk/arts-entertainment/tv/news/stranger-things-season-4-episodes-ted-sarandos-b2127235.html

Lindsey, C (2016) "Questioning Netflix's revolutionary impact: changes in the business and consumption of television", in McDonald, K and Smith-Rowsey, D (eds), *The Netflix effect: technology and entertainment in the 21st century*, New York, NY: Bloomsbury Academic, 173–184.

Lisa S [sic] (2018) "Lost in Space", *Common Sense Media*, https://www.commonsensemedia.org/tv-reviews/lost-in-space-0/user-reviews/adult

Littleton, C (2017) "Netflix to boost international kids content as viewership spikes", *Variety*, 15 October, https://variety.com/2017/tv/news/netflix-kids-guillermo-del-toro trollhunters andy yeatman-1202590366/

Littleton, C (2018) "Bob Iger Talks Disney+, Hulu Plans and his Vision for Enlarged TV Studio", *Variety*, 8 November, https://variety.com/2018/digital/news/disney-disney-streaming-service-launch-2019-1203023789/

Little Women (George Cukor, Film, 1933)

Liu, D (2015) *Raising Dion*, 25 August, *YouTube*, https://www.youtube.com/watch?time_continue=7&v=dW9EIxEqrJw&feature=emb_logo

Lizardi, R (2014) "The nostalgic revolution will be televised", in Lavigne, C (ed), *Remake Television: Reboot, Re-Use, Recycle*, Lanham MD: Lexington Books.

Lizardi, R (2017) *Nostalgic Generations and Media: Perception of Time and Available Meaning*, Lanham: Lexington Books.

Lizardi, R (2018) "Mourning and melancholia: conflicting approaches to reviving *Gilmore Girls* one season at a time", *Television & New Media*, 19 (4): 379–395.

Lizardo, O and Skiles, S (2008) "Cultural consumption in the fine and popular arts realms", *Sociology Compass* 2 (2): 485–502, 10.1111/j.1751-9020.2008.00101.

Lloyd, R (2019) "Q&A: Why is Netflix's 'A Series of Unfortunate Events' so superior to the movie? We ask Barry Sonnenfeld", *Los Angeles Times*, 6 January, https://www.latimes.com/entertainment/tv/la-et-st-barry-sonnenfeld-series-of-unfortunate-events-interview-20190102-story.html

Lobao, M (2018) "Netflix adding more granularity and transparency to its parental controls", *Android Police*, 5 March, https://www.androidpolice.com/2018/03/05/netflix-adding-granularity-transparency-parental-controls/

Lobato, R (2018) "Rethinking international TV flows research in the age of Netflix", *Television & New Media*, 19, (3): 241–256.

Lobato, R (2019) *Netflix Nations: The Geography of Digital Distribution*, New York: New York University Press.

Locke & Key (TV, 2020-2022)

Longo, C (2019) "Lost in Space Is Lifting Off With A Bigger Sci-Fi Quest In Season 2", *Den of Geek*, 10 December, https://www.denofgeek.com/tv/lost-in-space-is-lifting-off-with-a-bigger-sci-fi-quest-in-season-2/

Loock, K (2018) "'Whatever happened to predictability': *Fuller House*, post(feminism, and the revival of family-friendly viewing", *Television & New Media*, 19 (4): 361–378.

Lost (TV, 2004-2010)

Lost in Space (TV, 2018-2021)

Lotz, AD (2006) *Redesigning Women: Television After the Network Era*, Urbana and Chicago: University of Illinois Press.

Lotz, AD (2014) *Cable Guys: Television and Masculinities in the 21st Century*, New York: New York University Press.

Lotz, AD (2017) *Portals: A Treatise on Internet-Distributed Television*, Ann Arbor, MI: Maize Books, 10.3998/mpub.9699689

Lotz, AD (2018) *We Now Disrupt This Broadcast: How Cable Transformed Television and the Internet Revolutionized it All*, Cambridge, Massachusetts: The MIT Press.

Loussikian K (2019) "Netflix gets approval to classify own shows after two-year trial", *Sydney Morning Herald*, 20 January, https://www.smh.com.au/business/companies/netflix-gets-approval-to-classify-own-shows-after-two-year-trial-20190120-p50sim.html

Luke Cage (TV, 2016-2018).

Lury, K (2005a) *Interpreting Television*, London: Hodder Arnold.

Lury, K (2005b) "The child in film and television", *Screen* 46 (3): 307–314.

Lynch, A (2022) *Quality Telefantasy: How US Quality TV Brought Zombies, Dragons and Androids into the Mainstream*, London: Routledge.

Lynch, A and Scarlata, A (2023) "Streaming video on Demand (SVOD): A place for (outer) space?" in Hawkes, A, Christie, C, and Nienhuis, T (eds), *Science Fiction Television and the Politics of Space*: 71–94. New York & London: Bloomsbury.

Lynch, J (2018) "Sci-fi and fantasy are dominating Netflix – and subscribers can expect a lot more in the future", *Business Insider*, 28 April, https://www.businessinsider.com/netflix-is-focusing-on-sci-fi-to-meet-increasing-demand-data-2018-4

MacDowell, J (2010) "Notes on quirky", *Movie: A Journal of Film Criticism*, 1, 1–16, http://www2.warwick.ac.uk/fac/arts/film/movie/contents/notes_on_quirky.pdf

Macek III, JC (2013a) "The Lost in Space Family Robinson", *Pop Matters*, 3 June, https://www.popmatters.com/172206-the-lost-in-space-family-robinson-2495751035.html

Macek III, JC (2013b) "The Lost in Space Family Robinson Part II", *Pop Matters*, 26 June, https://www.popmatters.com/172965-the-lost-in-space-family-robinson-part-ii-2495745327.html

Madrigal, AC (2014) "How Netflix Reverse-Engineered Hollywood", *The Atlantic*, 2 January, https://www.theatlantic.com/technology/archive/2014/01/how-netflix-reverse-engineered-hollywood/282679/

Maesar, E (2022) "Movie: The Series *The Dark Crystal*", *Movie Jawn*, 23 March, https://www.moviejawn.com/home/2022/3/23/movie-the-series-the-dark-crystal

Maglio, T (2017) "Netflix's *Series of Unfortunate Events* tops *Luke Cage* in TV Ratings (Exclusive)", *The Wrap*, 18 January, https://www.thewrap.com/lemony-snickets-series-of-unfortunate-events-tv-ratings/

Magnusson, K (2012) "Lemony Snicket's *A Series of Unfortunate Events*: Daniel Handler and Marketing the Author", *Children's Literature Association Quarterly*, 37 (1): 86–107.

Mahlknecht, J (2015) "Three words to tell a story: the movie poster tagline", *Word & Image* 31: 414–424.

Malina87 [sic] (2021) "Lost in Space", *Common Sense Media*, https://www.commonsensemedia.org/tv-reviews/lost-in-space-0/user-reviews/adult

Managan, L (2016) "Stranger Things Review: A Shot of 80s Nostalgia Right to Your Heart", *The Guardian*, https://www.theguardian.com/tv-and-radio/2016/jul/15/stranger-things-review-a-shot-of-80s-nostalgia-right-to-your-heart-winona-ryder

Mannheim, K (1997) "The sociological problem of generations", *Collected Works of Karl Mannheim*, London: Routledge, 163–195.

Marniie [sic] (2018) "Top 10 Differences between A Series of Unfortunate Events Books & TV show", *YouTube*, 28 March, Accessed 11 Nov 2019, https://www.youtube.com/watch?v=LkNSL1SoieI

Marshall, R (2019) "*The Dark Crystal: Age of Resistance* makes CGI, puppetry, a winning combo", *Digital Trends*, 3 September, https://www.digitaltrends.com/home-theater/dark-crystal-age-of-resistance-cgi-puppetry/

Mascio, A (2021) "Sponsored Things: audiences and the commodification of the past in Stranger Things", in Mollet and Scott (eds), *Investigating Stranger Things: Upside Down in the World of Mainstream Cult Entertainment*, Cham, Switzerland: Palgrave Macmillan, 227–243.

Mathijs, E and Sexton, J (2011) *Cult Cinema: An Introduction*, New York: Wiley-Blackwell.

Mayer, R (2010) "Robinson Crusoe on television", *Quarterly Review of Film and Video*, 28 (1): 53–65.

McCabe, J and Akass, K (2007) *Quality TV: Contemporary American Television and Beyond*, London: I.B.Tauris.

McCabe, J and Akass, K (2008) "It's not TV, it's HBO's original programming: Producing quality TV", in Leverett, M, Ott, BL, and Buckley, CL (eds), *It's Not TV: Watching HBO in the Post-Television Era*, New York: Routledge, 83–94.

McCort, JR (2016) "'In the Darkest Zones': The allure of horror in contemporary revisionist fairy-tale novels for children", in JR (ed), *Reading in the Dark: Horror in Children's Literature and Culture*, Jackson: University Press of Mississippi, 121–146.

McCreesh, L (2018) "Lost in Space ratings on Netflix have apparently been revealed", *Digital Spy*, 25 April, https://www.digitalspy.com/tv/ustv/a855590/lost-in-space-netflix-ratings-us-nielsen/

McDonald, K. and Smith-Rowsey, D. (eds) 2016. *The Netflix Effect: Technology and Entertainment in the 21st Century*, New York and London: Bloomsbury.

McFarland, M (2019) "*The Dark Crystal: Age of Resistance*: A Dark Fantasy very relevant to our current reality", *Salon*, 28 August, https://www.salon.com/2019/08/28/the-dark-crystal-age-of-resistance-a-seductive-fantasy-very-relevant-to-our-reality/

McHenry, J (2017) "Barry Sonnenfeld on Netflix's A Series of Unfortunate Events and why he's glad he was fired from the movie", *Vulture*, 18 January, https://www.vulture.com/2017/01/barry-sonnenfeld-a-series-of-unfortunate-events-netflix.html?regwall-newsletter-signup=true#

McLaren, M (2022) "Netflix just canceled this popular show that reached No. 1", *Tom's Guide*, 27 April, https://www.tomsguide.com/news/netflix-just-canceled-this-show-with-83-rotten-tomatoes-score

McNamara, B (2016) "'Stranger Things' Actor Gaten Matarazzo On Living With Cleidocranial Dysplasia", *Teen Vogue*, 13 September, https://www.teenvogue.com/story/gaten-matarazzo-stranger-things-cleidocranial-dysplasia

McRobbie, A (2007) "TOP GIRLS? Young women and the post-feminist sexual contract", *Cultural Studies*, 21 (4-5): 718–737.

Mehmedova, F (2019) "Netflix explains why it controversially cancelled One Day at a Time", *Digital Spy*, 12 June, https://www.digitalspy.com/tv/ustv/a27943312/netflix-one-day-at-a-time-cancellation-explained/

Melrose, K (2018) "How Netflix's Lost in Space Reboot Pays Tribute to the Original", *CBR*, 13 April, https://www.cbr.com/lost-space-neflix-easter-eggs/

Merrill, N, Booker, JA and Fivush, R (2018) "Functions of parental intergenerational narratives told by young people", *Topics in Cognitive Science*, 11: 752–773.

Messenger-Davies, M (2001) "Studying Children's Television", in Creeber, G (ed), *The Television Genre Book*, London: British Film Institute, 96–102.

Midnight Mass (TV, 2021)

Milbrand, L (2017). "I'm Binge Watching 'Stranger Things' With My Kids This Weekend. Should You?" *Parents*, 30 October, https://www.parents.com/toddlers-preschoolers/everything-kids/im-binge-watching-stranger-things-with-my-kids-this-weekend/

Miller, C (2022) "*The Dark Crystal*'s 40th Anniversary to Be Celebrated by Fans at the Jim Henson Lot", *Movie Web*, 11 July, https://movieweb.com/fans-of-the-dark-crystal-celebrating-films-40th-anniversary-this-year/

Miller, M (2016) "*Stranger Things* Is Officially Bigger Than *House of Cards* and *Jessica Jones*", *Esquire*, 13 August, https://www.esquire.com/entertainment/tv/news/a47629/stranger-things-ratings-success/

Mills, B (2013) "What does it mean to call television 'cinematic'?" in Peacock, Steven and Jacobs, Jason (ed), *Television Aesthetics and Style*, New York: Bloomsbury Academic: 57–66.

Misery (Rob Reiner, Film, 1990)

Mitchell, T (2022) "The best TV shows for you to stream in June", *The Age*, 2 June, https://www.theage.com.au/culture/tv-and-radio/the-best-tv-shows-for-you-to-stream-in-june-20220601-p5aqdj.html?btis

Mittell, J (2001) A Cultural Approach to Television Genre Theory, *Cinema Journal*, 40 (3): 3–24.

Mittell, J (2004) *Genre and Television: From Cop Shows to Cartoons in American Culture*, New York and London: Routledge.

Mittell, J (2015a) "Children's Television - Children's Television as Genre", in Creeber, G, Miller, T, and Tulloch, J (eds), *The Television Genre Book*. London: Palgrave Macmillan, 112–114.

Mittell, J (2015b) *Complex TV: The Poetics of Contemporary Television Storytelling*, New York: New York University Press.

Mogg, K (2018) "Recognizing the Children in *Alfred Hitchcock Presents* and *The*

Alfred Hitchcock Hour", in Schober, A and Olson, D (eds), *Children, Youth, and American Television*, New York and Oxfordshire: Routledge, 23–43.

Mollet, T and Scott, L (2021) "*Stranger Things* in a familiar land: mainstream cult entertainment in the age of Netflix", in Mollet and Scott (eds), *Investigating Stranger Things: Upside Down in the World of Mainstream Cult Entertainment*, Cham, Switzerland: Palgrave Macmillan, 1–21.

MommaFino [sic] (2020) "Lost in Space", *Common Sense Media*, https://www.commonsensemedia.org/tv-reviews/lost-in-space-0/user-reviews/adult

Momoftwoboys 123 [sic] (2022) "Good show, but rating is WAY off", *Common Sense Media*, https://www.commonsensemedia.org/tv-reviews/raising-dion/user-reviews/adult

Monji, J (2018) "Against the Odds: Netflix Brings Lost in Space to WonderCon", 28 March, https://www.rogerebert.com/chazs-blog/against-the-odds-netflix-brings-lost-in-space-to-wondercon

Montgomery, H (2019) "*The Dark Crystal: Age of Resistance* Review", *Radio Times*, 30th August, https://www.bbc.com/culture/article/20190823-netflixs-new-dark-crystal-series-is-weird-and-brilliant

Mom of two kiddos [sic] (2019) "Great family entertainment, very fresh and realistic", *Common Sense Media*, 20 October, https://www.commonsensemedia.org/tv-reviews/raising-dion/user-reviews/adult

Moore, K (2021) "The Netflix ID Bible – Every Category on Netflix in 2021", *What's on Netflix*, 29 September, https://www.whats-on-netflix.com/news/the-netflix-id-bible-every-category-on-netflix/

Moore, S (2017) "The most streamed shows of 2016 revealed", *NME*, https://www.nme.com/news/most-streamed-shows-of-2016-1936362

MPAA, "Classification and Rating Rules", 1 January 2010, https://www.filmratings.com/Content/Downloads/rating_rules.pdfi

Mudede, C (2018) "Netflix's *Lost In Space* Features Surprising Recognition of Race", *The Stranger*, 11 July, https://www.thestranger.com/film/2018/07/11/29029340/netflixs-lost-in-space-features-surprising-recognition-of-race

Murray, N (2018) "'Lost in Space': Sixties Sci-Fi Reboot Gets Netflix Blockbuster-TV Treatment", *Rolling Stone*, 10 April, https://www.rollingstone.com/tv/tv-news/lost-in-space-sixties-sci-fi-reboot-gets-netflix-blockbuster-tv-treatment-629155/

Naremore, J (1998) *More Than Night: Film Noir in its Contexts*, Berkeley, CA: University of California Press.

Nathan, I (2018) "Lost In Space - Season 1 Review", *Empire*, 18 April, https://www.empireonline.com/tv/reviews/lost-space-season-1-review/

Ndalianis, A (2009) "Enter the Aleph: superhero worlds and hypertime realities", in Ndalianis, A (ed), *The Contemporary Comic Book Superhero*, New York: Routledge, 270–290.

Neale, S (2000) *Genre and Hollywood*, London: Routledge.

Neale, S (2012) "Questions of genre", in Grant, BK (ed), *Film Genre Reader IV*, Austin Texas: University of Texas Press, 178–202.

Nedd, A (2019) "'A Series of Unfortunate Events' was right to change its finale from the books", *Mashable*, 4 January, https://mashable.com/article/a-series-of-unfortunate-events-book-ending-tv

Needham, G (2008) "Scheduling Normativity: Television, the Family, and Queer

Temporality", in Davis, G and Needham, G (eds), *Queer TV: Theories, Histories, Politics*, New York: Routledge, 153–168.

Negra, D (2005) "'Queen of the indies': Parker Posey's niche stardom and taste cultures of independent film", in Holmund, C and Wyatt, J (eds), *Contemporary American Independent Film: From the Margins to the Mainstream*, London: Routledge, 71–88.

Nelson, R (2007) *State of Play: Contemporary 'High End' TV Drama*, Manchester: Manchester University Press.

Nelson, S (2019) "Netflix's superhero drama Raising Dion struggles to find a Stranger Things balance", *The Verge*, 30 September, https://www.theverge.com/2019/9/30/20892045/raising-dion-netflix-tv-review-superhero-stranger-things-drama-michael-b-jordan

Netflix, S (2016a) "Lemony Snicket's A Series of Unfortunate Events | Teaser Trailer [HD] | Netflix", *YouTube*, 5 October, https://www.youtube.com/watch?v=6hlNVt-STn4

Netflix (2016b) "Netflix Is Now Available Around the World", 7 January, https://about.netflix.com/en/news/netflix-is-now-available-around-the-world

Netflix (2016c) "New Updated 'Lost in Space' Series Coming Exclusively to Netflix", Netflix, https://about.netflix.com/en/news/new-updated-lost-in-space-series-coming-exclusively-to-netflix-1

Netflix (2017a) "A Single Mom raises her Superhero Son in the groundbreaking Raising Dion, coming to Netflix", Netflix Media Center, 5 October, https://media.netflix.com/en/press-releases/a-single-mom-raises-her-superhero-son-in-the-groundbreaking-raising-dion-coming-to-netflix

Netflix (2017b) "Netflix Announces 'The Dark Crystal: Age of Resistance,' A Prequel Series to the Groundbreaking Jim Henson Film", 19 May, https://about.netflix.com/en/news/netflix-announces-the-dark-crystal-age-of-resistance-a-prequel-series-to-the-groundbreaking-jim-henson-film

Netflix (2018a) "Y'all need Jesus", Twitter, 1 May, https://twitter.com/netflix/status/991106838983655424?s=20

Netflix (2018b) "A Series of Unfortunate Events - Season 2 | Teaser [HD] |" Youtube. https://www.youtube.com/watch?v=_mZhfeDr88A

Netflix (2019a) "See you Yesterday Official Trailer [HD]" 22 April https://www.youtube.com/watch?v=8MVRWQ1PnMo

Netflix (2019b) "Your new Netflix ident animation (cue *Netflix Sound*)," Netflix Media Center, 1 February, https://media.netflix.com/en/company-blog/your-new-netflix-ident-animation-cue-netflix-sound

Netflix (2022) "What is Netflix," Netflix Help, https://help.netflix.com/en/node/412#:~:text=Netflix%20is%20a%20subscription-based%20streaming%20service%20that%20allows,10%20device%20and%20watch%20without%20an%20internet%20connection

Netflix Family (2019) "Top 10 Most Popilar Kids & Family Series Releases of 2019", *Twitter*, 31 December, https://twitter.com/netflixfamily/status/1211693300392050688?s=20

Netflix Family (2022) "Netflix Greenlights *Squid Game: The Challenge* Reality Competition Series", *Netflix*, 15 June, https://about.netflix.com/en/news/netflix-greenlights-squid-game-the-challenge-reality-competition-series

Netflix Technology Blog (2016) "Selecting the best artwork for videos through A/B testing", 3 May, https://netflixtechblog.com/selecting-the-best-artwork-for-videos-through-a-b-testing-f6155c4595f6

Newman, MZ and Levine, E (2012) *Legitimating Television: Media Convergence and Cultural Status*, New York and London: Routledge.

New York Times (1998) "'Titanic,' After 15 Weeks, Bows to 'Lost in Space'", 6 April, https://www.nytimes.com/1998/04/06/movies/titanic-after-15-weeks-bows-to-lost-in-space.html

Nguyen, H (2018) "'The New Legends of Monkey' Review: Beyond Whitewashing, Campy Update Erases Classic Tale's Chinese Roots," *IndieWire*, 29 April, https://www.indiewire.com/2018/04/new-legends-of-monkey-review-netflix-chinese-whitewashing-1201958569/

Ní Fhlainn, S (2021) "'What happens to us in the future?': stranger things 3 goes back to the future (1985)," in Mollet and Scott (eds), *Investigating Stranger Things: Upside Down in the World of Mainstream Cult Entertainment*, Cham, Switzerland: Palgrave Macmillan, 111–132.

Niemeyer, K (2014) "Introduction: Media and Nostalgia", in Niemeyer (ed), *Media and Nostalgia: Yearning for the Past, Present and Future*, Houndsmills: Palgrave Macmillan, 1–30.

Night Gallery (TV, 1970-1973).

Night of the Living Dead (George A. Romero, Film, 1968).

nika A [sic] (2018) "Lost in Space", *Common Sense Media*, https://www.commonsensemedia.org/tv-reviews/lost-in-space-0/user-reviews/adult

Novak, AN (2017) "Narrowcasting, millennials and the personalization of genre in digital media", in Barker, C and MWiatrowski, M (eds), *The Age of Netflix: Critical Essays on Streaming Media, Digital Delivery and Instant Access*, Jefferson, NC: McFarland, 162–181.

Nowell, R (2011) *Blood Money: A History of the First Teen Slasher Film Cycle*, London: Bloomsbury Publishing.

Obertova, A and Caitlin, R (2019) "Racial politics of Netflix series", 4 October, https://imagingglobalpolitics.wordpress.com/racial-politics-of-netflix-series/

Ofcom (2019) "Life on the small screen: What children are watching and why", 29 January, https://www.ofcom.org.uk/__data/assets/pdf_file/0021/134832/Ofcom-childrens-content-review-Publish.pdf

Ogre's Crpyt (2016) "Netflix Streaming Genres", http://ogres-crypt.com/public/NetFlix-Streaming-Genres2.html

O'Halloran, J (2018) "Sci-fi/fantasy content of choice for Netflix users", *Rapid TV News*, 26 April, https://www.rapidtvnews.com/2018042551844/sci-fi-fantasy-content-of-choice-for-netflix-users.html#axzz7Rursk6wU

O'Keefe, M (2016) "Is streaming killing the family show?" *Decider*, 19 August, https://decider.com/2016/08/19/streaming-killing-family-tv-stranger-things/

One Day at a Time (TV, 1975-1984, 2017-2020)

Orange is the New Black (TV, 2013-2019)

Orosz, J (2015) "John Williams: paraphraser or plagiarist?", *Journal of Musicological Research*, 34 (4): 299–319, 10.1080/01411896.2015.1082064

Painter, R (2019) "Netflix's 'Raising Dion' is a superhero origin series for kids and tweens, not adults", *KUTV*, 4 October, https://kutv.com/news/

entertainment/netflixs-raising-dion-is-a-superhero-origin-series-for-kids-and-tweens-not-adults

Pallister, K (ed)(2019) *Netflix Nostalgia: Streaming the Past on Demand*, Lanham, Maryland: Lexington Books.

Pallotta, F (2022) "Netflix loses subscribers, but stops the bleeding", 20 July, *CNN Business*, https://edition.cnn.com/2022/07/19/media/netflix-earnings/index.html#:~:text=New%20York%20(CNN%20Business)%20Netflix,would%20lose%20two%20million%20subscribers

Parents Television and Media Council (PTMC) (2022) "Stranger and more explicit things", https://www.parentstv.org/resources/2022-Stranger-And-More-Explicit-Things.pdf

Park, E-A (2017) "Why the networks can't beat Netflix: speculations on the US OTT Services Market", *Digital Policy, Regulation and Governance*, 19 (1), 21–39.

@PavelBains (2021) "My kid: How can you ride a bike with no hands?" *Twitter*. https://twitter.com/pavelbains/status/1413355423164375043

Pearson, R (2011) "Cult television as digital television's cutting edge", in Bennett, J and Strange, N (eds), *Television as Digital Media*. Durham, NC and London: Duke University Press, 105–131.

Peirse, A (2010) "A broken tradition: British telefantasy and children's television in the 1980s and 1990s", *Visual Culture in Britain*, 11 (1): 109–124.

Perkins, C (2012) *American Smart Cinema*, Edinburgh: Edinburgh University Press.

Perks, LG (2014) *Media Marathoning: Immersions in Morality*, Lanham, Maryland: Lexington Books.

Phillips, J (2019) "In a CGI-dominated world, Netflix's *The Dark Crystal: Age of Resistance* chooses puppets over pixels", *Los Angeles Times*, 27 August, https://www.latimes.com/entertainment-arts/tv/story/2019-08-27/netflix-dark-crystal-age-of-resistance-puppets

Piatti-Farnell, L (2018) "Blood flows freely: the horror of classic fairy tales", in Corstorphine, K and Kremmel, LR (eds), *The Palgrave Handbook to Horror Literature*, Cham, Switzerland: Palgrave Macmillan, 91–100.

Pickering, M and Keightley, E (2006) "The Modalities of Nostalgia", *Current Sociology* 54 (6): 919–941.

Piper, D (2022) "Netflix has a 'new' logo – and it's driving Stranger Things fans wild", *Creative Bloq*, 31 May, https://www.creativebloq.com/news/netflix-stranger-things-logo

Poltergeist (Tobe Hooper, Film, 1982)

Poniewozik, J (2018) "This Fall, Everything Old Is TV Again", *New York Times*, 5 September, https://www.nytimes.com/2018/09/05/arts/television/fall-tv-revivals-reboots.html

Porter, S (2019) "Netflix Parents – Watch Out For Graphic Content On Your Screens", *National Center on Sexual Exploitation*, 8 February, https://endsexualexploitation.org/articles/netflix-parents-watch-out-for-graphic-content-on-your-screens/

Prahl, A (2022) "12 '80s-Inspried Easter Eggs in *Stranger Things* Season 4", *Popsugar*, 30 May, Accessed 15 November 2022, https://www.popsugar.com.au/entertainment/stranger-things-season-4-easter-eggs-48841487

Press, J (2022) "The *Stranger Things* Season 4 Finale Leaves Hawkins in a Dark

Place", *Vanity Fair*, 1 July, https://www.vanityfair.com/hollywood/2022/06/stranger-things-season-4-finale-review

Proctor, W (2012) "Regeneration & Rebirth: Anatomy of the Franchise Reboot", *Scope: An Online Journal of Film and Television Studies*, 22 (February), https://www.nottingham.ac.uk/scope/documents/2012/february-2012/proctor.pdf

Proctor, W (2013) "Ctl-Alt-Delete: Retcon, Relaunch, or Reboot?" *Sequart*, 8 February, http://sequart.org/magazine/18508/ctl-alt-delete-retcon-relaunch-or-reboot/

Proctor, W (2017) "Reboots and retroactive continuity", in Wolf, Mark JP (ed), *The Routledge Companion to Imaginary Worlds*, New York: Routledge, 224–235.

Propp, V (1968) *Morphology of the Folktale*, 2d ed. Trans. Laurence Scott, Austin: University of Texas Press.

Pugh, T (2008) "What, then, does beatrice mean?: hermaphroditic gender, predatory sexuality, and promiscuous allusion in Daniel Handler/Lemony Snicket's a series of unfortunate events", *Children's Literature* 36 (2008): 162–184.

Pugh, T (2018) *The Queer Fantasies of the American Family Sitcom*, New Brunswick, NJ: Rutgers University Press.

Pushing Daisies (TV, 2007-2009).

Qualtrics (2021) "Determining sample size: how to make sure you get the correct sample size", https://www.qualtrics.com/au/experiencemanagement/research/determine-sample-size/

Quora (2020) "Is Stranger Things too scary for a preteen to watch?" https://www.quora.com/Is-Stranger-Things-too-scary-for-a-preteen-to-watch

Radillo, R (2022) "Stranger Things Season 4 Makes Its Biggest Flaw Glaringly Obvious", *CBR*, 10 July, https://www.cbr.com/stranger-things-season4-diversity-netflix/

Rainey, S (2015) "The days of talking TV at the water cooler are over", *Insider*, 22 January, https://www.theguardian.com/tv-and-radio/2017/aug/03/end-of-families-gathering-round-the-tv-as-binge-watching-grows

Raising Dion (TV, 2019-2022)

@RaisingDion (2022) "This season Dion is learning new skills at Biona but he's quickly discovering that energy never dies, it just takes another form", *Twitter*, 19 January, https://twitter.com/raisingdion/status/1483499516837859329

@Raisinguprebels (2021) "Thank you @Stranger_Things, my 7yo is obsessed with Motley Crue now", *Twitter*, 27 September, https://twitter.com/raisinguprebels/status/1442299704298000385

Relidzyńska, A (2021) "Anthropcene nostalgia for the 1980s in Netflix's *Stranger Things*", *European Journal of American Culture* 40 (3): 233–247.

Renau, A (2018) "Is My Kid Old Enough To Watch That? The Ins & Outs Of Parental Guidance", *Scary Mommy*, 26 January, https://www.scarymommy.com/parental-controls-movie-ratings/

Renfro, K (2019) "Here's what the cast of *The Dark Crystal: Age of Resistance* looks like in real life", *Insider*, 4 September, https://www.insider.com/dark-crystal-netflix-show-cast-voice-actors-2019-8#:~:text=%22Game%20of%20Thrones%22%20stars%20Nathalie,Crystal%3A%20Age%20of%20Resistance.%22

Return to Oz (Walter Murch, Film, 1985)

Richards, D (2013) "Old SF, new FX: exploring the reception of replacement special effects for older episodes of doctor who and star trek", *Critical Studies in Television*, 8 (3): 47–64.

Richards, RW (2021) *Cinematic TV: Serial Drama Goes to the Movies*, New York: Oxford University Press.

Richardson, D (2018) "Why Casting Amandla Stenberg In 'The Hate U Give' Is Problematic", *Study Breaks*, 21 July, https://studybreaks.com/tvfilm/amandla-stenberg-the-hate-u-give/

Rim of the World (TV, 2019).

Riverdale (TV, 2017-).

Robinson, J (2019) "The Dark Crystal: everything You Need to Know to Watch Age of Resistance", *Vanity Fair*, 30 August, https://www.vanityfair.com/hollywood/2019/08/dark-crystal-explainer-character-guide-what-happened-in-the-movie

Roman, D (2022) "Are *Stranger Things 4*'s huge episodes the next evolution of TV?" *Winteriscoming.net*, July, https://winteriscoming.net/2022/06/04/are-stranger-things-4s-huge-episode-lengths-the-next-evolution-of-prestige-tv/#:~:text=But%20let's%20talk%20about%20that,episode%20as%20a%20short%20movie

Romano A (2019) "Netflix's Dark Crystal prequel finds hope amid social collapse. With puppets", *Vox*, 30 August, https://www.vox.com/2019/8/30/20827743/dark-crystal-age-of-resistance-review-netflix

Roth, MS (2018) "Dear friends", email, in "Write-In: 'Commencement 2018: Lemony Snicket, Anita Hill, and Silencing Women of Color in the Age of #MeToo'", *Wesleying*, http://wesleying.org/2018/02/19/write-in-commencement-2018-lemony-snicket-anita-hill-and-silencing-women-of-color-in-the-age-of-metoo/

Roy Morgan (2021) "Subscription TV viewers soared to 17.3 million Australians during 2020: Netflix, Foxtel, Stan, Disney+ & Amazon Prime all increased viewership by at least 1.5 million", 12 January, http://www.roymorgan.com/findings/8606-subscription-pay-tv-services-september-2020-202101120113

Royal, S (2018) "How Netflix's Lost in Space reboot holds a mirror up to our humanity", *ABC News*, 29 April, https://www.abc.net.au/news/2018-04-29/how-netflixs-lost-in-space-reboot-mirrors-our-humanity/9704264

Royle, N (2003) *The Uncanny*, Manchester: Manchester University Press.

Ruddick, G (2017) "End of families gathering around the TV as binge watching grows", *The Guardian*, 03 August, https://www.theguardian.com/tv-and-radio/2017/aug/03/end-of-families-gathering-round-the-tv-as-binge-watching-grows

Ruderman Family Foundation (2019) "The Ruderman Seal", 14 November, https://rudermanfoundation.org/the-ruderman-seal/

Ryan, K & R 'Spider' G [sic] (2014) *Taking Down Goliath: The Digital Marketing Strategy for Beating Competitors with 100 Times Your Spending Power*, New York: Palgrave Macmillan.

Sabrina the Animated Series (TV, 1999-2000)

Sabrina the Teenage Witch (TV, 1971-1974)

Sabrina, the Teenage Witch (TV, 1996-2003)

Sahlins, M (2011) "What is kinship (part one)", *The Journal of the Royal Anthropological Institute*, March, 1(17): 2–19.

Salfen, P (2019) "Raising Dion: A Family Friendly 'Stranger Things'", *AMFM*, 3 October, https://www.amfm-magazine.tv/raising-dion-a-family-friendly-stranger-things/

Samsel, S (2022) "Report: *Stranger Things* keeps TV-14 Rating Despite Rise in Profanity & Violence", *CNS News*, 11 July, https://www.cnsnews.com/article/

national/stephanie-samsel/report-stranger-things-keeps-tv-14-rating-despite-rise-profanity

Sánchez-Eppler, K (2011) "Castaways: child bookmakers, and the possibilities of literary flotsam", in Vallone, L and Mickenberg, Julia (eds), *The Oxford Handbook of Children's Literature*, Oxford: Oxford University Press, 433–454.

San Filippo, M (2016) "*Transparent* family values: unmasking sitcom myths of gender, sex(uality), and money", in Dalton, MM and Linder, LR (eds), *The Sitcom Reader, Second Edition: America Re-viewed, Still Skewed*, New York: State University of New York Press, 305–318.

San Filippo, M (2017) "Doing time: queer temporalities and Orange is the New Black", in Barker, C and Wiatrowski, M (eds), *The Age of Netflix: Critical Essays on Streaming Media, Digital Delivery and Instant Access*, Jefferson, NC: McFarland, 75–97.

Sandra, D [sic] (2018) "Lost in Space", *Common Sense Media*, https://www.commonsensemedia.org/tv-reviews/lost-in-space-0/user-reviews/adult

Santas, C, Wilson, J, Colavito, M and Baker, D (2014) *The Encyclopedia of Epic Films*, Lanham: Rowman & Littlefield.

Sarner, L (2017) "All The Unfortunate Events in Netflix's '*A Series Of Unfortunate Events*", *Inverse*, 1 December, https://www.inverse.com/article/26208-netflix-series-unfortunate-events-primer

Sattelberg, W (2020) "Using Parental Controls For Blocking Shows On Netflix", *alphr*, 1 July, https://www.alphr.com/block-shows-netflix/

Science Fiction Theatre (TV, 1955-1957)

Schatz, T (1981). *Hollywood Genres: Formulas, Filmmaking, and the Studio System*, New York: Random House.

Schager, N (2019) "The new 10-part Netflix series, featuring many A-list voices (Lena Headey! Mark Hamill! Simon Pegg!), is an instant genre classic", *Daily Beast*, 30 August, https://www.thedailybeast.com/netflixs-the-dark-crystal-age-of-resistance-will-make-you-forget-about-the-end-of-game-of-thrones

Schober, A (2018) "Rod Serling's Damaged Children", in Schober, A and Olson, D (eds), *Children, Youth, and American Television*, New York and Oxfordshire: Routledge, 44–63.

Schubart, R (2018) *Mastering Fear: Women, Emotions, and Contemporary Horror*, London: Bloomsbury.

Schlütz, DM (2016) "Contemporary Quality TV: The Entertainment Experience of Complex Serial Narratives", *Annals of the International Communication Association*, 40 (1): 95–124.

Schwerdtfeger, C (2018) "The Specific Way Netflix's Lost In Space Will Pay Homage To The Original Series", *Cinema Blend*, 30 March, https://www.cinemablend.com/television/2395192/the-specific-way-netflixs-lost-in-space-will-pay-homage-to-the-original-series

Schwichtenberg, C (1987) "The Love Boat: the packaging and selling of love, heterosexual romance, and family", in H. Newcomb (ed), *Television: The Critical View*, 4th edn, New York: Oxford University Press, 126–140.

Schwindt, O (2016) "'Stranger Things' tests limits of Netflix's nostalgia strategy", *Variety*, 25 July, https://variety.com/2016/tv/news/stranger-things-netflix-fuller-house-nostalgia-strategy-1201822075/?sub_action=logged_in

Sconce, J (2004) "Science fiction programs", in Newcomb, H (ed), *Encyclopedia of Television*, 2nd edn, New York: Fitzroy Dearborn, 2026–2027.

Seelye, J (1990) "Introduction: *The Swiss Family Robinson*", *Children's Literature Association Quarterly*, 1990: 4–12, 10.1353/chq.1990.0003

See You Yesterday (Stefon Bristol, Film, 2019)

Seibold, W (2018) "How Netflix's Lost in Space Compares to the Other Lost in Spaces", *IGN*, 8 March, https://www.ign.com/articles/2018/03/07/how-netflixs-lost-in-space-compares-to-the-other-lost-in-spaces

Sesame Street (TV, 1969-)

Shadowhunters: The Mortal Instruments (TV, 2017-2019)

Shager, N (2019) "The Dark Crystal: Age of Resistance Will Make You Forget About the End of Game of Thrones", *Daily Beast*, 30 August, https://www.thedailybeast.com/netflixs-the-dark-crystal-age-of-resistance-will-make-you-forge-t-about-the-end-of-game-of-thrones

Sharf, Z (2022) "David Harbour predicted 'Stranger Things' would be cancelled after season 1: 'It was going to be a disaster'", *Variety*, 29 July, https://variety.com/2022/tv/news/david-harbour-stranger-things-canceled-season-1-disaster-1235329126/

Sheldon, L (1998) "The middle years: Children and television – cool or just plain boring?", in Howard, S (ed.), *Wired Up: Young people and the electronic media*, London: UCL Press, 75–92.

Shepherd, E (2022) "Media agencies weigh in on Netflix's $6.99 ad-supported tier in Australia", *Mumbrella*, 14 October, Accessed 15 November, https://mumbrella.com.au/media-agencies-weigh-in-on-netflixs-6-99-ad-supported-tier-in-australia-760107

Shetland (TV, 2013-2016)

Shulgasser-Parker, B (2019) "Rim of the World", *Common Sense Media*, https://www.commonsensemedia.org/movie-reviews/rim-of-the-world

Shunyata, K (2022) "The Antagonism of Blackness in Netflix's *Stranger Things*", 19 June, https://www.rogerebert.com/black-writers-week/the-antagonism-of-blackness-in-netflixs-stranger-things

Silverman, DS and Douglas, B (2019) "The Western didn't die, it just went off-world: Guardians of the Galaxy and the Final Frontier", in Brode, D and Brode, ST (eds.), *The Twenty-First-Century Western: New Riders of the Cinematic Stage*, Lanham: Lexington, 259–271.

Simon, R [sic] (2019) "Netflix rate this as 7 plus!!", Common Sense Media, https://www.commonsensemedia.org/tv-reviews/raising-dion/user-reviews/adult

Sinister (Scott Derrikson, Film, 2012)

Siranni, JM (2019) "Nostalgic things: *Stranger Things* and the pervasiveness of nostalgic television", in Pallister, K (ed), *Netflix Nostalgia: streaming the past on demand*, Lanham: Lexington Books, 185–202.

Smail, G (2019) "Raising Dion – the superpowers and supertwists: discuss with spoilers", *The Guardian*, 10 October, https://www.theguardian.com/tv-and-radio/2019/oct/10/raising-dion-netflix-discuss-with-spoilers

Smedley, K (2019) "Raising Dion: The Burden of being a Black Child", *Blue Note Soul*, 5 November, http://www.bluenotesoul.com/raising-dion-the-burden-of-being-a-black-child/

Smith, B (2020) "How Netflix beat Hollywood to a generation of Black content",

Baltimore Sun, 6 July, https://www.baltimoresun.com/consumer-reviews/sns-nyt-op-netflix-hollywood-black-culture-20200706-tbsmbgfvzrfijo44shyjqv72ku-story.html

Smith, KL (2022) "Here's what the *Stranger Things* kids look like now vs 2016", *PopBuzz* https://www.popbuzz.com/tv-film/stranger-things/cast-now-then-2022-2016/

Smith, K (2016) "Don't visit *'Miss Peregrine's Home for Peculiar Children'*", *New York Post* 29 September, https://nypost.com/2016/09/29/dont-visit-miss-peregrines-home-for-peculiar-children/

Smith-Rowsey D (2016) "Imaginative indices and deceptive domains: how Netflix's categories and genres redefine and long tail", in McDonald, K and Smith-Rowsey, D (eds), *The Netflix Effect: Technology and Entertainment in the 21st Century*, New York: Bloomsbury, 63–79.

Snicket, L [Daniel Handler] (1999a) *The Bad Beginning*, New York: HarperCollins.

Snicket, L (1999b) *The Reptile Room*, New York: HarperCollins.

Snicket, L (2000a) *The Austere Academy*, New York: HarperCollins.

Snicket, L (2000b) *The Wide Window*, New York: HarperCollins.

Snicket, L (2000c) *The Miserable* Mill, New York: HarperCollins.

Snicket, L (2001a) *The Ersatz Elevator*, New York: HarperCollins.

Snicket, L (2001b) *The Hostile Hospital*, New York: HarperCollins.

Snicket, L (2001c) *The Vile Village*, New York: HarperCollins.

Snicket, L (2002) *The Carnivorous Carnival*, New York: HarperCollins.

Snicket, L (2003) *The Slippery Slope*, New York: HarperCollins.

Snicket, L (2004) *The Grim Grotto*, New York: HarperCollins.

Snicket, L (2005) *The Penultimate Peril*, New York: HarperCollins.

Snicket, L (2006) *The End*, New York: HarperCollins.

Snowden, H (2019) "*The Mandalorian* beats *Stranger Things* as America's most-streamed TV series", *High Snobriety*, https://www.highsnobiety.com/p/the-mandalorian-stranger-things-most-streamed-show/

Sobchack, V (2009) "Vivian Sobchack in Conversation with Scott Bukatman,", *E-media studies*, 2:1, https://journals.dartmouth.edu/cgi-bin/WebObjects/Journals.woa/xmlpage/4/article/338

Solin, J (2016) "'Stranger Things' Star Responds To Fans Who Are Upset About Season 2 Casting News", *International Business Times*, 15 October, https://www.ibtimes.com/stranger-things-star-responds-fans-who-are-upset-about-season-2-casting-news-2432117

Sontag, S (1967) *Against Interpretation and Other Essays*, London: Eyre and Spottiswoode.

Spangler, T (2018a) "Netflix Bulks Up Parental Controls With New Features", *Variety*, 5 March, https://variety.com/2018/digital/news/netflix-parental-controls-enhanced-features-1202718101/

Spangler, T (2018b) "Netflix 'Lost in Space' Reboot Draws 6.3 Million Viewers in First 3 Days, Nielsen Says", *Variety*, 24 April, https://variety.com/2018/digital/news/lost-in-space-netflix-ratings-nielsen-1202785547/

Spangler, T (2021) "Netflix Releases New Data on Most Popular TV Shows and Movies", *Variety*, 27 September, https://variety.com/2021/digital/news/netflix-most-popular-tv-shows-movies-1235075301/#recipient_hashed=e9d3a942b75e924985ce93516c14498c08152df6cbd4145d30f1ef5f65b9ab6d

Spencer, S (2022) "Why 'Locke and Key' Is ending with season 3 on Netflix",

Newsweek, 7 April, https://www.newsweek.com/locke-key-canceled-ending-season-3-netflix-1695901
Spigel, L (1992) *Make Room for TV: Television and the Family Ideal in Postwar America*, Chicago: University of Chicago Press.
Spigel, L (2001) *Welcome to the Dreamhouse: Popular Media and Postwar Suburbs*, Durham, NC: Duke University Press.
Spooner, C (2017) *Post-Millennial Gothic: Comedy, Romance and the Rise of Happy Gothic*, London: Bloomsbury.
Sprengler, C (2009) *Screening Nostalgia: Populuxe Props and Technicolor Aesthetics in Contemporary American Film*, New York: Berghahn.
Squid Game (TV, 2021)
Srspashly [sic] (2019) "Raising Dion", *Common Sense Media*, https://www.commonsensemedia.org/tv-reviews/raising-dion/user-reviews/adult
Staiger, J (2005) *Media Reception Studies*, New York and London: New York University Press.
Stand by Me (Rob Reiner, Film, 1986)
Stanley, A (2022) "Netflix's Lost In Space tops streaming charts once again", *Slash Film*, 8 January, https://www.slashfilm.com/728445/netflixs-lost-in-space-tops-streaming-charts-once-again/
Star Wars (George Lucas, Film, 1977)
Star Trek: Enterprise (TV, 2001-2005)
Steenland, S (1985) "Prime Time Kids: An Analysis of Children's and Families on Television", *National Commission on Working Women of Wider Opportunities for Women*, Washington, DC, 1–16.
Stopera, M (2022) "These Pictures Show how Everyone From Stranger Things Seriously Transformed From season 1 VS Season 4", *BuzzFeed*, https://www.buzzfeed.com/mjs538/stranger-things-season-1-vs-4
Stranger Things (TV, 2016-)
@Stranger_Things (2022) "ST4 VOLUME 1 IS NOW STREAMING", 27 May, https://twitter.com/Stranger_Things/status/1530081377575649280?s=20&t=BC6yfzJf9NKg3tBgK7b_2Q
@StrangerNews11 (2021) "Stranger Things & Squid Game … ." 10 October, https://twitter.com/StrangerNews11/status/1446905880344137730?t=cJiib2CyiHlfj4h4w2EBwA&s=03
Stranger Universe (2022) "*Stranger Things 4* cost $30 million per episode", *Twitter*, 22 April, https://twitter.com/struniverse/status/1517180315621642242
Stuewe, V (2020) "The Netflix Curse? Why was *The Dark Crystal: Age of Resistance* Cancelled?", *Film Daily*, 29 September, https://filmdaily.co/news/netflix-dark-crystal-canceled/
Sullivan, C (2020) "18 Inspiring Netflix Shows Committed to Representing People With Disabilities", *PopSugar*, 30 January, https://www.popsugar.com.au/entertainment/netflix-tv-shows-with-characters-with-disabilities-47162727
Supplisson, M (2022) "41 Best *Stranger Things* Easter Eggs and References." *Telltales*, 19 July. Accessed 15th November 2022. https://www.telltalesonline.com/27703/stranger-things-movie-references/
Susan D [sic] (2019) "My 2nd Grader LOVES this show!", *Common Sense Media*, 9 April, https://www.commonsensemedia.org/tv-reviews/raising-dion/user-reviews/adult
Sweney, M (2022) "'Stealth mode': how Disney overtook Netflix in streaming wars",

The Guardian, 12 August, https://www.theguardian.com/media/2022/aug/11/how-disney-overtook-netflix-in-streaming-wars

Tamm12276 [sic] (2019) "Too many cuss words", 2 June, https://www.commonsensemedia.org/movie-reviews/see-you-yesterday/user-reviews/adult

Tanderup Linkis, S (2020) "'It's off-book!': developing serial complexity across media in a series of unfortunate events", *Children's Literature Association Quarterly*, 45 (1), Spring: 59–79

Tan, E (2019) "Dennis Liu and Marie Iida work to break the model minority myth with the comic book 'LING'", *NBC News*, 8 October, https://www.nbcnews.com/news/asian-america/dennis-liu-marie-iida-work-break-model-minority-myth-comic-n1063351

Tassi, P (2020) "Netflix's 'Lost In Space' is a unique family-friendly(ish) sci-fi adventure you should give a chance", *Forbes*, 21 January, https://www.forbes.com/sites/paultassi/2020/01/21/netflixs-lost-in-space-is-a-unique-family-friendlyish-sci-fi-adventure-you-should-give-a-chance/?sh=1b8ef7bf6dd4

Tassi, P (2021) '"True Story"' Dethroned In Netflix's Top 10 List By A New Show', *Forbes*, 3 December, https://www.forbes.com/sites/paultassi/2021/12/03/true-story-dethroned-in-netflixs-top-10-list-by-a-new-show/?sh=5a051b167c6e

Taurino, G (2019) "Crossing Eras: Exploring Nostalgic Reconfigurations in Media Franchises", in Pallister, K (ed), *Netflix Nostalgia: Streaming the Past on Demand*, Lanham: Lexington, 9–23.

Telotte, JP (2008) "Introduction: The trajectory of science fiction television", in Telotte, JP (ed), *The Essential Science Fiction Television Reader*, Lexington: University Press of Kentucky, 1–34.

Telotte, JP (2016) "Robby the Robot and the robotic persistence", *Mosaic: An Interdisciplinary Critical Journal*, 49 (3): 19–37.

Terminator 2: Judgment Day (James Cameron, Film, 1991).

Terrace, V (2013) *Encyclopedia of Television Pilots, 1937-2012*, Jefferson, North Carolina: McFarland.

The Texas Chainsaw Massacre (Tobe Hooper, Film, 1974)

@TexasAngry (2022) "My son just finished Stranger Things season 1 through 3", *Twitter*, https://twitter.com/TexasAngry/status/1498853228871655430

The Addams Family (TV, 1964-66)

The Archie Show (TV, 1968-69)

The Baby-Sitters Club (TV, 1995, 2020-2021)

The Black Cauldron (Richard Rich and Ted Burman, Film, 1985)

The Brady Bunch (TV, 1969-1974)

The Cell (Tarsem Singh, Film, 2000)

The Company of Wolves (Neil Jordan, Film, 1984)

The Conjuring 2 (James Wan, Film, 2016)

The Cosby Show (TV, 1984–1992)

The Dark Crystal (Jim Henson and Frank Oz, Film, 1982)

The Day the Earth Stood Still (Robert Wise, Film, 1951)

The Gate (Tibor Takács, Film, 1987)

The Get Down (TV, 2016)

The Graduate (Mike Nichols, Film, 1967)

The Guardians of the Galaxy Vol. 1 (James Gunn, Film, 2014)

The Guardians of the Galaxy Vol. 2 (James Gunn, Film, 2017)

The Haunting (Robert Wise, Film, 1963)
The Haunting (Jan de Bont, Film, 1999)
The Haunting of Hill House (Mike Flanagan, TV, 2018)
The Healing Powers of Dude (TV, 2020)
The Iron Giant (Brad Bird, Film, 1999)
The Jeffersons (TV, 1975–1985)
The Late Late Show with James Corden (TV, 2015-2022)
The Lego Movie (Lord and Miller, Film, 2014)
The Mandalorian (TV, 2019-)
The Monster Squad (Fred Dekker, Film, 1987)
The Munsters (TV, 1964-1966)
The Muppet Show (TV, 1976-1981)
The NeverEnding Story (Wolfgang Peterson, Film, 1984)
The Patty Duke Show (TV, 1963-1966)
The Perils of Nyoka (William Witney, Film, 1942).
Perils of Pauline (Louis J Gasnier and Donald MacKenzie, Film, 1914)
The Perils of Pauline (Ray Taylor, Film, 1933).
The Phantom Empire (Otto Brower and B. Reeves Eason, Film, 1935)
The Princess Bride (Rob Reiner, Film, 1987)
The Quatermass Experiment (TV, 1953)
The Twilight Zone (TV, 1959-1964)
The Walking Dead (TV, 2010-2022)
TheycallmeMaaaaaaa [sic] (2020) "Raising Dion", *Common Sense Media*, https://www.commonsensemedia.org/tv-reviews/raising-dion/user-reviews/adult
Thomas, Ebony Elizabeth (2019) *The Dark Fantastic: Race and the imagination from Harry Potter to The Hunger Games*, New York: New York University.
Thompson, H (1960) "New Version of 'Swiss Family Robinson'", *New York Times*, 24 December, https://www.nytimes.com/1960/12/24/archives/new-version-of-swiss-family-robinson.html
Thompson, RJ (2007) "Preface", in McCabe, J and Akass, K (eds), *Quality TV: Contemporary American television and beyond*, London: I.B. Tauris, xvii–xvx.
Thompson, RJ (1996) *Television's Second Golden Age: From Hill Street Blues to ER*, Syracuse: Syracuse University Press.
Thor: Love and Thunder (Taika Waititi, Film, 2022)
Thorne, W (2020) "*The Dark Crystal: Age of Resistance* Cancelled After One Season at Netflix", *Variety*, 21 September, https://variety.com/2020/tv/news/the-dark-crystal-age-of-resistance-netflix-canceled-one-season 1234778139/#:~:text=Netflix%20will%20not%20be%20returning,single%20season%2C%20Variety%20has%20confirmed
Thrower, E (2016) "*Stranger Things*: the Duffer brothers share the secrets of their hit show", *Empire Online*, https://www.empireonline.com/movies/features/stranger-things-duffer-brothers-share-secrets-hit-show/
Tiffany, K (2017) "How Netflix made *A Series of Unfortunate Events*, its first great TV for families", *The Verge*, 13 January, https://www.theverge.com/2017/1/13/14266208/netflix-a-series-of-unfortunate-events-interview-daniel-handler
Tiffee, S and Filoteo, J (2020) "Yearning for yesteryear: nostalgia and the politics and sentimentality in Chilling Adventures of Sabrina", *The Journal of Popular Culture*, 53 (2): 327–347.

Titanic (James Cameron, Film, 1997)

Torres, S (1999) "The caped crusaders of camp: pop, camp, and the *Batman* television series", in Cleto, F (ed), *Camp: Queer Aesthetics and the Performing Subject: A Reader*, Edinburgh: Edinburgh University Press, 330–344.

@TortoiseHound (2020) "Tonight my kid asked me 'what's that thing on my Stranger Things' sweatshirt", *Twitter*, https://twitter.com/TortoiseNHound/status/1338720132512804865

Travers, B (2019) "'Raising Dion' Review: Michael B. Jordan's Cutesy Netflix Series Is a Bit More Than Popcorn Entertainment", *IndieWire*, 4 October, https://www.indiewire.com/2019/10/raising-dion-review-netflix-series-michael-b-jordan-1202177813/

Trenholm, R (2019) "*Dark Crystal: Age of Resistance* on Netflix is *Game of Thrones* with puppets", *CNet*, 1 September, https://www.cnet.com/news/magical-dark-crystal-age-of-resistance-netflix-review-game-of-thrones-with-puppets/

Trigg, D (2006) *The Aesthetics of Decay: Nothingness, Nostalgia, and the Absence of Reason*, New York: Peter Lang.

Tryon, C (2015) "TV Got Better: Netflix's Original Programming Strategies and Binge Viewing", *Media Industries*, 2 (2), 10.3998/mij.15031809.0002.206

Turner, G (2019) "Approaching the cultures of use: Netflix, disruption and the audience", *Critical Studies in Television*, 14 (2): 222–232.

TV Guidelines (2021) *The TV Parental Guidelines*, http://www.tvguidelines.org/resources/TheRatings.pdf

Tyree, JM (2013) "Unsafe houses: *Moonrise Kingdom* and Wes Anderson's conflicted comedies of escape", *Film Quarterly*, 66 (4): 23–27.

Ugwu, R (2018) "Why the Creator of 'Dear White People' Is Doubling Down on Identity Politics", *New York Times*, 2 May, https://www.nytimes.com/2018/05/02/arts/television/dear-white-people-creator-doubles-down-on-identity-politics.html

u/iamzaizen [sic] (2019) "Raising Dion is awesome but really racist", *Reddit*, https://www.reddit.com/r/television/comments/ddrqd4/raising_dion_is_awesome_but_really_racist/

Unbreakable (M. Night Shyamalan, Film, 2000)

Urbanski, H (2013) *The Science Fiction Reboot: Canon, Innovation and Fandom in Refashi oned Franchises*. Jefferson NC: McFarland & Company, Inc.

u/PinkMoonrise (2018) "Age for Netflix's 'Stranger Things?'" *Reddit*, https://www.reddit.com/r/Parenting/comments/7yrva4/age_for_netflixs_stranger_things/

u/shmashes (2020) "Is stranger things, a kids show?" *Reddit*, https://www.reddit.com/r/StrangerThings/comments/gkn3fv/is_stranger_things_a_kids_show/

Vaage, MB 2015, *The Antihero in American Television*, London: Taylor & Francis Group.

Van den Bulck, J, Custers, K and Nelissen, S (2016) "The child-effect in the new media environment: challenges and opportunities for communication research", *Journal of Children and Media*, 10 (2): 30–38.

Van Esler, M (2020) "In plain sight: online tv interfaces as branding", *Television & New Media*, 20 May: 1–16.

Vaughn, S (2005) *Freedom and Entertainment: Rating the Movies in an Age of New Media*, New York City: Cambridge University Press.

Vee, Geoffrey (2020) "A Series of Unfortunate Events", *Common Sense Media*, https://www.commonsensemedia.org/tv-reviews/a-series-of-unfortunate-events/user-reviews/adult

Vehling, A (2019) "Synth musician, trailer composer Bryce Miller on the art of making things happen," *Vehlinggo*, 30 October, https://vehlinggo.com/2019/10/30/bryce-miller-interview/

Vera (TV, 2011-2017)

Voyage to the Bottom of the Sea (TV, 1964-1968)

Wainio, W (2019) "Lost in Space season 2, episode 7 recap: Evolution", *Show Snob*, https://showsnob.com/2020/04/06/lost-in-space-s2e7-recap/

Wallin, Z (2019) *Classical Hollywood Film Cycles*, New York: Routledge.

Wang, W and Lobato, R (2019) "Chinese video streaming services in the context of global platform studies", *Chinese Journal of Communication*, 12 (3): 356–371.

Warner, K (2010) *Colorblind TV- Primetime Politics of Race in Television Casting*, Dissertation Presented to the Faculty of the Graduate School of The University of Texas at Austin.

Warner, S (2020) "*Dark Crystal* star Mark Strong reacts to 'upsetting' cancellation", *Digital Spy*, 6 November, https://www.digitalspy.com/tv/ustv/a34600116/dark-crystal-netflix-cancellation-mark-strong/

Warwick, JF (1968) "What the humanities offer the social studies", *Art Education*, 21 (2): 29–32.

Waterson, J (2019) "Netflix to set its own age ratings for film and television programmes", *The Guardian*, 14 March, https://www.theguardian.com/media/2019/mar/14/netflix-to-set-its-own-age-ratings-for-film-and-television-programmes

Weaver, T (2014) *A Sci-Fi Swarm and Horror Horde: Interviews with 62 Filmmakers*, Jefferson: McFarland.

Weintraub, S (2021) "'Lost in Space' Producers Zack Estrin, Matt Sazama and Burk Sharpless on Season 3 and How they Figured Out the Series Finale", *Collider*, 31 December, https://collider.com/lost-in-space-season-3-ending-zack-estrin-matt-sazama-burk-sharpless-interview/

Wells, J and Dallas, K (2014) *American Comic Book Chronicles: 1965-69*, Raleigh NC: TwoMorrows Publishing.

Wertham, F (1954) *Seduction of the Innocent*, London: Museum Press.

Wetmore, K (ed) (2018) *Uncovering Stranger Things: Essays on Eighties Nostalgia, Cynicism and Innocence in the Series*, Jefferson: McFarland.

Wheatley, H (2012) "Uncanny Children, haunted houses, hidden rooms: children's Gothic television in the 1970s and '80s", *Visual Culture in Britain*, 13 (3): 383–397.

Wheatley, H (2016) *Spectacular Television: Exploring Televisual Pleasure*, London: I.B. Tauris.

Whitney, D (1966) "One Case Where Evil Triumphs", *TV Guide*, 18 June, 12–14.

Whittmer A (2022) "Stranger (and more explicit?) Things: Why Parents are Questioning Netflix's Maturity Ratings", *Deseret*, July 22, https://www.deseret.com/entertainment/2022/7/12/23204193/stranger-and-more-explicit-things-parents-question-netflix-maturity-ratings-children-netflix-graphic

Wild Wild West (Barry Sonnenfeld, Film, 1997).

Wilder, J (2020) "Not Representative of Sabrina the Teenage Witch", *Common Sense Media*, 25 April, https://www.commonsensemedia.org/tv-reviews/chilling-adventures-of-sabrina/user-reviews/adult

Williams, R (2015) *Post-Object Fandom: Television, Identity and Self-Narrative*, New York: Bloomsbury Academic.
Williamson L (2008) "Challenging sitcom conventions: From *The Larry Sanders Show* to *The Comeback*", in Leverette, M, Ott, BL, and Buckley, CL (eds), *It's not TV: Watching HBO in the Post-Television Era*, New York: Routledge, 108–122.
Willis, I (2017) *Reception*, London: Routledge.
Willow (Ron Howard, Film, 1988)
Wilson, M (2019) "*Netflix has a New Intro, Two Years in the Making*", *Fast Company*, 1 February, https://www.fastcompany.com/90299526/heres-the-new-netflix-intro-two- years-in-the-making
Windsor, M (2019) "What is the uncanny?", *British Journal of Aesthetics*, 59 (1): 51–65, 10.1093/aesthj/ayy028
Wired (2019) "*The Dark Crystal* Prequel is *Game of Thrones* with Puppets", *Wired*, 21 September, https://www.wired.com/2019/09/geeks-guide-dark-crystal/
Wise, J (2022) "*Netflix Statistics 2022: How Many Subscribers Does Netflix Have?*" *EarthWeb*, 12 November, https://earthweb.com/netflix-statistics/
Witty, P (1952) "Two studies of children's interest in TV", *Elementary English*, 29 (5): 251–257.
Wojcik-Andrews I (2000) *Children's Films*, New York: Garland.
Wolf, MJP (2012) *Building Imaginary Worlds: The Theory and History of Subcreation*, New York: Routledge.
Wood, R (2003) *Hollywood from Vietnam to Reagan … and Beyond, Revised*, New York: Columbia University Press.
Woolery, GW (1985) *Children's Television: The First Thirty- Five Years, 1946– 1981, Part II: Live, Film and Tape Series*, Metuchen, NJ: The Scarecrow Press.
Wright, A (2005) "Selling the fantastic: the marketing and merchandising of the British Fairytale film in the 1980s", *Journal of British Cinema and Television*, 2 (2): 256–274.
YayOMG [sic] (2019) "Ja'Siah Young on Raising Dion and the Superheroes Who Inspire Him", 8 October, https://www.yayomg.com/jasiah-young-interview/
Yeoman, K (2018) "Lost In Space Season 2 Is Already Being Developed", *Screen Rant*, 16 April, https://screenrant.com/lost-space-season-2-developed/
Yodovich, Neta (2022) "Like father, like daughter: The intergenerational passing of *Doctor Who* and *Star Wars* fandom in the familial context," in Kies, B and Connor, M (eds), *Fandom, The Next Generation*, Iowa City: University of Iowa Press, 58–67.
Zakarin, J (2019) "*The Dark Crystal* prequel is a horror about evil billionaires that will scare kids – and that's the point", *SYFY Wire*, 3 September, https://www.syfy.com/syfy-wire/netflix-dark-crystal-prequel-about-billionaires-scare-kids
Zicree, M (1982) *The Twilight Zone Companion*, Los Angeles: Silman-James Press.

Index

Kolibri 360 GmbH
Ferdinand-Jühlke-Straße 7
99095 Erfurt, Deutschland
produktsicherheit@kolibri360.de